MOTEL
I0820997

BLACK FLAG
BLACK FLAG
NEW ALBUM
DAMAGED
ARE YOU A VICTIM OF FEAR?
AUG.29
BLACK FLAG
FEAR
D.O.A.
45 GRAVE
SOCIAL DISTORTION
WHISKY
BLACK FLAG
ADOLESCENTS
DOA
MINUTEMEN
FRIDAY JUNE 19
at the SANTA MONICA CIVIC
CIRCLE ONE
STAINS
SIN 34
BAD BRAINS
TWISTED ROOTS
ADOLESCENTS
DESCENDENTS
45 GRAVE
SINS
RITZ
FEAR
WE'RE LOOKING FOR A FEW GOOD MEN...
ENLIST NOW!
PICO RIVERA SPORTS ARENA
SOCIAL DISTORTION
BAD RELIGION
OVERKILL
MINUTE MEN
The Season stirs with CIRCLE ONE
RED CROSS
AT VALLEY WEST CLUB
19657 VENTURA BLVD
DESCENDENTS
B PEOPLE
CATHAY DE GRANDE
FRIDAY JULY 31
SOCIAL DISTORTION
AGENT ORANGE
OVERKILL
ANGRY SAMOANS
LEWD
MARCH 13
GODZILLA'S
WASTED YOUTH
AT THE WHISKY
THE CROWD
THE STAINS
RED CROSS
45 GRAVE
UNKNOWNS
The Slits
VEX
SIN 34
WASTED YOUTH
CHINA WHITE
WASTED YOUTH
JULY 11, 1981
LEGAL WEAPON
WEIRDOS
MAY 5
STARWOOD
BLACK FLAG
ADOLESCENTS
STAINS
VEX
BLACK FLAG
DOA
FEAR
LEWD
CIRCLE-ONE
CRUCIFIX
FUCK-UPS
DOMINO THEORY
45 GRAVE
CHRISTIAN DEATH
Five Live Bands
RED CROSS
Salvation Army
Sackrin Trust
Youth Brigade
& Disposals
SUBSERVICE

WE GOT POWER!

HARDCORE PUNK SCENES FROM 1980s SOUTHERN CALIFORNIA

BY DAVID MARKEY AND JORDAN SCHWARTZ

AWN DEE
MOTEL
DISCOUNT
DISCOUNT
DELIAS SALON
Rubber Stamps
PUNK

Joe's Mom
BLACK
FLAG
SIN
34

WE GOT POWER:
Hardcore Punk Scenes from 1980s Southern California

First printing 2012 by

Bazillion Points
61 Greenpoint Ave. #504
Brooklyn, New York 11222
United States
www.bazillionpoints.com
www.wegotpowerbook.com

Produced for Bazillion Points by Ian Christe

Cover layout and design by Bazillion Points
Copyedit by Polly Watson
All-seeing eyes: Jennifer Schwartz

Additional photos by Joe Cole, Edward Colver, Jennifer Finch, Mike Guerena,
Rick Hostage, Naomi Petersen, Spot, and Jennifer Schwartz

Lyrics to “Rockstar” by Frank Navetta, © Alltudemic Music (BMI)

A bazillion thank-yous to Print Space NYC, Magnus Henriksson, Tesco Vee,
Vivienne, and Dianna

ISBN 978-1-935950-07-3

Printed in China

TABLE OF CONTENTS

EVERYTHING WAS HEAVY

HENRY ROLLINS

I arrived in Los Angeles in the summer of 1981 as Black Flag's new vocalist. I had been to the city before, but had never spent any significant amount of time there. It has, over the last thirty years, become somewhat of a home to me. It is not a place I miss. It is not a place I think about with any degree of fondness, but it is a place where I have seen and learned much.

A lot of the people I met when I first came to the city are gone now. Living in Los Angeles taught me that there are a lot of ways to be gone. You can be impossible to find and no amount of searching will lead anyone to your door; you can be dead; you can slip out, back to the nowhere you came from after the dream has gone bust. However it happens, L.A. seems to disappear people.

Black Flag was a very well known band. Our notoriety was always a double-edged sword, and it seemed that the band was often cut by both sides. There were people who liked us and those who didn't. A lot of the time it was hard to tell the difference. That can get to someone. It definitely did a number on me.

When not on the road, we spent a lot of time at shows. We rarely had enough money to get the whole band in and had to rely on guest lists or our dubious notoriety to gain entrance. Some of the most intense and memorable nights of my young life were spent in music venues, seeing bands like the Minutemen, Saccharine Trust, the Meat Puppets, the Stains, Descendents, Red Cross, and many others.

There was something about these shows that made them distinct. They were not always enjoyable. Quite often, the environment inside was tense and guarded. Violence came easily. There were undercover police at many of the shows, and frequently uniformed ones outside, waiting with video cameras to get shots of the people walking out of the club. Something was up, and we were all a part of it.

Black Flag had a song called "Police Story," which has a lyric that sums up that relationship very well: "They hate us, we hate them. We can't win. No way."

The people I saw at these shows, after-parties, and assorted gatherings became regular fixtures on my landscape. Some of them—many of them—were living so hard, so fast. I think it was only their youth that got them through some of their experiences, often chemically induced or motivated.

I wasn't like them. Not in the least. I had no interest in dying young, and I couldn't understand why they pushed their existence to the edge as almost a matter of course. I felt like some naïve Boy Scout voyeur around these people. I couldn't call them friends. I didn't feel anything in common with them, and, quite often, they let me know that the feeling was mutual.

It seemed to me that either they didn't take their lives seriously—that is to say, that they thought they couldn't die—or they in fact were trying to make an early exit and have a great time fanning the flames of their own immolation. I didn't know if it was

Facing page: *Jack Brewer of Saccharine Trust performs on one knee, drawing in SST luminaries including, from left to right: Kurt Markham of Overkill (in striped shirt), partially visible Greg Ginn, Chuck Dukowski, Bill Stevenson, Henry Rollins, and Joe Carducci. Black Flag rehearsal space, Unicorn Studios, Santa Monica, CA, early 1980s.*
JORDAN SCHWARTZ

fearlessness, insanity, or stupidity that made them this way. I had never met anyone like them. They seemed like they had seen so much, like they were veterans of some long-running urban conflict.

We were young, the music was great, and everything was heavy.

I would often leave Los Angeles for months at a time, touring all over, as bands do. Sometimes we would come back to find that someone had died, someone else had acquired a dope habit, someone else had fled the state because of warrants—or worse. There were worse situations than an outstanding warrant. An outstanding payment to the wrong person, and the vast deepness of Oregon would become a viable alternative. It's been a long time since I've seen that guy. Anyway…

One of the most memorable people from those days was a girl named Kim Pilkington. She was extremely intelligent, and I believe she had the lowest fear quotient of anyone I have ever met. I guess she was a bit crazy, but I think it was more her zero tolerance for boredom. Life didn't seem to be hitting hard enough or going deep enough for her. No matter how far out you thought you wanted to go, Kim had already been there, and was only getting warmed up, where you had long before backed off.

Many years ago, Black Flag's bassist Chuck Dukowski advised me to take LSD. I asked him why, and he said: "Because you're an asshole. It might help." The only person I knew who could perhaps locate some acid was Kim. So I called her and told her of my assignment. She said that she would score, but that I had to do it with her. She said that there was no way she was going to miss this. Having absolutely no idea what I was in for, I said okay.

She showed up a while later with some acid. She gave me two hits and told me to let them sit on my tongue. I did, and so did she. Minutes passed, and she asked me if I was high. Not knowing what I was supposed to be feeling, I said no. We both did another hit of acid. Nothing. At least nothing that I was aware of. She gave me another one.

We went out driving. We were stopped at an intersection and she asked me how I was doing. I reported to her that the wheels of the motorcycle next to her car were spinning. She told me I was officially high.

Next stop, Burger King. The idea of getting out of the car was much too much for me to handle—there were people out there. She told me it was going to be fine. We somehow managed to get some food. It was a miracle. The hamburger I was eating had morphed into a baby's head. I told her. She seemed unimpressed.

She then remembered that she had to do some kind of errand—for her mother, I think it was. We were both now tripping extremely hard. She drove expertly through traffic and went into some office building with me trailing behind her. She talked to some adults about something, and we left. I was out of my mind, but still in it enough to be amazed at how well she was able to maintain. We spent the rest of the day somewhere in Santa Monica, talking and being very high. I don't remember much of it, but she was definitely in charge.

For some reason, experiences like this are rarely left to stand alone as onetime and onetime-only events. Days later, Kim called me and asked if I wanted to do LSD again. It was an incredibly bad idea. Sure.

I think we both did four hits and went driving. We were somewhere near the ocean, driving through some large parking area, and Kim was driving at high speed, doing her level best to run people over. "I hate people!" she yelled. I was unable to breathe. I managed to calm her down, and listed people she didn't hate, and that seemed to do the trick.

Facing page: *The Minutemen, Grandia Room, Hollywood, CA, 1982. Most of the few people in the crowd played in other SST bands. At left is Earl Liberty from Saccharine Trust, center is Henry Rollins, and at right (in trucker hat) is Chuck Dukowski from Black Flag.* JORDAN SCHWARTZ

BLACK SHEEP
TENSION
SICKLES AND HAMMERS

Later on, we were driving on some winding canyon road, and she started driving very fast, going around cars. I asked her how she was able to do that. She said it was no different than playing a video game. Around this time, she gunned the engine and started driving near the edge of the road, which bordered on some very severe drop-offs. She said that it was time for us to die. If I had any objections, or reasons to stay alive, I was to list them immediately. She would consider keeping the car on the road. If she wasn't serious, I had no idea.

I listed a couple of justifications for us staying alive. They were not good enough. Time to die. For some reason, I yelled out: "I still have to finish the vocals on the *My War* album!" It was true. That seemed to register with her, and she slowed down.

She was more alive than any five other people you knew put together. Smarter, too. Life seemed to go too slow for her, or was somehow not real enough, and I had no idea how she was going to survive that. Due to touring commitments and life, I lost track of Kim.

I saw her years later at a benefit show I was part of at the Roxy. She was wearing a large hat, almost like she was in disguise. She said hello, and I didn't recognize her, she looked so different. She reminded me who she was, and as I was still registering my very real surprise, she just laughed and walked away. That was the last time I ever saw her. The next time I became aware of her was when I read that long-term hard drug use had taken its toll and she had died.

Time must have been incredibly hard for Kim to endure. Life for her was perhaps too much, or not enough. I don't know.

So many of the people from those days are gone, it is as if they were ghosts all along. It's like they had already left the building, and you got to hang out with their aftereffect, like getting caught up in the wind of a passing train. Sometimes I wonder if I ever met them at all.

It is strange for me to live in this city, and to drive these streets filled with so many memories, so many stories that had such bad endings.

Somehow, you and I are still here.

Top left and right: *Black Flag, Stardust Ballroom, Hollywood, January 1986.* JORDAN SCHWARTZ. Bottom: *Black Flag,* We Got Power *session, Towers of Power, Redondo Beach, CA.* DAVID MARKEY. Next page: *Flower punks.* JORDAN SCHWARTZ. Next page following: *This* We Got Power *session with Black Flag took place during the Chuck Biscuits era at locations in and around SST Phelan, on Phelan St. in Redondo Beach. Dez Cadena was in the band, but he was unavailable.* DAVID MARKEY AND JORDAN SCHWARTZ

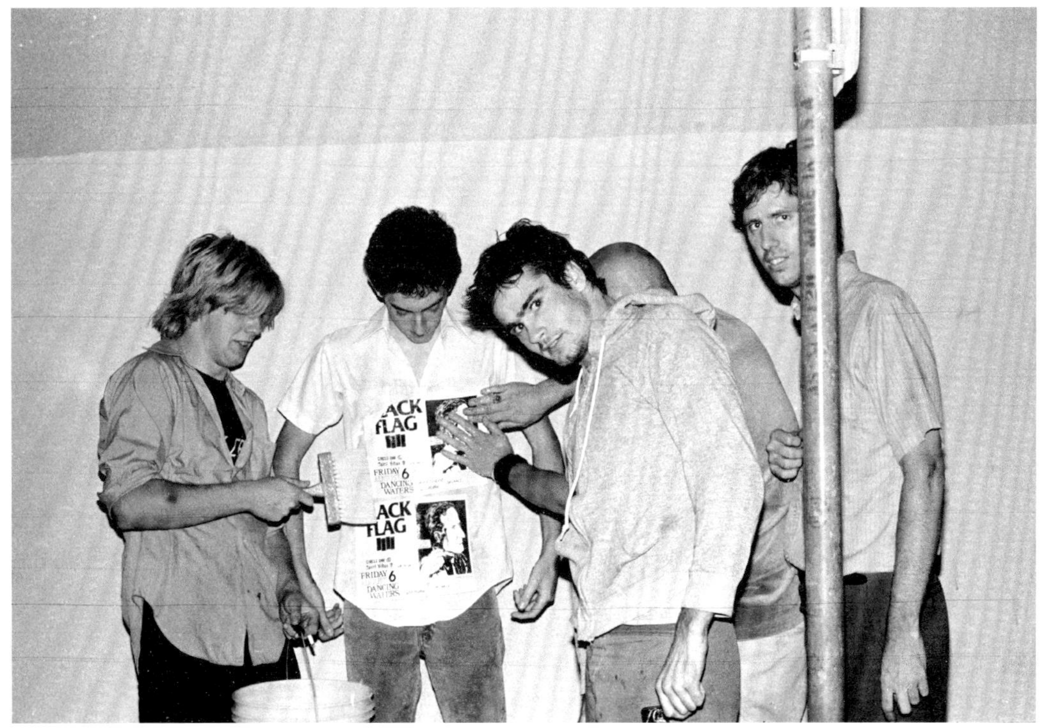
ACK
FLAG
FRIDAY 6
DANCING
WATERS
ACK
FLAG
FRIDAY 6
DANCING
WATERS

This page and previous: *Henry Rollins, Black Flag reality, somewhere in America, 1986.*
JORDAN SCHWARTZ

This page, clockwise from left: *Greg Ginn, Gone record store show. Ginn would play these afternoon spots, sometimes two or more a day, then at night perform for hours with Gone and Black Flag.* JORDAN SCHWARTZ; *Gone live.* JORDAN SCHWARTZ; *Black Flag, Stardust Ballroom, January 1986.* JORDAN SCHWARTZ. Facing page: *Black Flag minus Dez, SST Records Phelan.* DAVID MARKEY. Overleaf: *Black Flag avoids the light, 1985. Left to right: Henry Rollins, Greg Ginn, Kira Roessler, Bill Stevenson.* JORDAN SCHWARTZ

4200
THIS SIDE
CRÜE

PUNKS BECOME THE MEDIA
CAMERON JAMIE

The great photographer Weegee once claimed that New York newspapers paid him one dollar for each bullet shown in a shot of a dead mobster lying in the city streets. As an underage teen punk and amateur photographer, Jordan Schwartz was paid one can of beer for each backyard hardcore punk show he photographed for his underground fanzine. Together with musician and filmmaker Dave Markey, Jordan published the hardcore punk fanzine *We Got Power*. They were teenage kids who loved the most extreme hardcore punk music and still possessed an affectionate taste for popular culture and humor.

Like all great on-the-job photographers, Markey and Schwartz always reported to the scene of the crime. They documented punk happenings—a tiny house party at a punker's pad while the parents were away on vacation; a punk gig inside of a rented black discotheque in Watts—or simply snapping photos of their friends hanging out. Markey and Schwartz were teenagers looking into the subculture of teenagers. They wanted to reach out with their fanzine to promote hardcore punk to kids who felt the same about life as they did.

In *We Got Power*, they were way ahead of the game in mixing up popular film and TV culture references with hardcore punk bands. It might have been very uncool to love the popular TV program *Three's Company* while at the same time following one of the most extreme and feared L.A. hardcore bands of the scene, Circle One. But in their fanzine Markey and Schwartz never drew the line between these two very different sensibilities.

Southern California suburbia in the early 1980s was indeed a very strange and depressing place to grow up. Charles Manson must have been extremely jealous, because Ronald Reagan was the newly appointed bogeyman in the eyes of the new youth of America. During that time, Ronnie's wrinkled prune face was the '80s answer to Alfred E. Neuman, too. Humor and horror were both in the air.

Between 1981 and 1983, a massive infestation of teenage garage bands spread rapidly across the suburban landscapes around Los Angeles County, the South Bay, and Orange County. Isolated teenagers living in Southern California suburbs started to make punk music that was punctuated with violent rage and took a primal approach to playing and performing. The punk scene went more underground and became more "hardcore." As it became more fragmented and scattered, the variety of younger kids it attracted grew even stranger. These younger kids showed off their odd tastes and attitudes, injecting new definitions, ideas, and styles into the early-'80s chapter of hardcore punk in America.

We all know about the nihilistic violence and rage the kids felt against their parents, schools, cops, and society at large. But I'm surprised at how rarely popular culture and humor are discussed as a major drive in the development of hardcore punk attitudes and aesthetics.

Many hardcore punks who devoted their adolescent youth to this music movement were heavily influenced by, and em-

Facing page:
Alan Gilbert in his bedroom, 1981. I usually developed film in the school photo lab at Samohi. From the looks of the uneven pattern here, though, this one was probably developed by hand in the darkroom Jordan set up in the bathroom he shared with sister Jennifer in their mother's condo.
DAVID MARKEY

BLACK FLAG
FEAR
STAINS
YOUTH GONE MAD
CAUSTIC CAUSE
FRI. SEPT. 11
SIX PACK

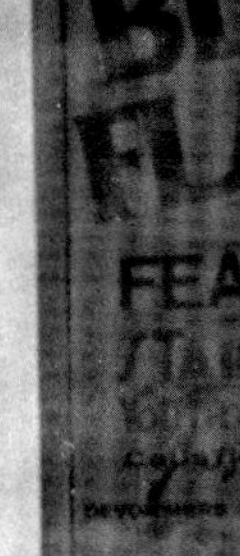

Uniting in Order to Divide
CAUSTIC CAUSE
NO AGE LIMIT
BARDS APOLLO
4417 W. ADAMS

AUG.
CIRCLE JERKS
PLUS
WASTED YOUTH
AT THE WHISKY

DON'T GO BACK TO SCHOOL PARTY
WITH
WASTED YOUTH

braced aspects of, popular media culture, even if they had serious contempt toward authoritarian social rules. The majority of kids in hardcore punk circles still lived at home with their middle-class families and had ready access to television. But while West Coast punks embraced television culture, they also used it as a major conduit for absorbing and expressing their disgust with humanity. As much these punks would enjoy taking part in the violent slam pits at shows to vent their antisocial anger, they would most likely end up back at home watching popular television reruns of *The Partridge Family*, *Fantasy Island*, *Adam-12*, and *Bewitched*. This casts a shameful and contradictory light on the image of the stereotypical outlaw street punk, which I suppose might be a major factor in why the issue is never raised.

Around this time, local tabloid television talk shows, such as *The Wally George Show*, and locally produced TV specials, such as the now infamous *We Destroy the Family: Parents vs. Punks* program, emerged and began exploiting and targeting punks as public enemy number one. This was several years before Latino and black street gang cultures started to make local and national headlines as the latest terror in Los Angeles. The outside world didn't realize that the punks were laughing along, watching themselves portrayed on television, completely understanding that the shows were pure exploitation fare. At the same time, punks didn't seem to mind the local attention, either.

What interests me most about any pictorial history of punk is not the iconic money shots of punk leaders from well-known bands. I've always been drawn to peculiar moments captured in the strange locations where gigs were held, mostly outside of the clubs in backyards, streets, and living rooms. It's an incredible sight to witness; in the far background of a photo from a hardcore show, a young nerdy kid with pimples and braces wearing a Hawaiian shirt, skanking in the slam pit. This speaks more to me about California youth culture than anything else. Who were those types of freaky suburban kids who were unconsciously breaking the stylistic rules and codes of hardcore punk? I've always been fascinated by those ultra-outcasts, because they reveal a lot about the specific reality of how kids really looked and lived in punk circles. Everything started getting really interesting during moments when the laws of punk were starting to warp, distort, and mutate, as punk rock ideology became more complicated and questionable.

The moment of *We Got Power* might seem very short-lived, but it obviously had a massive impact in forging the proto-independent attitude of music scenes throughout the mid- to late '80s and early '90s. As for Dave Markey and Jordan Schwartz, I can't help but think that they were two of the O.G. "beautiful losers" of their generation. They both documented a punk attitude that was, strangely enough, beyond punk. It was something weird and beautiful.

Facing page, clockwise from top left: *Unidentified hardcore band, Hollywood house party. Easily fifty bands scattered throughout Southern California looked exactly like this; most played a couple shows, then evaporated; Punk mom with injured son and daughter—the family that stage dives together stays together; Left to right: Blake Cruz and Ron Baird from Stalag 13, Mike Vallejo from Circle One; "It's not a gang, it's a club!" Circle One and Suicidal Tendencies fans side by side in homemade shirts at the Brown Box, aka Sewercide Hall, Culver City, CA.* PHOTOS BY JORDAN SCHWARTZ

CIRCLE

Becca 1982
POOTANG

This page: *D. Boon, Janet Housden, and Joe Baiza, Santa Barbara, CA, house party.* JORDAN SCHWARTZ. Facing page, clockwise from top left: *Kara Bjornlie; Stuart Bjornlie; Dream Delon (in varsity jacket) was ever-present onstage at Circle Jerks gigs, helping manage the chaos; Renee Smith on the sidewalks of Santa Monica.* PHOTOS BY JORDAN SCHWARTZ

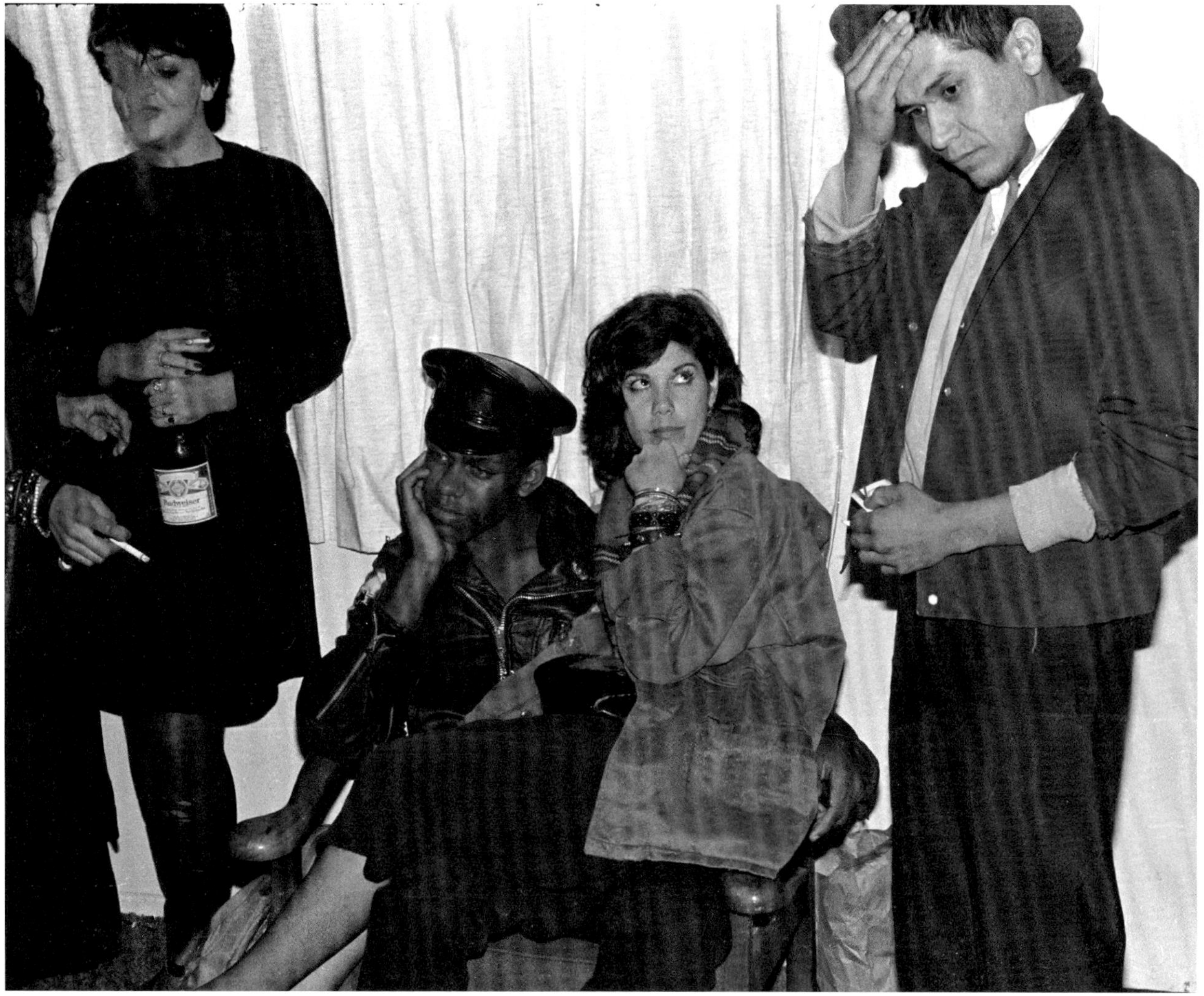

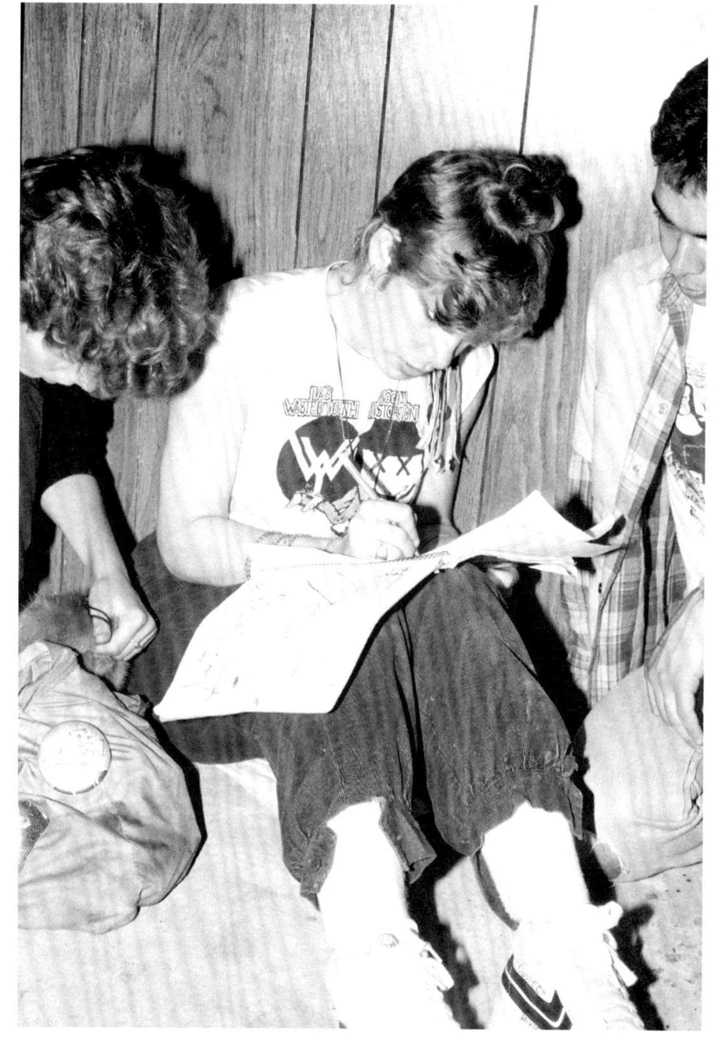

parents of punkers

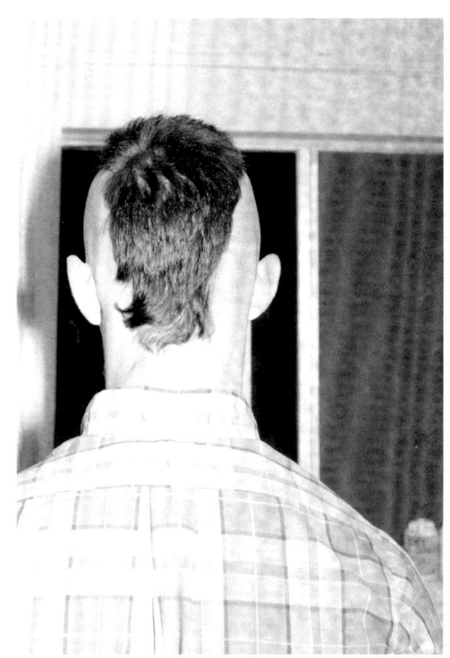

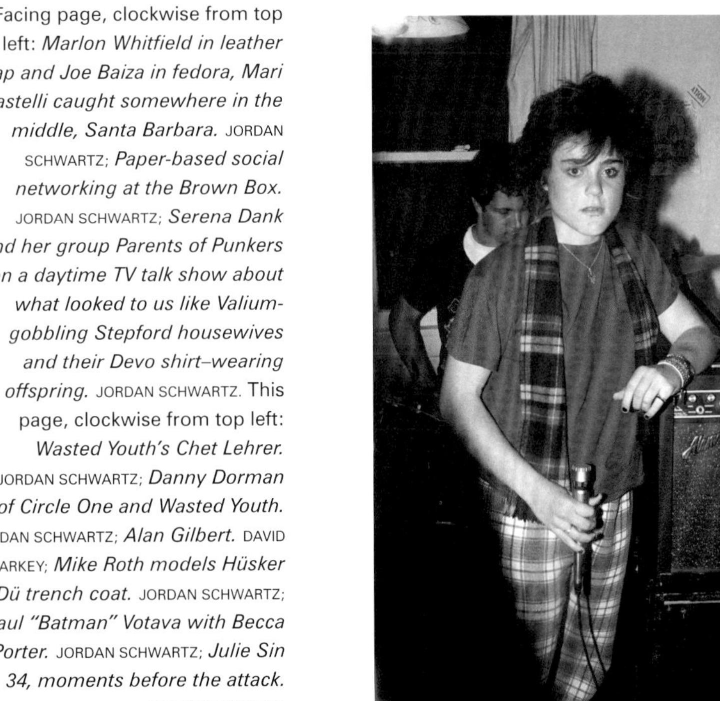

Facing page, clockwise from top left: *Marlon Whitfield in leather cap and Joe Baiza in fedora, Mari Castelli caught somewhere in the middle, Santa Barbara.* JORDAN SCHWARTZ; *Paper-based social networking at the Brown Box.* JORDAN SCHWARTZ; *Serena Dank and her group Parents of Punkers on a daytime TV talk show about what looked to us like Valium-gobbling Stepford housewives and their Devo shirt–wearing offspring.* JORDAN SCHWARTZ. This page, clockwise from top left: *Wasted Youth's Chet Lehrer.* JORDAN SCHWARTZ; *Danny Dorman of Circle One and Wasted Youth.* JORDAN SCHWARTZ; *Alan Gilbert.* DAVID MARKEY; *Mike Roth models Hüsker Dü trench coat.* JORDAN SCHWARTZ; *Paul "Batman" Votava with Becca Porter.* JORDAN SCHWARTZ; *Julie Sin 34, moments before the attack.* JORDAN SCHWARTZ.

WITH
FEAR
CIRCLE JERKS
CHINA WHITE
THE MINUTE MEN
FEB. 11
SPECTACULAR
STARDUST BALLROOM
In Hollywood
Wed. Nov. 26
SHOW
LONDON
the ORCHIDS
ONE
Full Bar
All Ages
HAVE A BREAST EXAM WITH
FEAR
+
LEGAL WEAPON
+
GUN CLUB
WHISKY
THU FEB 5
YOU MAY NOW METAPROGRAM
THE DECLINE
OF WESTERN
CIVILIZATION
RESERVED
TARWOOD
TUES
MAR 31
RHINO RECORD
BLACK
FLAG
adolescents
DOA
MINUTEMEN
The
Reagans
FEAR
SUN
JULY 5
CATHAY DE GRANDE
adolescents

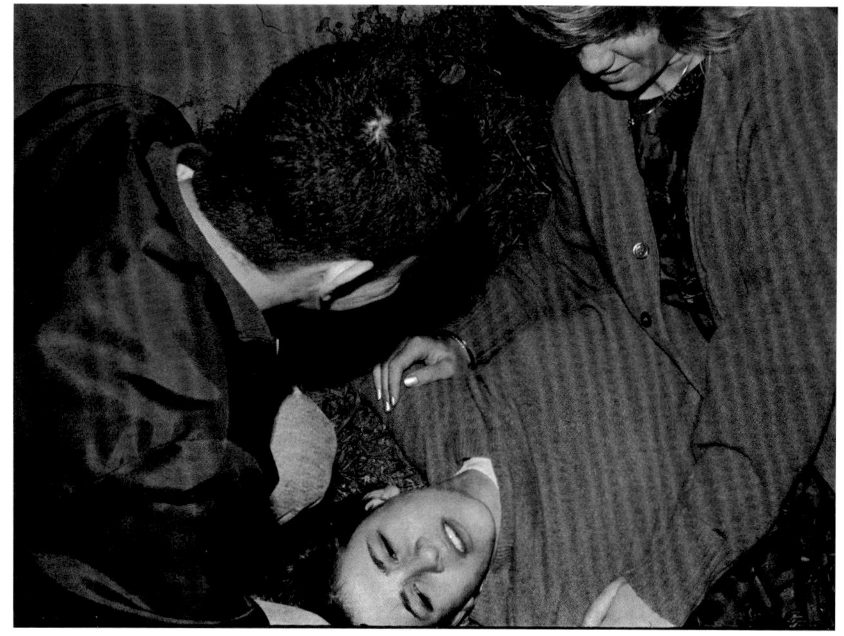

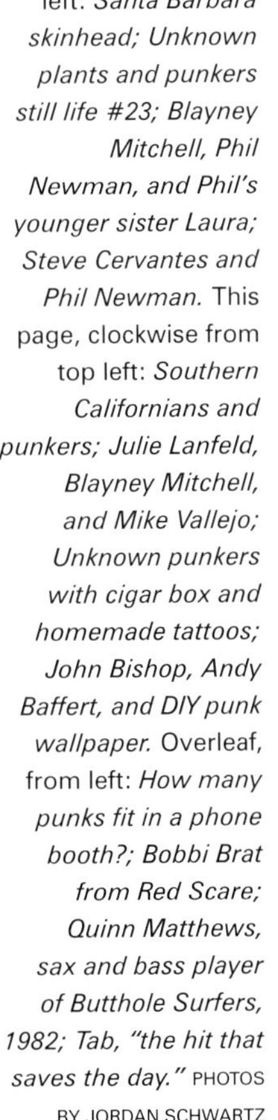

Previous page, clockwise from top left: *Santa Barbara skinhead; Unknown plants and punkers still life #23; Blayney Mitchell, Phil Newman, and Phil's younger sister Laura; Steve Cervantes and Phil Newman.* This page, clockwise from top left: *Southern Californians and punkers; Julie Lanfeld, Blayney Mitchell, and Mike Vallejo; Unknown punkers with cigar box and homemade tattoos; John Bishop, Andy Baffert, and DIY punk wallpaper.* Overleaf, from left: *How many punks fit in a phone booth?; Bobbi Brat from Red Scare; Quinn Matthews, sax and bass player of Butthole Surfers, 1982; Tab, "the hit that saves the day."* PHOTOS BY JORDAN SCHWARTZ

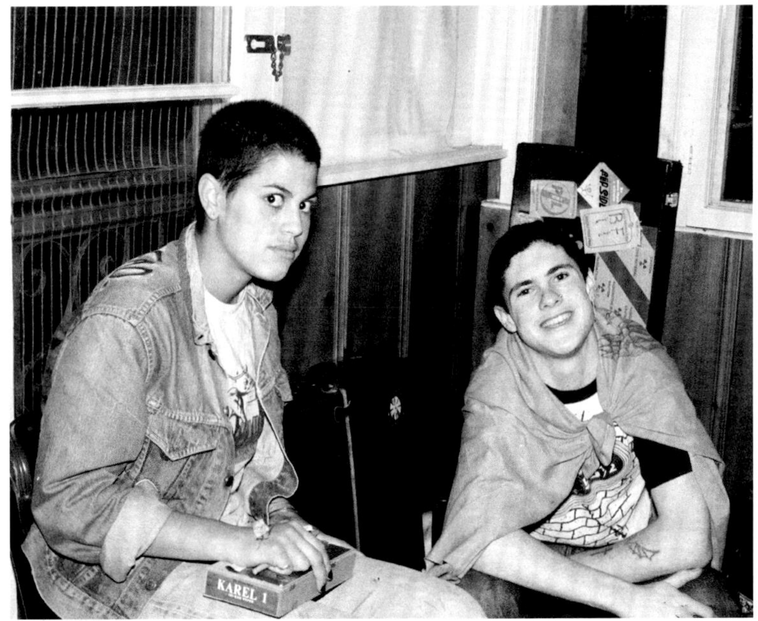

phone

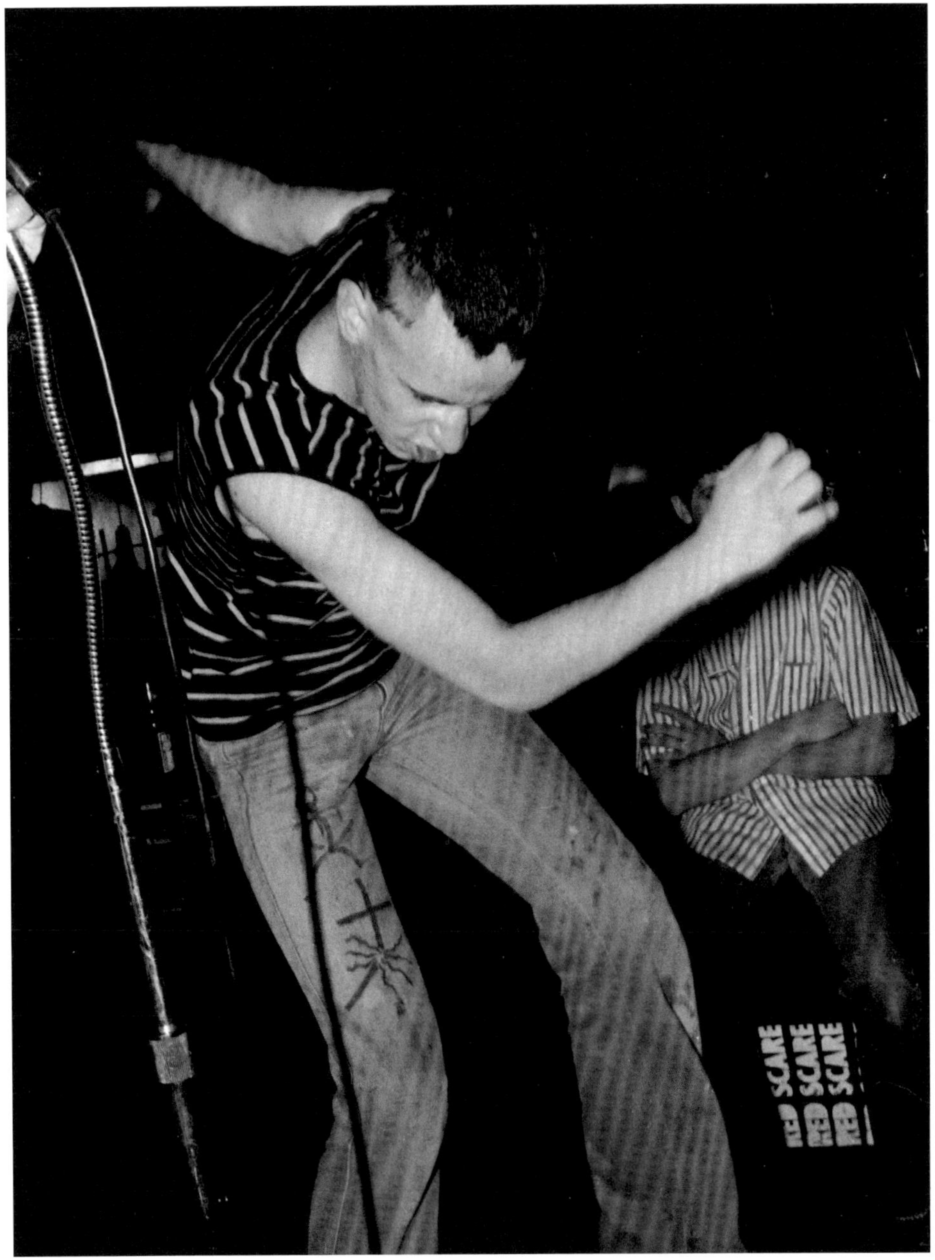
RED SCARE
RED SCARE
RED SCARE

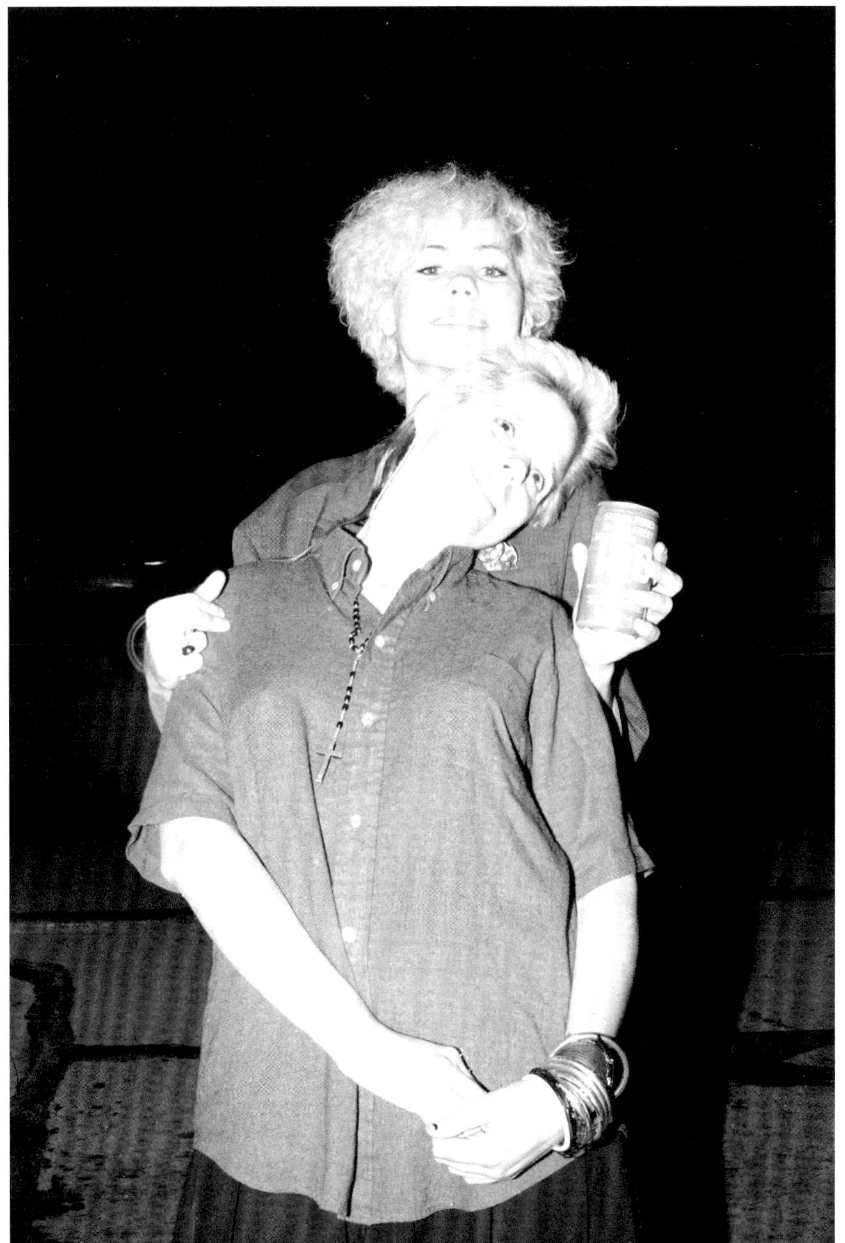

PARTY OR GO HOME
JORDAN SCHWARTZ

I first met Dave Markey in Santa Monica on a rainy fall night in 1979. I was cleaning out the underground garage of my mom's brand-spanking-new condo, which was flooded with about three feet of water from heavy freak rains the night before. As I was wheeling my bike out, along came Dave on a beat-up old skateboard, screaming down the concrete ramp from the street, splashing into the murky water. Being a skater myself, it looked like fun. He asked me if I wanted to join his teenage crew and skate the other flooded garages in the neighborhood.

This was a great chance to meet my new condo complex neighbors, one of whom quickly threatened to kill both Dave and me for skateboarding on his property. Dave just antagonized the guy for a few minutes until we moved on to skate our other neighbors' flooded driveways.

Dave and I were the same age, both sixteen, and he lived right around the corner. He had a few things going for him, including the *Neighborhood Journal*, a ten- to fourteen-page Xerox publication. That was like a fanzine for the neighborhood, although we wouldn't learn what fanzines were for another year or so. He also made Super 8 films using local kids. They were extremely funny, especially if you were a teenage street rat. When we met, Dave was working on a scripted feature-length Super 8 film called *The Omenous*, which was a spoof of two of my favorite horror films, *The Omen* and *Carrie*.

For me, that was the right place and time to almost literally run into Dave. My mom, my younger sister, Jennifer, and I had moved all over L.A. for the previous ten years. I never really clicked with any kids, and school was becoming fairly depressing. My sister and I were latchkey kids, a pretty common side effect of the '70s "me" generation. Our afternoons were spent watching many hours of sitcom TV, including *The Brady Bunch* and *The Partridge Family*.

Dave helped me get out of the house and see what was happening in the city. His motto—"When opportunity knocks, *you* open the door"—was the motivation for various urban adventures, which included a lot of trespassing, ditching school, light vandalism, shoplifting, publishing the neighborhood paper, and shooting and screening *The Omenous*. I hadn't really created anything until I began working with Dave, besides writing and delivering a five-minute stand-up comedy shtick when I was fourteen as part of an EST-type self-help seminar my mom dragged me to.

Dave wisely suggested that for my senior year of high school I transfer from the private school my sister and I were attending, Crossroads, to Santa Monica High, aka Samohi, where he went to school. That gave me the opportunity to learn some graphic arts and practice photography with Dave in our yearbook class. Meanwhile, Dave and I studied the L.A. music scene from afar. Every Thursday we would sneak out of our yearbook class, scour the *L.A. Weekly* band listings, check the reviews, scan Pleasant Gehman's gossip column *L.A. Dee Da* for its L.A. punk scene content, and read zines like *No Mag* and *Flipside*.

We were also able to take two amazing after-school classes

Facing page: *Jordan in his porkpie hat at the Punk Shack, Santa Monica. Jordan wrote* PRESS *on the back of a business card and stuck it in the brim of his hat like a character out of a 1940s movie. He used this to scam his way into shows in Hollywood. He would stare dead seriously at the person in the ticket booth: "I'm Jordan from* We Got Power *fanzine, and I'm here to review the show tonight. I need entrance plus one. Thank you very much!"* DAVID MARKEY

ONE LAW FOR THEM
MADNESS
FER YOUZ
FANZINE
BLACK FLAG
FEAR
YOUTH GONE MAD
999
FLORENTINE GARDENS
SPECIALS
ZEROX THIS
REAGAN'S IN
SKIN HEADS RULE
LEGAL WEAPON
NOMAG Benefit Show
SOCIAL DISTORTION
BAD RELIGION
45 GRAVE
AL'S BAR
OCT.30
45
AND I AM FOND
OF NO CRISIS
AND I SAW 2
PET FAWNS
GOVERNMENT
ISSUES

Carl's Jr.
CHAR - BROILED

at Beverly Hills High via the "Regional Occupational Program." The first was Television Production, where our class produced a weekly thirty-minute *Saturday Night Live*–type sketch comedy show we called *Rated G*. We used 1950s-era black-and-white, tube-based equipment, and the show aired on Beverly Hills cable. Dave and I commandeered the show. We wrote the nightly news segment, and Dave was the on-camera anchor—with a shaved head and and an *X* Magic Markered on his forehead. We brought in bands we liked as musical guests, like the Alcoholics, Gaudy Trash (who later became Symbol Six), the Smog Marines, and the B-52 Girls, featuring my fifteen-year-old sister, Jennifer Schwartz.

Our second class was Record Production, taught by legendary music mogul Neil Bogart of Casablanca Records. He had produced Kiss and Donna Summer, among other ubiquitous '70s bands. He would lecture us in his office while we sat around and read trade publications. Our homework included attending a Joan Jett concert at the Whisky A Go Go. Toward the end of the class we recorded a cheesy high school band at the Record Plant and released a 7" single. Dave tried to get Neil to sign Black Flag and the Go-Go's. Bogart declined, stating: "The Go-Go's will never go-go anywhere." Fourteen months later, the Go-Go's were number one on the *Billboard* charts and Neil Bogart dropped dead of a heart attack.

Facing page, from left: *Jordan mixing sound for* Rated G, *a weekly student-produced television show we did at Beverly Hills High, 1980. We were bussed there after school from Samohi; Jordan Schwartz, outside and inside.* PHOTOS BY DAVID MARKEY

We got into punk rock by way of new wave and ska—the B-52s, Talking Heads, the Specials, Devo, Madness, and so on. X's *Los Angeles* album and their 1980 gig at the Santa Monica Civic Auditorium with the Blasters and the Gears gave us a glimpse of the hardcore fun to come. While mellowing out after the show on the lawn in front of the Civic, we were verbally harassed by some booted, bandanna'd, and chains-wearing kids from "H.B."—Huntington Beach. They taunted us: "Why don't you get a haircut, hippie?!" We had not cut our hair yet, and we narrowly avoided getting jumped by a gang of kids because of that.

Until that point, music hadn't quite spoken to me. My suburban hippie parents played the Beatles and Rolling Stones during my formative years. This and other corporate rock was crammed down our throats: Led Zep, Nugent, Queen, Cheap Trick, and the like. All of it is great stuff, especially these days for automobile commercials, but back then you couldn't get away from it. After my parents divorced, my dad got me to listen to Dr. Demento on the radio every Sunday, complemented by George Carlin, Richard Pryor, Firesign Theatre, and Cheech and Chong records.

The hardcore punk transition record for me was the *Decline of Western Civilization* soundtrack, with Black Flag, Circle Jerks, Fear, X, and the Germs. We listened to that record every day, along with new releases like Black Flag's *Jealous Again* EP, Dead Kennedys' *Fresh Fruit for Rotting Vegetables*, and of course Rodney Bingenheimer's weekend radio show on KROQ. From there, I tape-recorded all the hardcore tunes on my ghetto blaster.

In those days before we even had our driver's licenses, I recall Dave's mom driving us to Hollywood in her Dodge Dart for the *Decline* premiere at the Egyptian Theatre. After seeing a hundred cops hanging out in front of the theater, we were too scared to get out of the car—not that Mrs. Markey was going to stop anyway. There was a Dead Kennedys gig at the Whisky, where the packed room and relatively low stage made possible one of my first stage-dive runs. I was also fortunate to have Jello involve me in an onstage impromptu pantomime during "Bleed for Me." He tied me to the mic stand, aimed his rifle, and shot. I died my dramatic death and flew off center stage into the churning pit.

By the time of the June 1981 Black Flag gig at the Santa Monica Civic, Dave and I had graduated high school. We were members of the L.A. hardcore scene and had the bruises to prove it. Not long afterward, Dave, Jennifer, and I were in Alan Gilbert's bedroom, making a mix tape of Circle One, the first Minor Threat EP, Crass, et cetera. We decided we would create our own fanzine. Jennifer sketched a picture of Alan's tiger pillow, which I assume he had had since he was a kid. Dave gave it an anarchy symbol necklace, and we had our first front cover.

Dave started laying out pages fairly quickly, building on the foundation of his *Neighborhood Journal* experience. I picked up a 35-mm camera as a graduation present and started to shoot, develop, and print my own pics. Kim Pilkington joined our crew. She was a bit crazier than all of us, but she actually had a car. *We Got Power* became our license to drive all over L.A. for any gig, band practice, or punk rock party that caught our interest. We built on that core team, meeting periodically in Dave's flyer-laden bedroom for editorial sessions. We took in contributions from local photographers we met in the pit, like Ed Colver and Alison "Mouse" Braun. Dave kept an eye on the mailbox for incoming scene reports from around the nation.

We printed interviews with Black Flag, Circle Jerks, Minor Threat, Dead Kennedys, Hüsker Dü, Misfits, and DOA. There wasn't much coverage of scene unity, like could be found in other fanzines, but it seemed like every story of some punk getting punched in the face made it into a gig review or a column somewhere in the mag. Perhaps the closest to unity we got was Kim's articles on scamming, which did involve kids "getting together." There were also lots of anti-police references. Of course, they made themselves a part of many of the big gigs back then, and harassed us by clearing out Oki Dog every Friday and Saturday night.

Humor was important from the beginning. We were the only fanzine I knew of to have a punk-themed maze ("Help the Punk Find the Safety Pin"). Our listing of best band names was mostly made up: the New Wave Secretaries, Street Wise Negroes, Chicken on Fire, True Fathers of Thrash, and Green Chompy. Six months after we published one joke—"Why did the punk cross the road? Because he was safety-pinned to the chicken"—it turned up in an episode of NBC's *Square Pegs.*

One of the side benefits of running a Circle One interview in the first issue was learning that the father of singer John Macias ran a printing press. That enabled us to have a well-printed magazine, with glossy cover and colored ink, from the very beginning. Our costs were low, and we sold enough copies so I would only have to kick in a couple hundred bucks from my pocket every time I picked up a new issue from Mr. Macias. We had a benefit at Godzilla's, in combination with another publication, *Fer Youz*, a free 14 x 18" Xerox poster zine of photos and graphic art that you could only get by hanging out at a gig or at Oki Dog. Bad Religion, Descendents, Minutemen, Sin 34, and Symbol Six, filling in for a flaky Circle One, played the benefit gig, while the *Fer Youz* folks showed slides of kids hanging out at previous shows.

Our publication runs started at one thousand for the first issue and expanded to twenty-five hundred for the fifth and final issue, which sold out fairly quickly. Dave handled sales to distributors such as Systematic, Greenworld, Rough Trade, and Dutch East India, and he took care of the mail order as well. Dave and I would both hit up the record companies via the phone and mass mailings for ads and copies of records to review. We would hop into Kim's car to hit all the independent record stores in L.A. and O.C. to sell mags on consignment. I also sold new issues at gigs; Maggie from Twisted Roots ripped me off for one out in front of the Whisky. I sold more than a hundred copies of *We Got Power* #3 at the BYO-sponsored Bad Religion blowout at the Hollywood Palladium.

We published five issues in a span of about two years. We also produced a compilation LP, *Party or Go Home*, featuring forty

Facing page, clockwise from top left: *Jordan hanging out in front of Rip City Skates. He hooked Black Flag up with Rip City, who started producing skateboards bearing Raymond Pettibon designs; Jordan and Jim McDowall, co-owner of Rip City Skates, save the universe via Aero Fighters. Video games came to Rip City and edged out the pinball machines, but the shop still has a pinball machine there today; Jordan lectures viewers in Black Flag's "Slip It In" music video; Jordan points to a flyer for a screening of* The Omenous *at the Bay City Jewish Community Center, Santa Monica, 1980.*
PHOTOS BY DAVID MARKEY

2709
828-0388
cal tranz
FIBREFLEX

The Comedy You'll Be Scared Of
THE OMENDUS
World Premier Screening
Friday Oct. 17 - 8:00pm
corner of 26th & S.M. blvd.
(BAY CITY COMMUNITY CENTER BLD.)

Nn Oo Pp Qq Rr S

American and Canadian bands doing one-minute songs, including 7 Seconds, the Minutemen, the Big Boys, Nip Drivers, JFA, Dr. Know, Tar Babies, Mecht Mensch, Dayglo Abortions, Rebel Truth, White Cross, and White Flag. Dave shot a Super 8 documentary film, *The Slog Movie*, which has some great live footage of Wasted Youth, Red Cross, Circle One, Black Flag, Circle Jerks, TSOL, the Cheifs, Sin 34, and Symbol Six. We started work on issue #6, which included an excellent cover contribution from Raymond Pettibon called "We Survived the Pit!" This issue was never completed or published, as we started working on the film *Desperate Teenage Lovedolls* while getting into weirder post-hardcore projects.

It seems we had a special group of people to cover—a very happening scene. Perhaps the lack of easy, everywhere, always-on media helped us keep our focus. These days, any song and most gigs can be downloaded to a cell phone, but that hardly compares to the sights, smells, and sweat of a one-dollar punk night Descendents gig with Frank, Milo, Bill, and Tony at the Cathay de Grande...

WE GOT POWER!

This page: *We made the best of what we found lying around. These wooden concrete molds were just waiting to be skated on.* DAVID MARKEY; Facing page: *Sidewalk scene at the strip mall across the street from the Punk Shack. When we finally decided to crop our long hair, FreeStyle charged us six dollars for new wave haircuts.* JORDAN SCHWARTZ

FREESTYLE
CLEANERS
DONUT KING

WE GOT NOTHIN'

DAVID MARKEY

The attempted assassination of newly elected president Ronald Reagan kicked things off. It was the spring of 1981, and the Los Angeles hardcore punk scene was in full bloom. The genre was more or less dubbed "hardcore" by West Coast Canadian punk band D.O.A. But, as far as I could tell, hardcore was really an offshoot of what was happening in Hollywood in the late 1970s, thanks to the blueprint written in 1979 by Darby Crash, Pat Smear, Lorna Doom, and Don Bolles—the Germs—on their unparalleled *GI* LP. Of course, Orange County's Middle Class put out their "Out of Vogue" 7" EP a year before that. Darby died at the dawning of this era, never knowing what his legacy would beget. Okay, so Sid beat him to the punch, but both of their images were selling an equal amount of T-shirts at the time in the two "post-punk" stores on Melrose, Flip and Vinyl Fetish.

Masque-era punk was fading. Only a few bands survived from the class of '77. A great divide emerged within the scene over punk proprietary rights. Some of the "old-timers" were not exactly thrilled with the second generation of fans of this music, i.e., my friends and me. They would scowl at us through their jet-black-dyed hair and doped-up jaded cool: "Where were you two years ago, when it mattered?" You see, at the time, two years was *a really long time*. All the really cool kids were eternally so much cooler because they were there first.

Granted, the first wave of L.A. punk was filled with incredible, diverse bands like X, the Weirdos, the Zeros, the Bags (R.I.P.), the Controllers, the Dickies, the Dils (who transformed into Rank and File), the Avengers (from S.F. and L.A., R.I.P.), the Alley Cats, the Plugz, the Deadbeats (R.I.P.), Black Randy and the Metrosquad (R.I.P.), the Screamers (R.I.P.), and the Go-Go's—who became the number one band in the nation in 1982.

Nonetheless, the fact of the matter was that it was time for a new generation to emerge. The new music was much more aggressive, faster, and the songs were shorter. The bands were younger, less urban or arty, and less learned musically. The fans were also younger, less urbane, and less art-school. We were suburban skate kids out to *fuck shit up*. The words of the prophets were written on the bus benches in Magic Marker: "Fuck art, let's slam dance!" and "Faster! Louder! Shorter!" Being hardcore for me meant REALLY BEING INTO IT. Rather than just be there for this music we loved, we started to document the scene through photographs, writing, and, when I could afford it, Super 8 film.

I was an avid reader of *Flipside*, the fun SoCal punk fanzine, and I had also seen *Slash* magazine on the stands at Rhino Records on Westwood Boulevard. I had sort of wanted to create something similar. This idea festered for a while, until a new acquaintance and local Westside punk enthusiast named Alan Gilbert took the initiative to actually get the ball rolling with *We Got Power*. Alan and I wholeheartedly agreed on music. For example, we both had a fondness for the Electric Eels' "Agitated" single; the debut Meat Puppets 7", "In a Car"; the Red Cross EP on Posh Boy; and a Half Japanese 7" that Alan had. In addition to doing some writing and photography, I helped put the first issue

Facing page: *David Markey surveying the slow demolition of the Punk Shack. Our hangout for the better part of a year was being demolished so another strip mall could be built. We had won the graffiti battle with the stoners, as one by one they began appearing at punk shows with their hair cut short. But we lost the war and had our beloved space consumed by commercial development of the Westside.* JORDAN SCHWARTZ

ADOLE
CENT
DARK
PART
CREEPING
KILL
T.S.

Sav on
RUGS

X
The BLASTERS
THE GEARS
OCT. 11
Santa Monica Civic

NEIGHBORHOOD
JOURNAL

Facing page, clockwise from top left: *Local kid Darrell Clark posing with a random patron of McDonald's. My films then involved things like Darrell go-go dancing for local senior citizens. He would eat Big Macs and puke them out on busses just to freak people out.* DAVID MARKEY; *1979, okay, another year with nothing to do. We were latchkey kids from broken homes with a lot of darkness on the edges. Without creative outlets and the ability to express ourselves, I am not sure what would have happened. Dave Markey and Scott Hittmyer pictured.* JORDAN SCHWARTZ; *Fake photo composite of Robert Peters advertising our* Neighborhood Journal *on a local billboard. We used the same rub-off letters for the* We Got Power *logo a year or two later.* DAVID MARKEY; *David and the telephone pole poster for our first big punk show—X, the Blasters, and the Gears, at hometown Santa Monica Civic, October 11, 1980.* JORDAN SCHWARTZ

together, along with Jordan and Jennifer Schwartz. I had already known the Schwartz siblings as kids from my neighborhood for a year or two before the L.A. punk scene engulfed us.

Although he doesn't remember doing so, Alan christened the zine *We Got Power*, after the Negative Trend song "I Got Power," which appeared on the local punk compilation *Tooth and Nail*, a favorite of ours. Alan soon bowed out, as he moved away to attend UC Santa Barbara and fell away from the L.A. scene. Santa Monica High School honor roll student (and Keith Richards/J. R. R. Tolkien fan) Kim Pilkington then became a part of our crew. We were bored teenagers, trying to amuse ourselves and spread word of these bands and their music that we loved. Music that meant something to us, something that we thought could change the world.

We dove headfirst into documenting and promoting this music and these bands. By now, the scene had shifted from small and insular "Hollyweird" to reach the teething masses in the outlying suburbs of L.A., primarily the beaches: Huntington Beach, Hermosa Beach, Long Beach, Oxnard, Santa Monica, Venice, and so on. The bands were Rhino 39, Black Flag, Circle Jerks, Fear, Gun Club, Suburban Lawns, Bad Religion, the Adolescents, the Stains, the Descendents, Saccharine Trust, the Minutemen, Social Distortion, TSOL, Red Cross, Agent Orange, the Last, the Urinals/100 Flowers, Angry Samoans, the Mentors, Suicidal Tendencies, Secret Hate, Shattered Faith, Channel 3, Agression [sic], the Cheifs [sic], RF7, White Flag, Wasted Youth, Decry, SVDB, China White, the Vandals, Youth Brigade, Christian Death, Overkill, Dr. Know, the Crowd, Legal Weapon, Mad Society, Sin 34, Caustic Cause, Lost Cause, Crankshaft, Red Scare, Symbol Six, Modern Warfare, the Crewd, No Crisis, the Hated, Hated Principles, Civil Dismay, Social Dismay, Anti, Mood of Defiance, Twisted Roots, Castration Squad, the Disposals, Naughty Women, the Atoms, the Oziehares, Toxic Shock, Manson Youth, Youth Gone Mad, the Patriots, Saigon, the Detours, and dozens of bands almost nobody ever heard of, which seemingly existed only on local compilation albums and gigged primarily at house parties.

Occasionally, West Hollywood nightclubs like the Starwood or the Whisky A Go Go would still host shows, at least until the Whisky actually "boycotted" hardcore punk. For the most part, hardcore gigs occurred in faraway suburban and urban spaces, in places like old movie theaters, bars, or warehouses. These off-the-map venues were usually in rough neighborhoods, like Bards Apollo in the Crenshaw and Adams district; the Vex, which had three different locations in East L.A.; Godzilla's in Sun Valley; the Brown Box in Culver City; Mendiola's Ballroom in Huntington Park; Happy Times Roller Rink in South Central; T-Bird Rollerdrome in Pico Rivera; Bob's Place in Watts; Shamus O'Brian's in El Monte; the Longshoremen's Hall in Wilmington; Dancing Waters in San Pedro; the Cuckoo's Nest in Costa Mesa; the Barn at Alpine Village in Torrance; the Cathay de Grande in Hollywood; and plenty of other one-off dives.

We knew very little about publishing, but we learned as we went. We were certainly not in it for money. We did sell a decent amount of ads, which helped subsidize the publication. The big rewards to us were getting into shows on guest lists and receiving a lot of free records, which Jordan and I and sometimes Jennifer fought over: "Okay, I get the *Rat Music for Rat People* comp, and you get the Zero Boys *Vicious Circle* record!"

By chance, our very first interview was with Pico Rivera's Circle One, a new band that impressed us with their cassette demo. The band was named after a Germs song, although they took great pains to explain otherwise: "'Circle' is a group of people bound together by common interest, and 'One' is united!" At one point during the interview, the tough, muscle-bound singer John

828-0388
cal tranz
OPEN
POWELL

Macias mentioned that his father ran a print shop. As fate would have it, John's dad, Mr. Macias, became our printer. Mr. Macias suggested the offset printing, Day-Glo ink, glossy cover, and high-quality paper after receiving our original pages for the first issue. He had the insight to recommend the best ways to preserve the zine for years to come, and he did this for us at a fraction of the normal expense. The quality of the paper was closer to that of a high-school yearbook, rather than newsprint or Xerox, and thus *We Got Power* was set apart from other fanzines at the time.

We Got Power had a unique sense of humor and did not take itself too seriously. We focused on people in the scene almost as much as bands and music. We printed the usual gig and record reviews, band interviews, photo collages, and scene gossip, all the while keeping our punk tongues planted firmly in our cheeks. Above all, though, *We Got Power* was really about the music. For those few in the know, scores of bands were ripping it up almost nightly in the L.A. Southland. The magazine brought us into contact with many of these bands, not only locals, but also national touring bands. Los Angeles was fortunately a major destination for the handful of hardcore bands that managed to get on the road. Dead Kennedys came through a lot; Minor Threat, a couple or a few times. We were at all the early Bad Brains shows in L.A.: the Anti Club, the Ukrainian Culture Center, and the Whisky—where for their encore the banned-for-life Black Flag appeared onstage and played "Rise Above," amazing! The Meat Puppets came through, as Phoenix is basically a suburb of L.A. Plus we saw SSD, Die Kreuzen, the Necros, Flipper, Butthole Surfers, Big Boys, the Misfits, and Government Issue (there's the Germs influence again). Before long, we had interviewed the cream of the crop of American hardcore: the Misfits, Jodie Foster's Army, Red Cross (as Redd Kross were called prior to the American Red Cross's cease and desist order), Saccharine Trust, Flipper, Circle Jerks, Dead Kennedys, DOA, Black Flag, Minor Threat, Jack Grisham of TSOL, Stevo of the Vandals, Bad Religion, Suicidal Tendencies, Hüsker Dü, and the Necros. We were probably the first publication to feature Henry Rollins on his own, outside of Black Flag.

Facing page, from left: *Our happy contest winner with his* We Got Power: Party or Go Home *limited edition penis-shaped skateboard; Drew Bernstein curb hopping on a virtually empty Santa Monica Blvd.* PHOTOS BY JORDAN SCHWARTZ

My bedroom became the *We Got Power* corporate headquarters, where I typed and put the zine together. That was the thing about hardcore: It really was about teenagers and their moms, as mostly everyone still lived at home. My mother Mary's tiny two-bedroom apartment and the neighboring Schwartz condo became pit stops for touring bands. I remember "In a Free Land"–era Hüsker Dü hanging out. Bob Mould played a rough mix tape of what would become *Everything Falls Apart* in my bedroom, and my mother asked me to turn the volume down. When in town, the Dayglo Abortions, JFA, and White Cross would stop by for visits, as would *Maximum Rocknroll*'s Tim Yohannan, probably to retrieve my L.A. scene report. We would usually end up at lifeguard tower 18 on Santa Monica Beach in the middle of the night, drinking cases of Lucky Lager beer, which had funny puzzles under the bottle caps. I also recall, back before Sonic Youth could afford to pay for hotel rooms, Lee Ranaldo and Steve Shelley spending a night or two at my mom's apartment. Henry Rollins once tripped an all-nighter at the Schwartz condo. After coming to the West Coast, the former Washington, DC, straight-edger was spreading his wings and freeing his mind. He started hanging out with Kim Pilkington, consuming large amounts of lysergic acid diethylamide. Who wasn't, thanks to Kim?

We were producing our sixth issue, dubbed "#666," when *We Got Power* ceased to exist sometime in late 1983. To the observant, hardcore was over midway through the decade, but for us the writing was already on the wall. In 1984, L.A. hardcore seemed to go straight off the edge of a cliff. The cops managed to shut down all the clubs, and they threatened the ones that remained open to avoid booking so-called punk acts. Many bands were evolving in a more "crossover" metal direction. Everything fell apart, bands broke up, friends disappeared, and the scene as we knew it died away or morphed into something else.

We all got into other things, mostly things that seemed to grow from our time with the zine. I was busy making records and touring, and of course making films. Jordan went to work for Chuck Dukowski's Global Network Booking, which handled the bands on SST Records. I, too, became a part of that *reality.* My band Painted Willie joined the SST roster, and we traveled across the continental US with Black Flag for half of 1986. Jordan ended up on the cover of Black Flag's *Annihilate This Week* EP.

As the 1980s wore on, many bands like Circle One vanished from the landscape. John Macias transformed into a street preacher, delivering his sermons on Westwood and Hollywood street corners, using the same intimidating macho-muscle-guy anger that he had used to enrapture hardcore punk audiences. The stage was set for his final performance. In late spring of 1991, Macias was shot and killed by the Santa Monica police in front of a shopping mall parking structure on Colorado and Main. Apparently, John had developed some serious psychological and biological issues, and he had gone off his meds. The John I had known had always had a problem with authority. As was equally true of many other hardcore bands, years before N.W.A or Ice-T, many of John's lyrics were anti-cop. Already the LAPD was long known for its rabid anti-punk agenda, hassling anyone who looked "punk," and raiding and shutting down shows umpteen times over. Keep in mind that this was prior to the public exposure of the corruption of Police Chief Daryl Gates's famously crooked Rampart Division.

According to witnesses and articles published in the *Santa Monica Evening Outlook* and the *L.A. Times*, Macias's rampage was set in motion by a security guard on the Santa Monica Pier. Apparently, John was interrupted in the middle of a sermon, and that's where the trouble started. John reportedly dropped the security guard over the side of the pier, twenty-five feet to the parking lot below. Fleeing on foot up the pier to Colorado Boulevard, Macias entered a McDonald's. He approached an elderly woman, a German tourist, who was enjoying a Big Mac. He snatched it out of her hands, punched her in the face, and stomped the burger into the floor. He then fled across the street, where he was seen running down the embankment of the 10 Freeway. Motorists reported seeing him in the McClure Tunnel, reaching out as if attempting to grab people from their quickly moving vehicles. He somehow reemerged on Colorado, where he was spotted by a passing squad car, which called for backup from the Santa Monica Police Station a half a block away.

Three squad cars and six armed cops surrounded him, guns trained on his upper torso. Unarmed, he charged at the six cops, professing aloud: "God is going to watch you die, pig!" Macias apparently was not going down without a fight. Reportedly, it took eight bullets to stop his advance. Many bands professed their disdain for the men in blue; not many of them followed through like John "Highway Patrolman, Fuck Off!" Macias. It was a tragic end for a troubled man. If not for John Macias and his father, *We Got Power* would never have been the publication that it was.

Facing page, clockwise from top left: *Dave getting rad...;...Until a rent-a-cop spoils the fun. The Man could never catch us, though; The infamous Goat Man, a full-time denizen of the Punk Shack, whose Satanic graffiti, pentagrams, and images of devils looked like something off a 45 Grave single. He would shit and piss there, and that bummed us out. Still, he scared us. He caused Jordan to fall into a hole, hence the photos of Jordan with his arm in a sling—the curse of the Goat Man.* PHOTOS BY JORDAN SCHWARTZ

CRAMPS

This page, from left: *Dave hanging in the McDonald's parking lot adjacent to the Schwartz condo, Santa Monica; David editing* Lovedolls Superstar *at EZTV, West Hollywood, 1985.* Facing page, clockwise from top left: *David singing with Circle One at a backyard party; A tool of thought; David and Blayney Mitchell; Death and bubble gum.* PHOTOS BY JORDAN SCHWARTZ

MIA

TOOLS OF THOUGHT
KAMAS COUNTY FAIR
MOTORHEAD
S.M.
HIPPI
RED

This page, clockwise from top left: *Sin 34 backyard party, Cerritos, CA, 1982; Sin 34 curbside in Silver Lake; Mike Glass and Phil Newman, Cerritos house party, 1982; Sin 34 on 26th St., Santa Monica, 1983.* Facing page: *Sin 34 and the Aquatic Marine Divers van, Broadway, Santa Monica, 1983.* PHOTOS BY JORDAN SCHWARTZ

SPEED
LIMIT
35
CALIFORNIA
1DGB245

This page, from left: *Dave in Painted Willie, Stardust Ballroom, 1986.* JORDAN SCHWARTZ; *John Macias from Circle One at a house party in Silver Lake, 1982.* JORDAN SCHWARTZ. Facing page: *Mike Roth in the Punk Shack during demolition, 1982.* DAVID MARKEY.

ADOLE
SCENTS
SIN 34 KIX ASS
BARDS IS BEST
SACCHARINE
TOXIC SHOC
PIL
ULTRA RIOT
FUCK OFF NAZI PUNK
KILL HIPPYS
COPS
PRESENTING
CIRCLE TWO
SIN 34
RED CROSS

1981: THE YEAR PUNK SUCKED

PAT FEAR

We Got Power? Huh? Awkward grammar; poor spelling; scribbled and badly typed and haphazard layouts; inane, redundant "the band rocked and got the crowd dancing" live reviews; Circle One; SVDB; Red Cross before the extra and alternate consonants; Bards Apollo; the Cuckoo's Nest; Dancing Waters; the Vex; Godzilla's; *the Cathay de Grande*. The name brings to mind weird two-color—but not *color*—printing, heavy paper, and glossy covers, years before L.A. firebrand *Flipside* even tried such feats—something to do with John Macias's father owning a print shop. NOFX's first gig was opening for Sin 34, whose drummer just so happened to also be the editor of *We Got Power*.

I remember the H.B.'s, punk violence, and printed *reviews* of police-instigated riots that happened *nowhere* outside of California, in particular in home base SoCal on a scale that you can't even imagine. Then came a really tall art-damaged guitar player from New York blown away that a West Coast mag reviewed his *Killer* fanzine *in* a fanzine; kids in Aberdeen or Los Alamitos getting schooled on the Huntington Beach, Valley, and Nardcore scenes; and an amazing compilation album, *We Got Power: Party or Go Home*. Not to mention an interview with some bald guy I first met when he was a roadie for the Teen Idles gig at the Hong Kong Cafe years earlier, who took Dez Cadena's place and became the last in a long line of charismatic singers for one of L.A.'s earliest and better South Bay bands.

We Got Power heard and published the resonating peals of those days. The photos and fanzines collected here are impressionistic sketches, each one illustrating and simultaneously *creating* its own sketchy times, replete with vague first names plus the band name in photo captions or references, plus some quirky details jotted down and printed out in a format that wasn't as flashy as the Internet, but had a lot more soul. It all meant more, because *everything* was harder then, from making the music to documenting and disseminating it.

These *WGP* guys were not from the original scene, any more than Monica West was a Chicago blues singer. I was, and the other twenty or a hundred or so of us L.A. punks who lived punk from 1976 onward, dragging glitter and metal into the gutter, pretty much resented the next few generations as a whole. During the premier screening of *The Decline*… with police hassles outside bordering on a riot (for a *movie*, for God's sake), one of the invite-only old-schoolers (four years old, really, in more ways than one) yelled: "Kill the second generation!" The theater erupted in rousing applause. Punk had already started to suck. Many gave it up, moved on, or died as it died out. We were now the old regime, and far too quickly the hippie-spoofing punk catchphrase "never trust anyone over thirty" had gone from an insider joke to a reality.

But these poor typists and Santa Monica middle-class miscreants somehow heralded a new "new," as hardcore was brewing. The energetic but often interchangeable music that was quickly sucking all the style, tunefulness, and creativity from the early music needed its own voice, its own subgenre instruction

Facing page, from left: *Punker with Mohawk on Al Bum's shoulders; Pat Fear, White Flag, the Vex, East L.A., 1983.* PHOTOS BY JORDAN SCHWARTZ

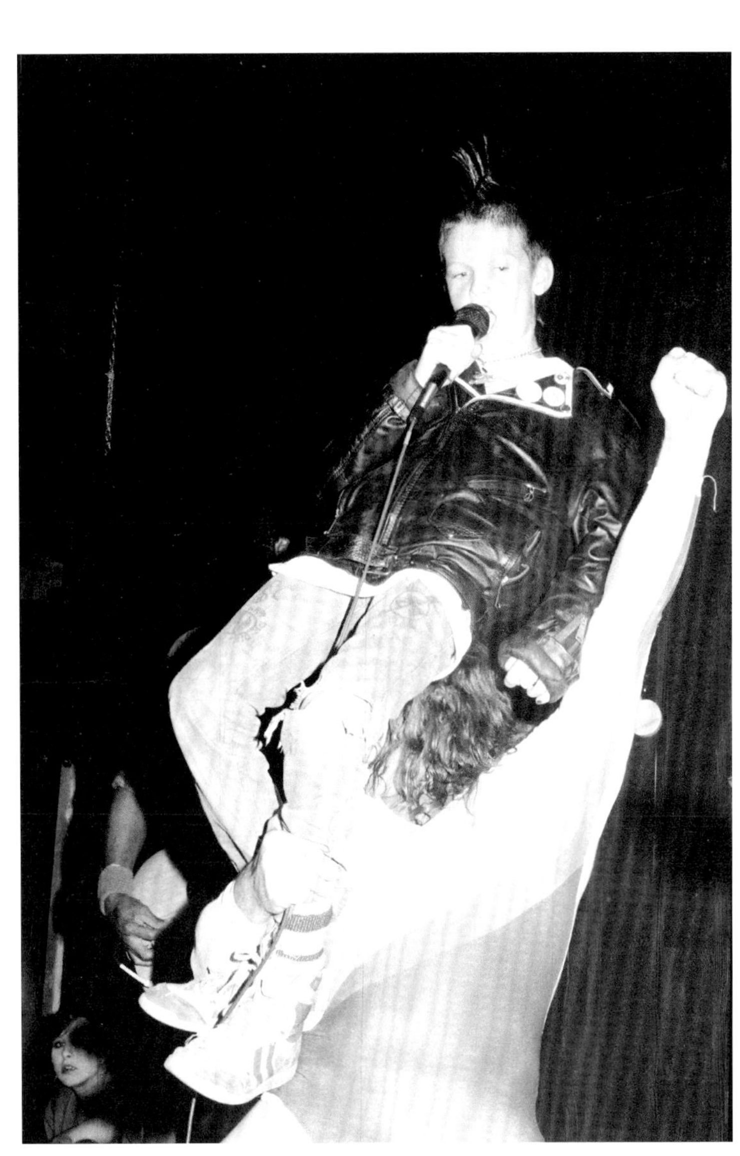

manual. The likes of X and the Germs were almost oldies by the first issue of *We Got Power* in 1981, usurped by the arrival of a larger audience for prime bands like Adolescents, Circle Jerks, and the Cheifs—whose deliberately misspelled moniker was only correctly written by a few publications at the time, including this minimalist mag. This was the document of the *real* decline, as the innovative spirit of the early-days scenesters was shoved aside, literally and often physically, by jock mentality, media pawns, and a few bright sparks of creative *power*, via hardcore's fast-as-possible chord changes doused in faked, or pointless, anger. Yeah, the same complaint us old-timers always have about the latecomers and later comers, so I should save the rhetoric, I know. But *this* Westside "gang" was, in their off-kilter approach, way more "hardcore" than fellow Dogtowners Suicidal Tendencies, who were actually really nice guys. These self-publishers really had a power, an often-mightier sword: the power of *print*.

Where these youngsters got the nerve to revive that original punk spirit, independent of any direct experience, and how they found each other's kindred spirits, are puzzles I never quite figured out. For that intangible reason, they were accepted. In return, they amazed us with some now-heralded Ed Colver cover shots; incredible live and candid time capsules by Jordan and Alison Braun, aka Mouse; left-of-center writers like Jennifer and Kim; and guest editorials by innovators like Spot and Keith Morris. They interviewed Nervous Gender and reviewed Vox Pop over and over again, luring Circle Jerks and TSOL fans into that psychotic mind-set that your average fifth-waver would never otherwise have encountered in any form. No failed-hippie faux politics of *Maximum Rocknroll*, no early scene cred of *Flipside* or Michelle Baer's *The Panic in L.A.*, but a mind-altering/alerting *power* of its own making.

The original zines barely made it out of California. Now they are posted online for the world to view in an instant; there's no more need for a desperate record store search or a mail-order treasure hunt crawling via the nearly extinct U.S. Postal Service across state and country borders. Yeah, this book is an *easier* conduit to the bridges between punk rock and hardcore, but it is still HARDCORE through its own insidious madness—and more tangible than something on an LCD screen. Smell the ink, touch the paper, lick it, smell the sweat and clove cigarettes, and maybe something will move you to think in grammar-poor English and find your own POWER.

P.S. Revisiting this time period has reminded me how many unique and talented people I knew or admired who were on the staff, depicted in pictures, named in reviews or interviews, or even just involved concurrently in the local punk scene during that era who are no longer with us: Rob "Graves" Ritter, Rozz Williams, Roger Rogerson, Dennis Dannell, Bobbi Brat, Todd Barnes, three out of five members of RKL (Bomer, Derrick Plourde, Jason Sears), Brent Liles, Gerardo Velasquez, Paula Pierce, El Duce, John Macias, Dave Dacron, Stevo, Rik L. Rik, Will Shatter, D. Boon, Frank Navetta, Mike Webber, Randy Turner, Drew Blood, Rene Gade, Joey 8, and, of course, *WGP* staffer Kim Pilkington. Sadly, this is in no way a complete list.

Clockwise from top: *White Flag, the Vex, 1983; Left to right, Al Bum, Pat Fear, Chris Gates of the Big Boys, the Big Boys' manager, Rey Washam of the Big Boys, and Spot, the Vex, 1983; Future Redd Kross guitarist Robert Hecker singing from the audience for White Flag, the Vex, 1983.* PHOTOS BY JORDAN SCHWARTZ

This page and previous: *The Gun Club, Cathay de Grande, Hollywood, January 20, 1982. Maybe fifteen or twenty people were at this show, and the band was on fire. I had already seen them opening for the Cramps at the Roxy.* DAVID MARKEY

This page, top left and right: *Civil Dismay—or Social Dismay? Both were real bands. The Barn, 1983.* Bottom: *Dude smoking weed at the Cathay de Grande.* Facing page, clockwise from top left: *Mood of Defiance, Dancing Waters, San Pedro, CA, 1982. They were very atypical for Southern California hardcore—almost psychedelic, but still really aggressive. Danny Dean Phillips on bass and Gary Kail on guitar were both also of Anti; Singer Hatha Watha of Mood of Defiance, the Barn, 1983. She was rumored to be the daughter of the hippies who rented the Church in Hermosa Beach to Black Flag; Gary Kail and backup singer, Mood of Defiance.* PHOTOS BY JORDAN SCHWARTZ

NOW

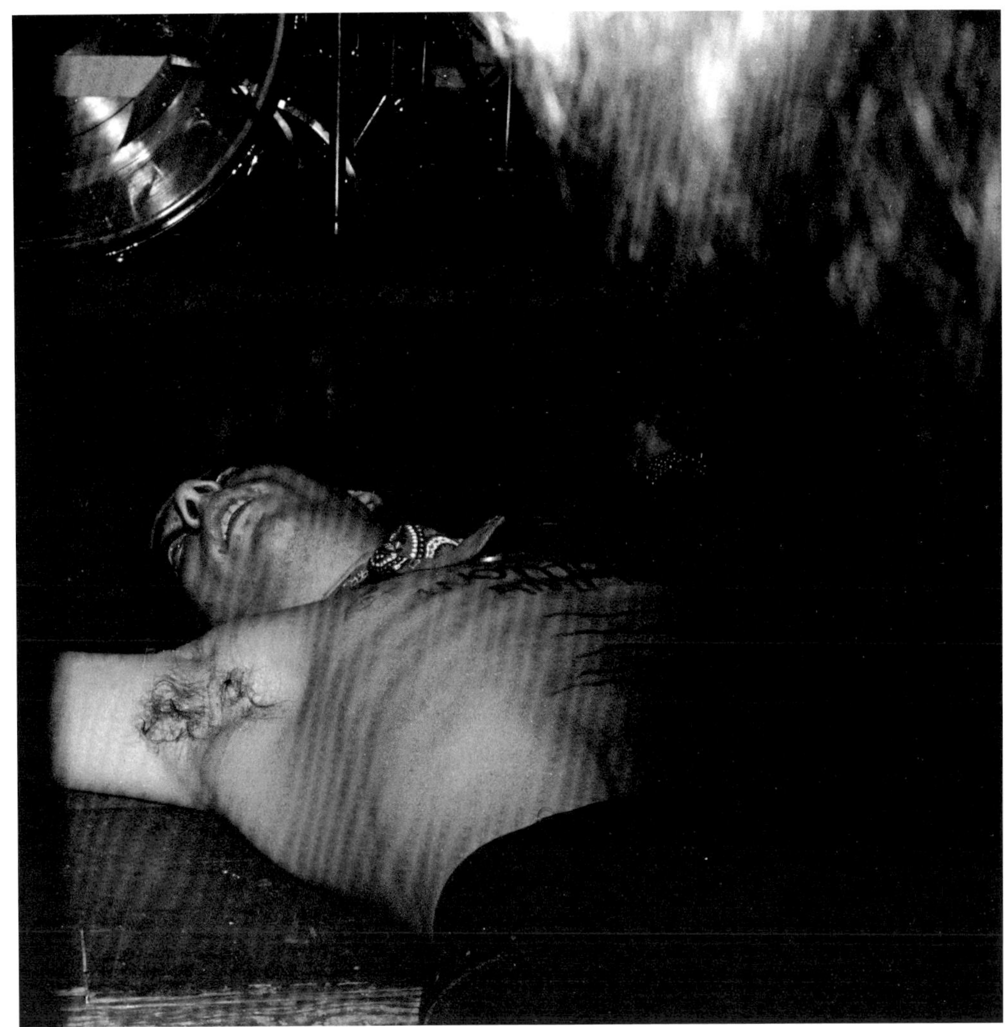

Facing page: *Vox Pop, Cathay de Grande, January 20, 1982.* This page: *Merrill Ward and Overkill, 1981.*
PHOTOS BY JORDAN SCHWARTZ

OUT OF VOGUE, WOMAN

JENNIFER SCHWARTZ

My first week at Santa Monica High School in 1980, I was headed up the stairs in between classes when I heard someone belting out "Mother's Little Helper" by the Rolling Stones, but with slightly different lyrics: "What a drag it is going to school." I saw this short, skinny, crazy-eyed, barefoot chick with a bad bleach job walking toward me. She was wearing black jeans and a sleeveless T-shirt and had a lock and chain around her neck. Making herself look even more insane, she had draped a hooded white velvet cloak over her shoulders.

I stood back—way back—and let this freaky hobbit chick pass.

I avoided her, but of course my friend Dave Markey—who had an affinity for weirdos, bums, and socially unaccepted psychotic misfits—was good friends with her. Her name was Kim Pilkington, but she took to calling herself Ruthallion Richards. She also happened to be an honor student with straight A's, who, aside from Dave, mostly stuck with her nerd peers.

I reluctantly started hanging out with Kim while we worked on *We Got Power* magazine. Kim was the only one with a car. Over time, Kim became more than just a means of transportation to me. She was a frequent contributor to the magazine. She loved being on guest lists. She wrote the "Ru on the Road" and "Scam" columns, in which she would offer tips to hopeful groupies on how to "scam" on—or hook up with, as they say these days—hot punk rock dudes. Kim embraced her inner sluttiness. In fact, she was really in touch with her outer sluttiness, too. A typical gig-going getup was bleached white hair, a slip, garter belts, fishnet stockings, tight black boots, and a black wide-brimmed felt hat with an ostrich feather sticking out of it.

When an issue of *We Got Power* was printed, she would load up her Gremlin and schlep Dave, Jordan, and me out to various record stores around L.A. and O.C.—Zed's in Long Beach, Vinyl Fetish on Melrose, Middle Earth in Downey, Moby Disc in Reseda, Rhino on Westwood—to drop off ten or so magazines that were sold on consignment for seventy-five cents a pop. The cover price was a buck. Go "Gremlin Distributors"! Pffft.

Kim weighed less than a hundred pounds, but she had huge, perfect breasts, and she was very proud of them. A little context: This was years before boob jobs, so big tits on a skinny chick was nothing short of a marvel. Even the most outrageous Mohawked punker would stop and stare when Kim walked into a club. A little more context: This was years before Madonna began whoring it up on MTV. Hard to imagine, but in 1980 slip wearing *was* scandalous.

Kim's presence, style, and personality were so memorable that bands would give her their own unique nicknames. Funny thing was that the names were all kinda similar, purely by coincidence. The Descendents called her "Vogue Woman." JFA referred to her as "Underwear Woman." I think it was Black Flag producer Spot (or maybe Bill Stevenson) who called her "Panic Woman." And I simply can't remember which band dubbed her "Hardware Woman."

Facing page: *Jennifer Schwartz, Rip City Skates, 1979. The Schwartz siblings both worked at Rip City. Jennifer assembled roller skates for twenty-five cents a skate. Of course, all the quarters went into the Space Invaders machine.* DAVID MARKEY

TRACKER

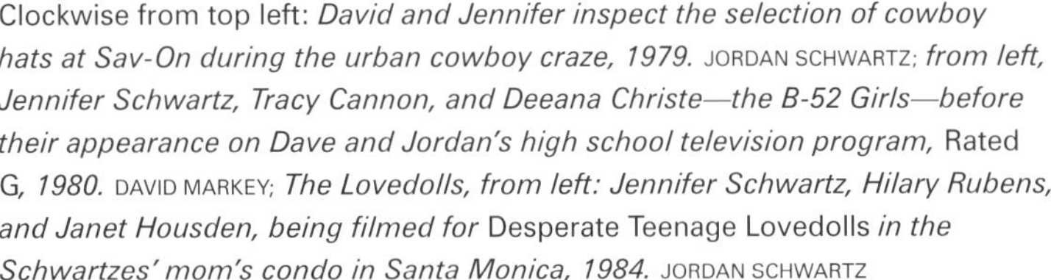

Clockwise from top left: *David and Jennifer inspect the selection of cowboy hats at Sav-On during the urban cowboy craze, 1979.* JORDAN SCHWARTZ; *from left, Jennifer Schwartz, Tracy Cannon, and Deeana Christe—the B-52 Girls—before their appearance on Dave and Jordan's high school television program,* Rated G, *1980.* DAVID MARKEY; *The Lovedolls, from left: Jennifer Schwartz, Hilary Rubens, and Janet Housden, being filmed for* Desperate Teenage Lovedolls *in the Schwartzes' mom's condo in Santa Monica, 1984.* JORDAN SCHWARTZ

Her reputation with band members went beyond nicknames. Kim loved dudes in bands—and she let everyone know it. Her favorites were SST bands, Black Flag being one of her longest and most enduring obsessions. But her *crème de la scam* was TSOL. She would gush about their all-American O.C. good looks, especially when she was around scruffy, dirty SST fans. "There are more cute guys at a TSOL rehearsal than at an *entire* Black Flag gig," she'd sneer. Funny, though, I don't think she nailed anyone in TSOL. She did once drive Mike Ness all the way to a Social Distortion show in Tucson.

After I rode shotgun alongside her in the Gremlin for a few months, Kim began to grow on me. She was ridiculously brilliant, had a photographic memory, had good taste in music (except for her obsessive love of Jimmy Page, which was annoying), and she was able to think on levels that I still don't understand. Context again: Kim was likely schizophrenic, or, at the very least, bipolar, but there were no meds back then to quell such genius/insanity.

She became my best friend. We were inseparable. It was a great friendship, especially for two people who had nothing in common. For all her overt sexuality, I was a relative prude. She dressed outlandishly, while I wore T-shirts and 501 jeans. She craved attention, while I was happy to lurk in the shadows. She drank and took handfuls of drugs... Well, we did have a few things in common.

Kim was an undeniable force who needed a partner in crime. I was fifteen years old, with a mom who couldn't give a fuck where I was or what I was doing. So I went along for the ride. And what a ride it was. Some of our most memorable escapades included hanging at Zero at 4 a.m. with David Lee Roth; interviewing Suicidal Tendencies in Mike Muir's living room; taking the red-eye flight from L.A. to S.F.—for $25!—to see Black Flag at the On Broadway (my mom thought I was spending the night at Kim's house, and I only had $20 in my pocket); doing drugs at the Cathay with Earthquake/Earache/Eric from the Stains; our entire four-person *WGP* staff tripping on LSD during a fucking race riot at a Misfits/Suicidal gig in Watts; smoking weed with D. Boon while he grilled the most amazing burgers; and avoiding a DUI thanks to Kim's in-depth knowledge of Led Zeppelin—yes, the cop let us go because he, too, rocked out to Zep.

And we started a band. But that's another story.

Kim died in 2005, far too young. Even though I knew the end would come early for her, I was still deeply saddened and shocked when I received the news. We went out on a bad note; we hadn't spoken for nearly fifteen years. But I'll always value the time I spent with Kim, and I'll never forget her, her nuttiness, or her little life lessons. For example, Kim would never leave the house without a weapon. She claimed the best weapons were things you find in a garage because they're heavy, durable, and totally legal. So Kim usually had a ratchet wrench or some sort of tool shoved in her boot. Her words proved prophetic, years later, when I avoided a late-night encounter because I had stuffed a tire iron in my jacket. Her odd wisdom saved me from an unspeakable outcome.

Thanks, Kim—or, actually, I should say: Thanks, Hardware Woman.

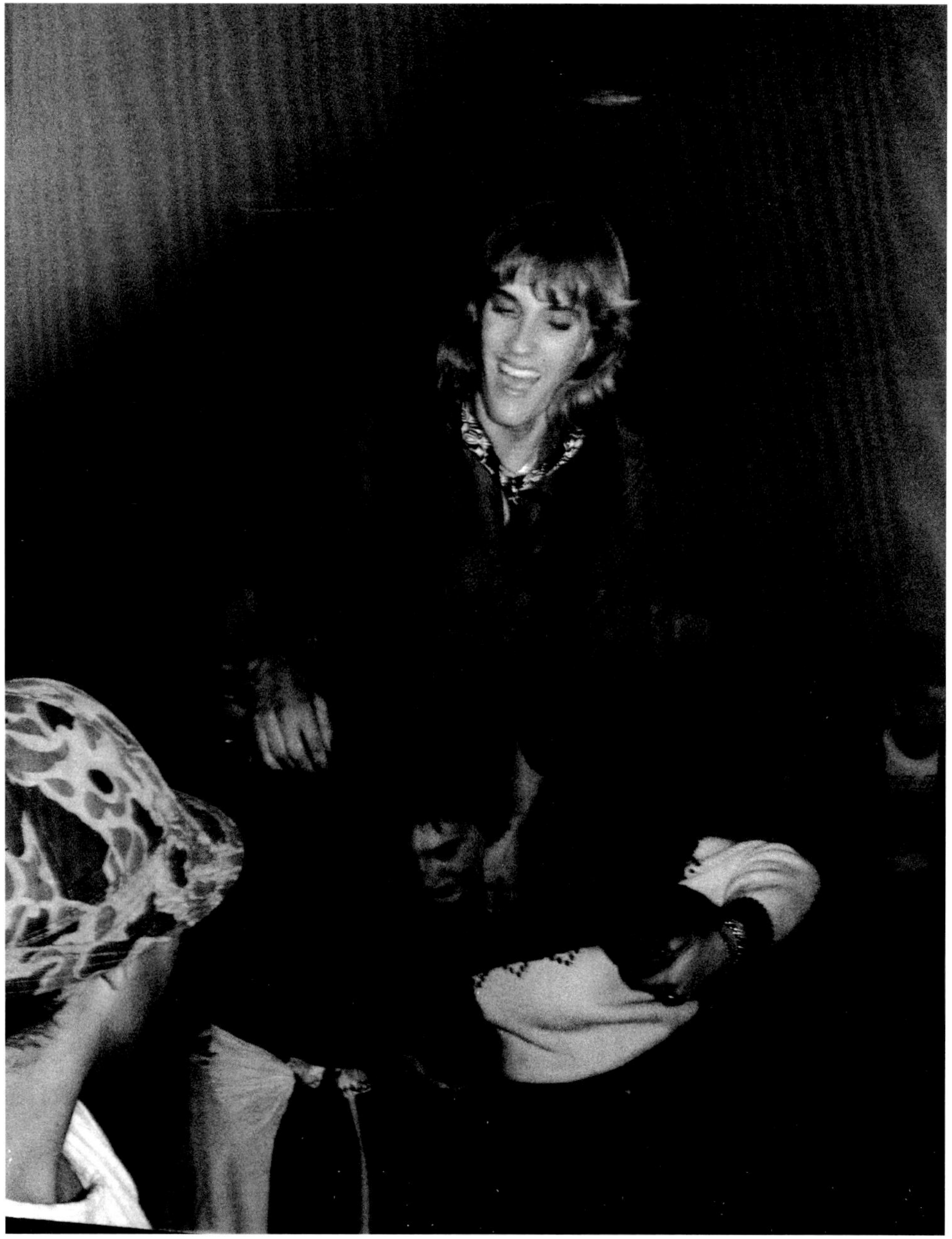

Facing page, clockwise from left: *Kim Pilkington slamming to Red Cross, the Brown Box, 1982; Kim and friends at Dancing Waters; Jennifer and Kim checking out Naughty Women (with Steven McDonald on bass), the Brown Box, 1982.* JORDAN SCHWARTZ. This page, from left: *Kim gassing her Gremlin, 1983; Kim on parade; Kim with the dolphins.* PHOTOS BY JORDAN SCHWARTZ

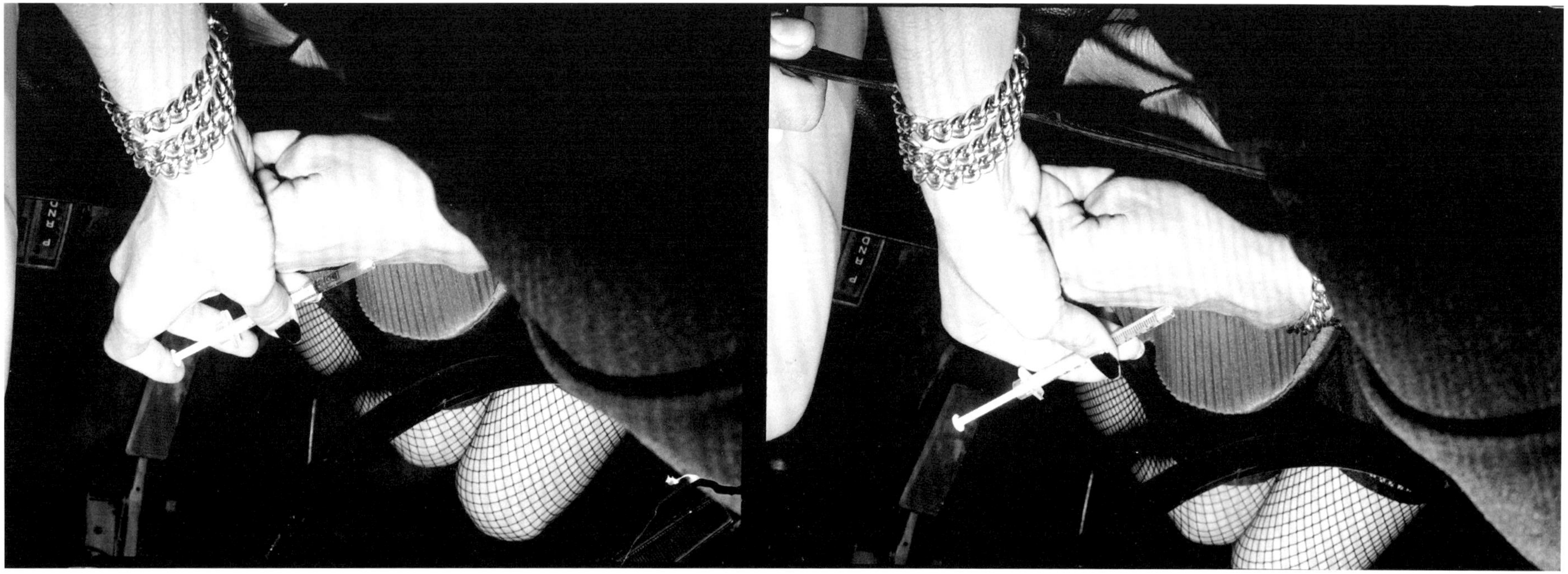

This page: *View from the backseat of a red 1974 Gremlin of punks doing drugs. This did not faze us. That's fucked up.* Facing page from left: *Jennifer and Samohi classmate Louiche Mayorga of Suicidal Tendencies; Jennifer Schwartz, Santa Monica, 1981.* PHOTOS BY JORDAN SCHWARTZ

LUNCH

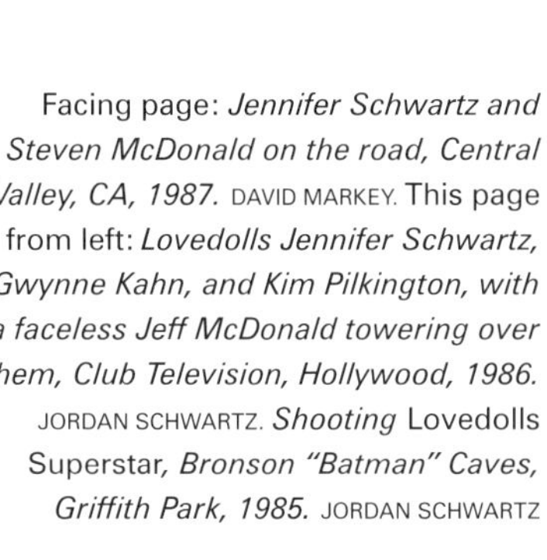

Facing page: *Jennifer Schwartz and Steven McDonald on the road, Central Valley, CA, 1987.* DAVID MARKEY. This page from left: *Lovedolls Jennifer Schwartz, Gwynne Kahn, and Kim Pilkington, with a faceless Jeff McDonald towering over them, Club Television, Hollywood, 1986.* JORDAN SCHWARTZ. *Shooting* Lovedolls Superstar, *Bronson "Batman" Caves, Griffith Park, 1985.* JORDAN SCHWARTZ

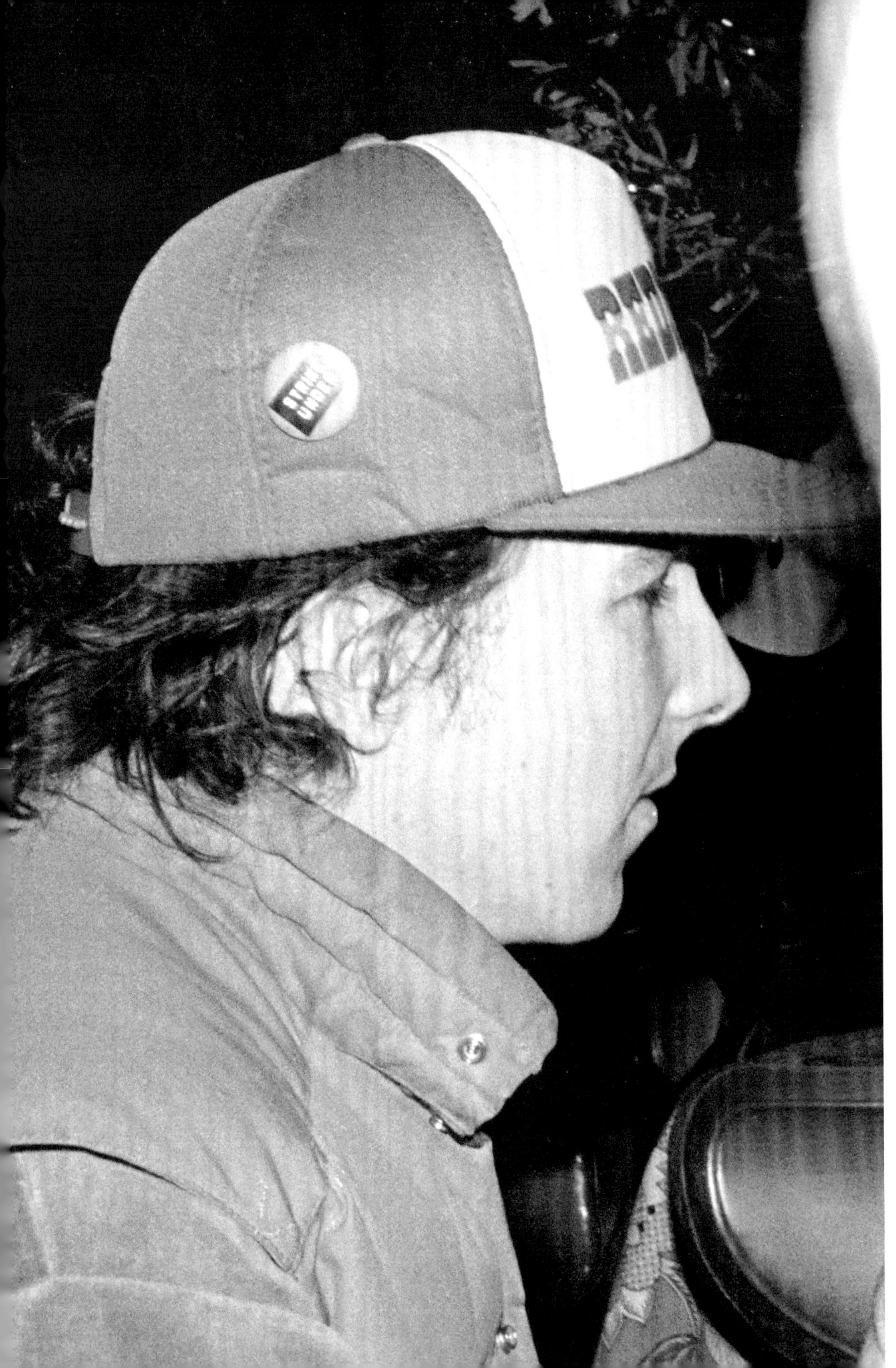

SANITY IS A LIE
CHUCK DUKOWSKI

My life and the lives of Jordan Schwartz and the rest of the *We Got Power* people became increasingly intertwined in the early 1980s Los Angeles music underground. For several years, Jordan I shared many a night of music and ideas, which led to us joining forces at Global Network Booking—a partnership of raw concept and manifestation that lasted for a productive six years. Everyone at *We Got Power*—Jordan, Jennifer Schwartz, Dave Markey, and Kim Pilkington—had so much energy and drive to do things. They coupled this with a fun, earnest, positive spirit; intense intellect; and the crucial courage to follow through.

We Got Power—it's a great name. They were more than fans, but epic supportive fans for sure. They were at every show. I used to take the bus from Redondo Beach to Hollywood to see my girlfriend. As I walked past the Grandia or Anti-Club, there would be Jordan, Jennifer, Kim, and Dave. Together we witnessed the awesomeness of seminal Minutemen and Saccharine Trust sets. There was wonderful music and a beautiful spirit. Then a couple of hours later I'd continue my walk on down the street. Every weird gig that Würm, Black Flag, and the Minutemen played—those guys were there.

The Black Flag bus rolled out to the San Fernando Valley to hear Minor Threat play. Jordan was there, looking like a reporter straight out of some '30s movie, wearing a trench coat and a fedora with a press pass in the hatband, holding a camera with an old-style flash reflector. It was a pivotal conceptual moment. The discussion took off with destruction as a personal metric in

Facing page: *Chuck Dukowski in* REDNECK *trucker hat with Strike Under pin, Grandia Room, 1982.* Following pages: *Dukowski at work, Global Network Booking/SST Records, 1986; Bill Stevenson's protégé, drummer Greg Cameron of SWA, hanging out at Global/SST offices, 1986; Chuck Dukowski and Rich Ford, Global/SST, 1986; Gone, left to right, Sim Cain, Greg Ginn, and Andrew Weiss.* PHOTOS BY JORDAN SCHWARTZ

skateboarding. We got to talking about freaked-out parents forcing their kids into mental hospitals, young people trying to put life together, feeling angst and hating school, getting into bad things like punk music or skateboarding, and maybe getting high and getting caught. From there we passed through selling earplugs as band merch, and riffed on to audio control units after Jordan said he had a job trying to sell hearing aids. I still think they're both good ideas.

When Jordan's parents were pressuring him to move out of the house, I invited him to come live in our parking lot. He slept in Black Flag's old broken tour bus. I paid him ten dollars a day for working as a press agent, advancing tours for Black Flag and the rest of the bands I arranged shows for at Global Network Booking. Exciting things were happening in music: The Minutemen, Meat Puppets, Black Flag, and Hüsker Dü were all finding larger audiences, and we were helping that come to pass.

For two years, Jordan and I and the rest of the Black Flag and the local SST music scene centered around the Global/SST space in Redondo Beach. Henry Rollins was interested in Charles Manson. We almost put out one of Manson's recordings, until one of his followers threatened to put a screwdriver through my eye. Then we got a phone call, and we learned that D. Boon had died in the Arizona desert. I wrote SANITY IS A LIE on a piece of paper and taped it over North Dakota on my giant wall highway map of North America.

For another two years, we kept the ball rolling, booking hundreds of shows, working on the Lovedolls movies, making the Black Flag "Slip It In" and SWA "Arroyo" videos, putting on generator shows, and organizing SST Fests. The music was wonderful. The concepts were powerful.

Reality is optional—make it serve you.

THE 1986 SST OFFENSIVE
DECEMBER
PAINTED WILLIE
and GONE
SAT. JAN 11
STARDUST BALLROOM
5612 SUNSET 8 PM
INFO LINE: 464-9320
TICKETS AT

SALE
TOP TWO
THRASHER
FRAGILE

DECEMBER
BLACK FLAG
BLACK FLAG
PAINTED WILLIE
STARDUST BALLROOM
BLACK FLAG

ELECTRIC FRIED WIENER
KEITH MORRIS

Yeah, we owned it! We had our little "*We Got Power* parking lot," a two- or four-car/band van/pickup truck–sized section of a small parking lot somewhere in San Pedro. It was the same story at any venue allowing something that resembled punk rawk musical stylings: Godzilla's out in the boonies of the San Fernando Valley, the Starwood in beautiful downtown West Hollywood, the Olympic Auditorium in the heart of Los Angeles, *y mas*. The Dancing (not Danzig) Waters club in Pedro only had a loose group of security guys patrolling the premises, which made things easy for our drinking, smoking, and carrying on outside the club like the carefree goofballs and goofballettes that we were.

Our clique could be made up of miscellaneous members from a small army of bands, including Bad Religion, Sin 34, Wasted Youth, "Redd Cross," TSOL, Circle Jerks, Adolescents, Minutemen, and lots of other pals and beer-guzzling Klingons. Our hangout scenario would always consist of us gathering in these types of places and loafing about, with all the fun conversations as to who went to this or that show, or who heard the new so-and-so record, or who was sleeping with who, and all the other fun gossip and hardcore soap opera bullshit. Everybody always had some dirt to spill.

The crew from *We Got Power* fanzine—Dave Markey, Jordan Schwartz, Jordan's sister, Jennifer, and Phil Newman—would show up with their cameras to take photos for their rag. Of course, they'd be accompanied by a couple other nitwits, and would end up being the happy hosts, hostesses, and royal partymeisters. They were just a buncha wiseass post-teenagers! On this particular occasion, in this particular parking lot, we happened to be celebrating a Circle Jerks/Bad Religion gig. I remember watching Jordan take about a four-minute hike across the lot to the mini-mart. He returned with a bag filled with liquid headache, or hangover-inna-can, and he had the craziest happy face beaming. His sitch looked as plum perfect as if he possessed a winning lotto ticket.

My favorite part of that day started with an extremely loud, bloodcurdling scream. The cry ripped through the air, and all of us looked at each other with puzzled faces. As it turned out, an inebriated character had decided to piss against the wall next to the mini-market, at the back of the parking lot. As it turned out, this store had an electrified pipe that ran the entire length of the building where the wall and asphalt met, an unfriendly addition meant to discourage drunks, winos, and any smart alecks from whizzin' on their property. When the paths crossed, an electrical current ran up the urine flow into the penis, and *bzzzt*: ELECTRIC FRIED WIENER!

Facing page: *Earl Liberty on bass and Keith Morris on face, Circle Jerks, Club Lingerie, Hollywood, 1984; Keith Morris, Club Lingerie, 1984.*
PHOTOS BY EDWARD COLVER

X
NEW WORLD TOUR
1983-84

This page, from top: *Circle Jerks, the Whisky A Go Go, Hollywood, August 3, 1981; Keith Morris loses his head. Assailant is Palm Springs punker Myke Bates.* PHOTOS BY EDWARD COLVER Facing page: *Spray-paint the Walls: David Markey and Oki Dog regular Carlton, Hollywood, 1982.* JORDAN SCHWARTZ

WE GOT POWER
CRANKSHAFT
BLITZKRIEG
7228

This page, clockwise from top left: *Cruising the Oki Dog parking lot, 1982; Dave "Ratman" Levine and Phil Newman of Painted Willie launching a model rocket before a gig with Black Flag, Indianapolis, May 2, 1986; Julie Lanfeld and Blayney Mitchell, Cerritos, CA. When David met Blayney and Julie in Westwood in 1980, they were totally punk, and called themselves "Ann Archy" and "Dee Kay"; Laura Newman and Mike Vallejo.* PHOTOS BY JORDAN SCHWARTZ.

Facing page, clockwise from top left: *Punk girl stranglers, the choker collar is not enough.* JORDAN SCHWARTZ; *Double date in San Pedro, D. Boon second from left.* JORDAN SCHWARTZ; *Circle One drummer Bill Ituarte at a Sin 34 party, Cerritos.* JORDAN SCHWARTZ; *Jordan Schwartz and Mike Vallejo.* DAVID MARKEY

MARKET

BEER

Neal Cassady

Van party tonight! Facing page: *Punks dug Neal Cassady too.* This page: *Los Angeles punks carpooling to a Black Flag gig in Santa Barbara.* PHOTOS BY JORDAN SCHWARTZ

Facing page: *Scenes from a backyard punk party, Montebello, CA.* This page: *Julie Lanfeld and Mike Brenson during a backyard Sin 34 and Circle One gig.* PHOTOS BY JORDAN SCHWARTZ

FRANK NAVETTA AND THE DESCENDENTS

JOE CARDUCCI

I wasn't aware of the first 45 by the Descendents, "Ride the Wild" b/w "It's a Hectic World." They recorded the single—catalog number Orca 001—in September 1979 with Spot at Media Art in Hermosa Beach, with help from Dave and Joe Nolte of the Last. The record was released in early 1980, and not distributed anywhere but at stores in Hermosa Beach and Redondo Beach, and at Zed in Long Beach. The first Descendents track I heard was "Global Probing" in 1981, on the second New Alliance compilation, *Chunks*. SST Records had pointed Mike Watt to Systematic Record Distribution, where I worked, to help get copies in circulation. At the time, Watt and D. Boon were working for Greg's SST Electronics company, assembling his tuners. Later in 1981, the Descendents' *"Fat"* EP came out on New Alliance, and I immediately ordered it for distribution around the country. It was one more idiosyncratic masterpiece of what was becoming known as L.A. hardcore.

On that first single the band was a trio: Frank Navetta on guitar, Tony Lombardo on bass, and Bill Stevenson on drums. I saw Frank and Tony again in 2006 at Bill's studio in Fort Collins, Colorado. Frank told me that the Descendents started with him and Dave Nolte woodshedding some tunes on acoustic guitars in the Noltes' garage in 1977. Dave was the youngest of the Nolte brothers and not yet in the Last. Bill knew the Noltes and loved their band. He lived in Hermosa Beach just around the corner from the Ginns but was barely aware of Black Flag, then called Panic. Nolte introduced Bill to Frank, and he Frank joined the Descendents in late 1978. Frank was sixteen. Bill was fifteen. Tony's age was then and still remains classified.

Frank and Bill had fishing in common. Bill's friend Pat McCuistion was, like Dave, a close associate of the band and cowrote or inspired songs, including "Weinerschnitzel" and "All." Bill told me that he'd go out fishing with Pat, and on bad days when they hated everybody, they'd troll small islands and rock piles off the coast and shoot seals. Bill writes in the *Hallraker* album liner notes: "Pat insisted that we quit writing 'stupid girl songs,' and start writing about things that really matter—like food and fishing." Pat, whom Bill refers to as the fifth member of the Descendents, was lost at sea in a 1987 storm. Bill wrote, "He had 15,000 pounds of fish onboard, so I guess you could say he died in heated pursuit of All."

The pair, Frank and Bill, practiced near LAX, and then down in Long Beach. Nearby, Tony's band shared a space with Rhino 39 and the Cheifs' guitarist. Tony heard the racket Frank and Bill were making and went over. Sure enough, they needed a bassist. From this early time, "Ride the Wild," written by Frank, shows the influence of the Last, with a relaxed '60s pop guitar and vocal approach. All three sang together, plus maybe Dave. "It's a Hectic World," written by Tony, points to the band's own sound with its speed and foursquare urgency.

Frank's dad prevented them from playing gigs, until finally Frank managed to escape and play a party in Long Beach. Bill's mom stopped them from playing what would've been their first

Frank Navetta, the Descendents, Dancing Waters, San Pedro, 1982. This club was a funky former dinner theater with a water fountain that came to life, set to disco music. Martin Scorsese had just finished filming Raging Bull *there—Jake LaMotta's club was Dancing Waters.*

JORDAN SCHWARTZ

gig, somewhere in O.C. Their second gig was on February 17, 1979, at the San Pedro Teen Post with the Plugz, the Alley Cats, Black Flag, and the Reactionaries. Good gig. It was Black Flag's second gig too, and the first for the Reactionaries—they soon morphed into the Minutemen. Dave still sang for these first gigs, and the Descendents continued as a trio while looking for a lead singer. They played one show with a girl named Gwynne Kahn singing, on November 9, 1979. It's hard to believe they even knew a girl back then. One can't exaggerate the extent to which the Descendents were uncool at school and put upon at home. Frank, Bill, and Pat found solace on the ocean. They didn't fish like I thought of fishing on lakes in Wisconsin; they pulled heavy, commercially desirable fish out of the Pacific Ocean and sold them for cash, the kind that if their classmates possessed was simply given to them by rich parents.

The band added Milo Aukerman on vocals in late 1980. Milo was a brainy, unhip kid. Later, while I was drawing the cover of the second album, after the style of the first, Bill told me that an old friend of theirs had drawn the cartoon of Milo on the first album. That was hardly true. Roger Deuerlein was actually a high school nemesis who had fixated on Milo to torment via cartoons and posters. Some friend. And some balls for Bill and Milo then to make Roger reprise his caricature—and thereby force it cool by his own hand—on the cover of their classic album! The new four-piece Descendents recorded the *"Fat"* EP the following March with Spot at Music Lab in Silver Lake. Spot writes: "It was definitely the 'bonus cup' era, so the vibe in the room was pretty manic."

In September 1981, I left Systematic in Berkeley for SST, when its offices were near the Tropicana in West Hollywood. That's where I first met Bill Stevenson. He did an emergency tour with Black Flag in December when their regular drummer Robo couldn't get back into the country after some UK dates. I really got to know Bill and his bandmates when we moved SST down to Redondo Beach in spring 1982. That June, Spot recorded the *Milo Goes to College* album at Total Access in Redondo. While Black Flag was away touring for the *Damaged* album, with Emil drumming, I went to every Descendents gig and got to know them well. The Descendents had a gig every weekend somewhere in the greater Los Angeles area. The gigs all seemed to be at small bars with one-foot-high stages. As they weren't a hardcore attraction yet, it was easy to listen to them from the best-sounding spot on the floor: just drums and vocals through the little house PAs. They drew twenty to thirty people. Bill filled me in on the Descendents' prehistory and gave me a copy of the first 45. Then I hooked him up with Joe Pope from the band Angst, who took over at Systematic when I left. At last that first single got out around the country.

Bill stopped by the SST office in Redondo Beach often. He worked at Jerry's Tackle on Aviation Boulevard. Jerry was Keith Morris's dad. Rob Holzman, drummer for Saccharine Trust and later Slovenly, remembers Bill and Frank in the hallway of Mira Costa High School before class, just in from predawn fishing off Catalina Island, their smelly clothes covered in fish slime. Bill was pointing out classmates as they walked past, noting: "I hate you…I hate you…I hate you…"

Milo Goes to College seemed like it would be a farewell album, but it turned out that Milo could maintain his involvement while he went to college. He was probably the best punk-era singer there was. Who was any better? H.R.? Johnny Rotten? Henry Rollins? Gary Floyd? Maybe, maybe not. The Descendents were never better than in the years 1982 and 1983. They played in East L.A. at the new Vex with the Nig-Heist and Suicidal Tendencies on July 8, 1983. Even though we expected it to be a

Facing page, from left: *Joe Nolte, the Last, the Barn/Alpine Village, Torrance, CA, 1982; Joe Carducci sleeping in his bed at SST Records, 1982.* PHOTOS BY JORDAN SCHWARTZ

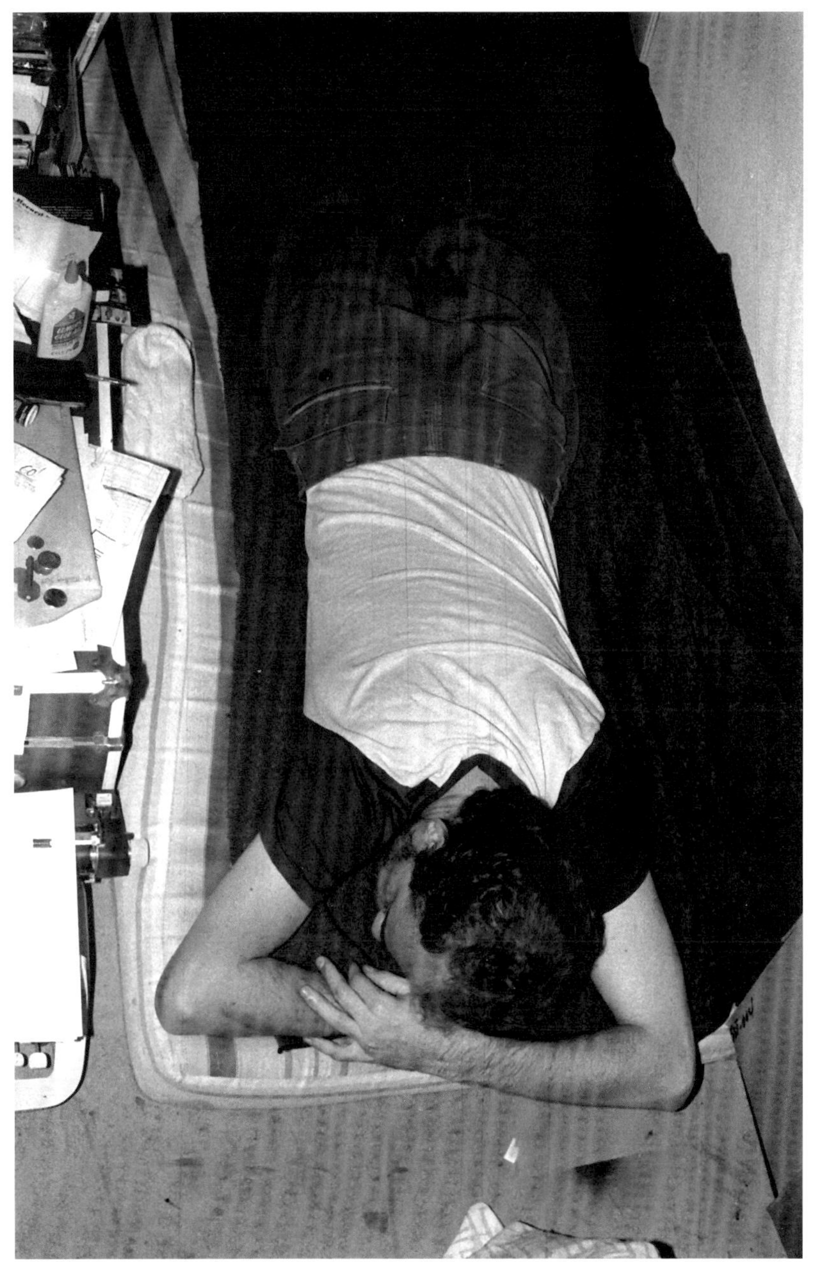

dangerous neighborhood, for some reason we all arrived early and had to sit around out front just waiting to be knifed. I sat in the Descendents' van with them. If it had been Black Flag's van, someone might have been getting a blow job in the back while the rest mind-fucked about music or bioanthropology. If it had been the Meat Puppets' van, there would have been a pipe being passed back and forth while the band members tripped out over the latest misunderstanding between them and the punk community. In the Descendents' van, they mostly just drank coffee and vibrated with bitter resentment at their place beneath the lowest rung of the social world. They were rungless! Black Flag roadie Mugger was seventeen then, and standing out front of the Vex with his arm around Gina, who seemed like his first real non-drive-by girlfriend. This was a bit much for Frank, Bill, Tony, and Milo to have to watch—particularly since they seemed to remember Gina as one of the unapproachable girls from Mira Costa High. These were still the years when the punk rarely got the girl, but in Mugger's case he taught even his elders how to get laid at home and on the road. It started in the van with Bill saying, "Look at that..." and went round and round, as Tony and Frank and Milo chipped in their umbrages over her preference for Mugger over any of them. Joe Vex took his time opening the doors to the club, so the umbrage piled quite high. It was a true Descendents moment I was privileged to witness, undoubtedly tempered by the fact that they knew I worked with Mugger at SST.

I also went up with them on January 1, 1982, when they first played San Francisco at the Mabuhay with the Effigies. Good gig. It was the farthest they had been to play, and I remember their impression was that San Francisco was like one giant urinal.

On Thanksgiving 1982, Frank invited me to his family's house for turkey dinner. We never turned down a meal at SST, but Black Flag, Mugger, and Spot were out on tour. I think Frank wanted to show me off to his dad, but how can I put this... His dad sucked. He was a great provider, a type A achiever, and the family—Mom, Dad, three sons, and three daughters—lived in a nice house in Manhattan Beach, but Mr. Navetta was severely disappointed in his son Frank. I don't remember how many of the other kids were there, but one of Frank's sisters was desperately trying to keep things light and positive. That didn't stop the father from insulting his son, founder of one of the most important bands in rock and roll history. Frank's sister Marie wrote me recently: "If anybody was trying to make peace it was either Barbie or myself. To tell you the truth, it used to break my heart to see the way Frank was treated by my dad. All of us suffered, my dad really did suck!" I got an eyeful and an earful, but I did get to eat, and I got to see where Frank pulled his great, no-BS classic Descendents bursts like "My Dad Sucks" and "I'm Not a Loser"—songs that still reach kids in a direct, honest, funny way. That first album of theirs is the best-selling record of that scene and era—it is a young kid's rite of passage. Frank also drew excellent artwork for their flyers and the *"Fat"* cover. Bill once marveled to me at Frank's guilelessness. Frank had left the *"Fat"* EP artwork lying around the house; his dad picked it up and saw "My Dad Sucks" in the track listing, triggering yet another round of abuse.

That summer, when I was alone at SST, Bill would often burst in after practice and vent his frustration with his bandmates. My favorite time was when he came in making retching noises: "Ugh! Achh! UGH!!! Milo thinks he can sing!" But when Frank told his bandmates that he would leave the band, I didn't hear anything about it. First, Ray Cooper was added as a second guitar, and they played for most of 1983 as a five-piece. Frank must have seen that things would be fine with the band. Only then did he leave, in November 1983. He left L.A., too, for the south coast of Oregon, where he fished and painted and got married.

Facing page: *Bill Stevenson, the Descendents, Dancing Waters, 1982; Milo Aukerman, the Descendents, Dancing Waters, 1982.* JORDAN SCHWARTZ

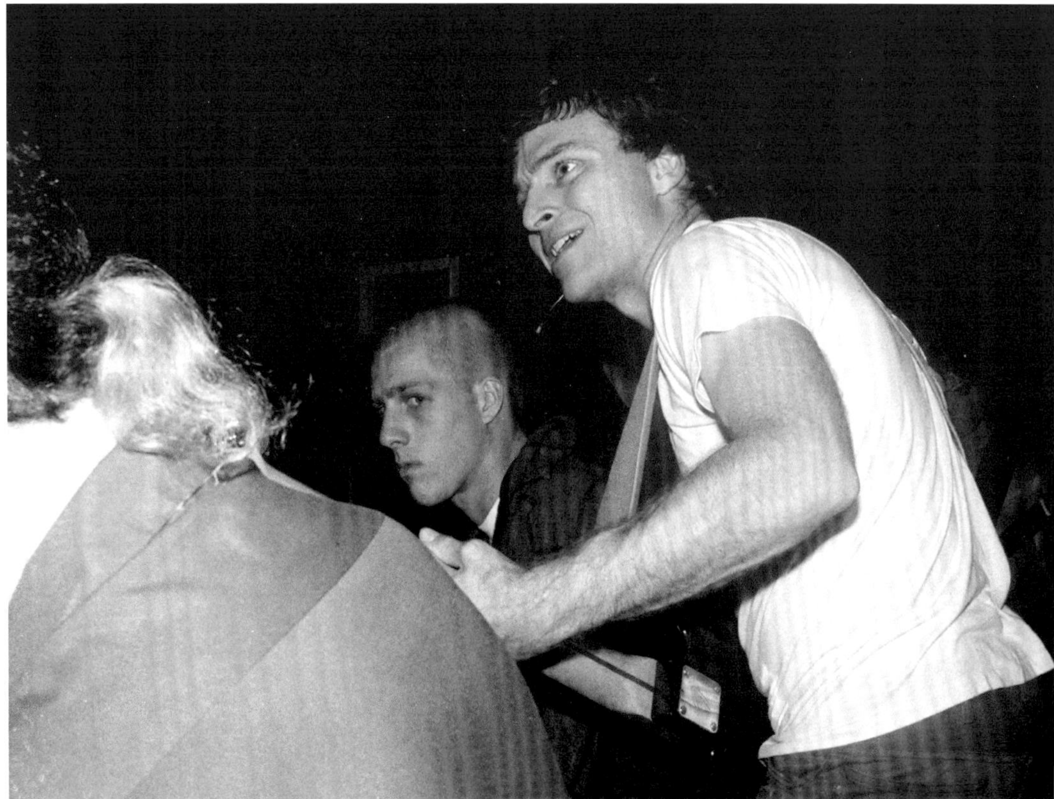

I left L.A. in mid-1986 and spent about ten years in Chicago. By then, the Descendents were reaching the Midwest regularly on tour. Then I moved to Laramie, Wyoming, and I got back into more regular touch with Bill Stevenson because he had moved his band, label, and recording operations just down the street to Fort Collins, Colorado. Tony was no longer in the Descendents. Stephen Egerton and Karl Alvarez were now in the band. Whenever Milo was too busy pursuing his academic career on the East Coast, Chad Price sang and made them the band All.

The Descendents were friends, and at first they were each other's only friends. Bill was good to Frank and kept him paid up on all royalties due from his old songs that were now selling so well. *Milo Goes to College* sold about five thousand copies in its first five years of release, and over a hundred thousand copies in its second five years. Frank was living in Bill's garage in Fort Collins one summer, having occasional trouble with still undiagnosed schizophrenia and bipolar disorder (according to himself and his sister Marie). I saw him then and he seemed himself, same hoarse high-pitched voice, a little fatter, a little hairier. He told me he was doing a lot of fishing back in Oregon.

In 2002, I drove out to L.A. to peddle screenplays and I stopped by the Ginns'. I read the papers over huevos rancheros at CaliMex, and later I walked around the last few streets of old-style beachside houses. Walking back up Pier Avenue, I thought I saw Frank, but it couldn't be. I had just seen him in Colorado. But it was him. He looked like a mountain man, with long hair and a beard, too. He said he'd just walked up from San Diego, and he looked it. I was afraid to ask if he was going to his parents' house. I thought Raymond Pettibon might like to see Frank, but didn't feel I could invite Frank to see the Ginns because I didn't really know what shape he was in. When I got back to Wyoming and next saw Bill, I told him I'd run into Frank on Pier. Bill was surprised, but then not so surprised, and he told me that he'd had to ask Frank to leave after some kind of fit had disrupted work at the recording studio.

I'm glad I got to see the Descendents often while Frank was in his band. During that era, they played only a handful of gigs outside of L.A. The rest of the country never saw Frank play. It's hard to explain today, but there was a desperation to play back then that accounts for the power many of those songs and recordings and bands have. Times changed fast. By the end of the '80s a band could be that good but not try very hard to keep it together, because they just didn't need it in the same way the bands I knew at SST did. The Descendents kept going, as Frank wanted them to, but I don't believe they could ever really replace him and his desperate energy. He started his band and followed through with it—despite being just about the last human being that the existing music audiences wanted to see up on stage. His actions may have made it so much easier for the kids who followed later that maybe they simply can't be as good.

I saw Frank, Tony, and Bill once more, in 2006, at the Blasting Room in Fort Collins, recording basic tracks for an album of new songs by the early lineup. I had arranged for Dave Lightbourne to record the day after the Upland Breakdown festival and was amazed to see the Descendents going at it in Studio B. I took a couple photos through the glass but I didn't want to interrupt them. I came back the next day to ask Frank and Tony a few questions about the beginnings of the band. I'm glad I did that. Frank died back in Oregon in 2008. According to the obit in the Florence, Oregon, paper, he left behind two daughters and a son.

Here's Frank's last song contribution to the Descendents, "Rockstar." The composition clocks in at thirty-seven seconds on the *I Don't Want to Grow Up* album, which was released in 1985:

Facing page, from left: *The few, the proud, early believers; Tony Lombardo, the Descendents, 1982.* PHOTOS BY JORDAN SCHWARTZ

Rockstar
Poser
Asshole
Loser
Satisfaction
Recognition
Leave me alone
Rockstar
See if you can do two things at once
Go away and leave me alone
Rockstar
Asshole
Loser
Satisfaction
Recognition
Leave me alone
Let's exploit rock and roll
To its fullest potential.

He wrote that song, recorded it, and then he bailed. Over the years he looked more and more like Jack London's Sea-Wolf. But Frank was much too nice a guy. He was just a sea dog.

Marie Navetta wrote me: "Frank forgave everybody before he passed away, his parents and everyone who hurt him; he was just full of love. He talked to us about his relationship with God, he was ready and really he couldn't wait to see the Lord."

It was Frank who named the band the Descendents in 1977. What do you think he meant by that?

This page: *Frank Navetta, the Descendents, 1982.* Following pages: *Singer Milo Aukerman and bassist Tony Lombardo of the Descendents, 1982. Glen E. Friedman with his camera visible in audience; Milo Aukerman and the Descendents, 1982; Bill Stevenson, the Descendents, 1982.* PHOTOS BY JORDAN SCHWARTZ

This page: *Guitarist Frank Navetta and Milo Aukerman of the Descendents, 1982.* Facing page: *Stage presence. Frank Navetta of the Descendents restrings guitar, Dancing Waters, 1982.* PHOTOS BY JORDAN SCHWARTZ

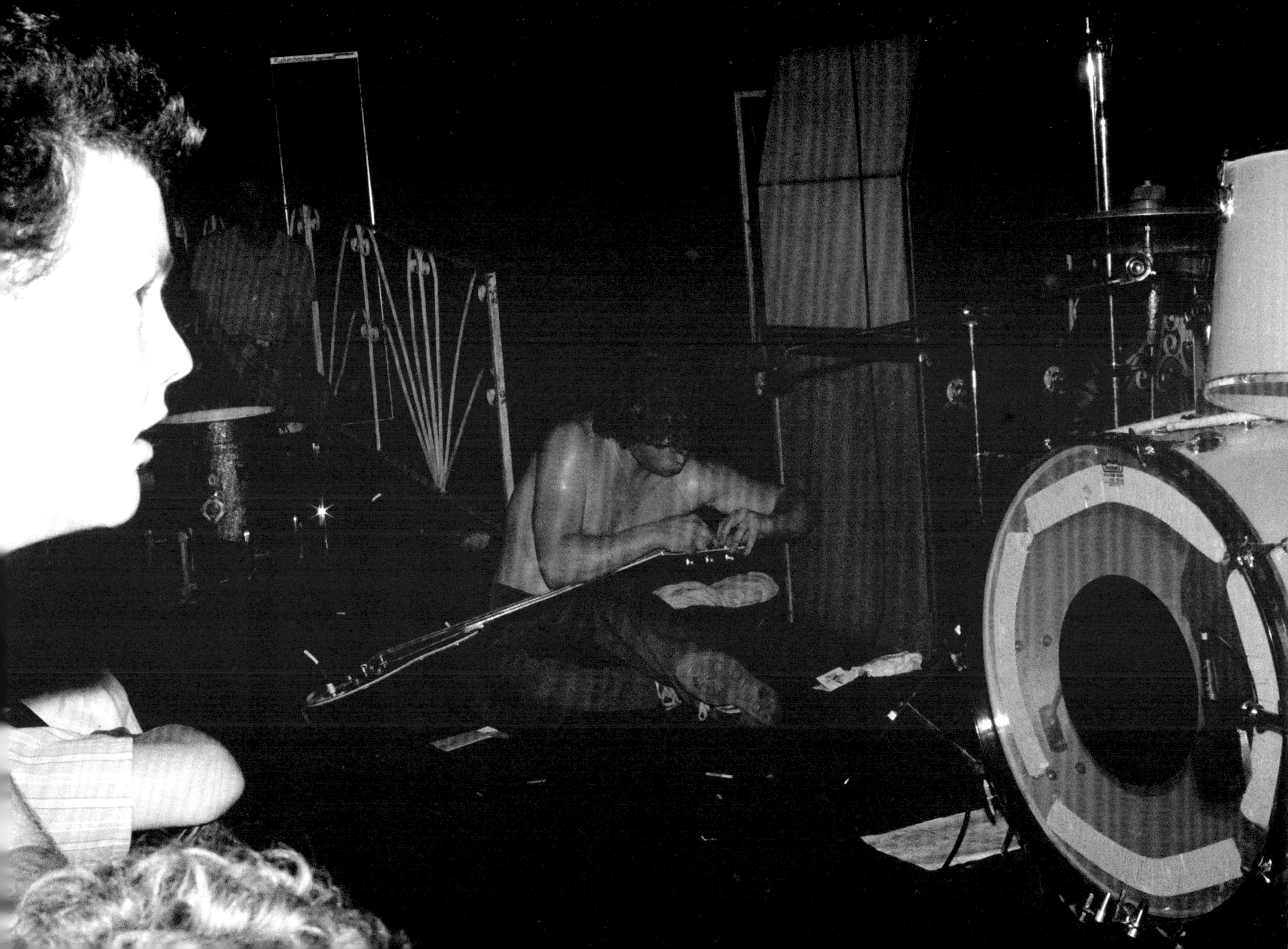
Rickenbacker

NOT ALL ONE BIG BEACH TOWN

MIKE WATT

It was trippy meeting cats up in Hollywood, where the scene mostly was, and learning their idea of anyone south of there. "Beach town," especially, were the words they used, like they thought we were all part of one big beach town. It was the kind of thing as if our Pedro town and maybe somewhere like Hermosa Beach were basically the same pad—or for that matter even Huntington Beach, which was in Orange County!

Humans seem to be pretty provincial. If we did rap with someone actually from Hermosa or H.B., then we'd most times very quickly learn they knew nothing of San Pedro. Likewise, we'd find the same thing about how ignorant we were of their towns, too. I guess what we had in common was that we were closer to the water than those in Hollywood. At the same time, we weren't Santa Monica or Malibu. I guess there was still some kind of understanding.

I don't know, but I guess I was feeling a little insecure when I wrote, "Nobody comes from Pedro," in a Reactionaries song that never made it to the Minutemen. (Actually, none of them ever did!) Or when I spray-painted PEDRO on my bass. The latter turned out to lead folks to think that was my first name, not where I lived.

I actually found out about Hermosa Beach because of Black Flag being from there, and not the other way around. Hell, my Pedro town wasn't that connected to the next town over, Wilmington, even though we both share the north and west parts of the L.A. harbor, let alone those pads northwest of us, maybe fifteen-plus miles away.

Anyway, Pedro faces east—the only "beach town" that does that. Why do you think all my photos are of sunrises? We're on one side of the Palos Verdes Peninsula. It wasn't just geography; it was also, in a trippy way, people. Why do you think Minutemen tunes are different than Descendents ones? You got it.

Facing page: *The Minutemen, house party, Hollywood, 1982. Mike Watt playing Earl Liberty's bass. The hepcat in the glasses to the left of Watt is Spot, producer of all the early SST records by Black Flag, Hüsker Dü, the Minutemen, Meat Puppets, and many others. The blonde woman is Janet Housden from Red Cross, the guy in the checkerboard jacket is David Markey, the guy behind Watt with the Aunt Jemima bandanna and raised fist is Henry Rollins, and the heavy-lidded fellow with glasses on the right is celebrated Black Flag roadie Davo Claassen. Earl Liberty looks on at far right.*
JORDAN SCHWARTZ

FLAG
ANTS
CONTACT
EARL
LIBERTY
"PAGAN ICONS"
Roadster

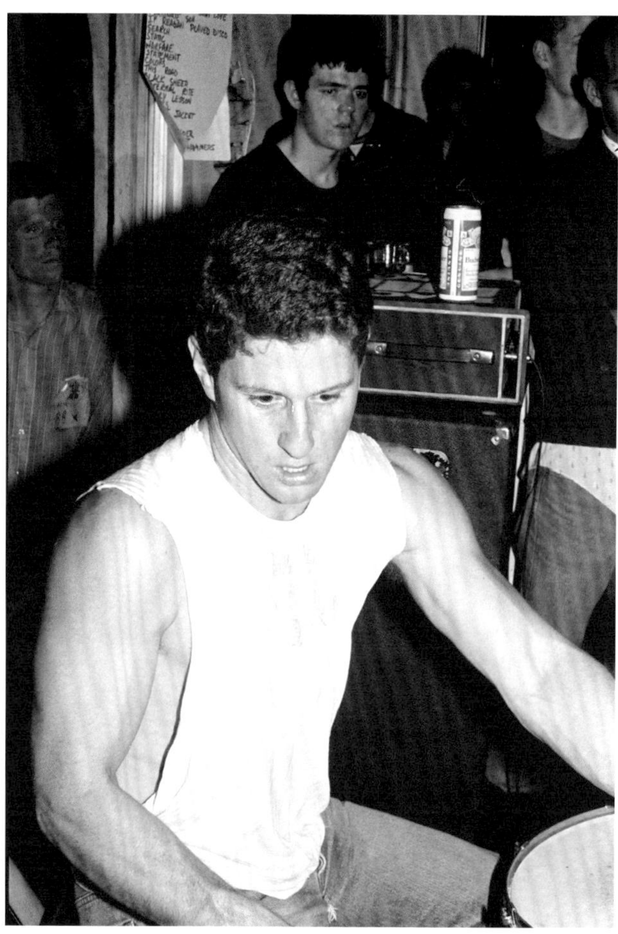

This page: *The Minutemen playing Black Flag's rehearsal space, Unicorn Studios, Santa Monica, except drummer George Hurley at far right, playing a Hollywood house party, early 1982.* Facing page: *The Minutemen, situation unknown.* PHOTOS BY JORDAN SCHWARTZ. Following page: *Mike Watt and George Hurley write the set list at the Grandia Room, 1982. With all the short songs, the titles took more time to write than to play.* Subsequent page, clockwise from upper left: *Mike Watt and D. Boon share a mic in the living room at a Hollywood house party the Minutemen played in early 1982 along with Red Cross, Saccharine Trust, and a couple forgotten hardcore bands. The Sunset Strip clubs had enacted a ban on punk bands altogether starting around '81, which led to a lot of house party shows. This one ended the way they all did—with the LAPD busting in and marching everyone out; Boon at the same house party; Watt and Hurley warm up at the Grandia Room, 1982; The Minutemen at El Senorial, Downtown L.A., 1982.* PHOTOS BY JORDAN SCHWARTZ

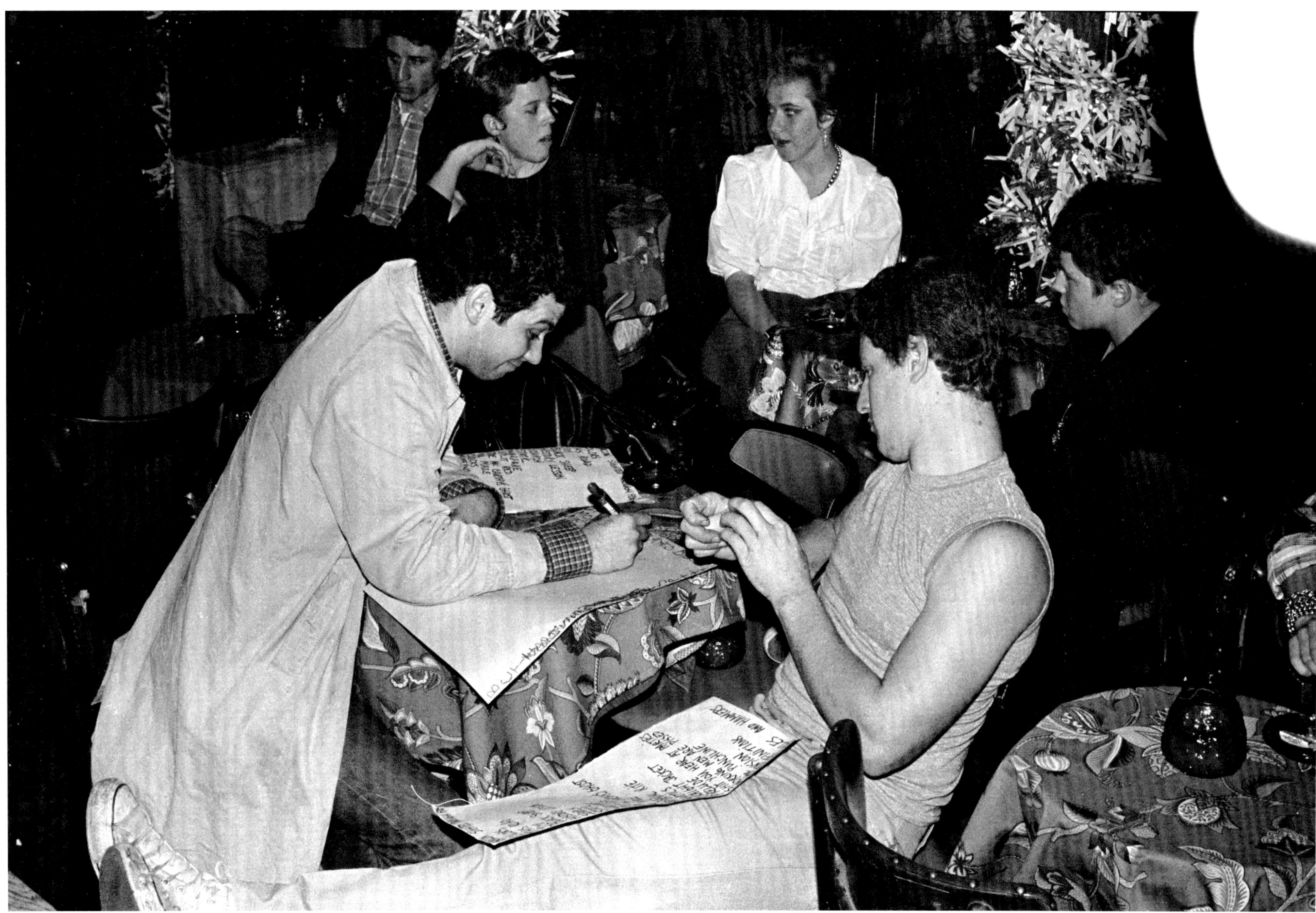

This page from left: *Mike Watt got power, Santa Barbara, 1982; D. Boon: "Time becomes a critical issue."* Facing page: *George Hurley, Grandia Room, 1982.* PHOTOS BY JORDAN SCHWARTZ

This page and next: *fIREHOSE, first show, Catholic Church Hall, San Pedro, 1986.* Lower left: *Joe Baiza and George Hurley, backstage.* PHOTOS BY JORDAN SCHWARTZ

TALES FROM THE SOUTH BAY
DEZ CADENA

When my family moved from Newark, New Jersey, to Hermosa Beach, California, in 1974, it was like moving to a completely different planet. Newark was a tough town. Hermosa was the complete opposite: a laid-back surfer/skater community rife with longhairs sporting puka shells, people who were into kicking back, cranking some Steely Dan, Eagles, Jimmy Buffett, or Fleetwood Mac. Even the skateboarders at the time, who eventually became the punks, didn't understand what was going on with this new music coming out of Hollywood. That scene was centered around Scotland-born Brendan Mullen and his Masque club, where bands like the Germs, Dils, Weirdos, Screamers, and X played. A handful of South Bay locals knew about these bands via DJ Rodney Bingenheimer's show on KROQ, broadcasting then on both FM and AM signals.

My father, Ozzie Cadena, had a backhouse in Redondo Beach, with a garage in front and a big front yard. He used to run garage sales in this yard all the time. He would put me in charge whenever he had to run errands in Hermosa. One Saturday, while I was playing my stereo loud, a short Puerto Rican kid wandered up. He had messy hair, a ripped jean jacket with patches and buttons, safety pins, and thin Devo wraparound shades. He asked me: "Do you like this music?" I think the Damned was playing on my stereo. I told him yes, and we became friends. His name was Ron Reyes. He asked if I wanted to go see a punk rock band rehearse down in Hermosa at an old church, which was now an artist's space. He mentioned their name—Panic—but said they would probably be changing their name to Black Flag, as there already was a British band using the name Panic.

A couple days later, Ron stopped by again, and we headed off to meet these guys. We walked a mile or so and reached Pier Avenue. We just happened to be standing directly in front of the Hermosa Beach police station as we spotted a guy with shoulder-length hair walking toward us, carrying a six-pack of Colt 45 tall cans in a bag. His name was Gary McDaniel; he was the bassist of Panic. He was heading down to the Church to practice, and he said we should come on down and hang out (remember: actors rehearse, musicians *practice*).

When we wandered into the Church, my first thought was: "Okay, a bunch of hippies took over this church." Black Flag, or Panic, rented a section in the back. I met the rest of the band: Keith Morris, the singer; Greg Ginn, the guitar player; and Robo, the Colombian drummer. Ron and I stayed there all day and into the night, watching the band play. I remember thinking I had stumbled into some sort of other world, a separate reality. I started to hang out there regularly. We would go to the Church every day instead of to high school. Up to that point, Black Flag had never played an official show. They had played parties at the Wurm Hole in Hermosa, and that was about it.

I always felt I wanted to play music. I didn't know what I wanted to do exactly, but the Church was a great introduction to band life. Then I met Jack Brewer and Joe Baiza during the Hong Kong Cafe era of the L.A. punk scene. The three of us became

Facing page, from left: *Dez Cadena checking out the Minutemen at the Grandia Room, 1982. Oftentimes, nobody was going to see these bands except their friends in other bands. The Minutemen didn't really have a crowd until* Double Nickels on the Dime *in 1984; Steven McDonald and Dez Cadena, Redd Kross, Cove Theater, Hermosa Beach, CA, 1983.* PHOTOS BY JORDAN SCHWARTZ

good friends, and we started a band called the Obstacles. I was crashing on the concrete floor of Baiza's father's garage in Wilmington, in the middle of winter, with space heaters and a down comforter. One night I nearly caught the garage and myself on fire when the comforter became caught in the heater. I awoke to find Joe above me, stamping out the blanket blaze.

Our band was constantly lacking a rhythm section. At one point, a girl named Phoenix played bass; she was in Castration Squad. We also had a girl drummer named Lou for a while. One day, Brewer called with word that he found a drummer and a bassist in San Pedro that he wanted to audition for our band. I agreed, and the next day we drove to an apartment in downtown Pedro, where I met Mike Watt. George Hurley was there; he played drums. Living upstairs was a guitar player named Dennes Boon. Watt, Hurley, Boon, and Martin Tamburovich had played in a band together called the Reactionaries, but they had broken up.

The "audition" started with us showing Watt and Hurley our repertoire of five songs, including "Dog's Liberation," "I Am Right," and "We Don't Need Freedom." Watt seemed very high-strung and nervous. He wouldn't sit still. He had a comment about every song. "These songs are way too complicated...," he remarked sarcastically, when in fact most of them only had two chords. George was quiet and just played his drums. We rehearsed our set of five songs three times with them. We drank beer, got drunk, and then we left. On the way home, Brewer asked me what I thought of Mike and George. I said: "George was a great drummer, good technique, very powerful and steady. Mike Watt was a great bass player, but I think he should be in a band with four Mike Watts." Soon enough, Watt and Hurley reconvened with D. Boon and started the Minutemen. I ended up joining Red Cross. Joe Baiza and Jack Brewer and the Obstacles became Saccharine Trust.

One day in June or July of 1978, the heat of summer in the South Bay, Greg Ginn from Panic announced that he planned to rent the Moose Lodge in Redondo. He wanted to invite the Alley Cats from Lomita and Rhino 39 from Long Beach to play on a bill with the newly rechristened Black Flag. That name came from Raymond Pettibon, who also created the amazing four bars logo for the band. The plan was for Black Flag to open, Rhino 39 to follow, and then the Alley Cats would headline. The Alley Cats had a single at the time, "Nothing Means Nothing Anymore"; Rhino 39 had a single, "Prolixin Stomp"; and Flag's debut EP, *Nervous Breakdown*, was about to come out.

Ron and I now lived two blocks away from the Moose Lodge. The Lodge was two doors down from a liquor store, convenient for underage kids to have their older friends buy them alcohol. Black Flag opened the night with their twelve-song set, clocking in at under a half hour. Toward the end of the set, Keith Morris grabbed one of the American flags hanging over the stage. He pulled it down, threw it to the ground, all the while bellowing about authority. This excited the crowd of about seventy people gathered from all around the South Bay, Hollywood, and Long Beach punk scenes, but it upset the elder management of the Moose Lodge. The owner grabbed the mic and said: "This band is banned from the Moose Lodge FOR LIFE!" Strangely, he allowed Rhino 39 and the Alley Cats to play their sets.

Meanwhile, Black Flag decided they would play another set that night after the Alley Cats were done, disguising Keith in a long-haired hippie wig. All of this happened in the presence of Rodney Bingenheimer, who had brought the Dead Boys' Stiv Bators along with him. Shortly afterwards, Rodney began playing Black Flag's "Nervous Breakdown" regularly.

This was Black Flag's first official show, and it pretty much put South Bay punk on the map. Until 1980, surfers from Orange

Facing page and following: *Black Flag, post-*Damaged *lineup with Bill Stevenson on drums, Henry Rollins singing, Chuck Dukowski on bass, Greg Ginn on guitar, and Dez Cadena on second guitar, Santa Barbara, 1982.* JORDAN SCHWARTZ

County to the south only wanted to start fights with us "Devo fags." But at the turn of the '80s, something happened. All the longhairs shaved their heads and started showing up at Black Flag and Circle Jerks gigs.

While I joined Red Cross, Ron joined Black Flag and recorded the *Jealous Again* record. Right on top of that, Black Flag was featured in *The Decline of Western Civilization*. Ron stayed in the band for all of six months. Then Black Flag went without a singer for another six months. They were considering having Brendan Mullen sing. They booked a gig with him in Culver City. Brendan was very nervous, and after drinking half a bottle of scotch, he only made it through three songs. Keith Morris was there, and the crowd pushed him onto the stage, and he finished the set of another six songs or so, much to the dismay of Black Flag.

Gary McDaniel began using the moniker "Chuck Dukowski," not in honor of Charles Bukowski at all, but because he found an engraved Zippo lighter in Hermosa that read, CHUCK THE DUKE. Incidentally, Greg Ginn's father, Regis, took to calling his sons by nicknames. Greg was "Kierkegaard," after the eighteenth-century Danish philosopher and theologian, and Raymond was "Pettibon." Supposedly it was intended to mean "petite boy," but Ray always said he was named after Richie Petitbon, football player for the Chicago Bears in the '60s.

While hanging out at the Church one afternoon, I was offered the gig singing with Black Flag. Chuck was drinking warm Burgie beer out of the can in the bag, out of the trunk of his car. He offered me one and asked me if I wanted to try out for the band. They had a tour booked, starting one week later and hitting S.F., Portland, Seattle, and Vancouver. I did the practice that day and everyone liked it. That's when the damage was done.

Black Flag planned to move from the Church at the end of that tour, after much hassle from the Hermosa Beach Police Department. They decided to throw a farewell gig at the Church, inviting SST's entire mailing list of Orange County H.B. ruffians over to Hermosa. More than two hundred of the most violent *Clockwork Orange*–type hooligans showed up. I wore a Quaalude Rorer 714 T-shirt, American flag bell-bottoms, and Peter Max sneakers, and I dyed my hair red. I sang through a guitar amp. The crowd proceeded to destroy the property, breaking windows and smashing everything inside and outside of the Church. It was a demolition party.

The Hermosa Police Department showed up in full force, threatening Chuck and warning him never to return to Hermosa. The following day, the local *Easy Reader* paper reported that the Hermosa police had successfully kicked Black Flag out of Hermosa. But we had already moved out and relocated to Torrance. The band left on the short tour, and from that point on my life was never the same.

EXIT

AN ESSENTIAL PART OF THE PLAN
JACK BREWER

I was going to start my thesis with: "I'm glad we never faked it." Then I looked at the photos, and I'm not so sure. Maybe it was a scene of pretending. We were all just beginning the transformation from being children and teenagers to adulthood. Make-believe was over. The world was corporate, and owned by somebody else. But we couldn't stop seeing as we saw. Couldn't stop hearing what we heard in the shoveling of night, in the uneasy breathing of dreamers.

Please, not the name; "Saccharine Trust" used to embarrass me in the beginning. We weren't punk enough to be "Wasted Youth," or feminine enough to be "True Sounds of Liberty," though I liked both of those bands. I'm not sure if I knew then what or who we were, or why we came to be. We felt our music was right to exist. We weren't going to turn our heads for approval or compatibility. Once our music was recorded, the records could wait for the listeners to find them. We didn't have to slow down. We just kept moving until we were stopped. Then we moved again. And still we move.

SST Records was the greatest place to hang out. There was always a band rehearsing there. At night, tents were set up over desks, and you could hear cassettes blaring and girls laughing. During the days, amid phone calls to New York and ads being cut up, I would always run into someone I just met at a party the night before, who had suddenly become a new employee. Everyone there eventually became a mystic. And I felt empowered as our records were unpacked from boxes. Everything was on a rage. Soon, they bought a computer. Mugger told me of its coming, on the wings of Hüsker Dü.

The business of SST was made by men smarter than me. They set a place for us, and I believe we fulfilled their aspirations. We were an essential part of a plan that succeeded. The success was maybe or maybe not ours. But what does it matter? The details of this cosmic hailstorm will be sorted in the calm and gray that precedes our final reflection.

Facing page: *Jack Brewer, Saccharine Trust, the Barn, 1982.*
JORDAN SCHWARTZ

FLAG
ANTS
CONTACT
EARL
LIBERT

Facing page, from left: *Earl Liberty, Saccharine Trust, Unicorn Studios, Santa Monica, early 1980s; Joe Baiza, Saccharine Trust, the Barn.* This page, clockwise from upper left: *Jack Brewer sings to crowd including Mike Watt, Junior, Davo, Kurt Markham, and Greg Ginn, Unicorn Studios, Santa Monica; Jack Brewer and the Pope, San Pedro, 1986; Brewer at a Saccharine Trust gig in a Hollywood backyard.*
PHOTOS BY JORDAN SCHWARTZ

RAG IN CHAINS

DANIEL "SHREDDER" WEIZMANN

I first met the staff of *We Got Power* on the Sunset Strip outside a Dickies show at the Whisky. The evening was notable for me for many reasons, not the least of which is that it was the first time I attempted to illegally purchase alcohol as a minor. Since I was a smallish thirteen-year-old, this was extremely ambitious on my part, but my friend Scotty convinced me that he had a secret technique. I think he learned it from an episode of *Happy Days*.

"You just play with your keys when you enter the liquor store," Scotty said. "Then they think you have a car." In retrospect, this doesn't totally make sense, since a sixteen-year-old could drive, but you had to be twenty-one to drink. I guess that to us, everybody over the age of fifteen was a full-on adult.

Scotty and I had taken the bus from East Hollywood. We were terribly innocent, as eighth graders ought to be, but then so was the Strip in those days, in its crumbling way. At the very, very tail end of the desiccation of the '60s epoch, mom-and-pop pharmacies on the Strip still sold jokey Ziggy birthday cards, Holly Hobbie knickknacks, *Whatever Happened to*… paperbacks filled with gossip about old Hollywood stars, and "Your Month, Day by Day" astrological scrolls. Rock 'n roll Denny's was merely called Denny's, and the journey from Poseur to Famous Amos Cookies was a short one. Yet our mission that day was not innocent. We wanted booze.

Scotty and I entered Gil T's Liquor like a couple of hopped-up bandits. I hovered by the *Oui* magazines while he flipped the keys and made for the malt liquor. With a nod, I came toward him. We each took two giant brown bottles from the cooler to the checkout counter. The scraggly clerk looked at us knowingly. His stare was long and hard. He was sizing us up, and visions of jail time flashed in my child consciousness. We had no choice but to keep fronting. Our hearts were pounding. Then the clerk reached under the cash register. Was he going for a rifle? No. He pulled out a strange three-ring binder with a clear plastic pouch for rulers and pencils. And inside this bag were smaller clear plastic Ziploc bags. He said: "You dudes wanna buy some opiated thai stick?"

Later that night, during the song "You Drive Me Ape (You Big Gorilla)," the Dickies ripped open a bright orange beanbag over what is now referred to—rather vulgarly—as a mosh pit. We didn't call it moshing. We called it jumping for joy. Scotty and I had utterly triumphed. Everywhere, to the high-speed sound of freedom, it was raining white beanbag pellets. It was glorious.

A few months later, I was hanging out at Poseur after it already had moved to Melrose. Two or three people were browsing around the store, scoping the bondage gear. Suddenly, in walked Julie Lanfeld, bragging that she had just spray-painted—or sprayed with whipped cream?—SIN 34 on a Mercedes outside. She was waving the can in her hand and laughing. Well, *surprise*—the driver was in the store, new wave slummin' it! He spun around fully in his turquoise polo shirt and CHiPs moustache and yelled, "That's *my* car, dammit!"

Facing page, clockwise from top left: *"All I wanted was a Pepsi." Jordan Schwartz on newfangled closed-circuit liquor store security TV, 1982.* DAVID MARKEY; *Dave Markey and Herb Lienau, Hollywood liquor store, 1985. Sonic Youth played around the corner that night at Club Lingerie.* JORDAN SCHWARTZ; Rag in Chains *zine issues #1, #2, #3, and #4.*

Rag in Chains
ISSUE #1 ...... JANUARY 1981

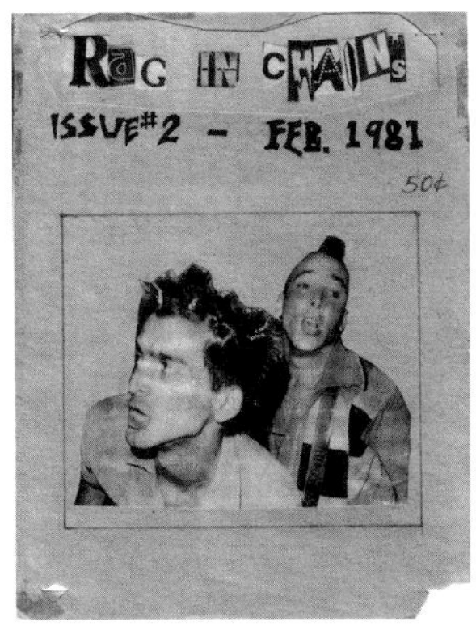
Rag in Chains
ISSUE #2 - FEB. 1981
50¢

Rag in Chains
50¢
ISSUE # THREE / APRIL 1981

Rag in Chains
ISSUE #4 JUNE '81
50¢

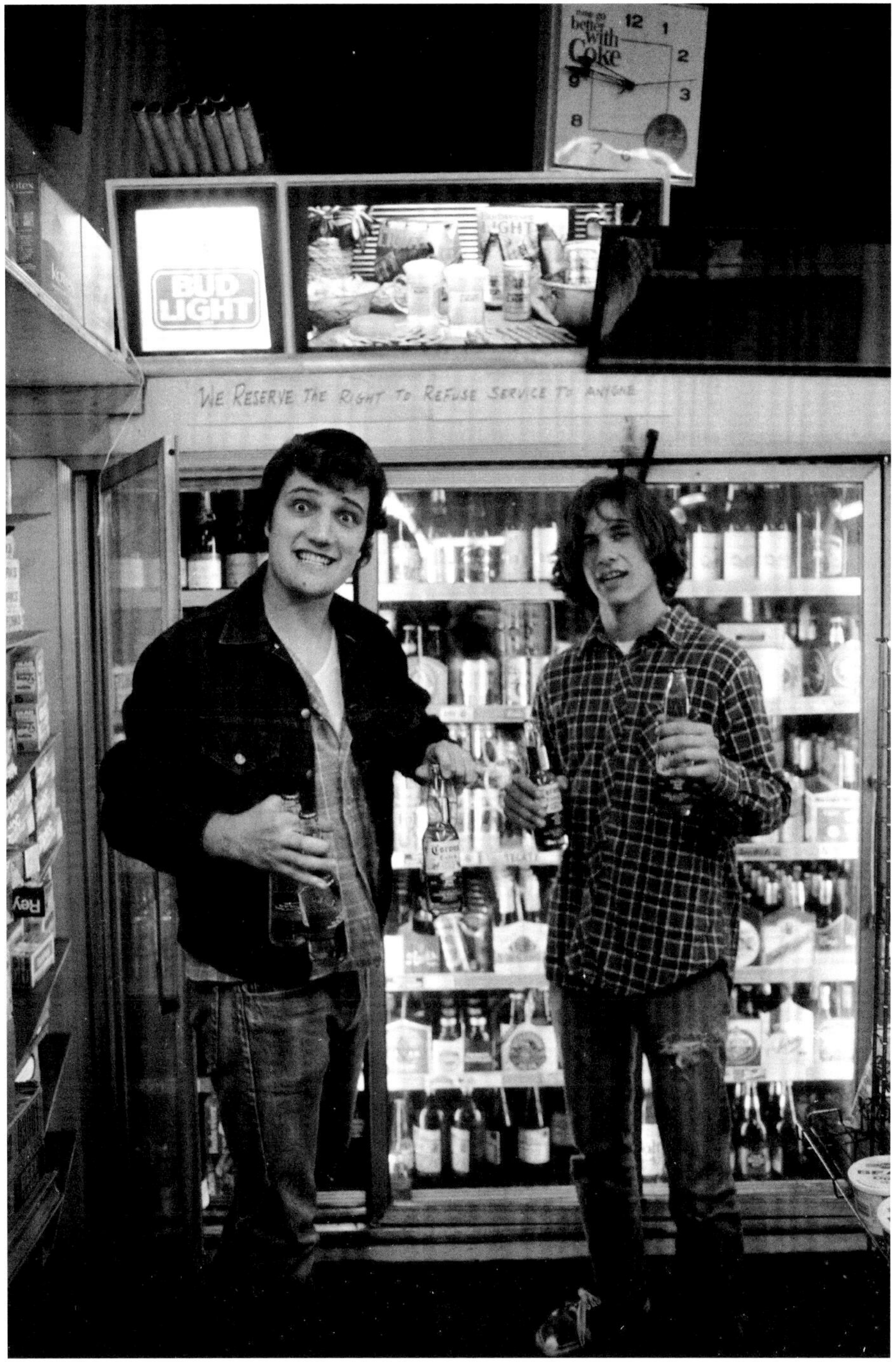

Julie tried to make a run for it, but Mr. Reaganomics leapt and blocked the door. Ah, the perils of a true heroine! I wish I could remember how that episode ended.

Now, time to trip out about the miracle of fanzines. Today, with "homemade" communication democratized, super-rad fanzines like *We Got Power* seem like something that fell to Earth from another planet. Even the names of the tools that went into creating these fanzine things sound alien: Letraset, X-Acto, and mucilage. I still wonder where the courage came from to bust out and go public, trying to be a poster-bearer for the collective trip—as I did with my own zine, *Rag in Chains*—but it was a gas.

Later, much later, when I thought about the "print environment" of L.A. at the end of the 1970s, I could see some of our twisted roots in brown-paper-wrapped contraband print material, religious pamphlets, porno newspapers like *L.A. X...Press*, political manifestos like that Tony whatsisname thing and Scientology, record trader cheat sheets, high-school slam books, poetry chapbooks, and so on. Plus, we had that particular Southern California–ruled lineup of checkout counter mags like *TV Guide*, *People* magazine, and *Tiger Beat*.

We Got Power captured the birth of an aesthetic that literally spread like a virus across the entire globe. In 1980, I visited my cousins in Israel, and I had short hair and a "No Values" T-shirt. Their cultural references were so lost that they made fun of me by saying: "John Travolta!" Today, every single teenager everywhere has a skateboard, listens to fast music, and aspires to radness.

Facing page, clockwise from top left: *Early metallic punkers Hari-Kari from San Pedro; cheery Hari-Kari guitarist; New Alliance band the Plebs from San Pedro, featuring saxophone player Martin Tamburovich. He was in the Reactionaries with Mike Watt, D. Boon, and George Hurley, and he wrote several Minutemen songs; The Urinals, or, as they were billed that night, 100 Flowers, Dancing Waters, 1982.* Following pages: *Jello Biafra as the president of the United States in* Lovedolls Superstar, occupying an *empty office adjacent to SST/Global, 1985.* PHOTOS BY JORDAN SCHWARTZ

ALMA HEIGHTS
ACADEMY

MR PRESIDENT

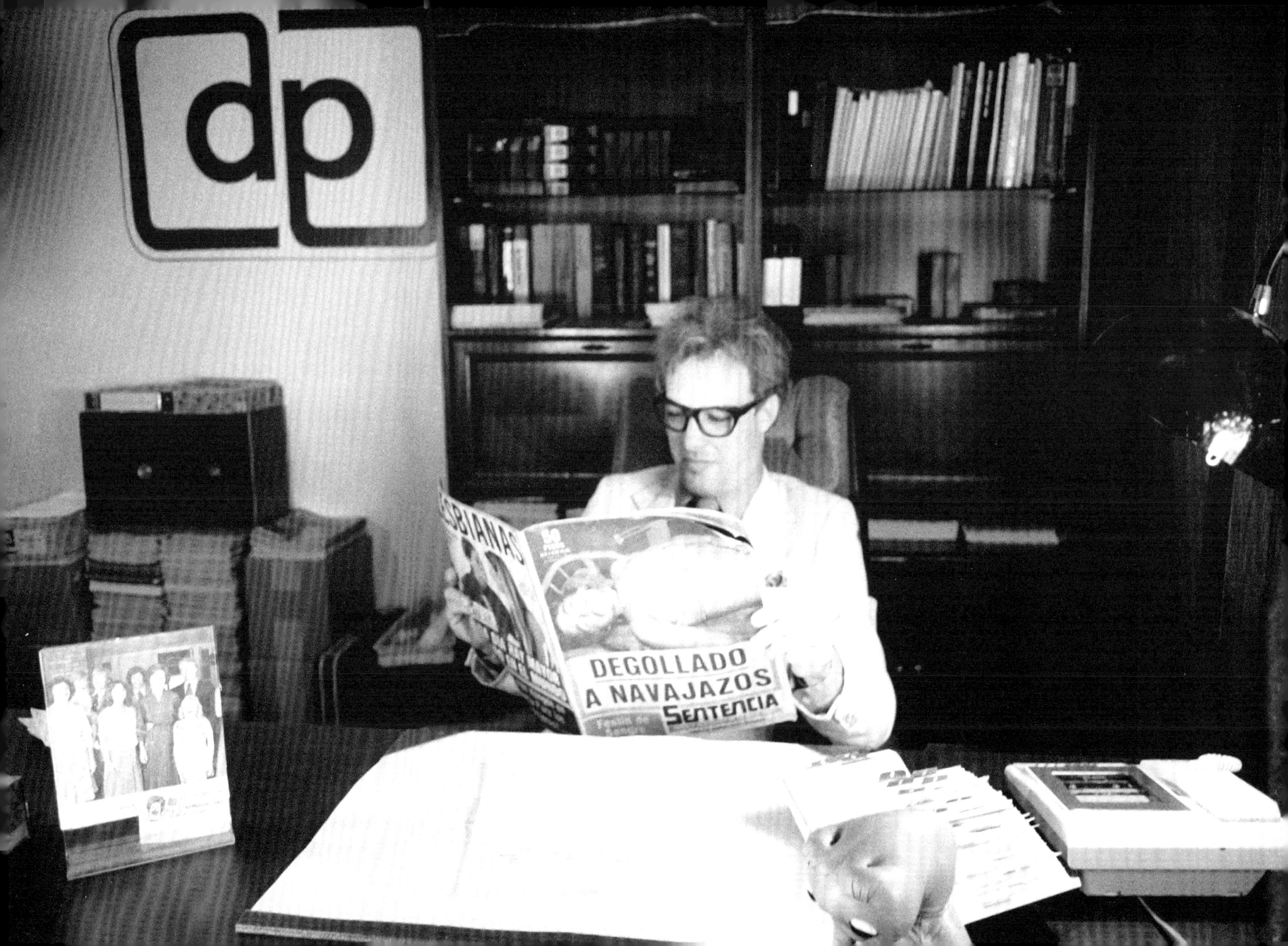

dp
DEGOLLADO
A NAVAJAZOS
SENTENCIA

THE VANDALS TOOK THE HANDLE

STEVE HUMANN

I joined the Vandals sometime late in 1980, after their drummer, Joe Escalante, asked me to try out on bass for his new friends, Jan Ackermann and Stevo. My bass had just been acquired in a typical takeover of a Vicious Circle/TSOL backyard party, somewhere in Huntington Beach. Some party cover band had been lured away from their equipment with the ruse that the keg was almost out, so they needed to hurry up front to get any of the remaining beer. Pat Brown, Todd Barnes, and the rest of the crew started throwing rocks and bottles. People ran for cover, and somebody turned out the lights. Equipment started going over the back fence to waiting hands. I ended up with a nice Fender P Bass. I remember thinking I really couldn't be too pissed about it when somebody else stole it from me at of the Cathay de Grande in Hollywood about five years later.

I had no idea how to play the new bass, but, for some reason, Jan kept at it with me until I could sort of keep up on his and Stevo's songs. The Vandals had been around for most of that year, but Joe had only recently joined them on drums. A year and a half earlier, Joe was the drummer for his and my own garage punk cover band. We had gone through various names, including Jim Jones and the Koolaids and Permanent Damage. I was the singer, while our guitarist was a friend who wasn't seeing the magic of punk himself. He wanted to play Led Zeppelin and Boston still. I think we lost him for good once he really heard the lyrics to "Belsen Was a Gas" by the Sex Pistols.

Nineteen seventy-nine was a great year for punk, which was why I couldn't understand Joe taking up with skate pro Steve Olson and a guy calling himself "Johnny Rockin'" to form the rockabilly band the Aristocats. They broke up soon, without catching the wave of success experienced by many rockabilly bands that year. Joe wasn't discouraged, though—he saw that punk rock was still economically viable. When slots opened up in the Vandals, he was quick to jump onboard, and he asked me to try to fill out the lineup.

Over the next few years, we had a hell of a time, several of the most crazy-fun years of my life. First came waking up in the morning and remembering with a grin how crazy things had gotten the night before. Then came the obligatory beer run, followed by hours of schemes and half-baked insanity, setting out to top the previous night's destructive bacchanalian splendor. It was all part of the plan. Most of us weren't there to hatch outlines for careers, college, or anything our parents had in mind for us. We were simply there to have fun and F.S.U.—fuck shit up. Destroying property was our random revenge on a society we hated.

The fact was, most non-punkers had only a few distorted media ideas regarding what we were about. Largely, everyone was scared of us for fearlessly looking stupid in the eyes of every other clique. In the late '70s we were in a serious minority; fewer than a half dozen kids wore any sort of recognizably punk attire at our particular high school of something like a thousand students. The difference between the people who chose to feel threatened by us and those who chose to actually do something about it was

Facing page: *The black-light posters identify this space immediately as Bob's Place in Watts. You risked your life by going there, but that was where the gigs were happening in 1982 and 1983. The last show there was raided by some locals who were clearly miffed that suburban white punks had taken over their dance hall. They raided the gig, mugging punks for their cameras. A girl was raped in the bathroom. That was the end of Bob's Place.* JORDAN SCHWARTZ

TSOL
BLACK

Punks in motion. From left: *It's not a fight, it's a dance; Anti-Hendrix; A flannel shirt tied around the waist.* PHOTOS BY JORDAN SCHWARTZ usually an age factor. There were regular gangs of mustachioed young adults with their own cars who would pull over and attack punk-rock teenagers walking to or from school. This made our lives a little less boring than we claimed they were, but it was all part of the landscape.

Later, once we were more established as a band, we played a lot of odd venues— a natural by-product of playing a type of music with a small fan base and lots of clueless people booking shows. This sort of mix-up was generally due to the fact that the Vandals were a band at least fifty percent determined to ruin anything and everything remotely related to what people used to like to call "the scene." We also had a minor radio hit with "Urban Struggle," based on the interesting non-coexistence between our punk club, the Cuckoo's Nest in Costa Mesa, and the urban cowboy bar next door known as Zubie's. Jan and Stevo's song was funny and catchy, so it rose through the ranks of KROQ's request lists until it hit some sort of almost regular rotation. KROQ was still a ways from taking over the ratings of classic rock stations like KMET and KLOS, but the money people were starting to notice the swinging pendulum only a year or two after the Sex Pistols broke up in a wash of cutouts. Because KROQ was also the place to go if you wanted to hear later new wave hits by the Cars or the Police, suddenly a little-known punk band such as the Vandals had a chance to be heard by—and then sell to—a whole new fan base. This was the band that people got when they booked the novelty funny-punk KROQ band with the funny cowboy song.

Jan, founder of the band and author of most of the music, was dabbling with various post-punk sounds and styles by this time. In any case, he wasn't really a fan of the drunken destruction that Stevo and I were capable of. Joe was seriously trying to turn the band into a business, so he, too, was always on Stevo and me to stop fucking things up. The Vandals weren't really known as a tight, cohesive musical unit—we were seen as a staggering chaotic mess, due to the presence of Stevo and me. We were more known for property damage, and possibly we were hoping for some good laughs while we were at it. This was the essential split in the band. Stevo and I were situated on the edges of what could be gotten away with, while Jan and Joey were largely unappreciative of our efforts to push the limits of our own endurance as well as the audience's. Stevo and I were equally unappreciative of Jan's extensive use of his flanger effect, and of Joe's business model. I clearly remember how Joe tried to insist that none of the songs on the second record could say "fuck" in them, because he was worried about airplay. Either Stevo or I said something about how lame that was, and that what we really should do was make sure that every song we wrote from then on should have "fuck" in it several times at least. The divisions in the band further fractured along these lines. We became a band divided unto itself.

I'm guessing that the USC frat house gig was probably the biggest booking mistake of my tenure with the band. I'd always avoided fraternity jock types like the ones who were around when we were loading in. Several times they asked: "You guys are the Vandals?" "Yeah, we sure are," we replied. "The guys who play the song that goes like…" They hummed a little of "Urban Struggle" just to rule out the possibility that they had the wrong band, and that we could be sent packing. No such luck. I grinned as I continued to load amps into the frat house. We'd just finished driving all over the southern U.S. for a mini-tour of largely ineffectual consequences. So we stank, as in we were unwashed. Musically, we were probably as tight as we ever were.

We immediately noticed a dearth of other punkers. These kids all had Izod shirts on and were clearly not our usual fans.

They looked at us warily, as well, as if they were unsure of what we might do. I was already starting to think about ways to vandalize the situation, because to me the frat kids were basically the embodiment of all that was not punk or cool in any way. Young, rich, legacy chowderheads being handed their leadership roles in life, but first we'll have a great big beer bash and we'll have a really cool "funny punk" band come play. I was further annoyed that Stevo was in the middle of some sort of post-tour snit and refused to show up. We'd asked our old friend Worm to sing for us, but this show was still going to be a disaster no matter what.

The frat house was a big brownstone-looking three-story monstrosity, with the first floor set about halfway underground and giant palatial steps leading up to a huge veranda. We were instructed to set up in a room that was to the left of the foyer; again of monstrous proportions. I'd guess it was maybe twenty-five by fifty feet, with us set up in the northeast corner of the building facing inward to the assumed audience area.

We set up and wandered around a bit, marveling at the Munsters' architecture and grabbing what little beer didn't involve hanging around with too many frat boys. It seemed a bit early, but someone told us it was time to play. So we walked into the nearly empty room, tuned up, and lit into one of our songs. This was Worm's first gig with us, but he'd learned the lyrics fairly well. People started to come in to the room. Almost everyone had a date to dance with, which was amazing to us. The alligator shirt crowd was in the house.

I don't think I had my own mic, but Worm seemed to be obliging when I thought of a new heckle for these aliens. By about the fourth song, I was taking to running out into the crowd of dancing couples and then running back to the band area, snarling up as many people as I could with my forty-foot bass cord. Though the sound guys would always tell me that anything over thirty feet would lose signal, I thought my bass was still plenty loud, and that extra ten feet came in handy sometimes.

I think I made it about eight songs in before I decided that this travesty needed to end. Jan was playing in front of a large plate-glass window in the building's east face. I'd say the window was around four feet by eight feet. Now Jan's about six feet tall, but he was kinda hunched over a bit, because he was playing. I decided what I was aiming for was somewhere in the top third of the window. My missile of choice was my Fender P Bass. My only real concern was that I might actually hit Jan in the face, so I aimed pretty high. Lucky for Jan, he saw my bass coming and was able to duck a bit. I forget what song we were doing, but I suddenly decided I was through and that it was time to quit. I made sure that my cord was on the window side of my legs. I unhooked my fire hose strap and threw that bass close to twenty feet, right through that window. Like a goddamn javelin. Without pausing, I ran over to Jan's stack and pulled it forward face-first onto the hardwood floor, before spinning around and diving backward into Joe's drum kit. I remember the dead silence in the room, punctuated only by Joe's distant screech: "Fucker, you fucker, fucker,

This page: *Steve Humann, the Vandals, USC frat party, 1982.* RICK HOSTAGE. Facing page, from left: *Kids at the Brown Box; Mike Muir with skanker on his shoulders. The youngest kid behind him is Junior.* PHOTOS BY JORDAN SCHWARTZ

you're a fucker!" as he repeatedly kicked me in the head. Then came the sound of my amp being thrown face-first onto the floor by Jan, followed by total silence again.

Seconds later, I jumped up to check out the hole my bass had made in the plate glass. It was amazing—it came off better than many movie stunts. There was a nearly perfect oblong hole near the center of the top half of the window—the rest of the glass had held perfectly! My torn-off-at-the-amp cord hung through the hole's dead center, like an unfinished swag lamp installation. Imagining my bass in pieces below, I ran outside through the still relatively shocked-silent crowd, down those huge steps, and around the side of the building. I couldn't believe my eyes. There was my bass, leaning upright against an evergreen hedge like I'd left it there. A thing of vibrant red beauty against the deep green natural background, all lit up from the lower floor's windows as if for a photo shoot. I guess the hedge had broken the instrument's nearly fifteen-foot fall, because, aside from a few tiny shards of glass stuck in the tip of the headstock, my bass was completely undamaged. Exultant, I ran back inside to explain the miracle. For some reason, nobody really cared. Jan wouldn't speak to me. Joe just kept bitching about what an asshole I was and how Jan had now quit the band. There was also a gathering posse of frat types starting to talk shit. There was one in particular who had the cutest little fuzzy beginnings of a mustache. He was attempting to marshal the troops to do something physical. I was lucky that he didn't have enough takers to rush me.

As the rest of the band gathered up their stuff, I could see that this was the end of the Vandals. I think in some ways it was. Actually, I came back to apologize a couple of weeks later. Lying through my teeth, I swore that nothing like that would ever happen again. We reformed for another year or so before I quit for good.

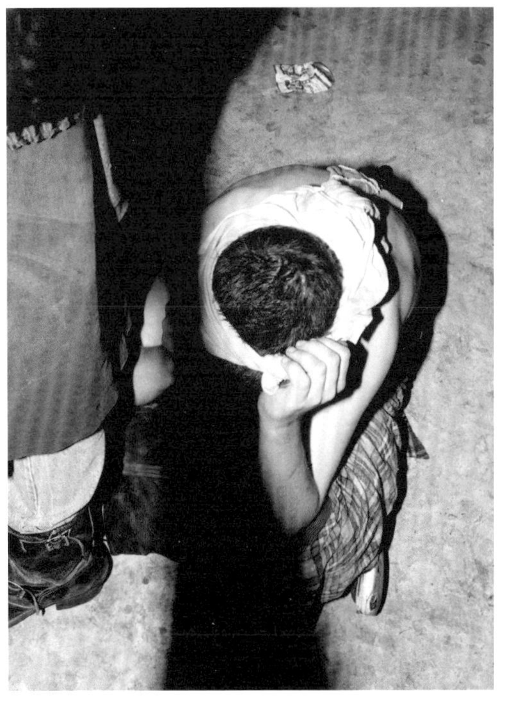

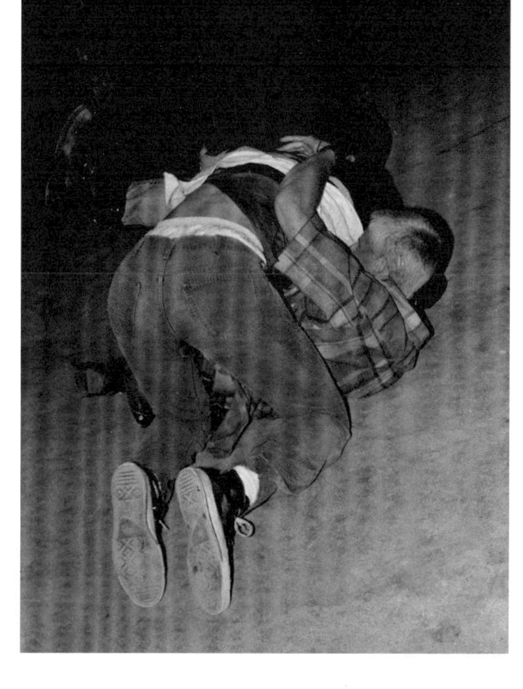

Facing page and this page: *Breaking pits and pit breakdowns.* PHOTOS BY JORDAN SCHWARTZ

HOLLY-WEST CRISIS

EUGENE TATU

In late 1979, at the age of fourteen, I moved into my first apartment, at the Holly-West Building in Hollywood at the intersection of Hollywood Boulevard and Western Avenue. I was born and raised in Los Feliz, just east of there. The Holly-West Building was originally built by United Artists film studio many years ago, and my apartment had actually been an office. My roommate at the time was named Dana Steverson. He was somewhat on the run from his hometown of Huntington Beach, basically for being punk rock. I fondly remember how Dana and I used to do our dishes by putting them out on the fire escape before it rained. That actually worked quite well.

Dana was responsible for starting what became known as the Skinhead Army. The leadership wing, which consisted of maybe twenty-five to thirty guys, was called the Wayward Caines. The whole idea started because a lot of redneck 4x4 types were assaulting punk rockers as they left shows. You might say it was open season on punks. People got crippled for life by these creeps, and some even died. The LAPD did not give a damn, as they were interested in shutting down this bizarre subculture themselves.

Soon there was a "war party" in my apartment, with all the heavies from Huntington Beach, including Jeff "Boz" Milucky, Chris Martin, and Borzoi and Bardia. The whole plan was hammered out, and it actually worked. The Skinhead Army grew into the hundreds and made it safe to go to punk shows (if you were punk!).

Around this time I joined my first band, the Atoms, which had been started by Monty Messex and Taz Rudd. Johnny Nobody, who later joined Red Cross circa *Born Innocent*, was the drummer. Around that time I met Mugger, Rob Henley, and Drew, through a mutual friend—Darby Crash. Later on, Mugger and I started the band Nig-Heist. Even back then he was already writing some pretty way-out songs.

The Holly-West Building was an amazing breeding ground for musicians. Right below my apartment, the Cheifs had their practice place, where they also lived. Below them, the Gears had their room, which I think they shared to some extent with the Mau Maus. We had quite a few neighbors in the building, as well: Michael Livingston, Scott Franklin, and Dewey Burns of the Mau Maus; and Avenue of the all-girl band the Anemics. She later became Eva O and formed the Speed Queens, and later she joined Christian Death. Brian Grillo, who later sang in Lock Up and Extra Fancy, lived right down the hall. Alice Malice of the Anemics and Timmy Turmoil were neighbors too.

The parties went on forever at the Holly-West, and you never knew who would show up. Snickers from the Simpletones would appear at the oddest times with Jack Daniel's and cases of beer, blaring Iron Maiden, Van Halen, or Dio from his ghetto blaster. Keith Morris was just starting the Circle Jerks and would be there all the time as well.

My favorite Holly-West story is how I became the roadie for the Cheifs—Darby Crash's favorite band (he produced their first

Facing page: *Wasted Youth's Chet Lehrer, Steve Cervantes, unknown punker girl, Circle One's Mike Vallejo, and unknown accomplice, Oki Dog, West Hollywood, CA, January 1982.* JORDAN SCHWARTZ

CHILI BURGER (C,M,P,O,T)
DANNY'S CHILI CHEESE BURGER
(SPECIAL CHILI SAUCE M,P,O,T)
DOUBLE CHILI CHEESE BURGER (C,M,P,O,T)
TRIPLE CHILI CHEESE BURGER (C,M,P,O,T)
HULA CHILI CHEESE BURGER (C,M,P,O,T)
TERIYAKI BURGER (P,O,T)
TACO BURGER (A,L,M,P,O,T)
EGG BURGER (C,M,P,O,T
OKI BURGER
ONION, TOMATOES,
STEAK SAND
TAQUITO
TERIYAKI TAQUITO
FRIED BURRITO
TERIYAKI BEEF BURRITO
TERIYAKI STEAK BURRITO
OKI PASTRAMI BURRITO
TOSTADA
GRILLED CHEESE
TUNA SALAD SAND.
FRIED EGG SAND.
BACON & EGG SAND.
BACON, LETTUCE, TOMATOE
BAR-B-QUE STICK
DANNY'S CHILI DOG
SOUR KRAUT & MUSTARD
MUSTARD, RELISH, ONION DOG
DOG (2 FRANKS, CHILI, CHEESE, WRAPPED IN
SANKA, HOT COCOA
ROOT BEER, GRAPE

DOGS
OKI DOG
CAR STEREOS
AUTO ALARMS
AND INSTALLATIONS
marantz
OPEN

single). I was in my apartment, having only moved in a few days before, and the Cheifs were practicing right below me. I plugged in the electric bass—a twelfth-birthday present from my foster father, Beat-era folksinger Hamilton Camp—and I began rather effortlessly playing along with the Cheifs as they practiced. The thing is, when they would stop below, I would keep on playing their songs—changes and all. Finally, the whole band came pounding on my apartment door. I opened the door and introduced myself. I was drafted into the job of roadie in short order. At this point singer Jerry Koskie and drummer Rabit, both formerly of the Simpletones, gave me the nickname "Euge." It stuck.

When Rabit and Jerry quit a few years later, the Cheifs continued playing for a while. I was loyal to the two of them, so I didn't really attend these shows—except one at the Whisky A Go Go, and then just to heckle. At one point, guitarist George Walker vanished, and the Cheifs—now with Gilbert from the Stains and a singer whose name escapes me—had booked a show at the O.N. Klub. I was the only person besides George who knew the songs on guitar. Besides, George had a very odd way of picking and playing that also had to be replicated. The bassist Bob Glassley came to my new apartment building, the Ponderosa in East Hollywood, and asked me to play the last gig with the Cheifs. Of course, out of respect for the Cheifs of old, I took the task.

When we actually had to once and for all leave the Holly-West Building, the new manager—who was being screwed over by his employers, the alleged owners of Holly-West— opened up the supply closet and gave all the tenants, basically a bunch of punk rock bands, buckets of paint and cans of spray paint. He just said: "Have at it." We really trashed that place good. Someone wrote "Holly-West Crisis" in black paint on the wall.

Facing page: *Sin 34 and friends at Oki Dog. From left: Phil Newman, unidentified, Julie Lanfeld, Jordan Schwartz, Mike Glass, David Markey.* JENNIFER SCHWARTZ

I relocated to Huntington Beach and hung out with Boz, Mosher, and the rest of the Skinhead Army and Wayward Caines. I went to a party at a house that had recently been sold. The former owner's daughter still had the keys, and she consented to letting a new band named China White play there. I was amazed by them, and called the Cheifs, letting them listen over the phone line. I insisted they get China White a gig in L.A., which they did, at the Starwood. That was China White's first L.A. show. Meanwhile, havoc ensued inside the house. Mosher was swinging from a chandelier, which promptly broke.

I went back to Hollywood to stay at the Skinhead Manor, where my friend Kevin Stench from San Diego lived. I joined the band No Crisis. I played my first show with them at a club in Burbank with the Circle Jerks and the Adolescents. I was so nervous that my knees were shaking, until Roger Rogerson from the Circle Jerks gave me some kind of pain pill that worked rather well. The No Crisis lineup was myself on the bass, Johnny Snot on guitar, Kevin Stench on vocals, and Ron Blast on drums.

The Stern brothers, who had the lease on the Manor, were formulating what would later become the BYO, the Better Youth Organization. I introduced them to the H.B. (Huntington Beach) people from the Skinhead Army and Wayward Caines, who in turn brought along the Long Beach contingent. I also introduced them to the Oxnard people. Kevin Stench brought up his friends from San Diego and things really started moving along.

At one point I left the Manor for Oxnard, where I joined Agression. I gave them some songs I had written: "Rat Race," "Locals Only," and "Money Machine." They later rerecorded most of their songs, including mine, and claimed full authorship. Mugger started up the band Nig-Heist, a name Johnny Snot and I came up with. Mugger had a lot of songs, and they all contained pretty obscene lyrics. We practiced wherever SST Records was at any given time. The LAPD and other police departments routinely drove them out wherever they went, or so it seemed. Nig-Heist was a lot of fun, as we could play whenever and wherever we liked. We would just show up at a show and announce that we would be playing, and that was that.

Facing page and this page: *Former Skinhead Manor inhabitants Youth Brigade. Live photos from Bob's Place, Watts, 1982.* PHOTOS BY JORDAN SCHWARTZ

THE SWEET LIFE
LOUICHE MAYORGA

I first became interested in music in the sixth grade. I was the second-youngest of nearly a dozen kids, and it was a good way to get attention. It wasn't until I was about thirteen that I started getting serious about the bass and guitar. My first bass was given to me by my godmother's boyfriend. I won't mention his name, but he ended fighting in the streets of Venice.

During a summer break from Catholic school, I worked and saved some money and bought my first guitar, a Hondo II candy-apple sunburst Les Paul copy that never stayed in tune. I would lock myself in the bedroom I shared with my brothers, turn on the suitcase record player, put a penny on top of the needle, and play along to whatever I was listening to. On the way to school in the eighth grade, I found a Chuck Berry record that someone had thrown out. I must have played "Johnny B. Goode" about a thousand times to learn the intro, and I never got it exactly right.

The first time I remember seeing Dave Markey was at John Adams Junior High School in Santa Monica around 1977 or '78. I wasn't sure if he was in the same grade as me, but he was wandering around the hallways brandishing matching forearm casts. I always wondered how he got the injury. A couple years later, farther down Pico Boulevard at Santa Monica High School, during tenth or eleventh grade I overheard the preppy students hanging out in "the Quad" talking shit and giggling at the sight of three freaks walking through the lunch area—Dave Markey, now with a shaved head, along with his pal Jordan Schwartz, and, I think, Jordan's sister, Jennifer. They were getting sweated pretty hard, but they kept their heads up. I sort of had an idea of punk rock, as I used to work at the Santa Monica Civic Auditorium, located across the street from Samohi. While on the clock there I saw Devo, on their very first tour, and the Buzzcocks.

You gotta realize, at the time everybody else wore OPs and Izod Lacoste shirts and corduroy pants. Girls and boys alike had long, feathered hair. *Everyone* looked the same: preppies in letterman sweaters. I really didn't fit in, either. I couldn't skate good and I couldn't afford fancy clothes. All I had was my bass and a few friends. So when I saw Markey, Jordan, and Jennifer, they were completely outta the norm. Outcasts. I admit that I thought they were a little strange. They were called "freaks," "geeks," and "dirty punkers." I think they really only had each other. People would throw stuff at them: gum, erasers, and sometimes they got spit on. Of course, back in those days punkers were expected to like to spit and be spit on. Although they were abused in my eyes, I thought they liked it, because they never changed; that was my philosophy. Stupid, huh?

Mike Muir wasn't a punker yet. I don't think his brother, Jim, was either. I think Mike left school in the eleventh grade, or he graduated early. Mike was going to punk shows, and at that point he had several ear piercings and was wearing swastika T-shirts, I think for the shock value. Then one morning at school there was a big ol' "hit-up" on the wall by the tennis courts that read SUICIDAL TENDENCIES. That was the first time I ever heard the name.

Facing page, from left: *Louiche Mayorga, Suicidal Tendencies, the Brown Box, Culver City, 1982; Mike Muir, Suicidal Tendencies. This was a very early Suicidal Tendencies show, before they'd recorded their first LP. This lineup included the Dunnigan brothers on guitar and drums. Mike Muir went to our high school, but he was expelled, supposedly for wearing a swastika T-shirt.* PHOTOS BY JORDAN SCHWARTZ

After graduating from Samohi and moving over to Santa Monica City College, I was standing in line to register for school, and Mike Muir just so happened to be in line in front of me. We start talking about his band, and he brought up the fact that he needed a bass player. We lined up an audition, and I was in Suicidal Tendencies that same week. The music was cool, too. The songs were short and simple but catchy. The first song he showed me was "Suicidal Failure." I liked the slow-and-fast approach. I remember thinking: "I got this!" All those years of jamming in my bedroom and in the basement were gonna pay off. I knew I had a lot to offer, being in this punk band.

I remember when punk was new. I knew I didn't want to get spit on. With my new crew I didn't have to dress like a punker. My brother was a gangster from Venice 13. The guys we were running around with kinda had the same look as that, but we had our own cause. It was all about the punk shows, and hanging out at Mar Vista Park with our homeboy attire mixed with a li'l punkness, like steel-toe boots and pierced ears. We thought we were the shit. Nobody looked like us. We ended up being very cliquish at the shows.

We started doing shows around WLA and the Westside. There was this little hall in Culver City called the Brown Box, which we later called "Sewercide Hall." There I saw David again with Jordan and Jennifer, and they had cameras—even, I think, a Super 8 camera. They had a fanzine called *We Got Power*, which I think was like fifty cents or a dollar, something real cheap. We ended up being interviewed in *We Got Power* #4.

Our first, self-titled record came out in 1983. I got really lucky being a cowriter of this song called "Institutionalized." That song really propelled us and set us apart from all the other bands. I could have never imagined on my best day ever coming out with something like that. The music I wrote for that track was something I borrowed from another ST song, "I Saw Your Mommy," and that was like a template for my writing in ST for years to come.

You know, we lived in Venice until I was about six years old. My dad moved us out of there because there was a lot of stuff going on. We moved to Third and Hollister in Santa Monica during the height of the Dogtown era. In Santa Monica, it was pretty safe to move around from place to place, unlike when I lived in Venice. When I joined Suicidal, I had just turned eighteen, and we were always in and out of Venice. Back when I was growing up, I was never allowed to cross Rose Avenue on the border between Venice and Santa Monica. Now I was all grown up and it was a beautiful thing. We could go through, we just looked straight, and we didn't look for no problems. Ahhhhhhh, the sweet life.

Facing page: *Suicidal Tendencies at the Brown Box, from left: founding member, bassist-turned-guitarist Mike Dunnigan; The other brother, drummer Sean Dunnigan.* PHOTOS BY JORDAN SCHWARTZ

SUICIDAL
TENDENCIES

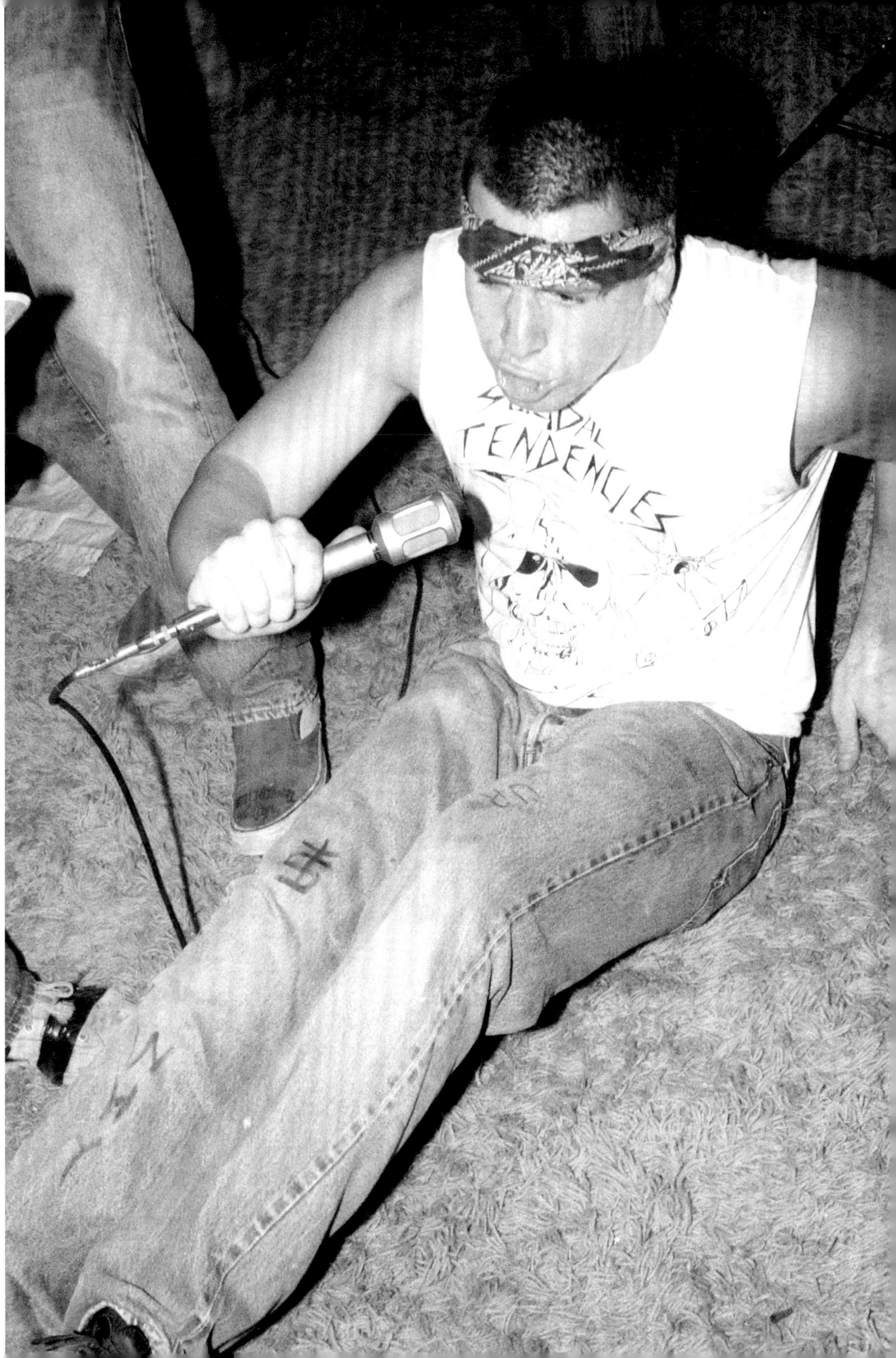

Facing page: *Suicidal Tendencies, the Brown Box. The band was already known on the Westside in 1982, as lots of kids with close-cropped heads and hand-drawn Suicidal shirts had formed a gang around the band.* This page: *Mike Muir of Suicidal, 1982.* PHOTOS BY JORDAN SCHWARTZ

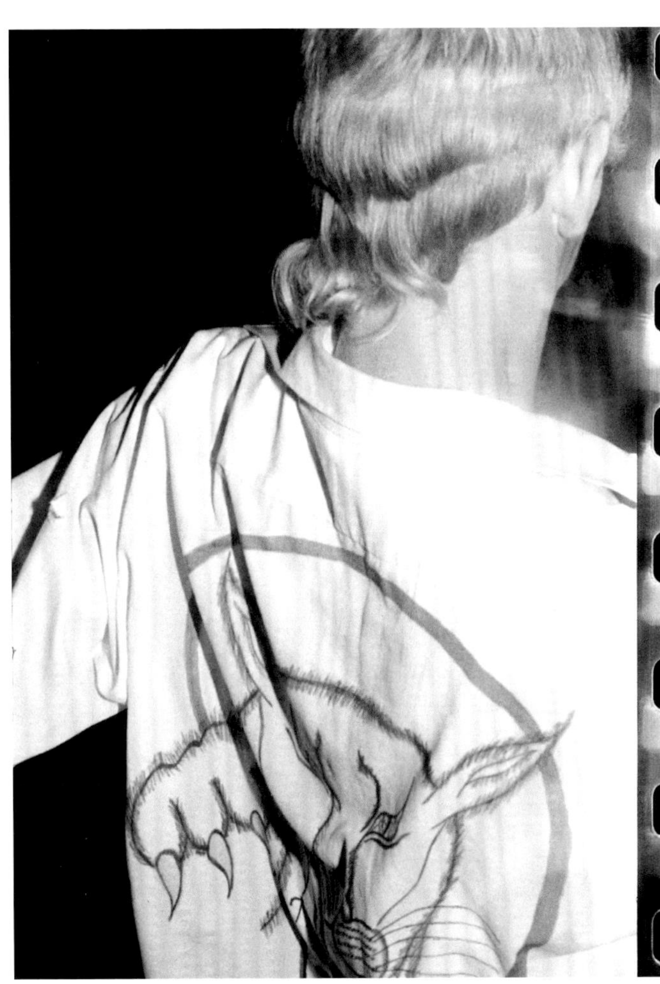

This page, from left: *Suicidal wearing homemade wild animal shirt; Vince, aka "Gore."* Facing page: *Louiche Mayorga and friends.* PHOTOS BY JORDAN SCHWARTZ

PALM SPRINGS: PUNK FROM THE DESERT
SEAN WHEELER

As memory serves, Myke Bates was the first committed punker in the dez. He wore the haircut, boots, bandannas, leather jacket, and other assorted punker gear, and he had a high-school band called Pretty Vacant around 1979–80 that played punk covers by the Pistols, the Clash, and whatever. He was older than the rest of us, and guys his age weren't making the commitment to being labeled freaks and suffering the harassment that would follow; Myke was on his own in high school. The rest of us were still in junior high, getting hip to this new wave and punk stuff largely through skateboarding. We would go to Big O skate park in O.C. and be too scared to go in the bathroom, 'cause Duane Peters would grab you and shave your head. Eventually, we willingly succumbed, and Myke Bates didn't have to punk out alone no more.

Myke was the only one old enough to have a license, so he would fill up his mini-truck and take us to shows in L.A. at the Starwood, Whisky, Vex, and, later on, Bards Apollo and Florentine Gardens and other hot spots. The key year in the desert punk scene was 1981. Black Flag came out that spring to play a place called Rumors. Dez Cadena was singing, and Greg Ginn's Dan Armstrong guitar was ripped off. At this point, Myke had an original band called Funeral Information, which disbanded and became Target 13—who recorded the "Rodney on the ROQ" theme on Rodney Bingenheimer's *Rodney on the ROQ, Volume 2* comp. Myke soon then formed Subservice with Herb Lienau, Scott Reeder, and Cary Abelardo.

Around the same time, my band Mutual Hatred began. Sin 34 came to Palm Springs in June of that summer of 1981 to play their first show ever. They taught Mike Vallejo from Circle One the songs in the car on the way down. Mutual Hatred played their first show that night as well, with Myke on guitar, notorious Indio punker Johnny Bloodstreak on drums, and Julie Sin 34 on bass. Subservice played as well, but according to Scott Reeder there were only six people still in the room, and he says he was still settling down from watching Dave Markey thrash on his drums.

In 1982, Johnny Bloodstreak got out of juvenile hall and started singing for Indio's Willful Failure. He tried stealing the name Mutual Hatred—I heard reports that he was spray-painting it all around Indio—but another stint in juvie slowed his efforts. At that point, Mutual Hatred had Alfredo Hernandez playing drums, Eric playing guitar, and Greg on bass. We had two big shows—one a house party in L.A. with Black Flag, which we never found due to being lost or getting bad directions; and another that Sin 34 hooked up for us, with them and Suicidal Tendencies in Culver City's Suicide Hall.

At the same time, Myke moved to O.C. and formed Uniform Choice, which later continued without him. Dead Issue was formed with Mario "Boomer" Lalli, Alex, Cary, and Scott Reeder on drums. Herb soon took over on vocals. That summer Herb and Scott Reeder moved to L.A., and Dead Issue recorded a song for the *Desperate Teenage Lovedolls* soundtrack album under the name Darkside, for some confusing reason. With Herb and Scott in Los Angeles, Boomer started other bands: the Yungins, the Breed, Yawning Man, Halo of Flies, etc. Mike and Mark Anderson, Gary Arce, Gary Burns, Mike Montano, and lots of other people went through these bands and lots of others.

Time pressed on. SST and many of its bands evolved from hardcore punk to jazz. Yawning Man turned into Sort of Quartet and then came Fatso Jetson. There were new punkers everywhere: Scabies Babies, the Unsound, Sons of Kyuss, Zezo Ze-Ce Zadfrack and the Dune Buggy Attack Battallion, Party Dolphin, and on and on. Many went on to do other things—some big, some small. Some ended up in prison, nuthouses, graveyards, or (worst of all?) nine-to-five jobs. It all depends who you ask.

From top: *Sean Wheeler on left with Joe Dillon, early 1980s.* UNKNOWN; *Rodney Bingenheimer in the studio.* DAVID MARKEY

Facing page: *Dirty Rotten Imbeciles, Shamus O'Brian's—a basement in City of Industry, CA, late 1983.* This page: *Kurt Brecht and bassist Sebastian Amok of D.R.I., Shamus O'Brian's.* Next page, from left: *Singer Randy "Biscuit" Turner and bassist Chris Gates, Big Boys, Grandia Room, 1982; guitarist Tim Kerr, Big Boys, Grandia Room.* Following pages: *First Butthole Surfers show in California, Grandia Room, 1982. Pictured are guitarist Paul Leary, bassist Quinn Mathews, and singer Gibby Haynes, putting clothespins in his hair. Gibby's Magic Marker tattoo reads "T-Asshole-L" —a pointed swipe at TSOL.* PHOTOS BY JORDAN SCHWARTZ

Fender

GLASS

Facing page: *Drummer Marc Alberstadt and singer John Stabb, Government Issue, Shamus O'Brian's.* This page, from left: *John Stabb of G.I., Shamus O'Brian's; Henry Rollins with Ted Falconi of Flipper, also a founding member, with Chuck Dukowski, of SWA, 1984.* PHOTOS BY JORDAN SCHWARTZ

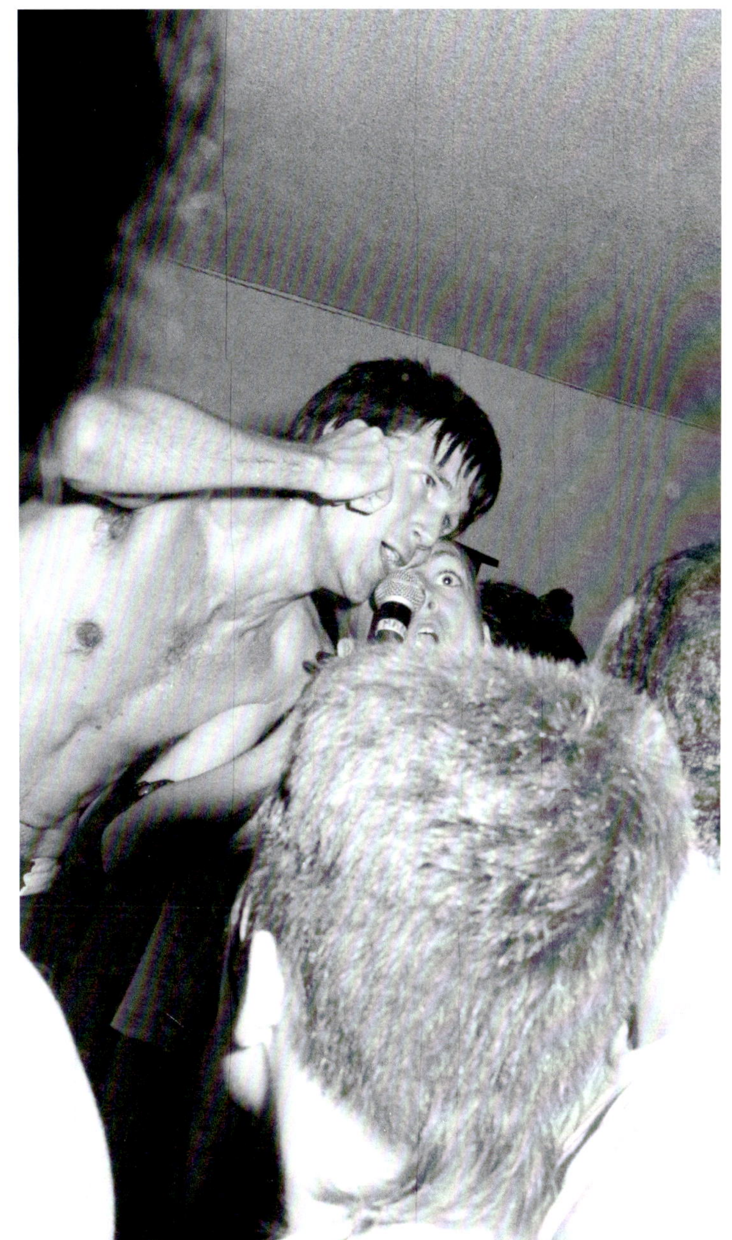

SLAM BOOK

TONY ADOLESCENT

Before spending too much time in retro mode, I must forewarn you that I am a creature of the present. While I do enjoy jawing about the past, I am more interested in moving forward, and not toward the *passed*. I am in a constant state of reevaluation, and while I love the histories that everyone shares, I prefer my world of wonderland to the more reliable half-truths that everyone else chooses to circulate.

Having said that, I want to compliment Dave Markey on his fine beard. We of little facial hair have beard envy, and for the last twenty-five years or so of the Adolescents' history, ne'er a day has passed when one of us hasn't randomly yelled "Beard!" simply for the sonic satisfaction of the word. I'm just saying.

First, I should pause for a moment to again apologize for ruining the Sin 34 set at the Cathay de Grande in 1983. I know that Dave Markey has spent years trying to erase all memory of the show from his brain data bank, possibly to allow me a semblance of dignity. Fear not, that dissipated years ago—this is what happened:

The Abandoned asked to jump on a show assembled by John Macias of Circle One. Our drummer, Chuy, was friends with Mike Vallejo and John, and arranged to squeeze us in to play the half-dozen songs we had been working on. Rather than change over another bunch of gear, the fine band Sin 34 loaned us a full setup. Bad idea. I fell into Mike Glass's guitar and broke three strings immediately. Mike freaked and started hollering at me. I then backed up and climbed up on Dave's bass drum, which Chuy was borrowing. Fearing that my 105-pound frame might be cracking it, Chuy hit me in the head with Dave's sticks, which made me lose my balance. I grabbed the ceiling, which was acoustic tile, and pulled down about twelve panels. Enraged, the bartender, Dobbs, came around the bar and began throttling me, Homer Simpson style. He then threw my sorry ass out the door, microphone still clutched in my hand. John Macias followed me up the street, where I humbly returned said microphone. Then I sat curbside with El Duce (another fine beard, but not nearly as impressive as Dave Markey's) for the remainder of the evening.

THE ADOPTED CADENA

Since the age of thirteen, I have lived using a succession of pseudonyms. This is a result of being involved in pen-pal networking. We used archaic methods such as postage stamps, envelopes, and handwritten letters to share our teen angst and musical preferences. The networking was enhanced by "slam books," which were little stapled insult books containing all kinds of personal information. We stuffed them into the envelopes with our letters, and then sent them to different people to be passed on, thus introducing ourselves to new groups of people. Think of it like a personal advertorial booklet. Through this network I met Rich Coffee of the Gizmos and the writer Gail Worley, and I learned about D.O.A., the Misfits, and a number of other bands that flew under the FM radio radar.

One of my pen pals, a hilarious man from Hillsdale, New Jersey, dubbed me "Tony Reflex." I began using that name in

Facing page: *The Adolescents, about an hour before a riot erupted, Baces Hall, East Hollywood, 1980.*
SPOT

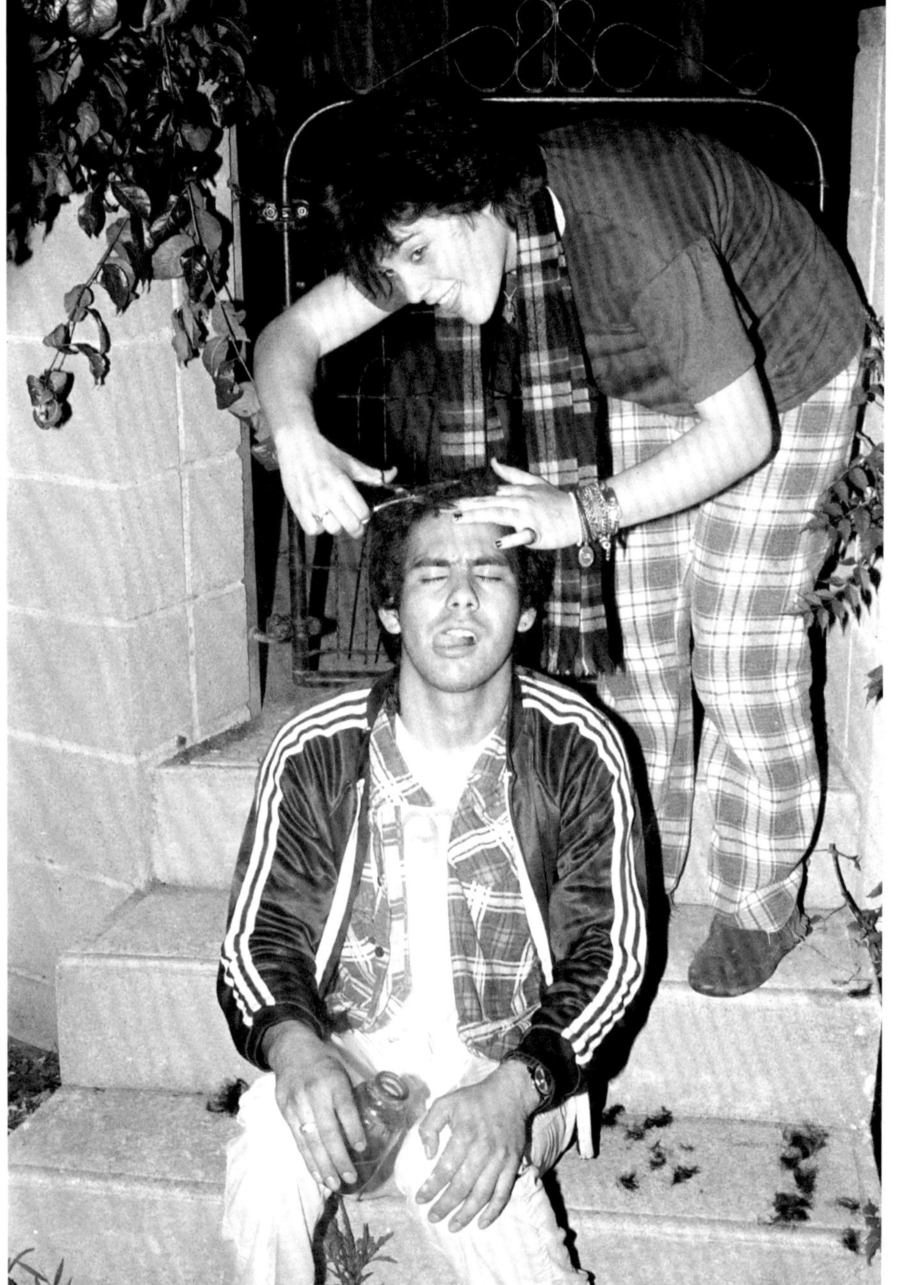

1978. Unfortunately, it did not transfer well. "Tony Reflex" began showing up in print as "Tony Flex," which I took as an intentional reference to my thin frame, and not what it was—a typo. I took on the name "Tony Cadena." By the time the Adolescents had begun playing around frequently, a couple years later, Dez Cadena was singing for Black Flag. People asked if we were brothers. I said, "Yes." It was as simple as that. People still ask me: "How is your brother?" I reply: "He's a Misfit." I love the way it sounds.

THE ORIGIN OF THE ADOLESCENTS

I was an annoying mosquito buzzing around the Agent Orange camp. I was the guy sneaking into shows, carrying in gear and losing it, jumping onstage and grabbing the microphone and singing, and generally making mischief. Building mayhem was easy, because Mike Palm and Steve Soto from Agent Orange were not able to grab the mic away from me while they were playing! Snickers from the Simpletones had tried to convince me that I should be in a band, as did General Hospital, aka Rikk Agnew—but neither of them wanted to try to generate the lasso to corral this little mustang. Soto took a chance and asked me to try something out with him and Frank Agnew. We ended up adopting the name of a garage band in Petaluma, from a pen pal who gave me her blessing, and we dubbed the band the Adolescents. With the encouragement of Jello Biafra, Rodney Bingenheimer, Eddie Subtitle, and our friends, we started recording and playing our songs at parties, high schools, youth centers, and stuff like that. The resulting fiascos are a book unto themselves!

Facing page, from left: *Jennifer Schwartz cuts Steve Cervantes's hair; Julie Lanfeld cuts Cervantes's hair.* PHOTOS BY JORDAN SCHWARTZ

DO THE "EDDIE"!

I stood outside of the Starwood one night in 1980 with Mike Patton and Mike Atta, watching Eddie Subtitle lurk around passing out flyers for a gig. I started trying to imitate Eddie's walk, as did the Mikes. It quickly became a standing joke, with the three of us circulating flyers while doing the "Eddie Walk." Then, in a move inspired by Frankie and Annette movies, I suggested a dance craze called "The Eddie," in which you kind of lumbered about. "Doing the Eddie" caught on wicked fast, as it was really fun to do, and really goofy to watch. The target of the joke, Eddie, seemed to like it as much as we did at the time.

WHAT REALLY WENT ON AT THE BLACK HOLE?

The Black Hole was an apartment shared by Mike Ness, Robert Omlit, Mr. Joe, and Kirby Jones. I knew Kirby from the pen-pal slam-book scene. She introduced me to a number of the freaks who were circulating around the *Rocky Horror Picture Show* crowd at the Fox Theatre in Fullerton and the Balboa Theater in Newport Beach, as well as a couple of bands—the Mechanics and the Naughty Women. It was a wonderful scene, full of bravado and misfits, mischief-makers, and escapees. They were really funny, wacky people, and the wild ride they took me on was brilliant—it was like Mr. Toad forgot to take his lithium and took peyote instead.

My guess is that Rozanne Omlit dubbed it the "Black Hole"—maybe as a companion piece to her VW bus, nicknamed "the Twilight Zone." Together, the two off-map spots were mobile parties, crash pads, and the stomping ground and birthplace of some of the most legendary stories in Fullerton's otherwise dull history. I have no problem saying that until rock and roll came to Fullerton in the late '70s, it was a flat, lifeless drone town.

There are too many tales of the Black Hole to enumerate, but suffice to say that chances are good that any legend anyone has heard or circulated about it is true. My favorites were Mr. Joe using Brylcreem instead of toothpaste, the fish tank full of stagnant water and stale beer, the Omlits' Zyklon-B-gas-the-house-in-their-sleep move, and Mike's inspired graffiti all over the walls. If someone told you they were there, the scene was small enough to either immediately support or discredit the storyteller. When the Black Hole finally went down, it was the most righteous destruction of any one-bedroom apartment known to mankind.

THE AGNEWS

What an amazingly talented family. What else can I say? I am truly blessed to have had the opportunity to meet, work with, and befriend Rikk, Frank, and Alfie, and to have the pleasure of knowing their parents, Sam and Leah, and that extends even more so to their children.

THE GERMS

I followed the Germs around for the last legs of their existence during 1979–80, and I had the joy of whacking the hornets' nest a few times. On a good night, they were easily the greatest band I had ever seen, and on a bad night they were still better than every shitty rock band I saw growing up in Anaheim. I don't care what anyone says about them, the naysayers, I mean. It's Tao, baby: Those who know don't speak, and those who speak don't know.

BILL BARTELL

The best mustache on earth belongs to Bill Bartell. He and Bruce Duff—those dudes are proof positive that higher life forms existed and landed in Riverside, then left their seed there to grow and prosper.

DISNEYLAND

I lived down the street from Disneyland. It used to be situated across from a Greyhound station. Anyone who knows bus stations knows that they are spots where hustlers, whores, junkies, and chicken hawks congregate. Even clean-cut John Wayne Orange County has an underbelly that it wants to hide from.

In the '70s, there was a serial killer wandering around killing teenage boys and stuffing them into trash bags alongside the freeways. I used to sell flowers out on the street in remote areas, and it was a fucked-up scene out there for a skinny little boy with a bucket full of roses for sale, let me tell you. All this shit was going down in the fifteen square miles around Disneyland, the Happiest Place on Earth. It was the cruelest of ironies—everything looked so spick-and-span on the outside, but it was wretched when the paint chipped off.

"The Happiest Place on Earth" usually wouldn't let us in. They would stop us at the door, insisting: "No punk rockers allowed." We had to go incognito, or sneak in by faking a hand stamp, then ride into the park on the monorail. The upside was that we could sneak in and catch a band like the Ventures for free. The downside was that guys dressed like the FBI would catch us and detain us like we were criminals for the offense of having purple hair.

For what it's worth, the hand-stamp-counterfeiting skills we mastered would be employed later to sneak into bars and clubs. In fact, the bravado that we used back then got us through many a doorway, and I can still get into most clubs these days using the same tricky little bastard moves I learned from at Disneyland. Thanks, Mickey.

Facing page: *The unknown traveling punk barber… always ready with shears in pocket.* PHOTOS BY JORDAN SCHWARTZ

ME VS. THE LORD OF DOGTOWN
JANET HOUSDEN

Hermosa Beach was a surf town, and despite what the movie *Lords of Dogtown* would have you believe, surfers and skaters weren't exactly down with punk rock—at least, not at first. In fact, as any 1970s suburban punk kid could tell you, surfers were the second-biggest anti-punk perpetrators, right behind jocks. Mostly they were content to just yell and throw things, but occasionally their anti-punk activities would escalate into yelling really mean things and throwing much bigger stuff. I once had a cinder block dropped on me from a balcony while I was waiting for the bus. It missed me by a couple of feet, but still!

The top three anti-punk slogans were "Punk sucks!," "Freak!," and, for some reason, "Devo!"—all preferably screamed from a moving car while the victim was schlepping to or from school. Heckling in the halls between classes was also popular. Once I tried to keep track of all the insults hurled my way over the course of one school day, and ended up losing track around lunchtime. I think I was up to ten "punk suckses" and eleven "Devos," not to mention a few random "dykes!" and "go back to Hollywoods!," before I gave up counting.

Not surprisingly, I hated surfers, despite the fact that prior to the coming of punk I'd been a puka-sporting hodad with a beavertail wet suit and a crush on Gerry Lopez. So imagine my righteous indignation when Tony Alva, who was at that time the Most Famous Skater in the Whole Wide World, and thus the Enemy, showed up at a Weirdos show at Baces Hall. Actually, I'm only assuming that I was indignant. I don't really remember, because, as usual, I was very, very drunk. I just remember someone saying, "Tony Alva is here!" and thinking it was a little odd (I should admit at this point that I used to have a poster of T.A. hanging in my bedroom, like every other 1970s beach kid), but not really paying much attention because—as I've already pointed out—I was very, very drunk, and the Weirdos were playing. I looooooooved the Weirdos.

I probably should have paid better attention, though, because then I might have had some clue as to what was about to happen next. I remember noticing a scuffle of some kind off to my left. The next thing I knew, I was flat on my back with a swelling eye on its way to becoming an enormous shiner. I'd been knocked out cold by something or other. Whatever it was, I never saw it coming, but boy oh boy was I pissed. Jeff McDonald, always the consummate troublemaker, immediately took advantage of this situation and said: "Tony Alva hit you!" Then he shoved an empty vodka bottle into my hand. For some reason, I accepted this rather startling news without question. Of course Tony Alva hit me. Why wouldn't he? He was the Enemy, and the Enemy was always doing stuff like that. I think it says a lot about the insanity of the times that it never occurred to me to wonder why a total stranger would just come up and knock me out for no reason, because unprovoked assaults were almost a daily occurrence for my friends and me. At any rate, my course of action seemed obvious. So, without further ado, I promptly marched up behind Mr. Alva and laid the bottle across his skull.

Facing page: *The City of Santa Monica had the genius idea to lure kids down to clean up the beach by having Red Cross play. It didn't really work—people just came to watch the show, then left all their food wrappers and beer bottles all over the place.* JORDAN SCHWARTZ

WALK

Now, everything I knew about violence I learned from TV. On TV, when you hit someone over the head with a bottle, they fall down. Apparently it doesn't work that way in real life, because all that happened was that Tony turned around and came after me. We were on the sidewalk in front of the club, and just as he grabbed me a bouncer grabbed him and I ran for my life.

I spent the next twenty-five years or so wondering what had really happened. The damn black eye lasted for weeks and caused me massive embarrassment in school, furthering my totally undeserved reputation as a violent psychopath (which did come in handy on occasion). A couple of years later, I met Tony Alva, and got my chance to ask his version of events. (When we were introduced, he just kind of rolled his eyes and said: "We've met.") He managed to convince me of his innocence, and he was actually pretty gracious about it, considering that I'd tried to kill him and all. Still, I was left clueless as to who or what had punched me out, and why.

A full quarter of a century had passed by now. I was at a party, and a mutual friend finally solved the mystery—although I suppose it wasn't much of a mystery, when you think about it. Of course the blame should have been placed on Jeff all along, but how he managed to knock me out, come up with an ingenious cover story on the spot, and totally get away with it (let alone why he would even do such a thing) still blows my mind. I mean, I had always suspected Jeff, but, really, who wants to admit that they have friends who would sucker punch them and then sic them on innocent strangers? That's kind of embarrassing.

I suppose there's some kind of lesson to be learned from this tragic tale, but hell if I can figure out what it is. Maybe it's something like: "Don't jump to conclusions and hit innocent bystanders over the head, because how do you know your best buddy isn't a scheming psychopath and is just playing you for giggles?" Or maybe: "Don't be mean to the weird kids at your school, because you'll make them all paranoid and crazy and then they'll assault random strangers with vodka bottles and it'll be your fault."

Perhaps the moral of the story is: "Punk rock was the devil's music, and it made nice teenagers bludgeon each other, so maybe it's a good thing that it's all corporate and lame now, so kids will just buy shoes instead of committing felonious assaults." Nah, that's definitely not it either. Let me know when you figure it out, okay?

Facing page, from left: *Red Cross, Santa Monica Beach Litter Walk, 1982* JORDAN SCHWARTZ; *Slamming in the sun, Santa Monica, 1982.* JORDAN SCHWARTZ. This page: *The enemy.* DAVID MARKEY. Overleaf and following: *Scenes from Beach Litter Walk, Santa Monica Beach at Station 26, 1982.* PHOTOS BY JORDAN SCHWARTZ

LITTER REDUCTION

This page, clockwise from top left: *Red Cross playing an upstairs bedroom at a Hollywood house party; Steven McDonald and Tracy Lea of Red Cross, the Brown Box; Jeff McDonald of Red Cross.* Facing page, from left: *Janet Housden, the newly rechristened Redd Kross, Dancing Waters, July 30, 1982; Jeff McDonald, Red Cross, the Brown Box.* PHOTOS BY JORDAN SCHWARTZ

This page, from left: *Jeff McDonald of Red Cross, the Brown Box, 1982; Janet Housden and Tracy Lea of Red Cross, the Brown Box, 1982; Steven McDonald of Redd Kross with B.C. Rich bass, Pomona Valley Auditorium, 1984.* Facing page: *Mike Muir takes the mic from Jeff McDonald, the Brown Box, 1982.* PHOTOS BY JORDAN SCHWARTZ

Ibanez

MY FRIEND MIKE WEBBER
JULA BELL

Mike Webber was the notorious lead singer of Nip Drivers, and he has been immortalized as kind of the South Bay's very own Darby Crash. Like Darby, he was brilliant, handsome, talented, persuasive, charming, fashionable, a master of witty on-stage banter, and he did a *lot* of drugs. Unlike Darby, he wasn't a narcissist. He didn't advocate violence. He wasn't concerned with starting a cult to take over the world. Basically, Mike Webber was just a genuinely nice, sensitive, funny, talented, impatient misfit who happened to be the most inherently hedonistic punk mofo around. He lived and breathed sex, drugs, and rock and roll—but spent a lot of his life living at his parents' house in Torrance.

Mostly, he just couldn't sit still—unless he was medicated, of course. Mike was extremely bright, open-minded, and well-read. He always had the craziest sexually explicit stories—sometimes hearsay, but usually firsthand—and he loved to "out" celebrities. Mike had the mind-set that punk was an avenue to be ironic and silly, and he derived infinite pleasure from poking fun at social norms, and debunking myths. He had a genuine love and respect for music of many different genres. At a time when a lot of punks in the scene were concerned with looking cool, Mike was very unapologetic concerning his offbeat musical tastes.

Nip Drivers formed in 1982 alongside a lot of other exciting bands in the South Bay area of Los Angeles. While new wave, metal, and punk were becoming a bit formulaic, Nip Drivers stood out with a quirky yet powerful sound. They released their debut LP, *Destroy Whitey*, on Mike Watt and D. Boon's New Alliance Records. The early lineups featured Kurt Schellenbach's assaultive punk guitar riffs and epic solos; Nick Passiglia's maniacal ass-whoopin' drum bashing and unconventional fills; and Janus Jones on bass with a smattering of crazed possessed siren vocals. The next lineup included Adam Bomb, the KXLU hardcore DJ, ripping the bass up with joyful vigor. I was proud to play bass in the final lineup, with the stellar South Bay skin beater Greg Cameron and shredding guitar taskmaster Dave Wakefield.

Sometimes watching Mike perform was was like watching an exorcism. He sang in an amazing whining falsetto, and would growl, moan, add a few tra-la-las, and scream his head off. He made all this sound while writhing around in a ripped-up dress, molesting the mic, dancing some weird little jig, or just standing there slumped over something with his eyes rolled up in his head looking like he was going to pass out.

Mike always picked the most eclectic non-punk songs that he could, and he would punkify them with glee. Watching burly South Bay jock punks slam to "Have You Never Been Mellow" by Olivia Newton John, "Fox on the Run" by the Sweet, "You Need Us" by the Honeybees (from *Gilligan's Island*), or "I Will Follow Him" by Peggy Lee was simply genius. The jocks would sing along to: "I love him I love him I love him / And when he comes I'll swallow, I'll swallow, I'll swallow." These homophobes had no idea that they were being captivated by a bisexual heroin addict hedonist who lived with his dad. Mike always bathed in the joy and glory of being ridiculous and breaking the gender role norms.

Mike was mesmerizing to watch, and every show promised some sort of unpredictable chaos. He was a total spazz. He had

Mike Webber and the Nip Drivers. Just when things were starting to fade a little, around 1983, the Nip Drivers came around and made things fun and exciting again. Top left photo features, from left, a guy who happened to be walking down the street and was pulled into the photo, vocalist Mike Webber, guitarist Kurt Schellenbach, drummer Nick Passiglia, and bassist Janus Jones. PHOTOS BY MIKE GUERENA

so much soul for a little white guy. A lot of people didn't realize that he could play almost any instrument, and rock it the fuck out. He was an impatient guy—sometimes he didn't have time to play the right chords and he liked to make up his own funny lyrics—but that didn't really matter. He was punk rock incarnate. He was an anti-perfectionist when it came to music, and that is what rock is about. He once admitted to me that he wrote all of the lyrics to one of the albums while on speed the night before recording. Needless to say, the lyrics were insightful and hysterical. Mike was one of a kind. He and the Nip Drivers influenced many bands.

In the early '90s while I was in Bulimia Banquet, Mike appeared at a show at the Gaslight in Hollywood. He was rambling on about the joys of Dilaudid, when all of a sudden he said: "Hey, can I do a song with you guys?" We said, "Sure," and he asked if we knew "Jealous Again" by Black Flag. We actually did—Dez Cadena had been in the band, and once in a while we had to kick out some Flag for rabid Dez fans. Although our show had been amazing all night, when Mike came out for the encore the whole place went *crazy*! He was a punk rock god. Half the crowd was stage diving and going nuts, while the other half was singing at the top of their lungs. It was one of those magical moments. That night I decided that I needed to do a band with Mike Webber.

Many years later, my band Bobsled had broken up, and I was disheartened. Mike said: "Hey, let's do a band together!" So we called it the Bob Drivers—just Mike and me acoustically with an Autoharp and guitar. We played a few shows together and it was amazing. We recorded a bunch of stuff on my home studio and then decided to do Marc Spitz Freestyle with Greg Cameron and Dave Wakefield. Eventually we became the new Nip Drivers. When we recorded, we were all fascinated by Mike's passionate vocals. No take was ever the same. He would sing with reckless abandon, completely wearing himself out by the end of each song. I have never heard anyone sing quite like Mike Webber.

Unlike most hedonists, Mike was loved not only for his talents and sense of humor, but also because he was a loyal son, brother, uncle, and friend to many. He took care of his mother, who suffered from dementia for many years, and he looked after his father very lovingly. As a friend, he would do his best to keep his word. If he were going to meet you at your house, he would show up. Sometimes he would be an hour early, without shoes on, or sometimes two hours late with some tired but smiley looking dude waiting in his car. But he would show up.

I never heard Mike talk poorly about anyone. He would just give this sort of special smile and say some quirky funny phrase he had made up that day, and all was understood. I really admired that about him. So many other older musicians in the scene were so bitter, but Mike just didn't seem to want to waste any of his energy on any of that. He was more intent on cracking you up with some kooky little nonsensical inside joke.

Mike had health problems throughout his life. He was born with a twisted spinal cord, requiring lots of operations. He was on strong pain medication since day one. By the time he passed away in 2006, he had lived with HIV for over 20 years. He used to jokingly call himself La Cucaracha, because he said he was impossible to kill. Shortly after a double heart valve operation, Mike arose, checked himself out of the hospital, and drove himself to the pharmacy where he got his fatal prescription of morphine. After a heart valve operation, most people cannot walk more than a few feet without passing out—but not La Cucaracha. Mike was just that sort of dude.

Like most of his good friends, I took Mike to rehab at least three or four times. We all had big hopes for him pulling it together. Mike Webber was a brilliant tragedy. His death on November 11, 2006, was an incredible loss to the music scene. He left behind a wonderful and very important musical legacy.

Facing page, from left: *Dave Dictor of MDC, Dancing Waters, July 30, 1982; JFA stopped by Santa Monica on their way from Arizona to Simi Valley to record a track for our* We Got Power: Party or Go Home *compilation LP.* PHOTOS BY JORDAN SCHWARTZ

Coke Is It!

Clockwise from top left: *Felix Alanis of RF7. Felix ran the crucial Smoke 7 Records, which released two compilations that featured bands including Red Cross, RF7, Circle One, Bad Religion, JFA, Youth Gone Mad, and Sin 34.* JORDAN SCHWARTZ; *RF7 on KHJ billboard after the station's short-lived switch from the beloved pop music of our youth to a country format. Fortunately, the urban cowboy trend died in 1981 before it fully arrived* JORDAN SCHWARTZ; *Jules of Sin 34 and Junior.* DAVID MARKEY

Symbol Six, featuring our Samohi classmates, left to right, Mark Conway, Donny Brooke, and Eric Leach, 1981.

PHOTOS BY JORDAN SCHWARTZ

Facing page: *Mike Ness, Social Distortion, playing the kitchen of Meg and Becca's apartment, Silver Lake, 1982. He had stitches in his mouth from some sort of fight or accident.* This page, clockwise from upper left: *An extremely sleepy Mike Ness, Social Distortion, 1982; Ness and drummer Derek O'Brien, Silver Lake, 1982; Punks levitate a six-pack—anything can happen at a punk rock house party; Founding member Dennis Dannell of Social Distortion, 1982.*
PHOTOS BY JORDAN SCHWARTZ

WE'RE A RIOT FIGHT

DAVID MARKEY

Naturally, there was a dark side to the L.A. punk scene—it came with the territory. There was always a fair amount of jocks and thugs at punk shows, and there was violence. Usually it was confined to those who were looking for it, and to the gang mentality types. Anyone blindly following the leaders seemed diametrically opposed to the true nature of punk to me: Think for yourself. I could detect the difference, and I noted the hypocrisy. I realized much of the crowd was not like me, and that's part of what killed it for me. Soon the scene was filled with followers, wannabe gangsters, and actual gang members. They weren't bringing anything into it but pose and senseless violence. These assholes proliferated, and the smart people pulled away.

Besides thugs, the L.A. punk scene had another problem plaguing its existence. Long before the Rodney King video was seen around the world, I saw the dark side of the LAPD. I witnessed several of the now infamous "punk rock riots" firsthand. It seems odd that the LAPD were threatened by primarily young white boys. The only retaliation I ever witnessed was a hurled beer bottle or two. Furthermore, there were never enough punks rioting. Far too often the LAPD had all the fun, with batons swinging and bashing, while Macing and tear-gassing kids at these shows. Just being there was reason enough for them to stomp you.

When the helmet-wearing men in blue showed up with their big plastic shields, you knew there was going to be a riot—which meant in short: *show's over*. These altercations were basically all the same. The cops would arrive en masse and take up a position either across the street or inside the venue. They dressed in helmets, shields, and batons; armed with tear gas and Mace ready for dispensing; standing shoulder to shoulder in a line. They moved in formation, without provocation, striking people randomly. It wasn't a fair fight. Punks were not armed or prepared with gas masks. Many of the punks were younger than driving age, or female, clearly no match for the football-player-size cops.

The LAPD had had it in for the punk scene in Los Angeles since the late '70s. These punks were primarily middle-class white kids, and not typically a menace under any other circumstances. The media loved a good teenage riot and really played up these events in print and during their live newscasts. This only brought more squad cars to the next big punk show. There was a series of infamous LAPD altercations at shows—from the Elks Lodge riot in '79, to the Black Flag riots at the Whisky in '80 and the Baces Hall riot around the same time.

These so-called punk rock riots happened with such regularity that a gig did not seem complete unless the cops showed up and shut it down. It became a running joke. Sin 34 played a show on June 24, 1983, at the Longshoremen's Hall in Wilmington with the Minutemen, D.O.A., and Youth Brigade, with the Dead Kennedys headlining. The heavy political subtext Jello Biafra espoused brought forward the largest contingent of combat-ready LAPD I had seen to date. Most of the show went off without an occurrence until after we finished our set. Then, slowly but surely, the riot squad started to arrive.

Facing page: *Cop car posted outside of S.I.R. Studios in the aftermath of a punk riot when TSOL played there, January 8, 1983. The police shut down Sunset Blvd. that night.* JORDAN SCHWARTZ

Ironically, the flyer for this show featured an image of a giant-size Ronald Reagan running a lawnmower over the tops of people's heads in a crowd. We watched the riot-geared cops gather by the truckload. There had to be a couple hundred armed riot cops deployed especially for this show. It quickly became apparent that the crowd was a bunch of sitting ducks. I locked all of our band equipment in Mike's van and secured myself near a rear exit door with a window, so I could see if anyone was awaiting me outside. There was only one small front entrance, and there was no way the massive crowd could have exited in any sort of orderly fashion as they had been instructed. I watched as the line of police swooped in on the crowd, swinging their batons as they stepped in formation.

This was an organized attack. You have to wonder where these orders were coming from. It was as if war had been declared, and we were the enemy. First-generation L.A. punk great Black Randy said it best, in "Trouble at the Cup": "There's war on the boulevard, and we're the enemy / Black-and-white cars are watching me / Fucking pigs, travel in pairs / Beat on my friends, nobody cares." In the years since, I was not surprised to see the image of the LAPD become tarnished with scandals like Rampart.

In the end, I was lucky enough to avoid any direct contact or injuries. As out of control as the police would usually get, there was always a way out. Or at least I was on the ball enough to find a path of least resistance. However, what I saw on my way out disturbed me. I only wish that I had had my camera on during those melees. Then again, I saw the people who did attempt to document these events getting special attention. Either their cameras would be confiscated outright, or the film would be ripped out of the camera and thrown to the ground—often along with the photographer.

Facing page: *This Hollywood house party ended like most parties, with the LAPD marching in and shutting it down. The Minutemen, Saccharine Trust, and Red Cross managed to play before that happened. Scott "Chopper" Franklin from the Mau Maus is being led into the cop car.* JORDAN SCHWARTZ

I witnessed, firsthand, LAPD cops ganging up on and beating the shit out of a non-punk photographer on assignment from the *L.A. Times* at Mendiola's Ballroom. You would have thought something would have appeared in the paper the following day about this occurrence. Instead, the news copy reflected negatively on the crowd, with a headline reading "Twelve Arrested at Punk Fracas." No mention of the photographer being beaten by the cops. No mention of innocent, unarmed teenage kids being Maced and assaulted. It was a harsh lesson in Reagan-era policies, and a preview of what was to come.

Witness the S.I.R. Studios riots in Hollywood: A defenseless fifteen-year-old kid facedown on the pavement was continually beaten over the back of the head by three or four cops in riot gear, towering in a circle over him. I was able to watch in disbelief somehow, without getting hit myself. Witness a line of fifty LAPD in riot gear taking over the front of the stage at Bards Apollo. The crowd slowly moved back across the old theater and spontaneously started singing, in prefect unison, key, and pitch: "O beautiful, for spacious skies, for amber waves of grain..." It was some of the greatest theater I have ever seen. Punks were great with irony. By the time the heartwarming ballad to our fatherland finished, the crowd was met by yet another column of helmeted and shielded riot squad cops—this one closing in from the back. What ensued as the punks were surrounded was not pretty. Thankfully, I escaped through a side door, at which point I spotted a cop smashing the storefront window of the neighboring business with his baton. This was standard at many of these riots, as the police anticipated the arrival of media. "Better make this look good for the cameras."

The neighborhoods surrounding these venues would be virtually shut down. Streets were closed and barricades would spring up from nowhere. If your car happened to be parked on one of these streets, you had better not take it up with any of the officers, as that would mean a sure ticket to jail, or a baton across the side of your head. I was so accustomed to the police after a few years of being on the punk scene, it all became just another part of the evening's entertainment.

The cops fucked up many shows—like the Ramones, Black Flag, and the Minutemen at the Hollywood Palladium in '84. Nothing like Mace burning your eyes to help you see the light. If you could open your eyes, you would see paddy wagons filled with punkers driving off to the pokey. I hastily jumped into the backseats of the cars of complete strangers to escape, returning safely returned to the Mecca of Oki Dog. There we would bond with our fellow punkers after we survived another riot.

The hassles were unrelenting. After the cops closed a punk show down, the West Hollywood Sheriff deputies would converge on Oki Dog, where they knew the after-show crowds would gather. They would assemble on the corner and around the parking lot where sometimes upward of four hundred punks might be congregating. Then the sheriffs would forcefully evict paying customers from the premises, punks and all.

After a while, the punks figured out that this would be par for the course and took to meeting in the city park around the corner. The sheriffs figured this one out soon enough. Punks were also known to be trespassing on Errol Flynn's long-abandoned estate at the end of Fuller Avenue in the Hollywood Hills. The property is now known as Runyon Canyon Park and is quite popular with dog owners and hiking enthusiasts. Sometimes there would be over a thousand punks running wild up there in the middle of the night. I recall one wild raid by the LAPD; that was a lot of fun, because it was a massive space with plenty of places to hide or outrun the cops, their German shepherds, and the police helicopters.

Years later, "punk" would come back and there was absolutely nothing the cops could do about it. They couldn't shut it down this time. This time it was sold safely through the malls and major retailers, and the shows began happening in the big city arenas and sports centers, and the tax dollars generated started paying cops' salaries. In contrast to the early days, "punk" is now the mainstream. Of course, now it's as safe as milk.

Facing page: *A fire in our neighborhood.* Overleaf: *Just some kids having a good time, prior to a riot erupting, January 1983. The crowd was way over capacity to see TSOL, Redd Kross, Social Distortion, Toxic Reasons, and Los Olvidados at "the Padded Cell," the back rehearsal room at S.I.R. Studios. The promoter, Gary Tovar, could only sell tickets to the show at the liquor store across the street; he promised the Korean owners a quarter for every ticket sold. Thousands of punks were crossing the street all day long in the heart of Hollywood that day. The cops arrived and kicked everybody out in brutal fashion, and some punks torched the barricade for a blazing finale.* PHOTOS BY JORDAN SCHWARTZ

California Greetings, Inc.

Danny's Dogs, aka Oki Dog, 7450 Santa Monica Blvd. at Vista St., before it was bulldozed to make way for Fatburger, late 1980s. Mentioned onstage by Darby Crash during the final Germs show on December 3, 1980, about a mile away at the Starwood, this hangout was immortalized by the Youth Gone Mad song "Oki Dogs," and appears in my 1982 film The Slog Movie. *The Oki Dog itself takes its name from Okinawa, but has a uniquely L.A. recipe: two hot dogs wrapped in a tortilla with pastrami and chili.*

DAVID MARKEY

Facing page: *The Go-Go's, the Whisky A Go Go, January 1, 1981. This was one of my first times going out in Hollywood, as a 17-year-old kid. They didn't let cameras into the Whisky, and I had to sneak in my Pentax K1000 35mm.* DAVID MARKEY. This page: *Scenes from Southern California hardcore punk.* Upper left: *Who dyed the cat green? Alan Gilbert, David Markey, and Jordan Schwartz.* JENNIFER SCHWARTZ. Others: *Night at the Valley West, December 26, 1981. The day after Xmas, lots of punks in sweaters to see Red Cross, Circle One, and RF7. Young punks visible in these photos include Carlton, Cathy, Paula, Nikki Fer Youz, Lino Lousy, Bob Bonehead, Jordan, Eric and Andy Baffert, Frankie, Mike Knox, Meg, and, from the looks of things, "Donald."* PHOTOS BY JORDAN SCHWARTZ AND DAVID MARKEY

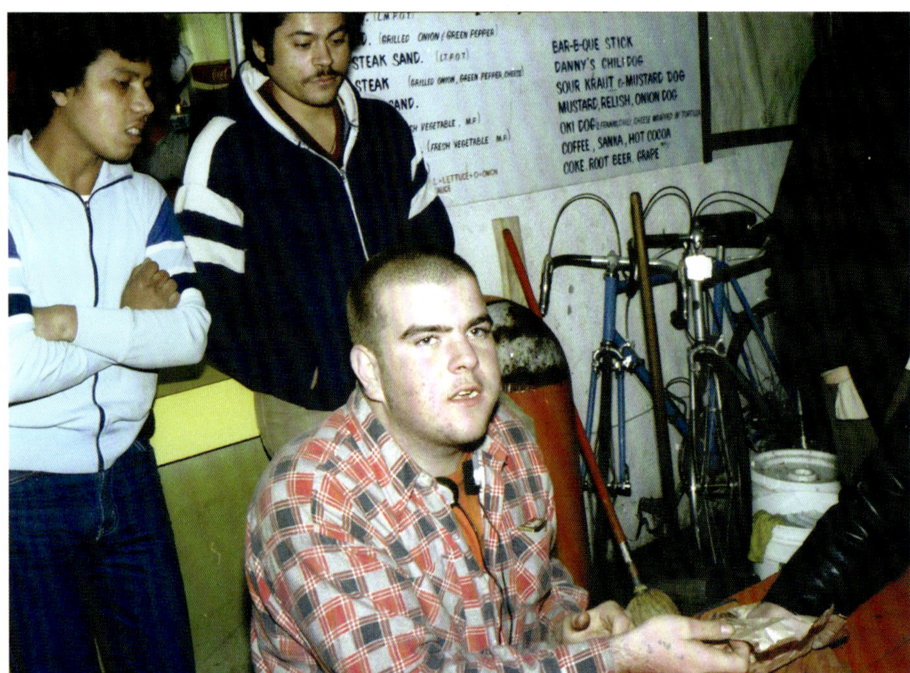

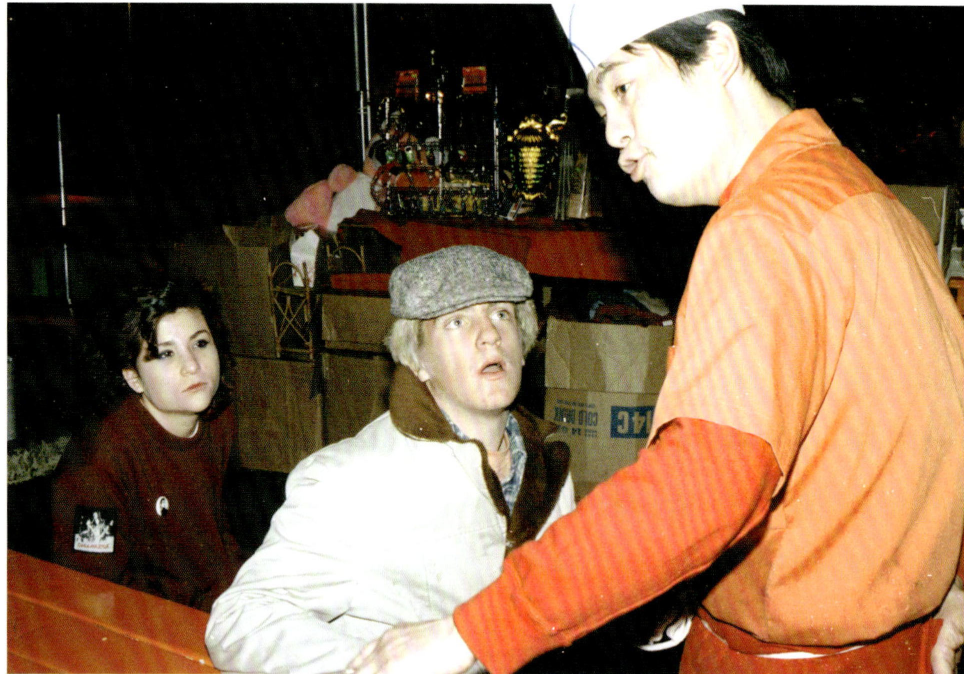

Clockwise from top left: *Fly at Oki Dog. Fly was in the Lads, or Los Angeles Death Squad, one of the big three gangs, along with Suicidal and Circle One. For the record, we were not part of any gang.* JORDAN SCHWARTZ; *The open-mouthed punker is named Tony. The fellow in the orange shirt was the most animated Oki Dog chef, behind the grill 24/7. We called him Arnold, à la* Happy Days. JORDAN SCHWARTZ; *Jordan Schwartz and Ronald McReagan, Christmas 1980.* DAVID MARKEY; *David Markey at McDonald's, Christmas 1980.* JORDAN SCHWARTZ.

Clockwise from top left: *Onetime Sin 34 guitarist Bob Bitchen, sporting a clean punk haircut, shows off a photo of himself in longer-locked days.* DAVID MARKEY; *Big Ed Draper and Mike Knox, Beverly Hills High punks of the band Rigormortis, Oki Dog, 1982.* JORDAN SCHWARTZ; *Marc Vachon, guitarist from Mad Society.* DAVID MARKEY; *Three punks drinking malt liquor in the Oki Dog parking lot, 1981.* DAVID MARKEY.

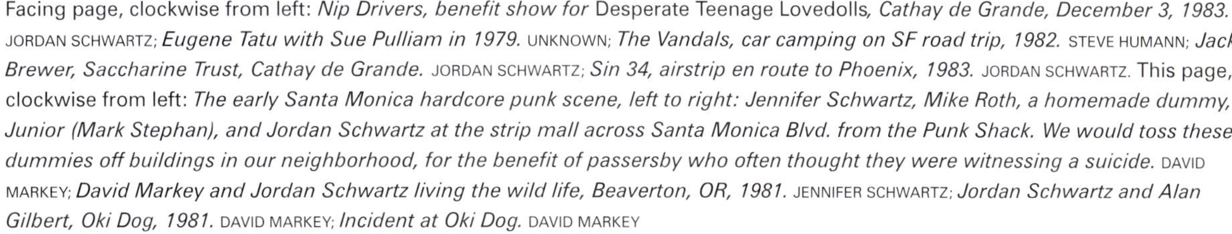

Facing page, clockwise from left: *Nip Drivers, benefit show for* Desperate Teenage Lovedolls, *Cathay de Grande, December 3, 1983.* JORDAN SCHWARTZ; *Eugene Tatu with Sue Pulliam in 1979.* UNKNOWN; *The Vandals, car camping on SF road trip, 1982.* STEVE HUMANN; *Jack Brewer, Saccharine Trust, Cathay de Grande.* JORDAN SCHWARTZ; *Sin 34, airstrip en route to Phoenix, 1983.* JORDAN SCHWARTZ. This page, clockwise from left: *The early Santa Monica hardcore punk scene, left to right: Jennifer Schwartz, Mike Roth, a homemade dummy, Junior (Mark Stephan), and Jordan Schwartz at the strip mall across Santa Monica Blvd. from the Punk Shack. We would toss these dummies off buildings in our neighborhood, for the benefit of passersby who often thought they were witnessing a suicide.* DAVID MARKEY; *David Markey and Jordan Schwartz living the wild life, Beaverton, OR, 1981.* JENNIFER SCHWARTZ; *Jordan Schwartz and Alan Gilbert, Oki Dog, 1981.* DAVID MARKEY; *Incident at Oki Dog.* DAVID MARKEY

Facing page: We Got Power *clan member Kim Pilkington.* JORDAN SCHWARTZ; *Fresh ink on Henry Rollins, 1984.* DAVID MARKEY. This page, clockwise from upper left: *Classroom scene from "Slip It In" video, Harbor College, Wilmington, CA, 1984. Location secured by Regis Ginn, father of Greg Ginn and Raymond Pettibon, who taught there.* DAVID MARKEY; *The Lovedolls, from* Desperate Teenage Lovedolls *promo session, Santa Monica.* DAVID MARKEY; *David Markey, couch slouch in the Punk Shack.* JORDAN SCHWARTZ; *Pat Smear of the Germs.* DAVID MARKEY

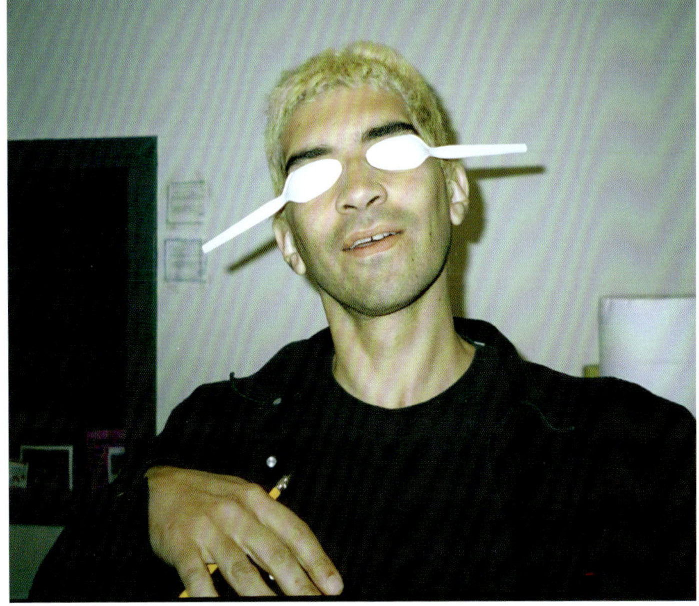

This page, from left: *Greg Ginn brandishing washboard.* JORDAN SCHWARTZ; *Henry Rollins with video costar, set of "Slip It In" clip directed by David Markey and Dave Travis, Palisades High, 1984.* DAVID MARKEY; *Chuck Dukowski live, circa 1985 with SWA.* JORDAN SCHWARTZ. Facing page, clockwise from top left: *Kira Roessler and Greg Ginn backstage, Black Flag.* JORDAN SCHWARTZ; *Henry Rollins modeling Painted Willie* Mind Bowling *tour shirt, 1986.* DAVID MARKEY; *Larry "Wild Man" Fischer and Dez Cadena, Hollywood, late 1980s.* DAVID MARKEY; *Merrill Ward and Chuck Dukowski of SWA.* JORDAN SCHWARTZ

BAGS KEY
USA
PACIFIC BELL

This page: *Word got out that the basement of the original Masque club was totally intact and untouched after all these years. So Dez Cadena and David Markey broke in and took a bunch of photos. We felt like we were raiding King Tut's tomb—it was like an archaeological dig into L.A. punk history.* DAVID MARKEY. Facing page, clockwise from left: *Ray Pettibon, the great Apple Pan, West L.A., 1988. He was pretty elusive at the time, but he was publishing comic books like* Captive Chains *and* Tripping Corpse *and selling them through SST Records; Kim Gordon of Sonic Youth, the Apple Pan, 1988. She grew up mere blocks away in West L.A., and was raised on Apple Pan burgers; Mike Watt of the Minutemen and Thurston Moore of Sonic Youth.* PHOTOS BY DAVID MARKEY

This page, clockwise from top left: *The Painted Willie/Black Flag tour dogs reality, 1986; Painted Willie (and Suzanne Somers) seaside at an SST blowout with Saccharine Trust, SWA, Lawndale, and Across the River, County Line, 1987; Devo man evolved—David Markey checking out Lawndale; Bubbles by Davo Claassen.* PHOTOS BY JOE COLE. Facing page: *Joe Cole, West L.A., 1988.* DAVID MARKEY

This page: *America? Sitting on a Youth Time Bomb Fast Asleep. Dez Cadena, the Masque.* DAVID MARKEY. Facing page: *Youth of America Unite! The rear of the Punk Shack during demolition. Local anti-punk surfers crossed out our Black Flag graffiti as part of an ongoing war. A year or two later, these same culprits would cut their long surfer hair and don Suicidal Tendencies shirts.* DAVID MARKEY

Youth of AMERICA UNITE
STAMP-RITE
Rubber Stamps
KILL JOCKS
SIN
PUNK
ROCKERS
PUNK

Mike Roth at We Got Power *headquarters—Dave Markey's bedroom—1982. Mike became a Calvin Klein model after being stolen from* We Got Power *by fashion photographer Bruce Weber.* DAVID MARKEY

WE GOT POWER #1

OCTOBER 1981

During my last semester of high school I took a photography class, and I started bringing my camera to shows. Soon Jordan started bringing his camera too. Dave had his Super 8 film camera, as he was shooting and editing *The Slog Movie*. We started talking to the bands, and nobody objected, so the three of us took lots of pictures unhindered. After developing some nice Circle Jerks shots, Dave and I talked about publishing a magazine. Dave insists I thought of the name *We Got Power*. I think he did. Anyway, Jordan and Jennifer thought it was a good idea, and as we were discussing it in my bedroom, Jennifer idly sketched a stuffed lion that was sitting on my bed. That became the cover of *We Got Power* #1.

We did our best to pull the first issue together. Following its publication, I went off to college in Santa Barbara. Although Dave and Jordan tried to keep me involved, by the start of my second year I was out. I did help sponsor a Black Flag/Circle One/Bad Brains show in Santa Barbara. The aftermath—with Greg Ginn doing Kim Pilkington in my bedroom, and Dave, Jordan, and me cruising around campus with Henry Rollins and Chuck Dukowski scaring college kids—almost got me kicked out of school. John Macias announced from the stage: "Party at Alan's dorm!" Everyone showed up and pretty much trashed my entire dorm, throwing shit like TVs and textbooks into the pool. The campus cops came the next day, but I somehow managed to say I had nothing to do with it.

—Alan Gilbert

What Makes Punks Tick?

The L.A. PRESS CLUB has closed its door to any new music shows, following what looked, on the surface, to be a very pleasant TWISTED ROOTS show. Though the bands all gave good performances, and the crowd seemed exceptionally cooperative (considering there were many so-called radical punks there), the Press Club complained of a broken drainpipe, smashed window, graffiti in the bathroom and several broken beer bottles. The show's promoter says most of the damage was done by three kids from WASTED YOUTH.

ALAN

DAVE

RUDY

KEITH

OLD

GOOD

WEIRDOS

HIT CITY

I won

For Shirley Lewis, the punk life makes shopping simple.

SIN 34

JULIE

FEAR

LA Bands Bounce Back

ray→

WASTED YOUTH

IM A FAN

"The club scene is only what the public chooses it to be."

Ready for a New Century

JENNIFER & JOHN

TR PAT

SYMBOL SIX

Red Cross

Surf Punk/Surf Violence

The American Red Cross, the country's largest humanitarian organization, celebrates its one-hundredth anniversary this year.

ARTICLES & SUCH

ONE OF THE TEN GREAT WONDERS OF BEAVER CREEK OREGON!!!

When it came time for me to pic the destination for my summer vacation I decided to go with the Beave Yes, I chose scenic Beaver Creek, Oregon, land of farming and T.V. watching.

Unfortunately, the Oregon teens aren't as "HIP" as L.A.'s modern young adults. The big fads are anima breeding, flare jeans, and teenage pregnancies.

The climate is usually cold and rainy but when I arrived it was in the hundreds. I could often be found swimming in the local rivers. Althou there are no poisonous snakes west of the Cascades I had to keep a watc out for drowning Oregonians who just couldn't handle the heat.

And the sun goes down in the Beaver Creek town for a night of Disco roller skating and Sheep reaming. Oregon is a must on the schedule for any L.A. jet setter.

-JORDA

L.A.'s WASTED YOUTH

WGP talked with Scranny Danny (singer) and Jeff Long (bass) outside of Coukoos Nest and at Jeff's house.

Jeff: I've been with Wasted Youth for three months now. Next big show is with Dead Kennedys Sept.11 in San Fransisco. Im anxious to see the SF scene.

WGP: What about your album?

JEFF: It was recorded at Mystic Studios. It has 10 songs, the test pressing is good. Should be out in two weeks.

WGP: What's it like to sing for WY?

Scranny: It's great! (Haha) All the guys, they say, they just love it! (Laughter). Oh, no, it's really great. I love it.

WGP: What about all the violence?

Scranny: Oh, I love it. I THRIVE OFF IT. No. (Getting serious) These Huntington people don't like us (refering to the crowd at Aug.26 gig with Black Flag and Cricle One at Cuckoos). I don't know what it is?

WGP: What are your inflounces?

Jeff:WY's inflounces are Crass, Discharge. Personally I like PIL, Discharge, & The Bags.

WGP: What are your favorite WY songs?

Jeff: UniHiBeefrag, Problem Child, Born deprived.

WGP: What are some of the problems you see with "the scene"?

Jeff: I hate punks who bother and hassle new punks. It's stupid. (Proudly points

JEFF - BASSIST - WASTED YOUTH

out, and smiles:) The LA Weekly says Wasted Youth & Wasted Youth Gang close down 3 clubs! But, in reality, the onl club we closed was LA Press Club.

WGP: What's the Wasted Youth gang?

Jeff: Kids. I don't know. I haven't me them.

Scranny: (Still upset about the crowd at the nest). People are too cool to dance! What did they cut their hair fc anywhays?

Jeff: I want punk to get intense, more violent- WY gang may do that. I'd like to see punks getting together and beating up people who hassle us.

WGP: Will you shave your head again?

Jeff: I'll shave it for big gigs, like the one with the Dead Kennedys.

NEWS FROM ....

PRINTED IN U.S.A.

SEND US NEWS OF YOUR AREA! See your name in print! For information on sending us anything, check out our back cover! Our adress is there!

LA:

OkiDog puts up "NO LOITERING" sign on an attempt to end, or curb locals from "hanging out". Jim says, "buy a coke & you can stay, the cops wont hassle you if your a coustomer." . . . The Whisky bans punk from it's confiendments... locals up in arms! Every Tuesday there is a **PUNK HANGOUT NITE** from 9-to-12 . . . **Rodney's show is cut again.** . . Charels of Bards fame claims Crass and Exploited are soon to play there. Don't you belcive it! . . . **Richard, also of Bards fame says he is soon to open a new club.** . . Scranny Danny keeps on saying "**Wasted Youth Lp** out in two weeks" all summer long! Their debut Lp should be out when your reading this. Maybe. More news as it developes. School started and kids didn't show for the big Minutemen/**Red Cross** show at the Nest. There were only 60 there, mostly membeers of Black Flag and the SST label staff. **Below are some good pix of the Minutemen** that nite. (pix by Alan)

OXNARD:

NO NEWS THIS TIME!!

Palm Springz:

Mike Bates **Subservice** breaks up again. But for how long? We need more news!!! Shawn and his band "**Mutual Hatred**" has been really coming along. They just added a saxaphone player. They have plans to play in L.A. real soon, and also have plans for recording a 45 called "**Tumbstone Religion**".

Up and Coming Band: Saigon

WGP: Who's in Circle One?
John: Me (singer), Mike V. (guitar), Bill (drums), & Mike (bass).
WGP: What does Circle One mean?
John: We didn't name ourselves after the Circle Jerks, or the Germs song. Circle means a group of people gathered together that share a common interest. One means united.
WGP: What are your favorite bands?
John: Black Flag, TSOL, Exploited.
Mike V.: Crass, Wasted Youth, Sin 34.
Mike: PiL, Black Flag.
WGP: What do you try to convey to people through your music?
John: We try to open their eyes to all the shit thats going on. We're the last generation if you go by what the Bible says. The war is coming sooner than you think. Especially that shit in the Middle East.
WGP: How did you guys get started?
John: It was Bill's and Mike V's idea to start a band. Then they got Bill's brother, Mike, to get a bass and then they got me.
WGP: What do you think of the cops?
John: I have a theory that there are cops and pigs. Cops do their jobs and pigs think they're God. Police like to hastle people that don't conform. Once you cut your hair you get a lot of shit from everyone...Pigs, society, hippys, parents, girlfriends. People believe what they see in the newspapers which is bullshit propoganda.
WGP: How long have you been into punk rock?
John: I've been listening to it for a year and a half but I've only been in the scene for thirteen months. He's been in it from the start.
Mike V.: I've been into it for three or four years.
WGP: Do you have any gigs coming soon?
John: We're playing with 45 Grave at the Cuckoo's Nest Saturday. We're only playing because we like 45 Grave a lot.
WGP: What do you like about skinheads?
John: Skinheads show that you're not part of society and that you don't care what people think. Someone said to me "Hey man, I heard you had a lot of followers and that you go around beating up people." That's a bunch of shit. Circle One doesn't have any followers, just friends.

PHOTOS BY: NIKKI & BRIAN - FER YOUZ

BALD HEADS!

WGP: Why did you shave your hair?
Bob: Well because it's cool. It's fucking punk rock.

WGP: Your hair isnt bald, but it's a grown out skinhead, tell us, why did you cut your hair?
Lino: 'Cos I got a haircut.

WGP: Why do you have a bald head?
John: To show people I am not part of society.

WGP: Why do you have a skinhead?
Vince: 'Cos it's a normal boys haircut.

WGP: How about you, why do you have real short hair, a crew cut, aka a skinhead?
Oscar M.: It's cool in the summer. I live on the streets, so it's no hassle washing it, or anything like that.

WGP: Why do you have one?
Alex: God told me to shave my head.

WGP: Whattabout you? Why a skin?
Lance: The bottom line is that it's easy to take care of. Practical.

WGP: Why did you once have a skinhead?
Julie: The clean cut American look- and besides, Im a dyke.

WGP: Tell us about your grown out skin-
Phil: I got a skinhead to show off my ears.
Vince: Hey, man, don't be ashamed of your ears!! Look at mine! (GGGGOOOORR)

Pam: Some people think skinheads are punk. THEY ARE FAR FROM IT. In England the skinheads and the punks are rivals.

John: I hate the wannabe English people don't you?

REVIEWS

RIC LEACH OF SYMBOL SIX

DETOURS, SYMBOL SIX, YOUTH BRIGADE, BLADES Bards Appollo Aug 29 **TSOL** had canceled. So had **Red Cross** and the **Descendents**. But we didn't despair. They had booked the **Blades** and **Youth Brigade** instead. After the Blades and YB **Symbol Six** came on. They put on a marvelous show. ALAN

45 GRAVE, SOCIAL DISTORTION, CHRISTIAN DEATH - Whiskey; Aug. 18: **Christian Death** freaked alot of the punks out with their **Siouxsie**-meets-graveyard music. The lead singer was dressed like a girl at a funeral, it was pretty funny. **Social Distortion** came on and tore the roof off the fucker! The floor was moving and they went over real well. **45 Grave** played GREAT, the kids who didn't dance were too busy falling in love with the singer. -DAVE

CHINA WHITE, RED CROSS- Whisky; August 16: WOW! What can I say about **Red Cross**! They are the best band around right now. They really did a tight set and they always looked like they were having fun. Every song they did sounded perfect, and the audience liked them all, even the slow ones. **China White** played too. -ALAN

STEVE OF RED CROSS

GUN CLUB, RIK L. RIK, UNIT 3, STINGERS- Cathay de Grande; August 25: We didn't go inside because we didn't have any money but we hung around outside for awhile. We couldn't hear too much from there though.-JOE

FEAR, TSOL, CHINA WHITE, CHEIFS, CROWD OVERKILL- Bards Apollo; August 22: **Fear** played a couple songs for a sound check. Kids started slamming & spitting to their sound check. **Overkill** came on and played pretty good. They did their familiaring songs to a gathering crowd. The **Crowd** played next and did another lively pop set. Even although there was little dancing, the crowd seemed to dig The Crowd. The **Cheifs** took to the stage and the new singer was great. The HUGE hall was nearly packed by now, and it was so hot in there! I missed **China White** because I went downstairs with a girl. All I know is their singer thinks he's John Denny of the **Weirdos** these days. The all new **TSOL** with Frank Agnew doing leads were GREAT! Still there were punks in attendence who thought is was cool to hate the band. **FEAR** was FUCKIN' GREAT, what more can I say except they had their set cut because it was too late and all the people who saw them in Decline didn't get to hear "I Love Livin' In THE SHITTY." -ALAN.

BLACK FLAG, WASTED YOUTH, CIRCLE ONE- Cuckoo's Nest; August 21: This was a strange show. It took place at 3:00 in the afternoon. They billed it as a "matinee". **Circle One**, the band everyone's talking about, came on first and probably did the best. **Wasted Youth** played fast and loud and everybody had a good time. They improve with each gig.(Their album sounds great!) **Black Flag's** summer '81 anthem "Six Pack" was the band's best song of the day. But when we all left at the end, it was hot and sunny outside! WEIRD. -DAVE

RED CROSS, MINUTEMEN, SACCHARINE TRUST, DESCENDENTS, SYGON- Cuckoo's Sept. 15: Everyone must be back in school alright, because the head count tonite was under 60. **Sygon** were real up & coming. The **Descendents** were real funny. The **Minutemen** were real tight. **Saccharine Trust** were real entertaining. **Red Cross** ran into a few problems. The P.A. wasn't on. Steve & Jeff were obviously in a quarrel. Their set was cut due to lack of time. -JOE

MEAT PUPPETS, VOX POP: Cathay DeGrand Sept. 9: **Meat Puppets** played very good. Sounded like the **Minutemen**, but lacked vocal diversity. The band appeared to be very excited about their music as they jumped and danced all over the small stage. The bass player played with his back to the audience, but only faced us to sing a few songs. **Vox Pop** were very funny. Paul was drunker than hell. Mary looked radient. They let everyone else sing a song (including **Circle Jerks'** Keith doing an imprompto version of Wild In The Streets). They had erratic lights and next backup slides. **Elvis Presley** joined them and did "Heartbreak Hotel". Vox ended the nite by their big hit off chunks, "Your my favorite", and an all inspired version of "American Woman" -Alan & Dave

BLACK FLAG, FEAR, STAINS, YOUTH GONE MAD, CAUSTIC CAUSE. CSUN Northrige September 11: I was warned about this place. But I got in for free (wow), so I went. Missed **Caustic** and **YGM**. The **Stains** I dont like that much. I watched a few songs, I do like "Sick & Crazy" though, they were sloppy fast heavy metal and they knew it. **Fear's** set was plauged by a person unplugging the power. **Black Flag** did a lot of slow physadelic stuff mixed with their reguar stuff. One more thing, the atmoshpehere here sucked. there. — JON

DEAD KENNEDYS, TSOL, 45 GRAVE. Florintine Gardens Sept. 5: I, like quite a few people, snuck in, since the guy with the guest list was really dumb. I got in towards the end of **45 Grave**'s set. I LOVED THEM as usual. Paul Cutler is the coolest! "Black Cross" had alot of em dancing, but most were too busy yelling "FUCK YOU!" Mary had all blone hair tonite, it looked like she enjoyed the crowd. They ended their set with a 10 minute wall of sound with guitar, synthezizer, and Don banging on his kit. **TSOL** came out with Jack wearing a red turbon. They ripped into "Superficial Love" and Jack took off the turbon and revealed a sporty new crew cut. Their whole entire set was fantastic. Their album is the best! "Code Blue" as an encore was a wise descion, also standing out in the set were "Silent Scream" and "Funeral March". Between TSOL and **Dead Kennedys**, the place got "trashed" as Two On The Town would put it. The bathrooms were flooded, someone broke an overhead pipe in the lobby, someone ripped off a fire extinguisher and sprayed it into the crown of over 22,00. It was so humid the the huge hall, and there were LOTSA FIGHTS! Outside cops were busting heads, I was told. People were T.P.ing the hall, it was funny. Dead Kennedys came on and played sloppy. I was looking foreward to seeing one of my favorite acts, but so were thousands of others. I still had a good time with them. DK's come down here twice a year, lets hope they pick a wiser spot to play next time. Florintine Gardens is WORSE than the S.M. Civic! Oh yeah, they did "Man With The Dogs", one of my old favorites. Too many dips got on stage, and Jello was frustrated. He said to one guy, "go back to your pick-up, Prick!" Anyhow, the whole thing was a treat for me. -DAVE

EDITORIALS & COMMENTS

ALL ABOUT "the SCENE"

MORE POLOTICS - EDITORIALS

At one point in my life, I was under the impression that **"punk"** suppose to mean somthing radical, entirely different from anything else. I thought it was a way to escape from fitting in . However, in many places fashion is what leads the scene- similar to our rivals, hippys, urban cowboys, and new romantic people. If you don't have a skin- skinheads hassle you- if you have a skinhead others bother you. Why can't some people be themselves? It's just not cool to put down or hassle others who don't fit up to your standards in fashion. BUT... there is something far more important than fashion, and that is **ATTITUDES!!** Yes, it is true, people with long hair can share the "punk attitude". The scene is reserved for no one. **EVERYONE** is eligible. Everyone counts. -DAVE

Police cheif Daryl Gates scams on the guest list at **Bards Apollo** for last night, Sept. 19, over 20 riot geared officers of the law marched right on in during a would-be Ch 3, Deprogrammer, Wasted Youth, **45 Grave,** Middle Class, Subhumans show.

The show was mellow enough, so many people paid and **GREAT** bands were scheduled. The police officers made their way to the stage like retarded boy scouts. Next thing the crowd of over 800 discovered our ~~brotherly~~ **pigs** were stoping the show, during the warm up acts set. We all were stunned. There was no reason for this. Some of us refused to leave and ~~trashed~~ the bar area of the club. About 50 protested by stomping up & down, singing "My Country Tis Of Thee" & **"America, America"** ~~to~~ the cops. The cops now started shooting friendly amounts of **mace and tear gas** at the kids who just got $6. ~~ripped~~ off from ~~them.~~ (The assholes made off with the cash box.) There was no way they'd give you your money back, so ~~alot~~ of us were upset.

They got everyone outside the club and into this beautiful neighborhood, infamous for muggings, rapes, etc. There was a faggot helicopter circling with a taped message of a siren. Do they think we are as dumb as dogs? Well, over **500 Kids** outside got even by throwing bottles at the police men and smashing 11 store front windows. Everyone ran, the pigs grabbed anyone they could. It was something out of **Quadrophenia.** Everyone went to **Okidog,** the pigs showed up, people went to **Errol Flyn,** where they were later arrested. (Over 15o, made up of punks, hippys, and vatos.)

PRINTED FROM FLYER AT OKI'S — MIDJETS.

OH BROTHER... OF ALL THE FAIRY STORIES I'VE EVER HEARD!

BE THERE BE COOL! —STARTING SEPT. 15TH.

THE BIBLE TELLS US—THAT SOON ALL THE TRUE BELIEVERS IN CHRIST WILL BE CAUGHT UP OFF THE EARTH TO MISS GOD'S COMING JUDGMENT!— THE TERRIBLE TRIBULATION, WHICH IS ALMOST UPON US!

"HANGOUT NIGHT" AT THE WHISKEY. PEACEFUL PROTEST OF PUNK BAN, EVERY TUESDAY. THERZ NO WHERE ELSE NOW, SO SHOW UP. 9:00-12:00

RECORD & TAPE REVIEWS

RECORD RATING

*****	= EXCELLENT
****	= GENERALLY GOOD
***	= FAIRLY WORTHWHILE
**	= BARELY WORTH IT
*	= CHEAP - SKIP IT

***

VARIOUS "THE FUTURE LOOKS BRIGHT"

Shattered Faith are okay. TSOL's cuts are dull (except Abolish Govt.) Social Distortion's "Playpen" is one of my favorites, the other SD cut is good too. CH3 get lost in mediocracy - they sound real up and coming though. MINUTEMEN have fantastic cuts including "Punch Line" and "Straight Jacket". Descendents - most famous for their "I like Food/Der Wienerschnitzel" ditty also do "My Dad Sucks", another classic. SACCHARINE TRUST's "We don't Need Freedon" is my favorite song of the week. Black Flag's "Six Pack" EP is included in its entirity in an obvious attempt at boosting sales. The tape ends with the Stains "Pre[illegible] Girls", which sums up this OK/almost perfect cassette pet. -DAVE

**

GERMS "WHAT WE DO IS SECRET"

Let's put it this way, it's only a 45 rpm, the two live songs sound worse than "Germs Live" 45. "Circle One" and "No God" are rare but are the same as the versions on the ond Slash EP. "Lesicon Devil" and "Other Newest One" are old news. Sorry kids, this is another ripoff, the Kim Fowley live album being the other one. How many other Germs albums are there gonna be?

*****

TSOL "DANCE WITH ME"

This is a great album even though the cover reminds me of Blue Oyster Cult. TSOL has changed a bit from their EP and they're still hot. My favorite songs are Code Blue, Die For Me, and Silent Scream. Don't forget, 'I'm Jonathon Harker. -JON

****

CIRCLE ONE "CIRCLE ONE"

This 7 song tape, most definatly a limited edition / collectors item, includes "Left Right Left", a favorite amongst local impresionares. I love "One Chord". Circle One has fast hardcore 17 second and slow 2 minute songs. Whatta nice mix. -DAVE

****

THE SPECIALS "GHOSTOWN"

Here are a few more hits from one of the best ska bands. Again, the Specials have changed their sound. You might have heard Ghostown on KROQ but don't worry, it's good anyway. Why? is an inspiring cut but the best song on the 3 song EP is Friday Night/ Saturday Morning which is sort Of a combination of the styles from the two previous themes. I don't care if you buy it or not. -JORDAN

MEDIA BLITZ

just to remind you that they're out there, watching you!!....

can possibly get, in addition to the punk and new wave "fad" bands that will probably be unheard of a year from now. You have to admit that Pleasant Gehman's "L.A. Dee Da" section should be really called "Punk Dee Da," since her column does not take in the L.A. musical spectrum but concentrates instead on the "fad" punk scene.

← Another letter to the L.A. Weekly from some poor, lost, inept asshole.

Clipping from a school paper from article on more "PUNK" violence! →

"I feel it's fair to say after my careful observation and analysis of our local club scene, that on the whole it is a rather monotonous, inane imbecility," said Uni senior Manuel Samaniego, "Indeed, I feel this rather absurd phenomenon has no place in our cities cultural development."

Black Flag don't say anything onstage because they're afraid they'll get their asses kicked by their own followers (who, incidentally, are so cool they don't have to applaud). But I doubt it.

Bam magazine's classic "BLACK FLAG VIOLENCE" article.

A LETTER to our favorite L.A. TIMES explaining punk rock →

Ahern hit the nail on the hammer. Punk will start World War III. The Beatles were responsible for the Vietnam War. Elvis initiated the Cold War, and the Lennon Sisters singlehandedly started the Korean War. And we must not forgive Glenn Miller for bringing us World War II.

J. M. TURNER

Big shit magazine "PEOPLE" found space for a cheap review of "DECLINE". Notice the last sentence.

People weekly

THE DECLINE OF WESTERN CIVILIZATION

If you believe Penelope Spheeris' engrossing, often hilarious and always outrageous documentary, rock 'n' roll has evolved into a new phenomenon known as "speedrock," in which rhythms of 300 beats per minute aren't unusual. Spheeris, hung around L.A.'s sleaziest rock clubs, interviewing club owners and often zonked-out fans. She also talks to post-punk band members and uncovers a nihilistic attitude toward just about everything. The result is both insanely funny and very frightening. The bands' names are indicative: Circle Jerks, Fear, Germs, Catholic Discipline and Black Flag are examples. Their songs are clearly intended to incite; the fighting in the audience and brawls onstage are all but part of the acts. *Depression*, *Revenge*, *Barbee Doll Lust* and *I Don't Care About You* are typical titles, often sung so fast Spheeris has provided subtitles in English. Is this just good clean fun, rock 'n' roll style? Maybe; at times, though, it looks a bit like the Hitler Youth Movement with guitars. (R)

FUN & GAMES

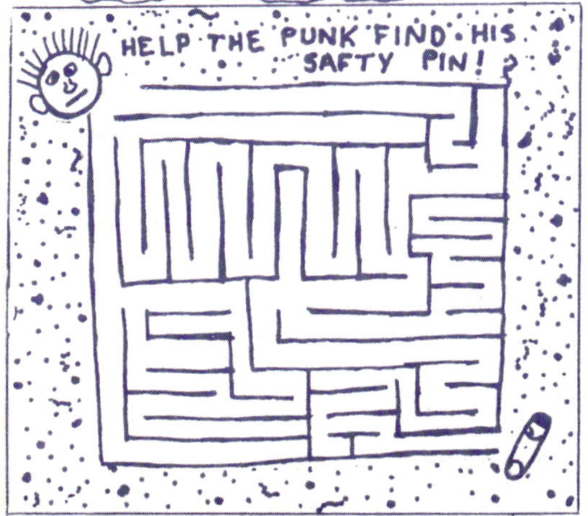

HELP THE PUNK FIND HIS SAFTY PIN!

TOP TEN T.V. SHOWS

1. Facts of Life
2. Stanley Siegel show
3. The Rookies
4. Benny Hill show
5. Dance Fever/Soul Train (tie)
6. Let's Make a Deal
7. Real People
8. Those Amazing Animals
9. Tomorrow show w/ T. Snyder
10. Wonderama

(Bring back "Get Smart" ch. 13!)

TOP TEN MOVIES

1. The Night the Lights went out in Georgia
2. Force Five
3. An Eye for an Eye
4. Condorman(Walt Disney prod.)
5. Comin' at ya'
6. Deadly Blessing
7. Endless Love
8. Private Lessons
9. Private Benjamin
10. Gong Show Movie

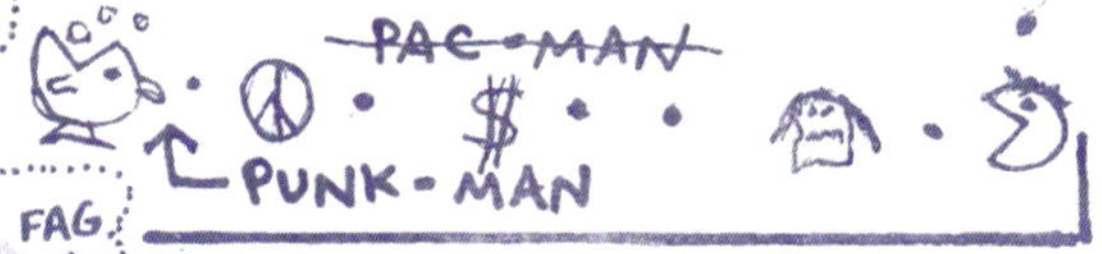

~~PAC-MAN~~ PUNK-MAN

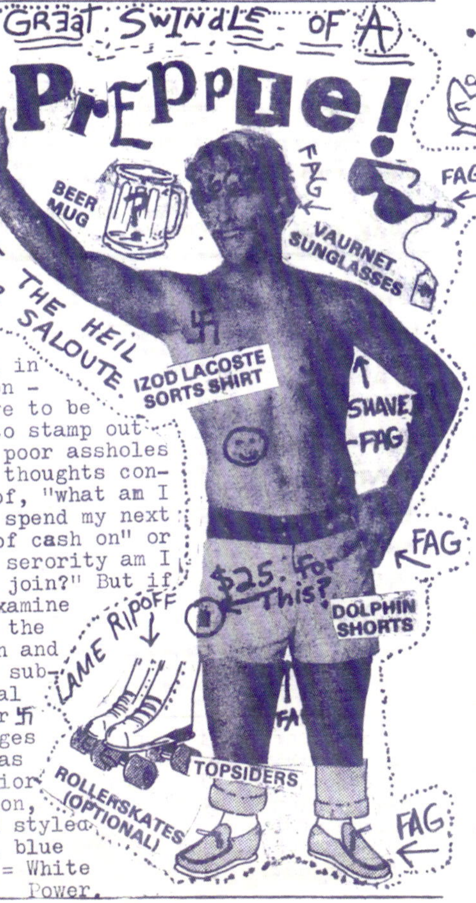

THE GREAT SWINDLE OF A PREPPIE!

FAG
BEER MUG
VAURNET SUNGLASSES
NOTICE HITLER THE HEIL SALOUTE
IZOD LACOSTE SORTS SHIRT
SHAVE -FAG
$25. For This?
DOLPHIN SHORTS
LAME RIPOFF
TOPSIDERS
ROLLERSKATES (OPTIONAL)
FAG

Well, with school in session - we have to be sure to stamp out these poor assholes whose thoughts consist of, "what am I gonna spend my next roll of cash on" or "what serority am I gonna join?" But if you examine them, the hidden and higly subliminal Hitler 卐 messages such as superior fashion, blond styled hair, blue eyes = White Power.

Find the missing word. First person to solve puzzle will win a pair of tickets to Billy Barty's roller fantasy. COMIC RELEIF!

1. Ihate cops to the _ _ X
2. LA's punk Judy Collins E _ _ _ _
3. Japaneese guy that works at Oki Dogs (HINT: was replaced by Al Delvechio) A _ N _ _ _ D
4. Cops best friend: _ _ _ E R _ _ _
5. Punk rock disease: _ A _ _ _
6. Hippies wear on head, while punks wear on boots _ _ _ _ _ N _ S
7. Both punks and your grandmother wears: FREE WORD! A R M Y _ _ _
8. Im a geekfag, I live in: O _ _ _ _ _ _ _

answers: 1. MAX 2. EXENE 3. ARNOLD 4. DOBERMAN 5. RABIES 6. BANDANAS 7. BOOTS 8. OREGON OR OXNARD

FLY-ING AROUND

This month the coveted "Best Flyer Award" goes to the legal-sized Fear-Wasted Youth at the Cuckoo's Nest. This flyer was unanimously voted as the months best flyer by the "Power" staff because of its originality and superb artwork. We hope to be seeing many more flyers of comparable quality from the boys in Wasted Youth.

FLYER OF THE MONTH

COMING SOON!!!!!!!!!!!!!!!!!!!!!!!!!!!!!
The SLOG movie!?!?!?!
Be prepared because SLOG will get you!
(What does SLOG mean?)

SECOND PLACE

Second in the race for best flyer was this effort for Black Flag-Wasted Youth-Circle One at the Cuckoo's Nest. The brilliant artwork of this flyer was surpassed only by the originality of the winning job.

PEOPLE ON THE GO

So ends another night at Bard's Apollo with Symbol Six, the Detours, Youth Brigade and the Blades. TSOL did not play. Back to people on the go. How about that foreign film star, Ray Grange? I don't know, I din't talk to him. What about Charles Dukowsky being named L.A. Punk spokesman by the L.A. Times? Again I don't fucking know; I've only seen the guy maybe once or twice. All I do is sit around at Oki Dog's and talk to the members of Circle One. I Dint even see Maggie and Eugeney on the Stanley segal show. If you want to find out about people on the go, go find out for yourself.- JORDAN

can you belive this is a real ad!

found in JULY '81 issue of "RIGHT ON!" a magazine aimed at the black young adult demographic! Really!!

DON'T READ THIS

VERY SERIOUS EDITORIAL FROM US:

Don't ask me why we stuck such an item of importance on such a page like this! Who cares. This is fuckin' punk. No. But seriously... we obviously need help. Help from anybody, in anyway! (Boy that really narrows it down, hugh?) It is harder than shit do create a fanzine or a magazine. Really. Why not send us photos of you? Nothin' sells a rag like people's pic being in it! We are presently low on our budget, so dont expect Life magazine, or even NoMag!!! Hey bands out there, send us photos & info, tapes or records (for reviews). We promise never to overlook anyone. Ha Ha! We would like to become larger, subscription wise, and production wise. So all you record and clothing shops, please take in our mag! Our address and more info can be found on our back cover (the last page!) Let's get our shit together! Eventually We Got Power will not only have reviews and interviews, but ALL ORIGINAL stuff from all over the continent! Send us news about YOUR area. Everybody counts. Maybe if all youz listen, our next issue will be even better than this one! (lets hope!) And now for our gimmicky production line we promised you: "IF YOU DONT LIKE IT, CHANGE IT! 'cos YOU HAVE POWER! Aw quit!!

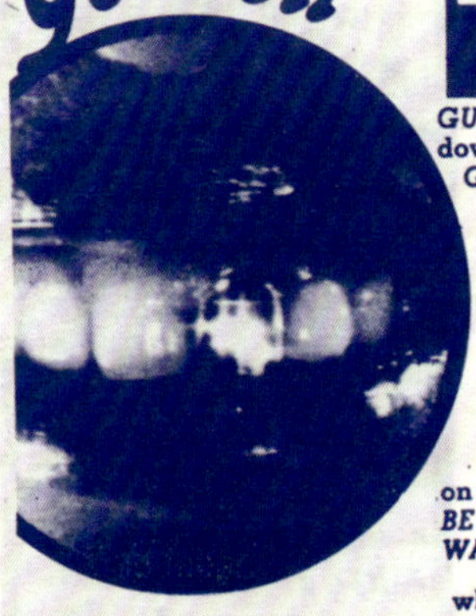

-STAFF WE Got Power!

at the Whisky a Go Go

Circle Jerks

AUG 3rd. & 4th.

Circle Jerks at Whiskey August 3&4 saw lotsa action. The Jerks did lots of new ones including "Trapped" and "Question Authority". When the next album gonna be out guys?

Keith

Greg

Overkill's Merryl and co. opened up for CJ's August 4..

Scranny of Wasted Youth played on the 3rd

Roger

Lucky

Photos by Alan

WE GOT POWER ! mag

your help

send us photos, cartoons, poetry, tapes & 45's, ideas, news, information about your band, comments, letters, suggestions, storys, and anything else! Send everything to us at:

WRITE US, PLease! →

WE GOT POWER
FONTAINEBLEU rm. 305/ 6525 El Collegio rd.
ISLA VISTA CA. 93017

← OUR Adress!!

annual subscriptions $12.50 (12 issues)

For advertising information send us a S.A.S.E

BUY ALAN

If You Hate it - CHANGE IT - BECAUSE You've got power. hT INC.

Merrill Ward of Overkill reading We Got Power *#2.* JORDAN SCHWARTZ

WE GOT POWER #2
FEBRUARY 1982

I took over as editor after helping Alan Gilbert put together *WGP #*1; we still used his UC Santa Barbara dorm room address. The bald man on the front cover is a crazed street preacher; Jordan took his photo in downtown L.A. in 1980 on a day that we ditched school.

Highlights include Kim Pilkington's salacious recounting of a lost weekend in San Francisco; a guest editorial from the amazing Spot, house producer of the classic early SST catalog; interviews with Henry Rollins—his first published solo profile—Overkill, and Saccharine Trust, all uncredited but conducted by me, with Kim here and there; my editorial "1981 to 1982, So What"; profiles of Nikki and Brian Tucker of local free photozine *Fer Youz* and Frank of the San Fernando Valley "for punks, by punks" club Godzilla's; Jordan's classic interview with Jeff and Steven McDonald of Red Cross; and a photo spread of the benefit for *We Got Power* at Godzilla's with Sin 34, Descendents, Minutemen, Symbol Six, and Bad Religion.

—David Markey

"punk is just not another fad"

This Is Sick!

Punk Rock

This week, an inside look at the punk phenomenon currently gripping America's youth.

Parents of Punkers Will Gather

Parents of Punkers, a support group ... cerned about their children's invol... will meet at 7 p.m. Dec. 9. Inform...

SHIRT

Oi! oi! oi!

1 AM (11) MOVIE—Drama "The Boy with Green Hair." (1948) A war orphan (Dean Stockwell) is ridiculed after his hair turns green overnight. Pat O'Brien, Robert Ry-

A Look at the American Punk Scene.

24 RIGHTEOUS APPLES —Teen-agers A record producer (Jerry Hauser) lures the Apples to Hollywood, secretly intending to turn them into a punk rock group. Neck: Mykel T. William-son. Ralph: Ray ...

OKI-DOG

Pic's BY: PHIL, MOUSE, ALAN, & JORDAN

WE got POWER

STAFF: publisher: ALAN / editor: DAVE / writers: JORDAN, LOU E, KIM "Ru", MARK, AMANDA, & JON / contributing writers: MARK (SB), DEBBIE, PHIL, & JENNIFER / photographers: MOUSE, ED CLOVER, PHIL, NIKKI & BRIAN, cartoonist: JORDAN / extra helpers LAURA, LINDA, MIKE, KATHY & MEG. others contribute who are not included above names are usually below their work.

front cover: JORDAN SCHWARTZ
back cover photo by: ED CLOVER

fucKin' Great FanzineS !

Lowest Common Denominator (issue #1, #2, .) Stick Time (#1), Outcry (#2), d. boon's "Prole" (#1), ray pettibone's "Tripping Corpse" (#1), Be My Friend (#2), Negative Army (#3), **Flipside (29)** Night Voices #5

Back cover photo taken at Dead Kennedys TSOL 45 Grave show at Florintine.

Having nothing better to do with a 150.00, my friend and I flew up to San Francisco on Halloween weekend to see **Black Flag, DOA,** & **Saccharine Trust** at The Elite Club. It was worth it, we got to see **Jello Biafra's** wedding at the cemetary, go to the reception at **Target** Video (where we stayed), meet DOA, and get into the show free. I did lose my camera however, so we have no photographic evidence of all this.

Anyhow we got into the show in the middle of Saccharine Trust's set. They were really good - I love Jack Brewer's voice. (There's only one Brewer, after all). The crowd really enjoyed them.

Flipper and **Minimal Man** played next but I was scamming with some guy during their sets, and missed them. All I know is they played too long. DOA had to cut their set because of this, but what they played was great. DOA are terrific- energetic, visually appealing, and their music is the best. The crowd went crazy, jumping off the stage, beating each other up, etc. If you haven't seen them yet, you're missing out, and Randy Rampage says their not coming to LA for a while.

Black Flag played three songs before their set was stopped. The cops, or some asshole, closed the slub. The crowd was, needless to say, upset, but there was no thrashing. What a dissapointment. What I saw of them was loud and obnoxious as usual. I wish they'd played longer, but I've seen enough of them anyways! By the way, their album "DamaGED" is out. Form your own opinion, Im not reviewing it right now. (Hilburn loves it.) - Rue

LETTERZ -

SUGGESTION: Why dont you accept tapes from new bands who dont have any public ity. Your zine could do a monthly article on some of the best up & coming bands. There's alot of underground bands who think they have talent but cant get recognition. If you were to do this, it would help many bands. Anyway, I think your mag is great. Keep up the good, clear pictures & dont stray away from the California Punk scene. -Mark Z.

WE GOT POWER: Just thought I'd write to help us both out. We need publicity and you need info, right? Im in a very interseting and unique band called Gumby Riot. We have our own sound a were from the Conejo Valley area. We are crazy and were; Greg (drums), Joe (guitar), Andy (bass), & Mike (aka Pokey)-(vocals). In due time we'll be able to send you tapes, photos, etc.
Thanks, Gumby Riot

Dear WGP: Got your first (?) issue the other day & decided to write. I used to write stuff in the SB/IV area from 77-80, but quit when I started getting static for having opinions. My printed opinions seemed to be omniportant by being printed in black & white and the slow-witted presented that there were people around me that couldnt ignore punk rock. I also didnt want to have a shitty or bad review follow me around like a tattoo on my asshole, but I really like your magazine, the styles of reviews in particular. So i wrote a few reviews for possible inclusion.
-Jon Beverly

A FEW OF JON'S REVIEWS ARE PUBLISHED IN THIS ISSUE ON SOME PAGE.-ed.

We Got Power: On a visit to Hollywood last weekend, I ran across your fanzine in Vinyl Fetish. The groups listed on the front cover & the title attracted me, and only $1. what did I have to lose? Im impressed with the format & pictures. It appears to be put together with personal thought and has the real local scene appearance. I go to shows now & then, and have many opinions about the music I listen to. Among my favorites are TSOL, Black Flag, Circle Jerks, Dead Kennedys, Bad Religion, Shattered Faith, Overkill, & CH 3. Since you seem interested in reader participation, I decided to sit down & devote some time to help you come up with some material for an upcoming issue. -Mark D. Henson

MARK'S ARTICLES ARE ALSO PRINTED IN THIS ISSUE ON SOME PAGE. -ed.

POLICE ON MY BACK!

Okay you homos, who said you could reprint my flyer for the hangout night? I cant thank you enough. "We Got Power" is a very hip fanzine, much needed, much appreciated. Its Sunday, the day after X & Subhumans at the Whisky. I picked up WGP on Friday and was totally amazed & impressed. Well anyways I just got out of jail. Another victim of the W.LA's sheriff roundup. It was the 3rd time for me, and Im still here, still showing up. You guys have to tell everybody to keep coming out, and not let these fuckers scare everyone away. They charged me & almost everyone else for Drunk & Disorderly conduct. (Funny, I dont even drink!) The sheriffs are just getting everybody now. Keep an eye out for an old beat up white dodge van w/ all windows covered. They got these two Texas rednecks in there, that are out for blood. Drunk and disorderly, but no one got a breath test They said thats only if your driving. Either way, their putting you away for being drunk. So we are seriously going to see about getting a law passed, so they have to give you a breath test, so it might make it harder to pick up & arrest us. You should say something about letter writing. It may not do anything, but it lets people know that were out here keepin an eye out. I write to everyone if they do something on punk. Included are a few examples. Unfortunatly the Tuesday hang out isnt working out good. I was hoping for a good turnout, which happened the first 2 wks. But it got less & less, and I guess it died. I figured the Whisky would just have to start booking punk bands or stop booking other bands. For everyone thats afraid of getting arrested, it's really no big deal. It's a pain in the ass, but also kinda fun! They just hold you for about 6 hrs, and let you go. If your 16 & under, your parents just have to pick you up. Try to make them understand just how unfair the cops are being. Let people know about it. In the wake of that football player dying in a Long Beach jail, everyone's up on the cops & the bullshit thats going on. These fuckers are trying to take away our livlihood. Shit, Im not gonna let those bastards keep me from having fun and enjoying my life. The more they fuck with me, the more wild I get. Nov 14 in Oxnard looks like the hot gig. You guys got all my support. If there's anything I can ever do, just let me know. Your fucking right, WE GOT POWER and nobody gonna take it away!

ZAPATA ESPINOZA.

P.S. MOHAWKS ARE THE COOLEST!

PIC BY ALAN

OVERKILL

"Im a geek... and proud of it!" -Merrill

Kurt and Ron from Overkill were interviewed at Okidog at 4:30 in the afternoon a while back.
WGP: Where is Merryl? Kurt: In the hospital. Ron: He's getting a brain scan. WGP: Where did you get the band started? Kurt: In South Bay-playing partys. We'd get shit throwen at us by the hippies. WGP: Didnt you used to have a different singer? Kurt: He left 'cos he didnt wanna work. He got lazy, so we booted him. WGP: Whose all in Overkill? Kurt: Myself (drums), Ron (bass), Merrill (singer), and were working on a new guitarist. Once we got Merrill this summer, things stared working out. Ron: After we played the Vex the first time, people saw us and wanted us for other gigs. Kurt: I think when we play, we give it everything we've got. If bands dont give everything they've got, they shouldnt be in punk. Ron: They should not be in MUSIC!!! WGP: What does your name mean? Kurt: To over do things. Ron: Not to over do, but to do everything to the max! WGP: What are your songs about? Kurt: Personal freedom, hate of conformity, refusal to be thrown out by society. WGP: And now a plug for your record... Ron: It'll be out soon. Kurt: It's on SST Records.

We found Merrill later on that nite at the Whisky. Well, here goes...
Merrill: Here's the phylosophy of Overkill according to me. I got into the band in July '81. I replaced the old singer basicly for the July 4 gig at Bards. Our drummer, Kurt, went to Spot, the producer, and told him they needed a new singer for Overkill. Spot immidiatly thought of me, he knew Merrill was the only one capibale! The music were doin' now is very simple, musically, However, the melodys and rhythems evoke a very energetic feeling. An almost physotic feeling.
In all music the performer strys to reach a certian level. That level is either reached - or not. Speed is a eliment. We are one of the faster bands in LA. THe only bands we rank behind in speed are the Descendents and Wasted Youth. Musically punkrock is asthetic. I enjoy punk for it's intensity. I would like to music alongthe lines of Gang of Four, Killing Joke, Joy Devision, The Cure, Human Leauge, etc. I am very commited to Overkill now. The commitment I have is very self centered. I have things I want out of this. 1. To have a good time. 2. MONEY. I love money! Ya know, the whole punk subculture developed from a swindle. 3. Girls. I get laid alot more often cos Im in a band. 4. Drugs, 'cos I do alot of 'em.
Personally, Ive never taken the scene too seriously. I feel people who take the whole thing seriously develope bad attitudes. I dont take any band in LA too seriosuly, although the Germs, Black Flag, and the Minutemen have some good ideas to offer. I think the whole idea is to have a good time. Now, I had a great time rousting 2000 kids as dressed up to Be Adam Ant at the Flag show at the SM Civic. Now that was great! I almost was killed.

we do it all FER YOuZ!

It's 12:45 at Okidog. The locals are busy moving back and forth from Okis-to-Astro, and Okis-to-the park. Two female fur-coated Bev Hills types show up and get hassled by 25 punks. They spit, through garbage, and spill beer on their Porshe, and on the two occupants. Jim shows up and kicks us all out of the lot. I spot Nikki and Brian in the midst of this. Next thing I know, we are interviewing Nikki and Brian inside Astro Burger, on the back of a flyer with a borrowed pen.

Nikki and Brian are not a band, but they play just an important part in the L.A. scene. The two produce that big sheet of photos you've seen, known as Fer Youz.

"We take photos of people, we never ask them to pose. They do what they wanna do." Brian explains. "They walk away, flip you off, pose; it's their decision."

Fer Youz was born in January '81 as a collection of punks and their clothing home-made t-shirts, flyers, tatoos, jewlery, haircuts, buttons- "body asthetics", for punks. There are not only photos of bands in performance, but band members "hanging out".

Nikki and Brian saw Fear two years ago at The Hong Kong, and were convinced there was something worthwhile going on here. Brian, as an artist, who draws punks, Nikki, writing a book on the L.A. scene, together they photograph punks. They like to be known as "caretakers" of their photos because "you can't own someone's image." They created Fer Youz as a favor in return for those who pose in them. "The picture belongs to the whole scene. It's history. It's important." Nikki exclaims.

When they first started, they felt the relationship between punks and photographers were rocky. Photographers seem to have a history of exploiting punks. There'd be an article on how terrible punk rockers are, and next to it would be a nice picture of you. "Hi mom!" Most parents aren't too happy about that!

people miss out on getting a copy due to the fact that Fer Youz is never on sale at record or clothing shops. They are handed out personally at Okidog once a month.

Brian ads about their publication. "People look at Fer Youz and say, 'oh I hate that guy!' But we put him in anyway. He is part of the scene. He is there!"

"Because we understand the movement we can be responsible with the pictures, and because we pay for it, we can be bribed in anyway to distort it." He summed up. -AL...

INTERVIEW WITH FRANK, OWNER OF GODZILLAS

WGP: Why did you open a club?

FRANK: I was goin' to other clubs since '78. I was a fan. I was a tile-setter, as a profession, and hurt my back - so I couldn't do that kinda work. So, I promoted a concert, "Razor Productions", Devonshire downs May 2 '81 with Adolescents headlining, TSOL, Cheifs, Wasted Youth (before they were famous), and the Stains. It was very successful. 1700 in attendence. So I started scouting for a club. I found this place.

WGP: Why did you pick this location?

FRANK: 'Cos it had lotsa parking & not too many neighbors & it was a funky old building - nothin' much to thrash, you could write on walls!

WGP: How is this club run in comparison to the others?

FRANK: Other club owners, what do they listen to when they go home? Barry Manilow. Jerry Roach doesn't go home and listen to Wasted Youth & Cockney Rejects I do. I already knew how to handle a club. There's no one really violent.

WGP: Tell us about your staff...

FRANK: Kids as old as 26. I know some of them. I hiered them. And then they hiered their friends.

WGP: What are the major problems that Godzillas is facing?

FRANK: The planning department - city hall - polaticians - and their inconsistant polocies. There playing God with my business. It's a big mix up. And the kids. 98 ./. are great, but that 2 ./. have been making problems - breaking windows.

WGP: Why do you call the place, Godzillas?

FRANK: Because this place is huge & Im into Science Fiction.

WGP: What's in the future for Zillas?

FRANK: We gotta OI package. Angelic Upstarts, Exploited, UK Subs. (Anti-Pasti have already played, they'll be back in July). DOA's comin' down. Slash records wants to do a live at Godzilla's comp. lp with up & coming bands. Hollywood movie & poster company wants to show movies in the other room. Texas Chainsaw Massacre, Three Stooges, etc. Oh yeah, and sci fi movies.

WGP: Anything else you wanna say...

FRANK: Kids openly drink beer outside of club, in front of police - thats whats hurtin' me. We'll get closed if this continues. I've got all my money invested inthis. So we want everyone to come down & support the club.

INTERVIEW BY DAVE.

News From ... SACRAMENTO

I'm Rats Ass,
Alias Patrick Thomas Stratford. I play 1st bass in the band the Square Cools., we will tour your ugly city L.A. , I used to live in east L.A., some fun. I'm ~~ma~~ married so to bad for for you disapointed girls. I was found, I was in our beatyful capitol city. Your probly thinking this band is a bunch of jokers well your wrong, we're one very serious band. Our ideas are going to save the world from satan. Naaa, just kidding! We're a band for fun like old rockabilly, rock and roll and punk. I always have fun at punk gigs. Our music is very energetic, radical, with fast cold beat and we're fucking fantastic! Fuck the Circle Jerks, we're the SQUARE COOLS !!!

LOVE ......

, RATS ASS

Santa Barbra:

The DUMPS have returned from their trip to San Francisco and should be playing again soon. The **STRAPPON DICKS** have broken up so that the members could go back to school ful time. **The TAN** is making a big name for themselves. The have headlined the Cathay, they have a record out, they have plans to open for the MOTELS at UCSB, and they are booked to open for FRAMPTON at the ARLINGTON. On September 25 and 26 the **REJECTORS** played the Shack in Goleta where every Tuesday is Punk/ New Wave night. Playing with them were **FOUND OBJECTS**, the **CONSUMERS**, and **MOD SQUAD**. The REJECTORS HAVE since dropped their name and are looking for a new bass player. -**ALAN**

News From Mt. Washington:

Mt. Washington is a neighborhood between Downtown and Pasadena. It's ajacent to Eagle Rock. The **only punks** I knoww about on my hill are about 5 (including ~~5~~ John Doe & Exene). The situation is pretty fuckin dead. We had a band called **SVDB** (St. Vids Dance Band) and after playing 1 ~~1/2~~ party, we broke up. Now everyone's in diferent bands. During the week Im stuck in boarding school. -IVAN

Send us news of your area! get up off your ass→!!!

NEW YEARS HAPPENINGS L.A.

If people were only like video-tape machines, they could of went to one of the many New-Years-1982 parties or big gigs, and taped the others. There was so much going on.

Some where in the wilds of Hollywood was a Mau-Maus party to celebrate that group's getting back together. We didn't get to go to this one, 'cos our car wasn't going that way.

Some of us unlucky people happeded to pass the "New" Olympic for the big "sell-out" Black Flag-meets-Suburban Lawns-meets-Blasters-meets-Fear-meets-Saccharine Trust. Rockabillys were all there. So were the hippies with sprayed color in their long hair, (they must of been "punking-out" man.). So were the first-timer punkrockers, even a few w/ brand new haircuts, who could of had long hair to spray colors in. Old lame art students from USC were there, observing "the punk culture". I wonder how Saccharine Trust & Flag did tonite. Joe Blow was with his Fear father, s, helping 'em out, 'cos they were

Palm Springz

Shawn Wheeler quits Dead Issue,fucking over the band, hoping to reform Mutual Hatred. LOCAL PUNKS HATE TARGET 13. Thrift-marts are ~~&~~ happening - new wave chicks love em. Bates Skates is broken into - Mike Bates unaware?

playing two gigs tonite. Right after they did their set, they packed on over to Sun Valley to Godzillas, where we all ended up.

Saccharine Trust were interviewed at SST Studios previous to their tour w/ Black Flag.

Earl Liberty- bass
Jack Brewer- tenor
Rob Holtzman- drums
Joe Biaza- guitar

WGP: What records are you guys on?

Earl: Cracks In The Sidewalk, Chunks, & Future looks Bright...

Jack: Yeah, we only do compolations! We know people will hear us. Our own album is coming out soon.

WGP: What are your influences?

Joe: Thats pretty diverse, we all have our own influences.

Jack: We dont like each other's music. We dont even like each other!! (laughs)

Oliver: What happened to your old bass player and your drummer?

Jack: Our drummer and bassist left on good terms. Our bassist quit 'cos he really wasnt into it anymore.

WGP: How did you find Earl?

Earl: Rob joined first. Rob met Joe at Polish Hall, the nite they had that big riot.

Rob: I was drunk in the parking lot and they found me and said, "hey, hey, your a drummer!" (laughter) Then I said,"yeah Ill practice with you." But I didnt really want to, but I was drunk!

Earl: I'd hang out at the practices & was familiar with the stuff. When the bass player quit, they asked me to join. Its pretty easy.

WGP: What about the tattoo on your arm (a "S" shaped snake nailed on a "T" shaped cross, their logo).

Earl: I got this after I got our of the hospital. I wanted a tattoo and I couldnt think of anything better to put on my arm.

WGP: So, tell us about your accident..

Earl: This party with Black Flag in Carson. Cops came and broke it up. One of the cops asked me if I knew the girl whose house it was, went out front, tryed to look for her. Cops out front told me to go home. My ride was in the back yard. One cop put a stick in my stomach. The two other cops came up and started pulling out their nite sticks, so I ran for it. It was a dead end street. I jumped a brick wall and hit a fence behind that, and fell 20 feet. Broke my leg. Knocked my teeth out. Opened up a hole in my jaw.

(Talk goes on to lighter subjects...)

WGP: How did you guys do in Frisco?

Rob: BURNED!

Earl: Fuckin' great!

Joe: I think we did okay.

Jack: We were more energetic.

WGP: What about your tour?

Earl: The tours gonna be mostly on the east coast w/ Flag.

Jordan: Are you guys gonna be on Saturday Nite Live? (Laughter...)

Earl: Black Flag suppose to be on Saturday Nite Live.

(Talk goes on about Jimmy Mack Theater)

Joe: We had parties there.

Earl: Me and Joe lived there. Our rent was to keep the place clean.

Joe: It turned into a hangout.

Jack: We had two really good parties there. Kids knocked holes in the walls, you could even spray paint!...

Joe: We got kicked out 'cos the manager owner lady came walking in one nite and saw people crashed out all over the place... beer bottles...

WGP: What are your favorite bands?

Jack: Salvation Army, Descendents, and th e Minutemen.

Earl: Dead Kennedys, Black Flag, jazz fusion. I wanna play jazz fusion.

Jack: I wanna raise great danes.

GUEST column:

On The Spot.... this issue's spotlight...

EDITOR'S NOTE: THIS MONTHS GUEST COLUM WAS PENNED BY FMOUS HOLLYWOOD PRO-DUCER, SPOT.

Im not gonna tell you about anything you think you wanna hear. Im going to praise NEOBOPISM. Yeah, you heard me you smelly little punks! Before this age ends and the next one begins Im gonna give you time to think you were here but you're not! No way, Jose!

Lately is seems like that good old Ⓐ is becoming a symbol of asthma. I mean you got your gigs that seem like someone's ides of an exploitation movie about "Punk Rock" complete with a "I say OI! You say OI!" type script. Dem songs be sounding da same, baby. Y' see, a wise man once snapped his fingers and said: "Anarchy is the trap of the Eighties..."

So in the meantime, five hardcore bands whose names will not be mentioned played a gig in some Chinese laundromat that specialized in dirty underwere. And the punkies be slammin' and doin' the bumpercar and in the midst of 10 back-flip stage dives someone calls the cops who protect and serve god's apple pie. Oh no! But Louie armstrong taps god on the shoulder and says: "Aw, c'mon! Them boys is jess having fun!" So he blows his trumpet and out of the sky fall 1001 records of the BEBOP & RIDDIM and BLOOZR and BAM!! Smacked them cops on the head! So Louie says: "Hah! That'll show 'em they cant mess with that jazz!" Then Sid sneered and asked: "Huh?" Louie answered: "You missed it you god-damn junkie! Now get your ass outta bed and go tell Darby to bring back my Duke Ellington records!" And on that trumpet note you'll find that there's a choice facing you. It's either more of that OI crap or you can learn the square root of 81. (Isn't it 82, Spot? -ed)

Yeah, Im praising NEOBOPISM.

the TAN

Interview with The Tan 10/17/81
Brad Nack- (guitar, vocals)
Paul Bergerot- (drums, vocals)
Joe Longo- (bass, vocals)
Spencer Barnitz- (vocals,guitar)

Q:How long has The Tan been around?
A:Two & a half years.
Q:What got you going? Inflouences?
A:Mostly local bands here in Santa Barbra. The music scene here in SB was from 79-80. It was great. It died... all the original stuff...
Q:You guys playing LA's Brave Dog?
A:Oct. 24, we'll be down in LA.(This interview was done a while ago -ed.)
Q:Does your music convey any messages?
A:No. Our music is meaningless for $! Besides, no one in SB would listen for any messages, anyways!
Q:What is the typical SB like?
A:Were pretty sarcastic, and some people dont pick up on the sarcasm. They think were serious.

We listen to earlt 60's music. I like Wall Of Voodoo-Brad. I like the Cramps -Joe. We have one ep out now, and we will have an lp out in 6 months. Weve got about 180 originals. The record out now is produced by Doors songwriter & guitarist, Robby Krieger. He even plays guitar on a few tracks.

The tan is cute surf pop with an ass-hole approach, fighting for workers of the world. Breaking those chains of economic bondage with one quick blow. -Brad Nack. Interview by Alan

RED CROSS a PUNKROCK PARTRIGE FAMILY

Part one of this interview takes place at world famous Dannys Dogs on January 8 at about 2 am. I used the straight forward approach.

WGP: Hey, do you guys want to do the interview now?
Jeff: Yeah
Somebody: What about the rest of the band?
Steve: They are our slaves.
Jeff: They've got nothing to say!
JORDAN: Okay, I have to get a pen. Does anybody have a pen?
Anybody: Yeah, brink it back when you are done.
(At this point Jeff and I sit down at a table next to two hippies).
Hippie #1: Do you know where I can get some drugs?
Jeff: I had some quaaludes earlier..
WGP: First question: what are your current plans for vynal?
Jeff: We're gonna have a record out on Smoke 7 records.
WGP: Really.
Jeff: Yes. We chose them 'cos we could have 100% creative right. We could do a Brady Bunch cover if we want.
WGP: How long have you been playing your instruments?
Jeff: Why dont you change that to, "how long have you been jamming your axes".
WGP: How long have you been jamming your axes?
Jeff: My brother started playing in 5th grade orchestra, so we could start up a band.
WGP: Your kidding.
Jeff: It was always my dream to start a kiddie band, we were the first Mad Society, before Mad Society was Mad Society. We survived cos steve was 12.
Steve: Then we learned how to play our instruments, and, ask me some questions.
WGP: Whats you name.
Steve: Steve.
WGP: The question we're on is, where did you learn to jam your axe...
Steve: What?
Jeff: I've been playing guitar for about a year and a half.
Steve: NO, no way, you've been playing as long as I have.
Jeff: Oh yeah, we used to do Runaways covers... and Ramones. Have you heard of Suzi Quatro?
WGP: Yes.
Jeff: We're doing a cover of one of her songs.

Pic BY: BOOTLICK CAVERN

WGP: What about TV. Facts Of Life
Steve: Way to go Tootie. Oh you have that flyer? (Note: Adolescents, Red Cross, Social Distortion gig at new old Vex July 17. The flyer had heart shaped pic's of Facts Of Life girls, Joe, Blair, Tootie, & Natilie.)
Steve: Tootie is a fox and Natalie is where it's at.
Jeff: Natalie used to go to my school.
WGP: Whats the deal with Greg Hetson?
Jeff: We ripped off "Cover Band" from The Leaving Trains, just the music. It was Greg's idea and we didn't make a cent on that album.
Steve: Greg stole the slow part of (some song). I wrote it about Connie Fransis getting raped.
(All at once the lights at Danny's go out. The sheriff's have arrived.)
JORDAN: Hey, who turned the lights out? TURN ON THE LIGHTS SO I CAN FINISH THIS INTERVIEW!!
Officer Malloy: You have 10 seconds to get out of here.
WGP: Shit.
(At this point I follow Jeff & Steve to their car)
Jeff: Maybe we can finish this interview some place else.
Steve: Be sure to come to our free gig.
WGP: Did someone say free gig?
Officer Reed: (Over bullhorn) You kids aren't moving fast enough.
(I walked away to our car and looked back to see the cops hasseling Steve & Jeff of Red Cross.) NOTE: We regret t that Johnny (drums) & Tracy (rhythm guitar) weren't present for the bigtime interview above. -JORDAN.

BENEFIT CONCERT

WE GOT POWER magazine & **FER YOUz**

GODZILLA'S, 8230 San Fernando Road (at Vineland). A large place, comparable to the Starwood, with a capacity of 1600. Music room, disco room, beer and wine, pool tables, pinball machines. Supported by the local bands, this place claims it's "for the kids, run by kids." Cover varies. For info, call 654-7472.

Thurs., Jan. 14—Benefit for We Got Power fanzine, with **Bad Religion, Circle One, Minutemen, Descendents, Sin 34.**

Sin 34

OPENED THE NIGHT AND THE CROWD WENT CRAZY.

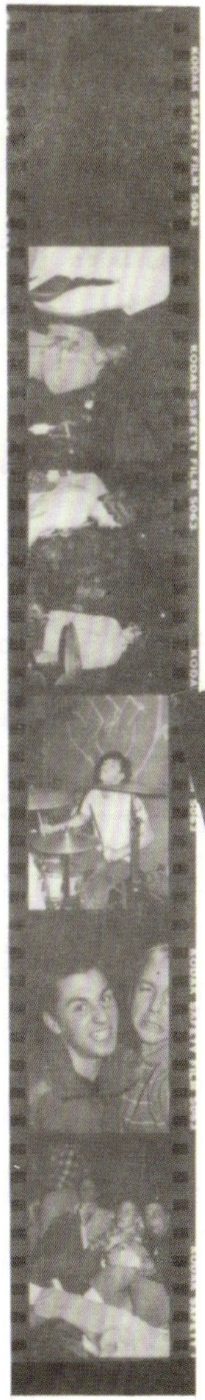

DESCENDENTS

PLAYED NEXT AND DID AN EXCELLENT SET OF TUNES, KEPT THE KIDS GOING NUTS!

Mike Watt - Minutemen ~~played~~ destroyed

symbol six

FILLED IN FOR CIRCLE ONE, WHO COULDN'T MAKE IT DUE TO PERSONAL TROUBLES. S-6 DID ALL THE STUFF FROM THEIR FORTH-COMING **POSH BOY** RELEASE.

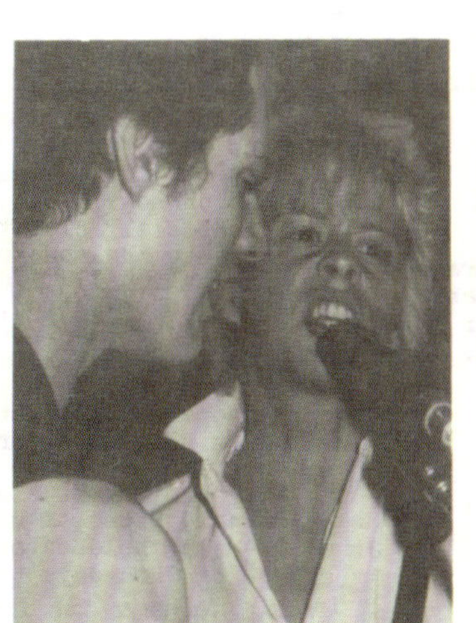

YELL

BAD Religion

HEADLINED THE NITE WITH A NEW DRUMMER.

Special thanks to all the bands & people who helped & Godzilla's...

Right before Bad Religion's set, Nikki & Brian screened their famous slides of the LA scene - went over great!

PHOTOS BY: **MOUSE, ALAN, & FER YOUZ**

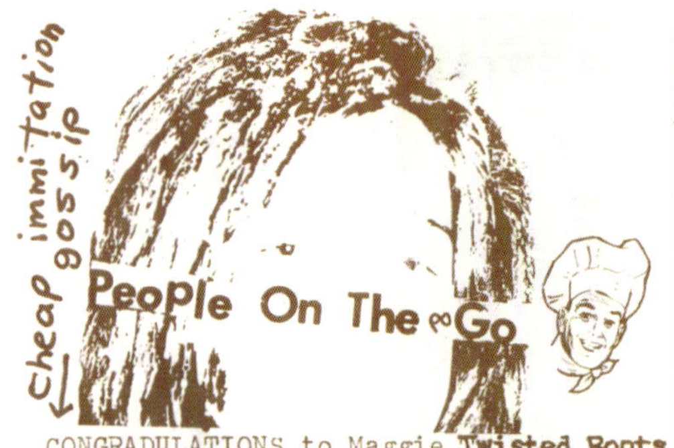

CONGRADULATIONS to Maggie **Twisted Roots** for being the first (and only?) person to steal a copy of **We Got Power.** ON THE FILM SCENE, I caught a sneak preview of **"The Slog"**, featuring home-movies and/or interviews with **Symbol Six, Circle One, Wasted Youth, The Cheifs, TSOL, Fear, Circle Jerks, Black Flag**, and a few others! On the subject of films, I was told Penelope Spheriis is getting together a **Decline** part **2.** SLAMMING BY CELEB'S; **Tar** (Juicy Hot) & **Keith Morris** sharing the slam/pogo floor at the **Dickies** return to the **Whisky.** Pat Smear Paul Rossler, Maggie & Co were seen SlAmMiNg it up at the **Starwood** for that episode of **Chips** on LA PUNKROCK. Pat was in a kilt! POGOING at Godzillas, film at eleven! John Belushi gets a mohawk. WASTED YOUTH NEWS; one week Chet says, "we gotta brand new bassist, from **Abandoned.**" One week later, Chet says "we got Lorna from the **Germs**". WHUT? It was also rumored that Jay from **Bad Religion** might fill in the gap that Jeff Long left. Jeff's been doin' well with **Africacorps** & also he's in a few other bands. RUDE BOYS OUT OF JAIL; **John Circle One** & **John Boy Bishop** were sharing hand-cuffs at Iggy Pop. **Fly** is on the lamb - and living fast, he refuses to give up his criminal tendencies. Speaking of tendencies, The **Suicidal Tendencies** hit up **Samohi** w/ some more great graffetti. VIOLENCE NEWS; **Teno** gets even with **Duane Peters**, & beats him up at **Godzillas.** Rumor has it **Tony-Okidog** got thrown in jail for thrashing someone with a green mohawk. John ① supposidly beat up Godzillas light man. **Jay Adams** gives **Alan** WGP a shiner. So what! John ① wants to get even with **Felix** of **RF7** & **Smoke 7**, for the fucked mixing he gave C1 on **Public Service.** FUN FUN FUN **Sticktime** fanzine is doing an interview with the creator of Parents Of Punkers. HAHAHAHAHAHAHAHA. Maybe we could go there & have punk hangout nite. Maybe we could get a flatbed truck and a PA. -JORDAN.

NIGHTCLUBS . . . .

NEW CLUBS REVIVE LA PUNK SCENE

Just when you thought all the clubs were closed, comes a whole new fleet of new clubs. Probably the most closest to the old Hollywood/LA scene is Sun Valley's GODZILLAS. Staffed by locals and Oxford-housers, GODZILLAs is like the Starwood 'cos it has a million rooms to go in. ZILLAs features a bar room, a video game arcade room, a MEXICAN resturant; if you can believe that!, a big disco room, two hangout rooms with tabels and chairs, and of corse, the big auditorium; all packed into a dingy/run-down building. They've been having all the big bands; Stains, Fear, Circle Jerks, Bad Religion, TSOL, China White, etc. etc. etc. This place is GOD.

The Ritz in Riverside has been doing really well these past few months. Booking 45 Grave to Circle One, this clubs also had Black Flag.

Punks not dead! It just took a nap for a while.

-SMIT

— brave doG article —

On December 18-'81 LA's Brave Dog club/bar was raided by neighboring LAPD officers who found BD to be selling beer to minors. As a result, the club is now closed indefinatly. The article below was written weeks before...

Its sits in the heart of Downtown El Lay, next to the infamous Atomic Cafe, at the ass end of Little Tokyo. 1st and Alameda to be exact. Around back, hidden to the unknowing eye, is the Brave Dog, a great small club that makes for a alternative to the monotony of popular clubs. Inside you'll find cool people, stimulating conversation, free beer, a cover charge never more than $5., 2 or 3 bands, all in an intimate atmosphere. The performers mingle with the crowd, & there is none of the pretentiousness you find in Hollywood, or worse yet, the Orange curtian. Co-owner by Claire and Jack, the "woofer" is also staffed by Shawna, Paul, Peter, & sometimes Mary & John! The club holds about 151 max and is opened on Saturdays (sometimes on Fridays). Anyways its fun, something different, its exciting, and almost always a good time.-Lou E

HERE IS SOME FORM OF PRESS RELEASE WHICH NERVOUS GENDER SENT TO US.....

exerpt from 'never to be released lyrics' interview:

BILL: I dont care! I still wont do Jesus' Clone because its sacriligious & I fear the wrath of God!

GERARDO: When Bruce (manager) and I finished mixing Jesus Clone (live at Target album) we went out to the car to listen to it. Bruce was parked down the street from a church and the cross on its steaple seemed to glare at me, like I was on acid. I told myself I would never do the song again, and I was going to write a personal apology to the pope.

EDWARD: Im more sane than they are, I can curve my childish Christian guilt.

DON: Ive had carnal knowledge of the devil.

BILL: That's so sacriligious! I dont want to hear about it!

GERARDO: Was he cute?

EDWARD: Was he cut?

GERARDO: How big was he?

EDWARD: Did he do anything kinky with his tail?

DON: He doesnt have a tail, his cock curves around his leg.

GERARDO: Could you take it all?

EDWARD: Did you take it all?

GERARDO: Whered he stick it?

EDWARD: What about his wings?

GERARDO: Did he fly across the room as he pegged you?

BILL: Stop it! Stop it. This is making me paraniod! I have enough problems trying to reconciliate with God without you guys agrevating him further! I hate sex! Im scared of shit blasphemy! I camt handle getting a job and my parent s are fucked to me! The band can never make any money. And I hate punk rock! I hate everything. But I cant hate everything, thats a dictomy! But I do hate everything! I hate everything!

GERARDO: Calm down Bill, do you want me to get you a coke?

BILL: And a hershy bar too. Or some rolos.

GERARDO —NERVOUS GENDER— DON EDWARD BILL

TUNA'S... TUNE

STAKIST, FUCK THEM MAN, I KNEW I WAS ONE TUNA WHO WAS NOT GONNA TAKE ANY OF THEIR,"TASTIEST TUNA AROUND" SHIT. SO I SPLIT.TO L A

THINGS WERE GOING BAD UNTIL ONE DAY LEE VING OF FEAR GOT A WHIFF OF ME, HE LIKED ME ALOT, HE SAID THAT I REMINDED HIM OF HIS MOTHER. SO IM OFF TO DO THE BAND"S SCRATCH N SNIFF ALBUM COVER.

JORDAN

oooOH HENRY

We walked into SST and found Henry & Spot listening to Wildman Fisher and answering letters. We talked to Henry for a while...

WGP: So, tell us about England:

Henry: Alot of the kids are real closed minded - they go with their gangs - liking what their gang likes - afraid to like bands like us. Reminds me of some scenes in the US. Im not into scenes.

WGP: Why?

HENRY: 'Cos scenes emply an "order", Im not into that.

WGP: What do you think there should be?

There shouldn't be rules. Im into doing what you wanna do. (Pause, as subject goes on about bands & songs). "Reagens In" fuck that... "fuck authority"...'over-throw government'... thats not the stuff that effects me. Emotions. Thats what Black Flag is all about. Emotions. Personal feelings. Frustration. Depression. Were not saying, "fuck punk", were not cutting down Wasted Youth. People hear Rise Above and think we mean we are better than all of this. Not true. The stuff we write; "What I See", is a love song by Chuck... his personal feelings. Were not saying, we are macho, we're tough. I can be broken. I can be hurt. Im not a fuckin' machine. Im a human being.

WGP: Whats it like when kids come up to you and say, "oh, your so great" etc.

HeNRY: It makes me feel good. People ask me for my autograph. I make them autograph it too! (Henry puts on Dicks/Big Boys record)

HENRY: The dicks are fuckin' great! (Talk goes on about his other favorite bands). MINUTEMEN. They make me roll on the floor. Saccharine Trust. Red Cross. Overkill, Sick Pleasure. Flipper. DOA. Subhumans. all DC bands. BAD BRAINS!!! One of the best bands EVER! Right up their with UK Subs...(who Flag met up with on their English tour).

WGP: What do you think of Flag's success w/ KROQ ("TV Party"), Headlining The Olympic, etc.

HENRY: I don't think of it on terms of success. I think of it as reaching people. If Black Flag lost everyone, we'd still play. Im not saying "we dont need you..." We're into, "lets play" & if people like us; great, if they dont like us, fine. Thats their right.

PIC-FER YOUZ

GIGS REVIEWS! GIGS

CIRCLE JERKS, LEGAL WEAPON, BLADES, SECRET HATE Godzillas 12/5

Secret Hate was a pleasent surprise, not your average slam 'n dive warm-up act, but an original sounding quintet from Long Beach. **The Blades** were your average slam 'n dive band. **Legal Weapon** were good, I had never seen them before. I've heard their stuff though, unaware it was the Steve Soto X-**Adolescents** plays bass, and they've got a female singer. The Jerks came on, and were nice and loud. At the end of the set, Roger threw his bass into the air, and it smashed on stage. Rumor has it Nikki & Brian of Fer Youz blackmailed them to play this gig. Thanks. -JORDAN

999 Circle Jerks & Wasted Youth, Florintine Gardens 11/25

Wasted Youth was real cool, they flipped off the bouncers & played a great set including my personal fave, "Punk For A Day". The best part was at the end when they did fucked-up version of "Rock Around The Clock" & Scranny jumped into the audience. I thought the bouncers were gonna have a collective coronary. The **Circle Jerks** were their usual thrash-selves. They did new stuff, which I cant remember because some HB jumped off the stage onto my head. At one part of their set, FG's manager stopped the noise & told the kids to act like young adults, or something. I never saw anyone get so much spit on the face before. **999** looked pretty awful. I never had seen them before, and hadn't heard much by them & was unprepared for those middle age Englishmen playing stupid newromantic disco. (New romantic??-ed.) The lead singer (looked about 39) stopped between songs long enough to tell us to calm down, cuz thats what the kids in England. Fuck England, this is L.A. -Rich

Subhumans, Detours, Circle 1, CH 3 September 26, Cuckoos Nest:

Arriving in Costa Mesa is always a shock since I usually am Hollywood & LA. Anyhow, I bought a ticket. The first band tonite, **CH3**, I'd seen, and alls I can say is that I wasn't excited about seeing them again. On the other hand, I was impressed by the next band, **Circle One.** From the audience reaction I forgot they weren't headlining. Some people say, Circle (1) is the next Flag. Next, **The Detours**, were terrible. The singer, right before their set, was swinging the mike stand at somebody, and the base flew off, and smashed a girl in the head. Blood poured all over the floor, and no one cared. Well, thats the Nest for you. This incident didn't exactly raise my opinions of this band. I was not too lucid when **The Subhumans** came on, but I thought they were great. Playing fast/danceable music, these Canadians are very fun to see. -Phil

New Music Festival: ZEALOTS, GROUP SEX, IRON CURTAIN, THE DUMPS, GHETTO BLASTERS, AK47, & others. This was being called "Santa Barbra Slam" by some. I went not expecting much, because the ratio of cool people to dicks here is 1 to 25. It started early, we came late, and left before it was over. **Iron Curtian** was far too synthesized & heavy cosmic ya know for this crowd. We wanted to move, not space out. **Group Sex** was ok. Their singer must have seen Decline once too many times cuz he thought he was Keith. **Public Enema's** violinist got her equipment locked in a car & couldn't play. too BAD! Thats all I can recall. We gathered up or Vodka and promptly left. -LouE

GIG'S

GIG'S

THE ATOMS AT AL'S BAR-

GIG'S

After two years of existence and an amazing number of ex-members to their credit, The Atoms finally made their debut at Al's Bar on October 23. It is debatable whether or not the product was worth two years effort, but they were not dissapointing.

They preformed six originals and the **Animals'** "House Of The Rising Sun" & **Johnny Thunders'** "Chatterbox". Their set was sloppy, but they were still enjoyable. Their music is very reminiscent of the **Sex Pistols**, good rock'n roll, and far removed from typical hardcore LA thrash punk.

The audience seemed to thoroughly enjoy the show, even asking for (but not receving) an encore. Jeff on drums and Harvey Oscar on bass provided a good, competant rhythem section. Monty sang well, but still needs to -uh- master the art of showmanship. At least he can carry a tune. Taz, on guitar was not nearly loud enough, but still appeared to be above-average and charismatic musician. By the way, I want my amp back Taz!

All in all it was a pretty good show. With a few more songs and some polishing up, they could go far.(Whatever that means!) I just hope it doesnt take another two years. -Ru

BENEFIT for some studio in HOLLYWOOD... Friday November 27 (or was it 26?)!!

This small practice studio was packed with 200 locals & lotsa bands played. **Flag** were playing when I went in, they were good sounding for a new band. **Bad Religion** kinda did an impromt·to set. I like their new stuff alot. "**Wasted Jerks**" played while we waited for Keith & Roger to show. Chet & Danny teamed up with Greg & Lucky and did **Red Cross** covers. **Circle Jerks** went on next and were great, as usual. Heavy metal has really taken over, I noticed on "Wasted" They dont say "I was a hippie" anymore. -DAVE

The Dickies, The Wigs; Whisky Nov.21

The **Wigs** were the most aggrivating nuvo wavo garbage I've ever had to watch They sucked. I HATE THEM. HATE. HATE. The **Dickies**, with their long awaited Hollywod return since death of C. Wagon were tight as ever. I dont like their new rythem guitarist at all.

Paul

Godzillas Sat. Dec 12.45 Grave/Social Distortion/Salvation Army/Red Beret

I was late & missed **Red Beret. Salvation Army** tried to be the Byrds. Cheezey. **Social Distortion** couldnt get their shit together. They blew out the two bass amps & broke guitar strings. I listened to their hits, got bored & went to the disco. **45 Grave** sounded good that nite. You could hear what Dinah was singing about. Don Bolles had a mike and sang a song. They handed out bubble gum cards & little plastic rings to the audience. -Jennifer

FEAR the crowd CH3, Dec 28 Al's Bar-

21 was the minimum age for this one However, a few lucky minors (including me.) were albe to find a way in. **Channel Three** opened the night with some biteing tones. The sound at Al's was excellent. The audience of art school drop-outs couldn't get into their great sounds. **The Crowd** was next with their unique style of homosexual rock. They are good musicians but dont do much otherwise. Finally, it's time for **FEAR** to stir the audience into riot form (exactly what Lee Ving wants) The older punks & under-age Fear Fanatics were up from the start. They did an excellent set, including the new favorite "Hank Williams Was Queer" and all the rest of the fun stuff. The audience wouldn't let them off the stage. Finally it was over, Philo said he had to go play golf & snort coke on his yacht so they couldn't stay. JOHN

PUNK MOVEMENT

ON THE RISE AGAIN

ANTI-PASTI, EFFIGY, CIRCLE ONE, Zillas January 1, 1982

Whatta way to wring in the new years! **Circle One** are getting tighter each show. **Effigy**, from Chicago are also very tight-sounding. They've got a record out, which should be worth buying. Beyond the ballyhoo of the "English Craze 'OI'", stands **Anti-Pasti.** This band told the kids to forget about England & that their glad to be here! The band seemed to enjoy what they were doing, and so did everyone else in this hall!

EDITORIALS

1981 to 1982 so what

I sit and ask myself what 13 years in school has done for me, and my mind draws a blank. It might of helped me a bit here and there, but it didn't make me think. For the most part, school left me feeling out-done. It certainly didn't teach me these "anti-society" lines that I come across too often. I had to learn most stuff on my own, but I was never told to. I wonder if Im being cheated, even as I cheat others. I just can't figure it out. Sometimes I think nothing makes sense, and that we all lie to ourselves always. Is it a "cop-out", man? Well fucking far out Im pist. Maybe its just that I refuse to. Well I don't know. It's so easy to look back on your past, and say, "oh, Im better now." You'll only be doing the same thing next year. Everyday is another problem. There's so much shit man! Well, I guess it's whatever your into. Is it better to just keep quiet? Everyone's off on their own trip, I guess. Your inflouences come from everyone else. Most ideas are cloned. Thats not wrong. What are you suppose to do? Decide for your self, but your decision is mainly based on pleasing others, as you please youself. Like I said, sometimes nothing makes sense. Everyday we are reminded to repeat one and other - and no matter what you do, it's been done before. Even if you don't know about it! Maybe I picked a wrong mood to be writing this essay, I don't know, You tell me. I need to hear the bull-shit from everyone. I need to be inflounced. I need to copy someone else's test answers, 'cos I didn't study. Well, maybe I can do my best at guessing. As long as I keep telling myself Im happy, and I wont die. -David

The "punk scene" seems to be changing rapidly these days. Apparently there are more bands, less clubs, and more long haired, middle of the road followers. Its pretty hard to beleive that a guy with hair hanging all over his shoulders likes Black Flag and TSOL, but there are more and more people like this. As a high school senior at a relatively "anti-punk" school, I've noticed that even us cool people who society has rejected can't get along with one another. Harassment from dead zepplin fans is bad enough, but when "punks" hate each other there is definately a problem. We have to learn to get along with each other, stop second guessing, or at least not hate because somebody dosen't appear devoted enough. Not everybody, especially those still living at home, can go out and get a skinhead or dye their hair. One must realize that we all share basically the same attitude, appreciate how commercial and stupid society can be, and listen to and support the same bands Please, if you want to fight--beat up a hippie, not a fellow punk. If you don't like another punk for superficial reasons--don't hassle him. Remember this, you belong to a minority, a Mr. Toughguy complex and disrespect to people who should be your friends can only result in the deterioration of our elite class.

-Mark
Seal Beach

WHATEVER YOUR INTO.

It's so easy to criticize by saying, "oh, that sucks!",,, but the hard part is explaining why it sucks! This is why the staff of We Got Power invites YOU to write us your comments, storys, interviews, photos, etc. It'll give us a turn at saying YOUR stuff sucks! Naw. Just kidding. But seriously, keep on sending you stuff in!

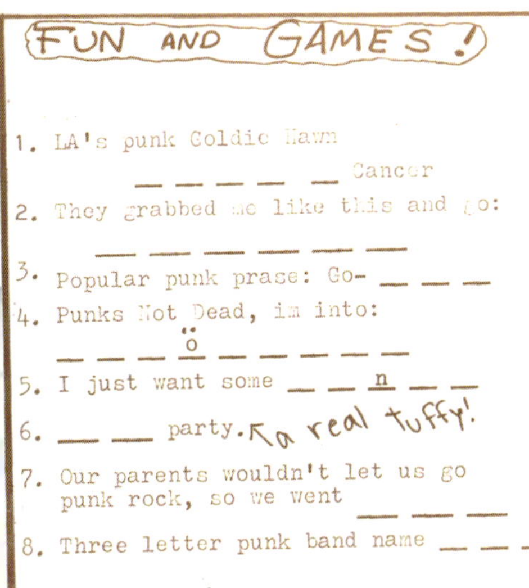

FUN AND GAMES!

1. LA's punk Goldie Hawn ___ ___ ___ ___ Cancer
2. They grabbed me like this and go: ___ ___ ___ ___ ___
3. Popular punk prase: Go- ___ ___ ___
4. Punks Not Dead, im into: ___ ___ ___ ö ___ ___ ___ ___ ___
5. I just want some ___ ___ n ___ ___
6. ___ ___ party. ← a real tuffy!
7. Our parents wouldn't let us go punk rock, so we went ___ ___ ___
8. Three letter punk band name ___ ___ ___

ANSWERS: 1.Dinah 2.Hippie 3.Die 4.Motör-head 5.Money 6.TV 7.Mod 8.it could be:MDA, IUD, DOA, SOA, MIA, IOU, PIL, AKA, TIA, SSI, DOI, etc!!!!!!!!

S N I A H C P I B L T I K B O O T S
K L S H I T G G A S B J F A Y R S C
A Y N N A R C S N M I A W R A U O I
N W Y M O O D O D E V O H N C V L T
K D E A D M A N A Y D U I E L S O A
B E E Y H C R A N A A X T Y E P S M
S I D F A R T U N O D A E H N I K S
D E C L I N E H A D I S C O S T K A
O P K A T G F A S O R E D N O P K L
A I L G O G O S M S Y D E N N E K P
J S O M I E N E H B A G O D I K P B
E T S I L R Z X R I R A E F V N O L
T O F D N M I Z A R D O F P E E T A
B L U E T S E S P H E R I S X S O C
S S E W I Z A R D O F O Z Z Y T P K
E R D X N B M O T O R H E A D Y S B
G F U C K M O H A W K B S K R E E J

Word Find Game. How many punk terms can you spot in the above puzzle

A REAL FUN GAME!

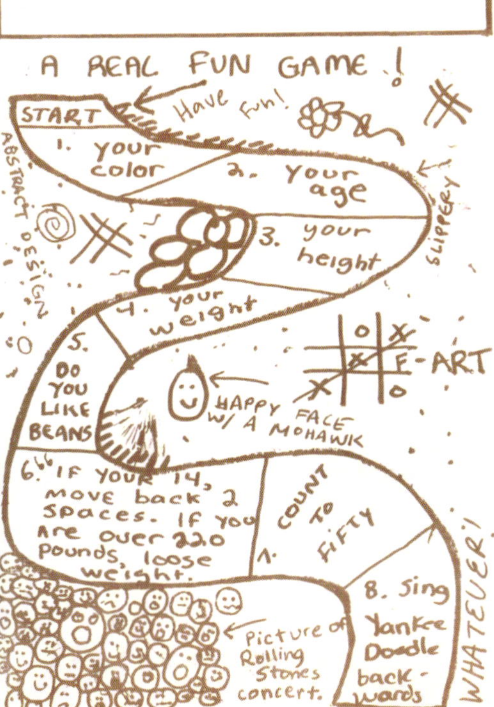

19 wgp's new 82
SKINHEADS INVASION

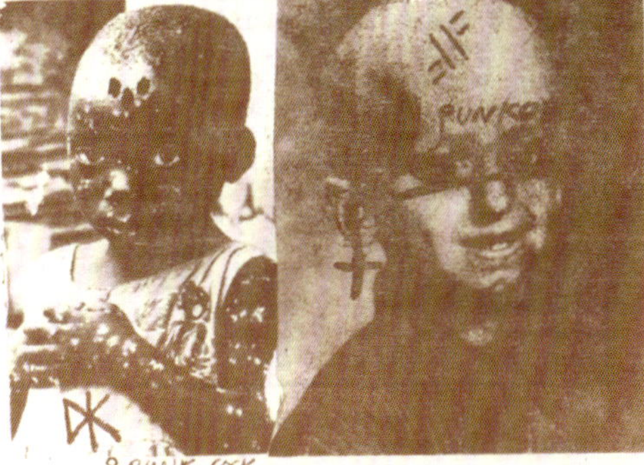

Malnutrition & PUNK ROCK leads to sickness and disease

For his parents (top), "Aaron remains the most important member of the family." Though disfigured by PUNKROCK the teenager remained resolutely good-natured: On his bedroom wall he pinned the motto: "Bald Is Beautiful."

Best Band Names....

Here goes another exclusive and all original section in We Got Power...... names of bands we thought were ggood.

Gnarley Buggers, Jews From The Valley, Racial Slur, Ethel & the Mertz Killers, Bloodflow, Invisible Zoo, Debt Of Nature, Fun Boy Three, Anti-Pasti, Ghoul Squad, Happy-Go-Lucky Youth, Red Youth, Red Brigade, Red Cross, Red Beret, Red Alert, Red Scare, Really Red, Green On Red, Red Red, St. Vidas Dance Band, Gumby Riot, Pillboy & The Anteaters, Flux Of Pink Indians, Wasted Youth, Youth Gone Mad, Manson's Youth, Reagens Youth, Youth Brigade, Social Youth, Youth Troup, Youthy Youth, etc.

Record + Tape Reviews

In God We Trust - **Dead Kennedys**
A fun 8 song hardcore ep with all the DK lyrics hitting up religious and political leaders etc. "Dog Bite" & "Rawhide" are comic relief... while you get "Religious Vomit", "Moral Majority", and 4 others. Nazi Punks Fuck Off.-DAVE

The Fartz - Hardcore from Seattle
This 9 song 7 inch 45 speed ep is quite a good deal. The songs are no longer than a minute & a half and no shorter than a half of a minute. Maybe your average punk, but it's something cool, ya.

Public Service (Various)
Circle One and Red Cross are the best. Bad Religion do the same songs off their single; their alright. RF7 are good heavy metal. Disibility are from the valley; ok. "Rejection" is good.
-MIKE 'NOT' ROTH

Hell Comes To Your House (Various)
EXCELLENT. Too good. Takes local LA acts and makes 'em sound better than anything you'd ever hear on KMET. All bands, esp. Secret Hate, Rhino 39, 45 Grave, 100 Flowers, & Social Distortion come off A OK. Red Cross do New York Dolls. Christian Death do death stuff. Conservatives do local punk scene polotics. All in all, best lp of month.

BLACK FLAG "Damaged"
This album is really stylin', it must be played at loudest volume for the best effect. Damaged is a well chosen title for this album. Six Pack & TV Party are two nice happy mello songs contrast with cuts like Depression & Damaged 1. This is an insane, hardcore album and wont rank as high as America's favorites, The GoGo's.-JORDAN

The Effigies HAUNTED TOWN ep
This is a good album, if you can find it. (On sale at Godzillas & Rhino records). Effigies have a good sound, like they know what they're talking about. See them live, if you can. (They have been hanging around LA, they're from Chicago.)

Modern Warfare -
Here's another loud/fast record. I really like the guitar work on this one. My favorite **Suburban Death Row** is on this 45, and the other two cuts are good too. I've seen lotsa extra copies of this record at **Tower records** in H WOOD. -JORDAN

Minutemen "Punch Line"
Fun. Funky/jazzy/energetic stuff w/ snappy lyrics. Happytime music from an intense three peice band with fresh ideas. The only thing better than their stuff on record, is seeing them live.
-DAVE

Bullshit Detector - (var. British bands)
Who Cares - (various L.A. bands)
Two comp lps that show the diffs of current Brit & LA punk thrashes. More variety on **BSDetector** due to 4x as many groups & varying recording tech (which adds tension, heart, etc.) Standard party line, no/war, no/nukes, no/system stuff, with **PIL** creeping in.
On **Who Cares,** its hard to tell one band from the next, although theres more concern and less hardcore stupidity. Best are **Cheifs** & **Shattered Faith;** Suspects sound good but have nothing to say; filler by Civil Disobedience and Political Crap. -JON

Saccharine Trust - PAGAN ICONS
The long over due (it was recorded last April) lp from one of the more imaginative acts in Southern California is finally out. Catchy rhythems & good back-up vocals ad to Jack Brewer's unusual intense vocals with some clever lyrics. "I Have" & "Human Certainty" - sound excellent. Also on this record are 3 songs from Posh's Future Looks Bright tape. -DJCM

FLY-ING AROUND

It seems like every mag, rag, butt-wipe paper is doing a reader's poll. So WGP decided to jump on the bandwagon and ask our readers the deepest innermost questions. Pleeze cut this out and mail it to WE GOT POWER Fontainebleu rm.305 6525 El Collegio Rd. Isla Vista CA 93017.

1. Male ()   Female ()   Both ()
2. Why did you buy this mag?__________
3. What do you like best about this mag?__________
4. What bands do you like?__________
5. What records have you bought recently?__________
6. Everyday I... ()go to school   ()go to work   ()school/work   ()Im in a band   ()bum around   ()get stuff done
7. When I go to shows I... ()sit down/stand up & watch the bands.   ()get drunk before, usually have a good time.   ()Slam-dance.   ()Pogo.   ()get into the music -if I like the band-.   ()I rarly go to shows.   ()hang out & be popular.
8. My favorite club is __________
9. My favorite group is __________
10. What is the best show/gig/concert you saw last year -'81-?__________
11. What groups do you hate?__________
12. What is your favorite style of music? ()disco/funk-ska/reggea   ()New Romantic   ()Hardcore punk.   ()Softcore "Mod"   ()Just Rock n Roll   ()OI   ()Heavy metal   ()Other__________
13. Are you in a band? (If so, tell us the name)__________
14. Where do you get your cloths at?__________
15. What do you have one your walls? ()Flyers of gigs   ()Posters.example: Plasmatics, Sex Pistols, etc.   ()Nothing   ()Everything
16. My favorite pastime is__________

haha

smallest FLYER OF THE MONTH

the above flyer was the smallest we could fit into the alloted space. It may not be the best.. who cares.

Media Blitz

taken from: Catholic Twin Circle, Sunday, October 4, 1981

Sex Pistols member Sid Vicious showed by his lifestyle that the group were not mere performers. Their hatred and despair were genuine. Vicious murdered his girlfriend while on a concert tour of America, and then killed himself with an overdose of heroin, given him by his mother, also a heroin addict.

this month's reminder of distorted media coverage of Punk is another big laugh! enjoy!

"The heart of Christ says deny yourself. This music says indulge yourself. The message of all these songs is that drugs are great and that youths should have as many sexual partners as they can get. The music prepares youths psychologically to respond positively to occa-

As Flipper says... HA HA HA

Parents against punk

On the Westside, Dank works with a boy who "ran a knife up and down his arms." Whenever he gets mad at his parents, he opens the wounds and lets "the blood drip out on the floor."

In another family, "the daughter was burning cigarette holes up and down her arm" — in the punk vernacular, these are called "germ burns."

12/26/81 Valley West for Circle One. RedCross, Gig

Godzillas for Anti-Pasti 1-1-82

NOW BALD

...the upper and middle class suburbs of Southern California "the last bastion of punk in America."

NIKKI   LENO   CAT-TOP

punkers

Dream

Don't let your building look like a bathroom wall.

"Punk started as a spoof."

DONALD

LOUIE

NICE PREP... D. SPIRA

SLAM JUNIOR

"I look at kids today who are 11 and they are definitely living life in the fast lane. No way would my mother let me out of the house if I was punked-out with make-up on and my hair vaselined."

WE GOT POWER

WE GOT POWER
PIC. BY ED COLVER

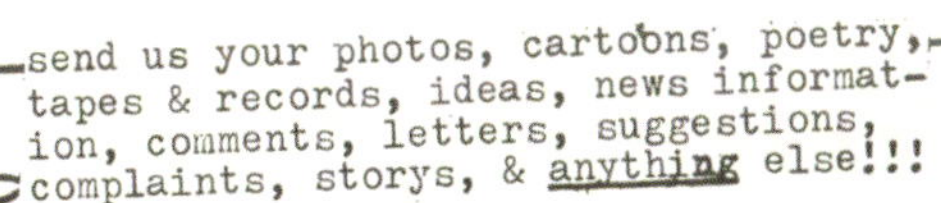
send us your photos, cartoons, poetry, tapes & records, ideas, news information, comments, letters, suggestions, complaints, storys, & anything else!!!
WE GOT POWER
FONTAINEBLEU rm. 305/ 6525 El Collegio rd.
ISLA VISTA CA. 93017

Mike Roth and Jordan Schwartz hold an editorial summit in Dave Markey's bedroom. DAVID MARKEY

WE GOT POWER #3

MAY 1982

This cover, a reader contribution, was a portrait of a skeleton at the beach with his surfboard and the Black Flag bars. Dave added the line "toy surprise inside" to give the mag that exciting cereal box feel. We fortunately caught the Misfits, D.O.A., and JFA, for interviews as they came through town. We ended up taking D.O.A. to the beach.

One of my favorite pieces here is the SST ad—"Carducci: The Man, the Shirt"—put together by coworker Mugger in tribute to the new partner, Joe Carducci, and highlighting the first Minutemen and Saccharine Trust LPs.

Among the reviews is a tribute to the end of Godzilla's, which we called "L.A.'s last hardcore club." That didn't exactly turn out to be true, since the Cathay de Grande soon hosted dollar punk nights, and Joe Vex would opened another version of the Vex in East L.A. Still, the death of Godzilla's was a milestone.

For light entertainment, Dave created a connect-the-dots happy face, and a maze titled "Help the Punk Find the Liquor Store That Sells to Minors." Fortunately, the maze was tougher than actually scoring beer back then. Kim also debuted her scam column, describing pickup lines various punkers had laid on her.

This issue also contains an editorial from Lino Lousy, one of my favorite heavy metal burnouts, arguing that punks shouldn't fuck with metalheads who liked hardcore. Sure enough, *My War* was coming in another two years—the metal issue would need to be sorted out.

—Jordan Schwartz

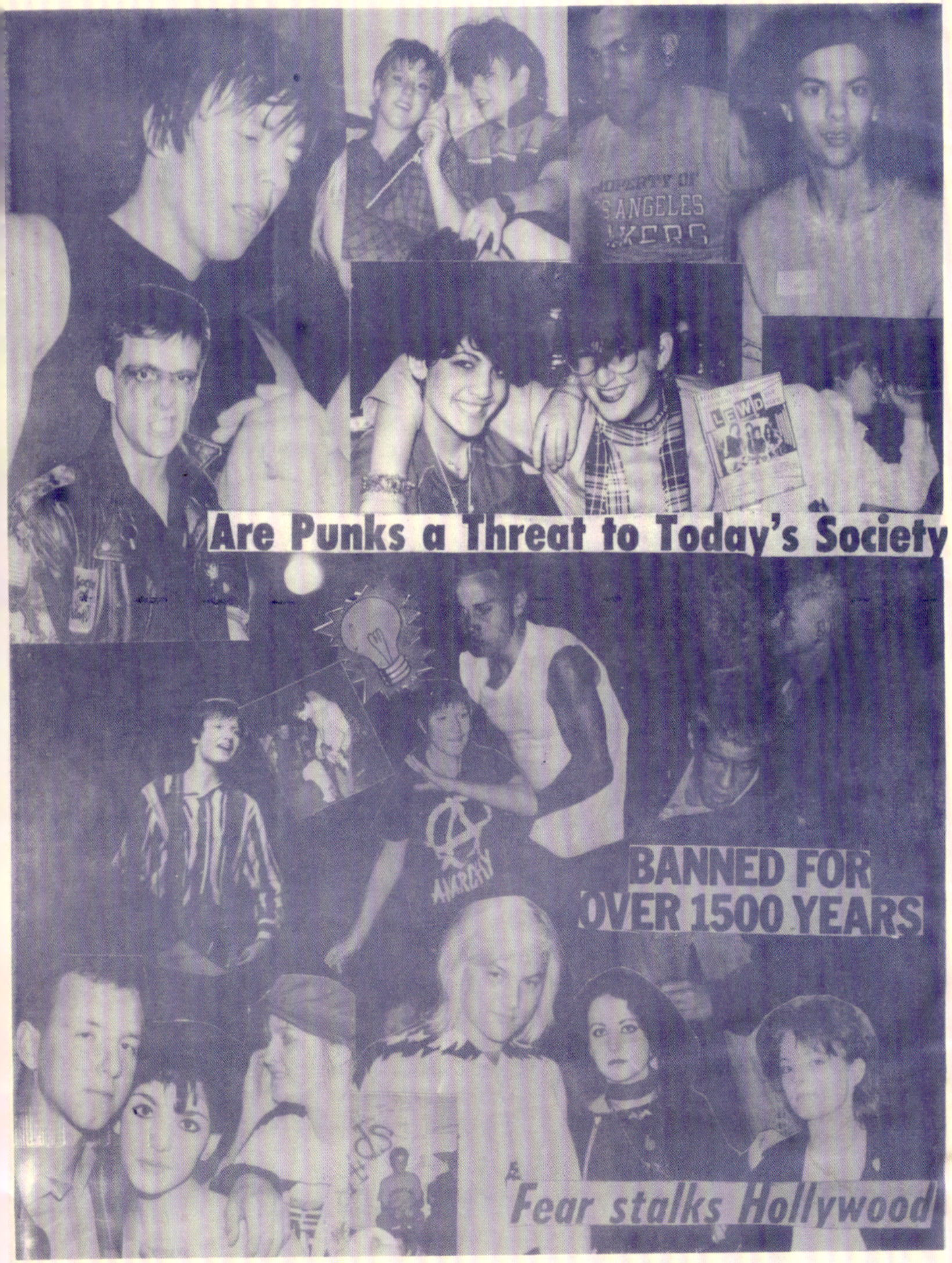
LEWD
Are Punks a Threat to Today's Society
BANNED FOR OVER 1500 YEARS
Fear stalks Hollywood

ROACH HOTEL.

Once upon a time, maybe a couple of years ago, lived a family of cockroaches: Betty, the mother, and her three children, Julie, Greg, and Rodger. One day their home burned to the ground, and they found themselves on the streets. Then someone told Betty about a nearby sleazy nightclub called the Starwood where a lot of homeless cockroaches had lately been seeking refuge.

It didn't sound like a very nice place to her but, faced with no other alternative, she and her children made the long, hard, six block journey by foot to The Starwood. They lived happily for a few days, but then Tuesday night came. The kids were in bed early, but around 10:30 Julie got up to use the bathroom and came back running excited.

"Mom! Greg! Rodger! Come see! Come see!" As one, the three jumped to their eighteen collective legs. "Is the place on fire?" Betty cried. "No mom, it's the people out there! They've got funny hair cuts that're green or red or blue and some of them have no hair at all and they're all wearing chains and big boots

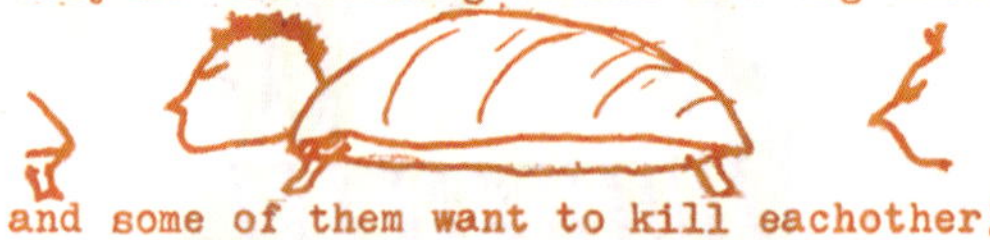

and some of them want to kill eachother! Come see!"

They looked and saw that it was true. "Wow! I'm gonna paint my shell purple like that guys hair!" Exclaimed Rodger.

"Can I put chains and sprikes around my ankles? Mom, please!" Begged Greg.

"Wow, look at all that beer on the floor, I bet we can get real fucked up later on!"

"Don't talk like that!" Cried the mother. Shocked. "Go back to bed. We'll hear no more of such nonsense."

"Bed? With this blairing noise?" Asked Rodger. "It's certainly terrible," said Betty. "Who is this?"

"Black Flag, and they're great!" Said Greg. Betty nearly screamed!

"Black Flag? Thats terrible! Your father died of that! These people are anti-life! Next thing you know, they'll be fumigating!" Dispite the children's protests, they cought a ride out of the club on a patron's pants cuff that very night, getting out at Okidog's ten minutes later. Unfortunatly, the food there was too bad to survive on. So they went to live at the Pondorosa, up the street a few miles, and lived happily ever after and had millions of friends and neighbors. -~~XXX~~ RU

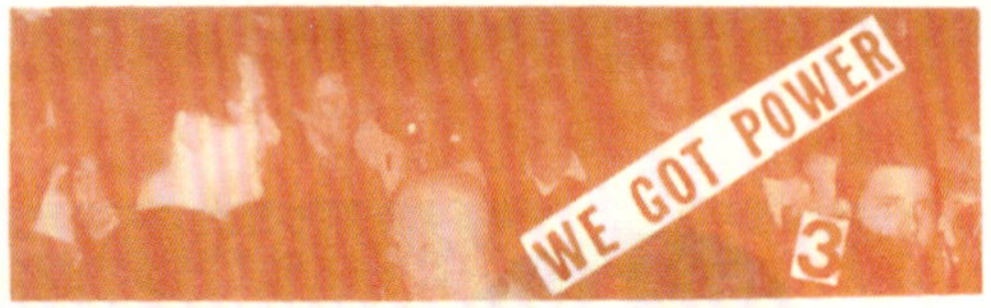
WE GOT POWER
3

WE GOT POWER trys it's best to include most everything we receive. We try to put "something for everyone" in each issue. We cover the bands we see. We use photos that are good and BLACK & WHITE! We print many different views in our editorials, features, reviews, etc. We often let local personalities sound off whenever they get their shit together and write! By no way does anything that it written by these dudes reflect the publishers etc, this is why the person's name is signed after their work. WE GOT POWER anxiously awaits news from your city, your band, your fanzine, your record label etc. Remember there's loads of people to be heard (our mail intake proves this) , so don't expect us to publish your book! (In other words, try to keep it short, to the point!). We have so many fucking people to thank! If we were to start listing names, we would have to fill twenty pages! So, THANKS TO EVERYONE. Thanks for buying and supporting this mag. And now on with the show......

staff

created by: ALAN
published by: JORDAN
edited by: DAVE
writers: RU, JENNIFER, JON, ROB MOSS, ALLISON, ALAN, MIKE, KEITH, etc.
photographers: MOUSE aka ALLISON, PHIL, JORDAN, anyone else...
thanks for help: GREMLIN DISTRIBUTION. LAURA,

NEW ADDRESS!!

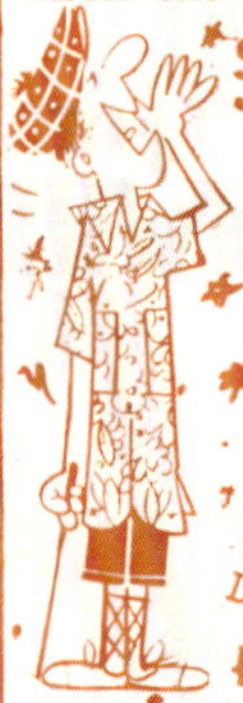

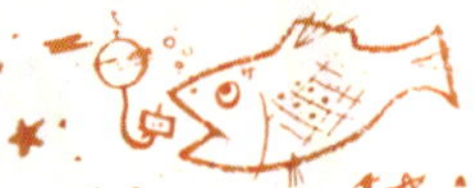

WE GOT POWER
3010 santa monica blvd.
no. 310 santa monica CA
90404

FUCKING GREAT FANZINES:
FLIPSIDE, NOISE, TOUCH & GO, BURP, BACKLASH, LOWEST COMMON DENOMINATOR, BLIND OBEDIENCE, NEGATIVE ARMY, PUNK LUST, ATTACK, SICK TEEN, SLAM, PARANOIA, THE PROLE, STICK TIME, NIGHT VOICES, PHENIS, ARTSY FARTSY, FORCED EXPOSURE,

LETTERZ

Bouncers Are Fucked

Last Thursday me and some of my friends went to the Hollywood Palladium to see TSOL Adolescents Wasted Youth Social Distortion Youth Brigade AKA. Outside news people with cameras and stuff, got in some shots. The Palladium is a cool place for gigs but the fucking bouncers were fucked. You try to go for stage-jumps, you get your ass kicked. Wasted Youth had they mellow for part of their set, Flush The Bouncers klinched the whole thing. Why can't the nonecks just do their jobs. They get carried away and kick people in the face. -HARRY C. BOYLE

Dear Sirs,

I would love to own a copy of WE GOT POWER but I can't seem to find it at my local record store PooBahs. Could you please tell me where I can get it and how much it costs?

-Charlotte

HEY CHARLOTTE: IF YOU CANT FIND EM AT YOUR LOCAL SHOP, ASK 'EM TO OREDER THEM THROUGH OUR ADDRESS. IF YOU WANT TO ORDER WGP THROUGH MAIL, SEND $2. FOR EACH ISSUE. (POSTAGE INCLUDED).

FUCK OFF, SERENA!

This is to you, Serena Dank. I hope you read this. I hope some dumbfuck mother finds this here magazine in her child's bedroom and brings it to one of your Parents Of Punkers meetings. I hope you all sit around and discuss the contents of this magazine.

Ms. Dank you are an ugly lesbian. If only you knew about punkrock teenagers as much as you know about biting tit. No Mag's interview with you absolutly made me furious! (If you can't already tell.) You admitted to being naive at first, but now you rave about Soft Little Finger's, a punk band that has positive messages. Dank you suck!

You said "punks are into self mutilation." Well cuntface where's your fucking degree from John Hopkins? I bet they kicked you out of high school 'cos you were so damn ugly. WHY DOES NATIONAL MEDIA PAY ATTENTION TO DAMN IGNOROIDS LIKE YOU? HOW CAN YOU CLAIM TO HANDLE PUNKS IF YOU DON'T KNOW THE SLIGHTEST THING ABOUT THEM? -JOE

To WE GOT POWER:

Today I saw the Phil Donahue Show with Parents Of Punkers. I feel that punks were not represented right and those on television were interupted by rip-roaring old ladies that still live in 1820. The image of the punk-rocker was that of one who lived for drugs, massive sex, and loved to break laws. Well I hate to dissapoint you, but most punks go to gigs to enjoy the music and have fun. HOW IMORAL IS THAT I ASK? None more that society to ridicule the younger generation for speaking out, well wake up, we're sick of war, corruption and gay polotics. -JEFF (VIOLENT DEEDS).

To We Got Power:

There are two basic differences between the music of today and yesterday. Exploitation. Will modern music's new generation suffer the same fate as yesterday heroes?

LA's scene is for the people - by the people and as long as everyone remembers that fact the music, the clubs, and the bands will not be ruined.

Many of us overlook the advantages of living in Los Angeles in 1982. We can see a few shows a week, while the typical fan waits two years. We also pay reasonable prices for seeing bands and usually quite a few bands at a time. But the most important aspect of todays scene is the people. We do not make our performers into gods (oh, really? -ed.) that are untouchable and unrealistic (it depends!-ed.). Our audiences & performers accept each other equally.

In fact although we do not realize it, alot of us are spoiled. Would any of us go to a concert, pay twenty five dollars to sit in a seat and watch one band play to 200,000 other lost souls? No way.

So when we complain the scene has become mainstream, just remember there is no one above us shoving records down our throats. We buy records because we want to! Everyone puts down punk. Punks are freaks and society's misfits, but are we the stupid fools who stand in line? -ERICA

THERE ARE LINES AT PUNK SHOWS! DID YOU GO TO THE PALLADIUM?!! -ed

KEEP THEM CARDS & LETTERS COMIN', YA hear?

NEWS FROM...

SANTA BARBRA

Tagalong & Ghoul Sisters party w/ Affliction (formerly the Dumps w/ Brad from The Tan). Everyone gets personalized invites no one wants to go. Sorry tuna. Urban Assault change name to Secret Service, fire manager after he gets shot by low-rider. They give the job...to me! WOW. Does anyone wanna book some bigheads??? The Miserables, getting songs together, hope to play someday. Do you guys really know how to play instruments? Pretenders BowWowWow show dont sell out, but people camp out 2 nites for tickets. B-52's to play UCSB gym. Devo cancels. U2 rumored to play whenever. Final decision... everyone in Santa Barbra is a degenerate. -ALAN

MID CITY... L.A.

Lots of news & lots of bands are starting to come out of this portion of the city. The band Why (no they are not Discharge clones). They consist of Nighiest (drums), Mike (bass), Mostafa (guitar). Black rediculous. These guys are a great mixture of aggressive punk & little bit of comedy. Look for this bandin the future. Another band is Stanic (Ex Bloodflow). Other bands in this area are Bad Example, Urban Gorillas, Apathy. -ERNIE

(HEY ERNIE, HOW CAN YOU DO A COLUMN ON MID CITY AND NOT MENTION KRANKSHAFT & LENO & THE M.C.P.'s?-ed)

THE BAY AREA

some more news from

WHIPPING BOY and REBEL TRUTH are going to tour during the summer, they should be making an appearance sometime next month at The Whisky, at least Whipping Boy will. Some people right now saing who the fuck is Whipping Boy?!? Rebel Truth?! Soon the answer will be revealed. They are the newset, hardest, raspiest shit out of the Bay Area (no thanks to those bands from SF that dont mention them). Whipping Boy has got not only a brutal looking band (w/ a guitarist whi is 6'6", 225 lbs, the scariest looking black guy on vocals coupled w/ 2 mild looking characters on drums and bass, btu they play hot & hard. Rebel Truth=scathing. Anyway, now that I've finished beating off about how good they are, I will bid you farewell.

-EUGENE ORGAN

Palm Springs

Mutual Hatred still going strong! Drummer plays a snare only, which they ripped off from a church! Nazi-Punk band from Indio (15 minutes away), called, "Family Butcher", locals hate 'em. Shawn tries out for Target 13, but shines it on. (Guess your not "mod" enough!! -ed). Tribe Of Six disbands. Sin 34 comes to PS and plays... again.

-SEAN

MALCOLM RIVIERA

WASHINGTON D.C.

Let me start with a run down of DC bands and general info on DC records, fanzines, & clubs. GOVERNMENT ISSUE: My favorite local band, & a new line-up since their EP (Dischord #4). John Stabb is still doing vocals & Marc still on drums, new guitarist is Brian Baker (ex bass for Minor Threat), and bass- Tom (from Beaver). Played up in New York w/ Bad Brains at CBGB's a little while ago. Played w/ The Misfits & Necros at 9:30 club... VOID: From Columbia, MD. Been around for a while and finally learned their songs and in the process became incredible. COMMON CAUSE: Brand new band, haven't seen them yet. SOme friends of mine saw them practice & said they were real good... CAPITOL PUNISHMENT: Real young, age & history wise. Fast & raw. I like them alot... FAITH: Getting alot of attention. Featuring Alec MacKaye & ex. SOA... DEADLINE: DC's resident "creepy" band. They don't dress in Halloween fashion, but play slow & creepy. They're also getting alot of attention... DOUBLE O: Ex Yøuth Brigade, Red C, Untouchable members. Sounds a bit like Yøuth Brigade, but Eric (vocals) make a difference, espically live... BLACK MARKET BABY: Great band, sound a bit like English pre-OI. They have a single on Limp Records... IRON CROSS Play English Skinhead OI style, w/ OI views, not my personal favorite. BAD BRAINS: Although they reside in NY, they're a DC band. Their the first band in the world to play fast, this is true. Single - Pay To Cum, also on Jellybeans. Just came out with an album leigth cassette. Incredible... ARTIFICIAL PEACE: My band. So far we've only played the Peppermint Lounge in NY w/ Bad Brains. Pep Lounge ripped us off, they suck... Anyway, the scene here is different from California. Most of us dont take drugs or alcohol, but few do. The number of punks involved is fewer than LA. So we all know each other. No fights but not everyone is friends. Club shows are fairly scarce the only clubs that occasionally have shows are 9:30 & Chancery. Alot of places open up and get shut down by the fire marshall (thrumpted up charges that no club/bar could pass). Like Bad Brain's club, Rhumba/Rumble Club. Most of the time we're playing parties & high schools. We played at a talent show of the high school 3/4 of us graduated from. It was pretty funny, and they even want us back.

I'll be keeping you up to date on what's up to date in your Nations Capitol. If you want to write me or my band, write to Rob Moss, 10301 Dickens ave. Bethesda, MD 20814. -ROB

HOUSTON SPRING 1982

Appearing at U. of H. Cullen Auditoreum, the Plasmatics displayed there shock rock antics. U2 played at Cardis Rock Club. In the red light district gay Disco Numbers held a rare live concert of Siouxie and the Banshees. Alley Rock Club is now advertising themselves as Z street. New Wave disco. HATES performed on 3-15-82 at the Caribana. Weeks earlier HATES were on local television. Anti Nowhere League U.K. Subs on 3-26-82 played at the Island. They were more heavy metal than punk. -Christian Arnheiter

PHENOIX, ARIZONA

AKA - PHENIS

Well, Mad Gardens closed. The muscle dick owner had too many bouncers being dicks, the cops found it a good spot for a hassle and the "redecorating" inside made it useless for shows. Saccharine Trust, the Plebs, & the Minutemen played the last show there. Minutemen ripped. The scene is saved by the opening of the Salty Dog, a by-the-bands-for-the-bands kind of club. Some great shows there recently. Conflict, a really hot hardcore band from Tuscon, gained somePhx respect there recently. A new Phx HC band, Soylent Green have also gotten some new fans there. SG is now going through personnel problems. They threw out the physco guitarist. 45 Grave played two nights to a small crowd, I thought the place would be packed. Other shows- Seldoms from Tuscon semi psychadelic real original. Green On Red very drunk PRANC folk music for punks- cool. Couple of JFA shows. Crowds have been thin but the place is the best! Grant And The Geezers (Rockabilly), JFA, & Soylent Green went to Tuscon with a small army of skins to cause a riot, get rude w/ Tuscon girls & skate. Tuscon sucks, no scene just good bands - Seldoms & Conflict. Oh yeah, Bad Brains play the Dog & shocked the Phxpunx, what a great band. Meat Puppets played too. MP are the best, never a bad show ever. WRITE PHENIS FANZINE AT: 1347 W. 10th PL. TEMPE, AZ. 85281

ORANGE-TUSTIN - EAST Santa Ana

There are some damn good bands here.... Convicted, mainly from Tustin, plays an energetic tight sounding set. The lead singer sounds like Jack TSOL, check 'em out at Dungeon or Ritz. Lost Cause, from Orange County w/ a single out, are doing well. They do a good pipeline but mostly do intense punk... Human Restraint is another one of these upcoming bands to watch for. They have alot of influonces but play a sound of their own. Max & Mary have had some great late night parties in their room at the Fireside Hotel, complete with punk graffetti on the wall and the "best" SOUNDING THRASH punk band, Saigon, from Tustin... excellent songs like "Anti-Vouge". Get their single "Anihilation" it's fuckin' hot. Todd Hall (lead singer) gots a voice that wont quit ...Free outdoor gigs on the weekends now in Orange at Heart Park. This is for legalization of marajuana campaign. Hippy and punk bands. Lost Cause played a few times. The latest club here is the Dungeon which opened in March, since the pigs closed the T.S.O.L. show at old Broadway Theater. The Dungeon is at Main & Bradway upstairs with lotsa room and parking. Even the pigs leave the place alone usually. Bands that have played here include Social Distortion Ch. 3, Saigon, Legal Weapon, Super Heroins, etc. This cheezy pad only cost 3 bucks for 4 to 5 decent bands.

Oh ya, there's also a christian punk band that plays around here alot called Lifesavers, you can always hear them on Rodney.

That's too much for now. Punks alive and kicking in Orange and Tustin so come out and see us, there is always room for a few more good ones! JASON V.

WE Got POWER's "BEST BAND NAMES OF THE MONTH:"

HAROLD, LITTLE RICKYS, SWOLEN MONKEYS, PARTY BOYS, DUCK BRIGADE, STUPID DISCO, MORAL DECAY, FRIED ABORTIONS, DAY-GLO ABORTIONS, QUEER PILLS, CARREERGIRLS, WARM BEER, BEERGUTS, BORED YOUTH, ADAM 12, ½JAPANEESE, KILLER PUSSY, BILLSPURM, THE DAPS, 100 PUNKS, MY 3 SONS, RIBSY, WHIPPING BOY, DEAD GRANDPA, BIG BOYS, Mc DONALDS 7 SECONDS, HUSKER DU, AK47, SECTION 8, CIVIL DISMAY, SOCIAL DISMAY, DISMAYED TODAY, DISARRAED YOUTH, PLASTIC MAN, THE PLIMWHIPES, BLUEGEIODIONED PIGIONS, LEZ MISERABLES, RUDIMENTARY PENI, DISCKAKA, EVEN WORSE, MEATMEN, MINUTEMEN, 4 GARCIA's, DICKS, RED DESCENDING SOCIAL YOUTH ARMY, REAGEN YOUTH

DOA

Don't Eat Yello snow

)OA were interviewed in their van
›utside Devonshire Downs 4-17-82
›efore they were to play...

Chuck: Alright, this is DOA interview, take two! (The first tape broke, and we had to start over.) My name is Chuck Biscuits.

RON :My name is Ron, Alan.

Joey: Im Joe Shithead, Im the straight man of the bunch.

Ron: We've been cooped up together a little bit too long on this tour!...

Dave: This is Dave talkin' at ya...

Joey: It's okay being in this van, but being cooped up with Dimwit, that's the problem!

Dimwit: I was kicked out of my last band

Joey: Dimwit used to be in a band called Primate Stool.

Dimwit: Lets give the readers some useful info... if your ever in Canada, dont eat yello snow.

Joey: People have this misconception about Canadians being a bunch of ignorant louts... (laughter)

Dave: Actually, a bunch of ignorant louts who cut wood and fuck beavers.

Dimwit: ...Louts who collect welfare and sit on our butts.

Anyways, we're down here in L.A. to record for a compolation...

Joey: Clem from ICI is puttin' together. (Talk goes on about future and past record deals...) Thats been a problem all along, being from an obscure place like Vancouver...gettin' stuff distributed.

WGP: Ya, they dont have mail out where you live. (laughter etc.)

Joey: Dogsleads take it out pretty regulary, but sometimes...

Dave: ...it falls in the ice sometimes!

WGP: So what goes on in Canada with DOA?

Joey: We played a few times. A couple hall gigs, basically we've sorta slowed down, we haven't done too much because we got a new bass player.

Dimwit: We've got a problem with drunk indians! They're really mean. They hang out at a place called The Windmill. They made it a real drag to be there.

WGP: On the back inside label on Hardcore '81 (LP) that picture of all those people jumpin' around...

Joey: That picture was taken at a gig called "Hardcore '81" before the album came out last Febuary. In Canada. (Talk goes on about Vancouver bands etc.) and (L.A. gigs, touring US, Canada's scene)

WGP: Do you guys cause alot of problems, controversy in Vancouver?

Joey: Off and on. Basically it's the same thing as, say, Black Flag and bands down here... Tryin' to find gigs and it is just impossible.

WGP: In Canada, what's the differnce betwen the laws, hanging out, and shit.

DAVE: Basically it's the same as here.

Joey: Your intitled to get your rights read down here, that stuff never existed in Canada. Now we have a new constitution. (Talk goes on about polotics etc.)

Joey Shithead ↑
DAVE GREG →
D.O.A. live at CSUN-Devonshire.

Joey:I ended up getting real thumped one time. Fuckin throttled and kicked in the head. Woke up back of the police van, caughing up blood... I actually got on t.v., being interviewed, this fuckin' stupid woman. Police brutality. I said, "well let me show you the bruises" so I go like this, (lifts up his shirt) and this big roll of fat & the bruises. (laughter..)

Dimwit:I remember seein' that on t.v. I had a black & white set you couldn't see your bruises, you saw a big roll of flab hanging out over the edge of your pants!

Dave: When we through that Hardcore '81 Gig, the cops clued into that Black Flag was comin' up here. Our police phoned down to the Huntington Beach Police and asked, "What should we do about this..."

Joey: They actually went out and rented an office across the street from the hall, took film, videio film of everyone goin' in. Dave:Every cop in Vancouver knew what was happening! -JORDAN & RU

J.F.A

DESERT SKATE RATS

Jody Fosters Army was interviewed at Dennys by Mouse & Chryl. Also present were Rodney B. & Posh Boy & Ru.

WGP: And your names are? Bam: Bam-Bam, I play drums. WGP: And you're Brian, you sing, right? Brian: Ah ya. Don: And Im Don, I play guitar. Mike: And Im Mike, I play bass. WGP: All right you guys, attention!! When did you first come out here? Mike: The first time? WGP: No, before your last LA gig (w/ Bad Brains). Mike: About 30 minutes before we were suppose to play. WGP: Oh no! All the way from Phoenix? Don: We blew out a tire. Brian: And we took alot of drugs. Don: The forbidden zone. WGP: The what? Don: 300 miles of desert. Bam: Ha ha ha! WGP: How long have you all been together? Mike: 19 days after Reagan was shot. WGP: What are your inflounces? Don:TSOL old Germs. Bam: Wasted Youth. Don: The Adolescents. Mike: I like funk. Bam: Ya funkadelic's great! JFA: We like the Meat Puppets, they're great! Bam: We like skateboarding. (Talk goes on about skateboarding.) WGP: How did you get your name, "Jody Foster's Army"? Brian: The guy who shot Reagan said he loved Jody Foster. Mike: Don't ask him, he doesn't know anything. Brian: Our band was named something different, but we won't tell you! Bam: No, no! Don: Jody Foster's Army was a song in our set. We just evolved into JFA. WGP: What about the real Jody Foster? Don: Ya if she sues us she'll get 4 skateboards & a borrowed amp. Rodney: The REAL Jody Foster was suppose to be here, BUT.... WGP: Met any interesting groupies yet? Bam: Not one groupie. Don: Your not a band untill you get girls. WGP: What does your mother think of all this? I mean your 15 years-old, your driving off changing states. Mike: Bam Bam was grounded. Don: His mother doesn't believe he's in a band, she thinks he's making it up so he can get out at nite. WGP: Have you been to Okidogs yet? Danny: (JFA Roadie) Ya, we had an okidog and we thought they were great! Everyone said we would hate them! WGP: Whats the scene like in Phoenix? Don: Like here, but smaller. Mostly skaters. WGP: Any good clubs? MIKE: The salty dog. Bam: A lot of hippies! WGP: Is there anything else you want to say? Don: Skate or go home! Bam: But not today, hippy! (Then we all left and went skateboarding. The end. -MOUSE aka ALISON McMOUSE

The Misfits were interviewed at Rachel's house after their April 13 Whiskey show. Dave, Ru and Jordan talked mostly with singer Glenn Danzig. Doyle (guitar) and Googey (drums) were also present at times.

Dave: I wanted to ask the bass player why he smashed up his bass onstage, but he's not here.

Glenn: Because he's fucking cool. He said it didn't work, so he fucked it up.

Ru: Can you compare the New York scene to the way it is here, like with the cops, etc.?

Glenn: Cops are cool in New York. They know that they got better things to do than be bothering little kids. They're assholes here! And the kids would crack a few heads if they knew what was good for them. They should just take the cops and beat the shit out of them. If the cops got guns, they should get guns. Because it's ridiculous here. It's more than just harassment. You should take the cops out and shoot 'em around here.

Jordan: Is there a good scene in New York?

Glenn: Now there is. It died for a while 'cause people were watering it down with faggy disco new wave shit.

Dave: What L.A. bands do you like?

Glenn: Black Flag.

Ru: That's it? That's all that appeals to you!

Glenn: That's it. Black Flag.

Jordan: What kind of people go to your gigs---like, are they punks, or paying customers, or..

Glenn: 'Punks'?? What do you mean, "are they punks?"???

Ru: Uh, Glenn...try to lower yourself to our level, please.

Dave: Yeah...we're kinda stupid.

Glenn: Well, do you mean trendy mohawk people, or people in leather jackets, or skins? We got everything. L.A. isn't the only place with people who're into punk music. That's another thing I don't like about L.A., they think they got the market cornered on punk. We had a thousand people at our last New York show.

Ru: Is Washington D.C. happening?

Glenn: No. Not anymore. Maybe now that Minor Threat's back together it will be--when they broke up, the D.C. scene sorta fizzled. It was real good. But the Midwest scene's the best. Better than L.A. or New York. Detroit, especially.

Jordan: So when are you coming back to LA?

Glenn: In June or July.

Ru: Have you ever played in L.A. before?

Glenn: No. They wouldn't let us last time. We played at the Nest, and a couple gigs in Frisco in November. We tried to get some dates in LA but they told us we were too violent, too loud, too fast, and there'd be lots of fights. Slash got us the show at the Whiskey--that's the only reason we got it, because of Slash.

Googey: (entering room) So, like, what kind of magazine is this?

Dave: A really good fanzine.

Glenn: Tell your readers to send us all their skulls. Any skulls you got. We collect 'em. If your baby brother dies, just cut off his head and send it to us. I collect horror movies, too, shit like that...horror posters. I like blood.

Dave: What about your name, "The Misfits"? Do you think that fits in with the skulls and all?

Glenn: I think it's a great name. I don't care if it fits in or not. What do I care? If you don't like it, don't come see us. Don't buy our records. What do we care? But you will, 'cause you'll love us.

Dave: Tell us about the Fiend Club.

Glenn: It's a fan club. It's basically so we can get feedback from our fans, and we send 'em free shit. Whenever new buttons or pictures come out, we mail 'em out free. They can order t-shirts through us for five dollars instead of ten. Print our new address:

MISFITS FIEND CLUB
P.O. BOX 3112
GRAND CENTRAL STATION, N.Y.
N.Y., 10163

Dave: What's the radio scene like in New York? Do you get much airplay?

Glenn: Yeah. Timmy Summers has a hardcore show, he always play us. There's the New Afternoon show on right before that on Wednesdays.

Ru: What other N.Y. bands get airplay?

Glenn: He plays a lot of British stuff lately, but some good N.Y. bands are Reagan Youth and Kraut. That's about it. The Beastie Boys were good, but they broke up. I don't like N.Y. bands that say, "American music sucks. The British are more emotional, more into what they're doing." I hate British bands. There's more talent in one acre of America than there is in all of fucking Britain.

Dave: It's kinda ironic, how the LA Oi scene really seems to like you guys a lot, and you're definitely American. They hate every LA band.

Glenn: Do they like Black Flag?

Ru: They despise Black Flag.

Googey: They're assholes then. Besides us, Black Flag's the best band in Ameriaa.

Glenn: Oi is alright. It's just like everybody singing along and shit. I'm into singalongs. Besides me having a good time onstage, I want ather people to have a good time, too. --RU

Interview with Saigon in the parking lot of Stone Fox during the NoMag party 3/26/82 by Alison and Jordan. Eddy-bass. Todd-vocals. Adam-drums. jess-guitar.

WGP: When did your 45 come out? Todd: June '81. Jess: We produced it with our own money. Todd: We lost all out jobs. WGP: And got kicked out of your houses, right? How did you get money for your 45? Jess: I once had a good job but Reagen screwed me over. Adam: Im a pump jockey. WGP: How long have you been together? Todd: Almost a year. All of us were in other bands, we used to be hippies. (Ya, ya -ed.) Todd: Actually we're serious musicians. WGP: How long have you been playing drums? Adam: Seven years. I also play with Legal Weapon. Charly joined the army. WGP: What were you into before punk? Todd: Iggy, heavily, and surfing. WGP: Do you still surf? Todd: Nope. Jess: I had curly long hair and a beard. Eddy: I had hair to my knees at a continuation school. WGP: What are your favorite places to eat? Todd: Jack In The Box. WGP: How did you name your band? Todd: We live in Japville. Adam: A place that doesn't exist anymore. WGP: How does it feel to play a place and everyone get in free? (tonite) Todd: Everyone we promised that would get in free and didn't come, tough shit if you didn't come. Eddy: There's a gig in my pants. WGP: Where are you from? Todd: Tustin. WGP: In your opinion, what would be a good gig? Todd: Saccharine Trust, Legal Weapon, & Saigon. Adam: We'd like to play in New York with the Bad Brains.

channel 3 CERRITOS SUBURBIA

Kim; guitar, Mike; guitar & vocals, Larry; bass, Mike; drums

WGP: You have an album out, don't you? Kim: We have an EP on Posh Boy... Mike: The album comes out April 15. WGP: Got any big plans or anything? Kim: We're playing Florintine Gardens w/ The Professionals on April 30. Mike: It will be great to play with members of The Sex Pistols. WGP: How long have you been together? Kim: Two years. WGP: Where are you all from? Band: Cerritos. Kim: Suburbia. WGP: Whats is Cerritos to do? Larry: Drink. WGP: You've been together two years, why did you wait to put out vynil? Mike: We were still playing the garage when Posh Boy heard us. Kim: We made a demo tape. He got a hold of us, we didn't even know who Posh Boy was! We played a couple parties you know we never played any clubs. It was funny, we just sent in a tape and he liked it. Mike: Robby's cool. He helps out alot of bands. WGP: Are you going to go on tour soon? WGP: Frisco? Kim: The country. We're playing May 1st in Vegas. We are playing the 7 & 8 in Phoenix. Mike: Ya in Vegas we are going to jump over the fountains at Ceaser's Palace, in our van! WGP: How did it feel to sell out at the Whisky? Mike: We had high hopes because there were two shows that night. We sold out at 9:00, it was great! Kim: When they found out we sold out they tore up the guest list and my sister could'nt get in. Larry: I heard they do that at The Whisky. Kim: Hopefully we'll play the Whisky again next month with The Bags. (Talk goes on about clubs like The Godzilla Club.) Hello The Godzilla Club! Mike: We got arrested after we finished playing at Godzillas. The cops arrested us and said we were drunk in public, but we weren't. They took us down to the station and didn't even print us or anything, and then they let us go. (Kim returns to announce they have to play.) -ALISON McMOUSE

LIVE LA HARD CORE 82!

↑ merrill overkill reads his favorite mag! P.S: he is not in Ⓐ anymore!

LACK FLAG, ADOLESCENTS, CH3, OVERKILL
OLETA VAL. COMMUNITY CTR. S.B. MAR. 5

We actually got there on time! verkill played first, and were the ost interesting band of the evening. errill was in top form, tearing off is KISS shirt in mid-set to reveal, ANOTHER ANIMAL" scrawled across his nest. The crowd, mostly hardcore, of orse, didn't seem to understand the eavy metal music but they tried slam-ing anyway. CH3 went on next. I missed ost of their set but from what I saw he crowd enjoyed them and they played ell. The newly reformed Adolescents ere competant but not overly thrill-ng. They did a fairly tight run hrough of the same old tunes at an asy-listening volume level. It was as uch fun as listening to the album, and as reportedly better than the Pallad-um show. Since I sat on the edge of he stage for the headlining thriller, lack Flag, I couldn't hear much but istortion. I could tell they weren't ll that tight and were somewhat out of une at times. Of course no one noticed r cared- the crowd loved them, clam -red for an encore, which they received. ll of the Descendents played drums, xcept for the encore with rumored fu-ure drummer Emil. They both did well. ersonally I thought the high point of f the show was Dave and Mugger singing ackup vocals on "TV Party". I was dis-ppointed that they didn't do "Louie ouie" so I could watch my hero, Dez adena sing. Oh well. -RU

GODZILLA'S reviews

1-30-82 WASTED YOUTH, CH3, ABANDONED, and WHY NUT.

Why Nut, another new band, were a pleasent surprise... 3 peice - good material. Abandoned capitolized on the Adolescents w/ Tony X-Adole singing & doing "Wrecking Crew" & "House Of The Rising Sun". DULL. CH3 were introduced as "the powerful Channel Three, and they are. Wasted Youth headlined with Scranny's fake blood- passed it off as if someone kicked him in the face. After all, this is Hollywood.

FRI FEB 12: BAD RELIGION, CHRISTIAN DEATH, CRUCIFIX.

No one was here tonite. Crucifix were okay, typical-sounding complete with Darby vocals. C.D. did faster stuff 'cos they be playin' a punk club. We left.

SAT FEB 13: CH3, SHATTERED FAITH, NO CRISIS

Attendence picked up, the place wuz packed. No Crisis ripped the stage apart! Definatly one of the more happening bands around these days. Shattered Faith were stupid. I've always disliked them, but tonite they were even worse →One of the more tedious bands around! CH3 were the best I've seen 'em. DAVE

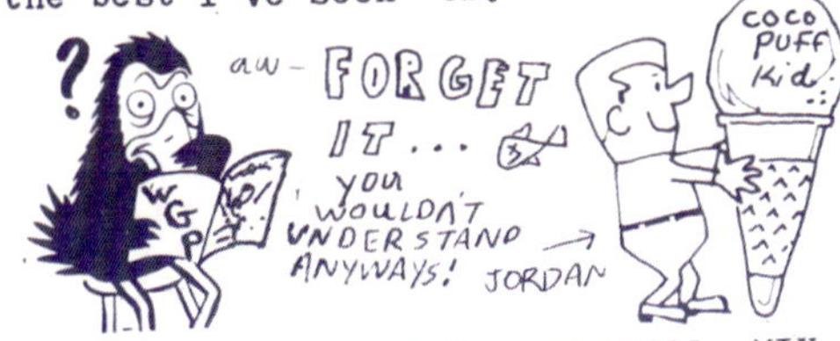

2-19-82 ANGRY SAMOANS, OVERKILL, MINUTEMEN, ANTI, ARYAN DISGRACE.

Aryan D. started & a little more practing and songs couldn't hurt. Missed Anti cuz I was talking to Red Cross. Minutemen were very good, best live band I've seen in a while. Even got Chuck Dukowski slamming. Overkill, heavy metal with punkrock connotations (or maybe the other way around) were loud! Angry Samoans were really great, thanx to Frank who had enough balls to book them. They dedicated Get Off The Air to "that Faggot New Wave D J and all the LA bands that suck up to him". -JORDAN

MAU MAUS, RED CROSS, SIN 34, SEDITONARIES, & MORAL DEKAY FEB. 20

Moral Dekay were real good! They've got an OI singer. Seditonaries are new romantic fags, they played for too long & were slow. Sin 34 were good, played new songs and got cut off. Red Cross got cut after 10 minutes! But they kept on playing. We went home, 'cos my ride left.
-MIKE NOT ROTH

DID THE MERIC SYSTEM TAKE OVER YET

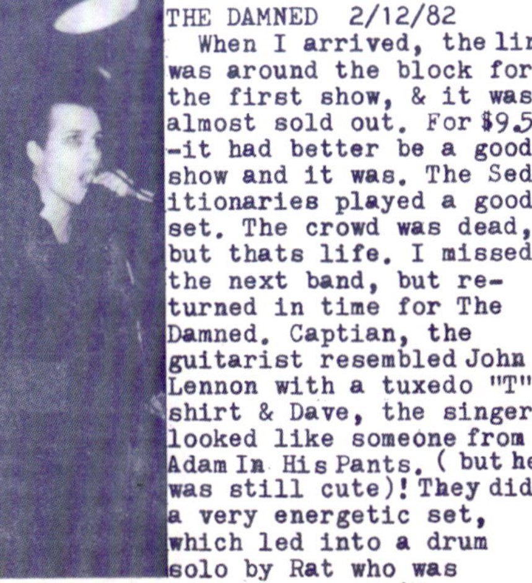

THE DAMNED 2/12/82

When I arrived, the line was around the block for the first show, & it was almost sold out. For $9.50 -it had better be a good show and it was. The Seditionaries played a good set. The crowd was dead, but thats life. I missed the next band, but returned in time for The Damned. Captian, the guitarist resembled John Lennon with a tuxedo "T" shirt & Dave, the singer, looked like someone from Adam In His Pants. (but he was still cute)! They did a very energetic set, which led into a drum solo by Rat who was Excellent. It was well worth the cover charge. -MOUSE

WE DON'T NEED THE ENGLISH, DO WE NOW?

FRIDAY MARCH 19 MAU MAU'S, CH3, MINUTEMEN, CAUSTIC CAUSE.

Little did we know this was to the the last show ever to take place in the infamous Godzilla. Even although it was run shitty, usually dull and a rip off (coustemers & bands), we all spent every weekend there for four months! I guess I'll miss it. The best thing about it was I never paid to get in. Too many bad memories of everyone getting arrested and harrased by the pigs. Maybe I won't miss it. ANYHOW, Caustic Cause were unusual... punkrock w/ sax and doin' covers like Peter Gun. Minutemen were, as usual, highly enjoyable. Music for everyone. They slammed to 'em. (can this mean their getting BIG?) And the older people (like Chuck Dukowski) bobbed they heads & waved their arms! WEEE! CH3 were good, although I've seen them better. I think CH3 played this club once too many times, as did alot of other bands. Mau Mau's are definatly ready to record and become BIG, if they stay together this time! But, well, we knew the time was comin' for Godzillas to close. No one was surprised and no one cared. BUT there's no where to go. Well, back to "the underground". DAVE

SUBHUMANS, SOCIAL D, YOUTH BRIGADE, SACCHARINE TRUST - Contempo Hall May 1st

Saccharine did their last gig in LA for a while cuz their goin' on tour. They were happenin', Merrill came up to sing back-ups on "Human Certanty". Youth B came up next and people started slammin' YB did a song called Violence just after a drunken Mike Ness was punched by one of the Minutemen. After a while Social Distortion came on. Lotsa slammin' and shot. Mike Ness was more intoxicated than usual but still managed to do pretty good but they took too long betewwn songs. I guess alot of people left after SD, but they missed Canada's Subhumans who were real cool. They made a good first impression, and I'd like to hear their record before I see them the next time. -JORDAN

DESCENDENTS, Anti, Resistance, Hari Kari, at the Dancing Waters.

Dancing Waters is too hip, there's this funky water fall that runs behind the stage. Hari Kari warmed up and they were really energetic and fun to watch. Resistance came on next and did a bunch of covers. Anti played hardcore punkrock. They were pretty cool, Snickers of the Stains slammed and did cartwheels during their set. The Descendents played a whole bunch of cool tunes. Everybody should check out the South Bay scene, they have lots of gigs on Wednesday, Thursday, and Sat.night.

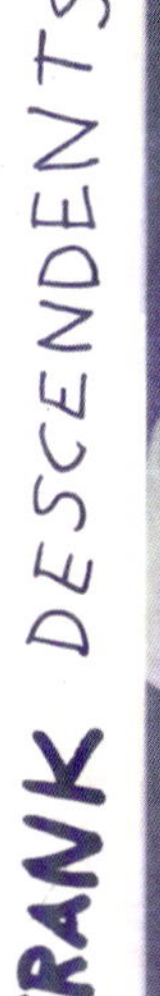

MORE LIVE 'CORE:

REVIEW FROM WASHINGTON D.C. ...
Feb. 28, 9:30 CLUB. MISFITS, NECROS, & GOVERNMENT ISSUE.

The Misfits, definatly a visual band. i Like the Bullet EP & their soundcheck was great, but when they went on, they had too much distortion and volume than this place could handle. Raw is one thing, inaudible is another. The Misfits are "Horror"core, but not like alot of the "horror" bands that come off like Casper The Friendly Ghost. the Misfits are more like the Groovy Ghoulies (on Sabrena The Teen Age Witch) gone hard core. They're definatly not wimpy. NECROS were great. Fast & extreemly tight. Their EP is really good, but live is when they're at their best. They're the best band in the mid-west, and can hold their own with any DC or California band. Government Issue did a great set. John Stabb's electric green suit had to definatly be seen. Their new songs are incredible. They just recorded last week for the Bad Brains Compolation. GOV. ISSUE has a totally different sound than that recorded on their ep. now that the ep's isnt good, They are just a little more complex. -ROB MOSS

GET SERIOUS

THE LAST & SACCHARINE TRUST plus others at The Barn, April 1st

I didn't catch the opening bands, saw part of Mood Of Defiance. They were okay lotsa noise and screaming, screachy vocals from Rachel, she was backed that night by Anti from Hawthorne or is it El Segundo? Next up were Saccharine Trust who are a great band, haven't heard their record yet but it has to be great (notice how I use the word great twice cause this band is - great!) I didnt watch as I was at the bar with Mr. Watt from the Minutemen getting shitfaced. The band sounded fantastic and hope to see these guys more often. Last but not least were The Last and man are these guys the coolest. Joe Nolte is easily one of the best front men in Los Angeles, California, United States or in the world. If you ever want to see a band that is totally into their music onstage this is the group to see. They play very aggressive heavy pop type of music, never lightweight. They very seldom get on bills like this but the next time they do GO SEE THEM!! You wont be dissapointed.-KEITH MORRIS

BAD BRAINS, BAD RELIGION, LEWD, JFA...
UKRAINIAN CULTURE CTR. MARCH 12

Jody Foster's Army (JFA), were pretty fun. The Lewd sounded good, great music to read Flipside by (Al gave me one for free!)Directly after SF's - Lewd, the infamous LAPD busted in and discharged lots of kids & maced them. Luckily the show went on, 'cos I've been dieing to see the Bad Brains! Bad Religion went on and . . . .Anyhow, Bad Brains were the best live band I've seen, EVER! REALLY! Henry Rollins (or is it Garfield?) sung on Pay To Cum and it was FUCKING GREAT! The crowd loved all their material, even the reggea stuff! - MM

BAD BRAINS & BLACK FLAG!! -WHISKY 3/25

Everything I want to say about the Bad Brains was said in the above review! After their set, SURPRISE, Black Flag took to the stage! Yes, thee band who'se been BANNED from this club for more than a year is playing! THE KIDS WENT NUTS and they did Rise Above and everyone got to sing! FUN! DAVE

T.S.O.L., D.O.A., SIN34, PUBLIC NUISANCE, DEVONSHIRE DOWNS 4/17/82

I arrived in time to see Sin 34. They seem to be getting better and Mike Geek didn't break any strings. D.O.A. Put on a great show, they played a real tight set. T.S.O.L. was too boring to watch. I don't like their new style,(whatever you want to call it). The hall was filled with a bunch of lame anarchy punkers diving off the stage and skanking. That's the last hall gig I'll ever go to! They cost too much and the sound sucks. -JENNIFER

The Last Tribute To Godzilla's

RIP GODZILLAS (DEC. '81 - Mar. '82
LA's last hardcore only nightclub is no more. Do you miss it?

YES ☐
NO ☐

No CRISIS

No Crisis were interviewed at the Pondo in Hollywood, their home.
Dave: My name is Dave, I play guitar.
Kurt: Kurt Mosher. And I sing.
Ian: I'm Johnny. And I play bass!
WGP: Okay, you can sit in for Johnny.
Kurt: We have another guy in the band named Mark, he plays guitar also.
WGP: Don't you have a drummer?
Kurt: Yeah, a bunch of 'em. WGP:So what are you going to do about a record?
Kurt: We have a couple tunes we recorded in December at Perspective w/ Tom Wilson. We're gonna do a couple more and put 'em an a 12" ep. We did a couple tunes for Roger Rogerson's comp album that's gonna have Secret Hate, The Crewd; from Long Beach, Circle Jerks, and No Crisis.
WGP: What are your musical inflounces?
Dave: (from bed) Heavy metal!!
WGP:Balls out metal? Dave:Yeah, exactly. Balls Out Metal, Black Sabbath, early guitar stuff. Kurt:I like hard punk & country and western. And Elvis. I like Stiff Little Fingers and Sham 69 best.
Dave: Johnny likes Kiss and The Ramones.
Kurt: Mark likes The Cure...Ask us our sexual prefernces. WGP:What are your sexual preferences? Kurt: We are strictly heterosexual.. In and out, a little wham-bam. Ian:Cleaning the yard!
Dave: Mine's John Holmes, he influenced me to have a big dick.
WGP: What are your favorite LA bands?
Kurt: The Dickies and... what's the other band I like? Ian:Youth Brigade?
Kurt: We hate the Youth Brigade. I wanna say something, you know the BYO? It's a communist plot. Join the club, pay your dues, and they'll let you hang out. Their big line is, "Yeah, we wanna help the scene, we wanna put on shows", but all they wanna do is get rich...
WGP:Do you like to fight?
Kurt: I don't like to. I will if I have to. I beat up Mike Muir. I beat up quite a few people. (At long last, Johnny and Mark arrive) Johnny:Anyone wanna get high?
WGP: Tell us the No Crisis story...
Kurt: Here's the story. Johnny lived in New York and he bought a Ramones record, and he thinks, fuck! I could do that! But what am I doing in New York, these guys were already there. I think I'll move to Hollywood and corner the market.
WGP: Yeah, start a scene there...
Kurt: So he took the bus out to Hollywood and found this guy and said, "hey, hey, I'm gonna teach you how to plam drums! So he got a couple tin cans, a couple pencils, and all of a sudden...
Johnny: BLAM! There was the scene!
WGP: Do you guys consider yourself a hardcore punk band? Kurt:I consider myself hardcore. I condiser it hardcore. I don't know about the rest of 'em...
Johnny: He's about as hardcore as you get
WGP: Alot of bands are getting "Anti-Punker". Are you anti-punker?
Johnny: No. The music of the band is punk rock. That's exactly it. WGP:Some bands deny playing punkrock, they tell you their just playing "their music".
Johnny: That's the problem with punk, it's so distorted. (Talk goes on about how everyone has their own ideas what the scene should be like, etc. etc.)
Kurt: Are you gonna ask us if we have a mascot? WGP:Well.. Kurt:His name is Eugene. Affectionatly known as Hagi Denagi
WGP:What do you do for a living?
Kurt:Im a tile setter. I work with Frank of Godzillas...Godzillas was my brainchild (Talk goes on about cockroaches etc.)
WGP: Johnny, you've been in the scene a long time. Do you think it's dying?
Johnny: No. WGP:Didn't you say punk will be around until 1990? Johnny: Yes. There's a great similarity between it & the 60's thing. A cult scene building up. There's more and more people gettin into it each day. It'll go until 1990 and then there may be a need for a change as far as each individual is concerned. It all depends how you handle yourself. The way alot of people are going nowadays in a few years alot of 'em won't have their brains. I think life nowadays is stamina and pride in yourself, being able to stand up and say "no" or "I don't need that". Individuality. That was the whole punk movement anyways, just stand up for yourself...
WGP: Any final comments?...
Johnny: No Crisis. Fuck everything else.
Kurt: I'd like to say hello to the Wayward Caines. -RU & JORDAN

HATES TEXAS

WGP: When did you start playing? HATES: Since 1978. WGP: Are you all the original members? HATES: No. HATES currently consist of Paul Minot/bass, Lawrence Baker/drums, and Christian Arnheiter/guitar and vocals. WGP: Does your name have significance to your music? HATES: Yes. The name of our band describes the tone of the music. HATES is to be used as a verb. We are HATES, not THE HATES. WGP: Do you have any touring plans? HATES: Not at the moment, but if the opportunity arises, yes. WGP: When did you record your EP? HATES: The first EP was recorded in spring of '79. We did it in three hours! WGP: How well did the record do? HATES: It was number one on a radio record chart in California. WGP: Do you have any future recording plans? Are you going to do a album? HATES: As soon as possible we want to make at least a 4 song EP featuring "What Am I LIving For" & "Punk 1301". WGP: Whats the scene like in Texas? HATES: Texas isn't the most ideal place to play, but it is growing! The rock clubs give into such touring acts as Iggy Pop, Ramones, Siouxie, etc. WGP: What are the Texas police like? HATES: I can't really describe the Texas police because there aren't that many punk concerts to draw a conclusion from. Bouncers have been a problem. In the past. WGP: What are your favorite bands? HATES: We mostly listen to British bands. WGP: What are your stands on drugs? sex? liquor? HATES: I don't believe in telling other people how to live. WGP: What is the basic phylosophy of HATES? HATES: HATES music is based on a depiction of the social and darker side of life by presenting it in a hardcore minimalistic form. -INTERVIEW BY ALAN PAUL

HATES 4200 W34th Box 132
Huston, Texas 77092.

Q. WHY DID THE PUNKER CROSS THE ROAD??

...he didn't care if he lived or died.
...Darby was on the other side.
...Because the cops were at Oki's.
...Because he was safety pinned to the chicken.
...Because DEVOwas playing.
...Because it was the latest thing from England.
...He wanted to get on the guest list.
...To beat up the old lady on the other side.
...To piss on a front lawn
...Because he was ditching school
...Because their was a dime on the sidewalk.
...Because he's been in the scene since '77
...Because they were giving away free beer
...So he could disrupt the parade

S C A M

Ever wonder how come people seem to scam so easily on members of the opposite sex, while others go for weeks trying, unsuccessfully, to get laid? WE GOT POWER, recognizing the enormity of this social problem, has sent in investigatory reporters disguised as harmless observers in an effort to see how it's really done. What we have came up with are an amazing collection of facts, myths, d dont's, and insights about the greatest of all co-ed sports, SCAMMING. Our o vati will be printed over the space of several ssues in a monthly column. Thi sue will cover: "OPENING LINES" . . .

One of the most important tors in any sc ttempt is definatly the come o proach. Opening lines shou display style, inality and taste. For example, we'll take a look at a favorite lines used by some local well-known personalities. -GREG HETSON's ev popular, "Hey baby, what's your sign?" Subtle, yet darling. -DANNY SPIRA's "Come on over to the love palace." Romantic and intriguing, definatly a lady's man approach. -MUGGER's well known (and much used) collection of such graceful phrasings as "Hey baby, lets get it happening."... "How about a blow-job?" and "Fuck me, I know you want it!" The straight forward approach - quick & to the point, it's a surefire winner.

Of corse, you could resort to such familiar stand-bys as, "Do you come here often?" or "Excuse me, but I couldn't help but noticing your lovely spiked bracelet, where did you get it?" but we fell such approaches are trite, and should be avoided. One of the scene's top scammers, who requested not to be identified, was interviewed by WGP at Godzillas and told us, "It's an ego thing, really. I tell a gal she's pretty or say how smart she is and she'll fuck me for making her feel good about herself." Another point to ponder, kiddies!

After the all-important opening line you must, of course, try judge whether or not it went over well, but if you can't do it for yourself you've got serious problems. Well, we're running out of space, so we'll have to continue this next issue. If you have anything on SCAMMING, send it into us. -RU & MIDGE

FAST-ITY

NEW EXCITING SHIT FROM THE ALLIANCE!
here we go with 4 brand-new releases:
HUSKER DU "in a free land" 3 song EP
PEER GROUP "rhetoric and hands" 5 song EP
PLEBS "a collection of question marks" EP
"feeble efforts" a 10 tune compilation EP featuring top-notch closet cases

COST TO YOU: $2.50 each post paid

1/20 the price of a record I could learn how to kill the russians

send 75¢ for a copy of D. Boon's "the prole" mag. ALSO: Ray Pettibon comix "Captive Chains" & "Tripping Corpse" $2.00 each

AND GET THESE IF YOU DON'T HAVE 'EM

MINUTEMEN "joy" 3 song EP
DESCENDENTS "fat" 5 song EP
SALVATION ARMY "mind garden"

$2.50 each ppd.

new alliance records
p. o. box 21
san pedro, CA
90733

GET YOUR BACK ISSUE'S

WE GOT POWER MAGAZINE OFFERS YOU ALL A SECOND CHANCE !!

ORDER ANY AMOUNT OF OUR BACK ISSUE's TODAY!

WE GOT POWER!
NATIONAL ENQUIRER $1.00
Circle One
Wasted Youth
Interview
circle jerks at the whisky
bards apollo riot
Reviews
DK's
FEAR
Red cross

WGP #1 with CIRCLE ONE, WASTED YOUTH, BARDS APOLLO RIOT, plus photos & revie w/ FEAR, MINUTEMEN, DEAD KENNEDYS, and CIRCLE JERKS pix at the Whisky!

WGP #2 with OVERKILL, RED CROSS, GODZI CLUB, SACCHARINE TRUST, HENRY B.F., THE TAN, BRAVE DOG, photos cartoons games fun w/ ANTI-PASTI, SUBHUMANS, & more!

Order through our address: WE GOT POW 3010 SANTA MONICA BLVD.#310 SANTA MONIC CALIF 90404 - only $2. per issue! postpai

RECORD REVIEWS

BAD BRAINS, FLESHTONES On (ROIR)
Bad Brains cassette-only album (ROIR A106) surprised me. Not only great D.C. harDCore, but also some terrific reggae songs. The mixture makes for a tape you'll want to listen over & over again.
The Fleshtones cassette-only album (RIOR a107) is also a very good effort on the part of the band. Their music is very energetic, though not hardcore. Combinds soul-punk-&surf pop, which is fun to listen to. -ALAN

QUEER PILLS (ANGRY SAMOANS)
Although this ep is no where nearly as good as Inside My Brain, it still has it's merits. For one thing, songs are short (25,35,39, longest being 1:42 Their songs are still pretty lame, even with the new name & haircuts. With lyrics like; "they saved Hitler's cock, hid it under a rock" & "Stupid Jerk" reminds me of "You Stupid AssholE" -JON LIU

RF7 "WEIGHT OF THE WORLD"
This album has a different sound than most of my records, they call it heavy metal, but the guitar ain't loud enough. The guitar player is good but the most emphasised sound on the album is the vocals, which are loud and harsh and get monotonous after a while. I like "Jesus Loves You". -JORDAN

CIRCLE JERKS "WILD IN THE STREETS"
Half of this is great, half of this is lame. The title cut is soo cheezy, you almost don't wanna listen to the rest. But "Letter Bomb", "Question Authority", "Murder The Disturb" etc. are worthwile. -DAVE

ANTI NOWHERE LEAGUE
Streets Of London / So What (WXYZ)
Whats the big deal? Banned in England. What a joke. All they say is some "nasty words". "So What" isn't even as good as "Streets" a cover song. Buy it at Rhino for 95¢, I don't think they have any left -JON LIU

RED CROSS - Born Innocent
This album includes some hits like Linda Blair and look up from the Bottom They often resemble The New York Dolls and very early Stones, but there is still alot of originality in it. They must be seen live to be really appreciated! Red Cross have since kicked half the group and are a three peice band once again with a different drummer. JENNIFER P.S. = Cool cover concept!

FLEX YOUR HEAD comp (Dischord)
Okay. Here is the ultimate comp from the overly healthy Washington D.C. hardcore scene... from one of the best fuckin' labels ever... hosting eleven acts including Artificial Peace, Void, Red C, and these other kickass bands who have 7 inchers out on this label; SOA, Minor Threat, Government Issue, & Youth Brigade. GET IT ASSHOLE! - DAVE

BATTALION OF SAINTS ep
A pretty cool sounding record, even although this San Diego band over-endulges their self-images on the back cover and slick inside poster, which looks like they borroed the idea from Crass sorta. Oh well, at least this band has enough brains to form their own label, which alot of bands could be doing!

ANTI-NOWHERE LEAGE AT THE COUNTRY CLUB
PIC: DINA DOUGLAS

PUNK AND DISORDERLY (various)
Anyone vitally interested in British politics should get Posh Boy's new comp "Punk & Disorderly". This LP features 15 British bands and one old Dead Kennedys tune, and barrages the listener with political & social statements, gripes & warnings. Though few songs are great, most are redundant with trite messages.
The best cut is the first, Vice Squad's "Last Rockers". The music is imaginative, though it features typical blame-the-government-because-we're-gonna-die lyrics. Side one's other great cuts are Peter & The Test Tube Babies' "Banned from the Pub", Red Alert's "In Britian", & Blitz's "Someone's gonna Die" featuring an OI OI OI backup chorus. Others are the Addicts, UK Decay, Disorder, & the Disrupters ranging in that order from OK to terrible. Side two opens with "Kill The Poor", for some dumb reason, and moves on to it's best cut, the Partisan's "Police Story". Abrasive Wheels "Army Song" is pretty good, as is Chaos UK's "Four Minute Warning". All others, Demob, the Outcasts, the Insane and GBH are passible. -RU

MEDIA BLITZ

This issue's reminder of USA's fucked up and distorted press coverage of this thing they call... 'punkrock' is from Erica of Van Nuys. The following exerpts are from a editorial on 'punkers' which appeared in her high school paper.

We all go through changes; changes in maturity, in physical appearance and co-ordination, and even popularity. These changes are readily acceptable and normal. However, when you see your average "Punker" walk-by in his/her dog collar with spikes on it, and his/her hair shaved in various designs, or colored to an astonishing brilliance, and his pathetic wardrobe of boots and drab green army coats, you have to wonder what could make someone desirous of looking like a Salvation Army reject.

Why would someone, in this case "Punkers", want to go to the extreme of re-arranging their values and morals to the extent that violence, brutality, and an anti-American belief would be normal? Have we, the leaders of the future, lost the love and desire for peace that so many Americans have fought to preserve, so that we're desirous of a daily culture of meaness that thrives on cruelty to others and even their own bodies, by disfiguring themselves with bizarre hair cuts and a pathetic style of dress? I think not.

MORE MEDIA BLITZ — MORE HUMOR!

parents and taxpaying citizens we were outraged at the "Punk Day" demonstration which was held at Los Nogales School Friday (Jan. 22) and which was front page news in the Sunday, Jan. 24

It is hard enough as it is to raise children to be decent law-abiding citizens and to teach them Christian moral values in this day and age without the public school system adding to the burden by condoning and promoting the "punkers" philosophy.

What is next — "Pot and Acid Day" or "Free Sex Day"?

THIS COMES FROM A CAMARILLO PAPER

EDITORIALS & COMMENTS

POLICE ON MY BACK

I cant beleive that any cops would be more fucked than those in LA. I used to say that too, until I moved to Isla Vista. For anyone who doesn't know, I V is just north of Santa Barbra and is there primarily to house students from UCSB (University of California Santa Barbra). The school is known among many as the "Party School", which means there is an overabundance of beer & drugs. I can remember one time when I went to a Dumps/Rejectors/Aggression show at The Closet when I got popped for drinking a beer. Now, normally, a cop would just say, "pour it out & go". I can remember times when a cop just questioned us and let us go, with the beer! Not here. We were sitting in the park next to the Closet drinking a six-pack, there were four of us, one & a half beers each, when two cops walked up unnoticed. We were questioned, asked to pour the beer and them, given tickets! One of us got away with a fake name, two had to pay $40 and I had to pay $35. Those cops are fuckin' dicks. Another time, Jordan, Lou E, and I and some friends were walking to get breakfast on a Sunday morning when a cop rode up and told one of us to take off his wrist spikes. The cop said that spikes were illegal weapon and proceeded to hastle and search selected members of the group. Last Thursday two cops tried to get into my apartment, luckily I locked the door. They had to settle for peering in my window and going next door, where they just walked in without knocking. -ALAN

EDITORIAL REPLY

I read a part of your magazine. This guy named Mark from Seal Beach, talking about people should not have long hair in the scene. That to cut it or dye it. Thats stupid! Do we all have to look the same? Thats real Punk Rock! asshole, who ever you are. And whats wrong with liking more than Punk. We should look the way we want. And if you want to beat up a hippie, try me! Punk came from heavy metal, Don't get me wrong, I like punk bands. But who has the right to tell people how to dress. Thats wrong. Or look, be yourself not whats cool. You know it gets me mad, some dick, thinks it coll to beat up people just cause the way they look, and you cry about harrasment, This guy is probably new. P.S.-HEAVY METAL RULES!
-LINO LOUSY M.C.P. #13 CRANKSHAFT

PEOPLE ON THE GO

D. Boon
Minutemen

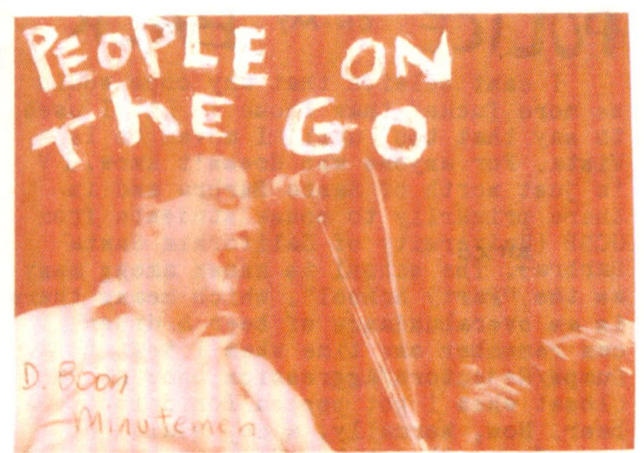

Lino rumored to get another mohawk. Mouse gets pic's in No Mag. Descendents slow down & Saccharine Trust speed up. Mugger, Kim, & Jack go to New York to find the true meaning of anarchy. Chuck Duko = plastic man. Mike Negative Army forms band called Street Wise Negros. Does sex sell records? Vox Pop album cover doesn't measure up! Tourists put out vinyl. Aggression: Speedrock, Oxnard. Nikki (Aka Lumpy) home safe from hospital. Lino, Fly, Bob Bonehead get busted for gunning fags. Fear plays at John Belushi's funeral. Bad Brains play Whisky to buy weed. G. R. Ginn sprains ankle playing basketball with the Brains! Now walks with a rad limp. Pac-Man gets broken into at Okidog. I don't want an okidog, it gives me diareah (sic)? YGM. Frank, of Godzillas defame wants to relocate in Mexico. Junior rips off Unicorn Salvation Army whimprock insense trend catches on. Red Cross still KING of the whimprock w/ a kickass Partrige Fanily-like LP. Suicidal Tendencies: Venice. TSOL ads syntheziser (sic). Circle One doesn't break up, they're getting two new members... their album delayed due to the fact that the engineer lost their tape! BYO doing comp w/ Soch D., Blades, Youth Brigade, etc. Country Club Whisky, & Devonshire provide LA HC entertainment. Zapade shaves mohawk! Rodney can't read, Rodney can't talk. RF7 graffetti's Brian's artwork at CASH. Don't expect to see RF7 on Fer Youz. Charred Remains- cool HC cassette by Noise mag of Ohio w/ loads of US & Canadian bands. Flex Your Head, great DC comp on Dischord. 2 record set comin at ya On Alternative Tenticals with 40 bands. Hell Comes To Your House 2. Rodney On The Roq volume 3. Roger's Circle Jerk's U.S.H.C. putting out a comp. Spinhead records comin' at youz. LA Rocks, a cassette mag w/ Flag, Trust, YB, 7, etc. Get it! -JORDAN & DAVE

YOUNG ACHIEVER

Jack T.S.O.L.

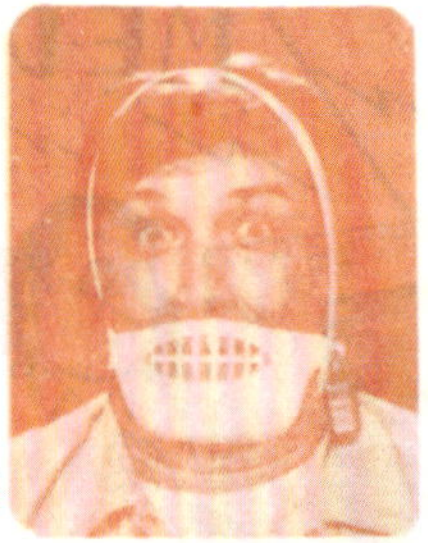

After a hectic night at Devonshire Downs show with TSOL, DOA, SIN 34, & Public Nuisance, I managed to have a chat with Jack Groggors, front-man of TSOL. It seems the white face image of TSOL has permantly abolished due to the fact that the make-up keeps getting stolen.

TSOL are serious musicians when it comes to their music, however, when it comes to performing, they are just out to have a good time whether they play good or not.

Jack's spaced-out antics carry right off stage, you can see this while talking with him. It seems he got a 14 year old girl pregnant and has to either marry her or go to jail. Jack states that after marrying his child-bride, he will fuck her when she is 9 months pregnant and take her to all the gigs and beat her up.

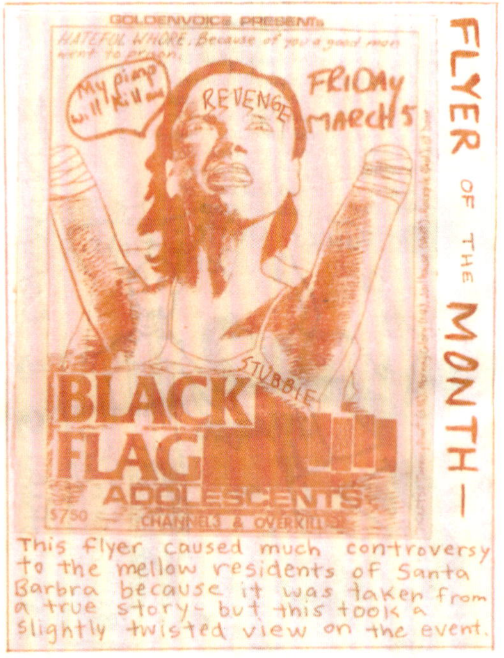

FLYER OF THE MONTH—

GOLDENVOICE PRESENTS
My pimp will kill
REVENGE
FRIDAY MARCH 5
STUBBIE
BLACK FLAG
ADOLESCENTS
CHANNEL 3 & OVERKILL
$7.50

This flyer caused much controversy to the mellow residents of Santa Barbra because it was taken from a true story- but this took a slightly twisted view on the event.

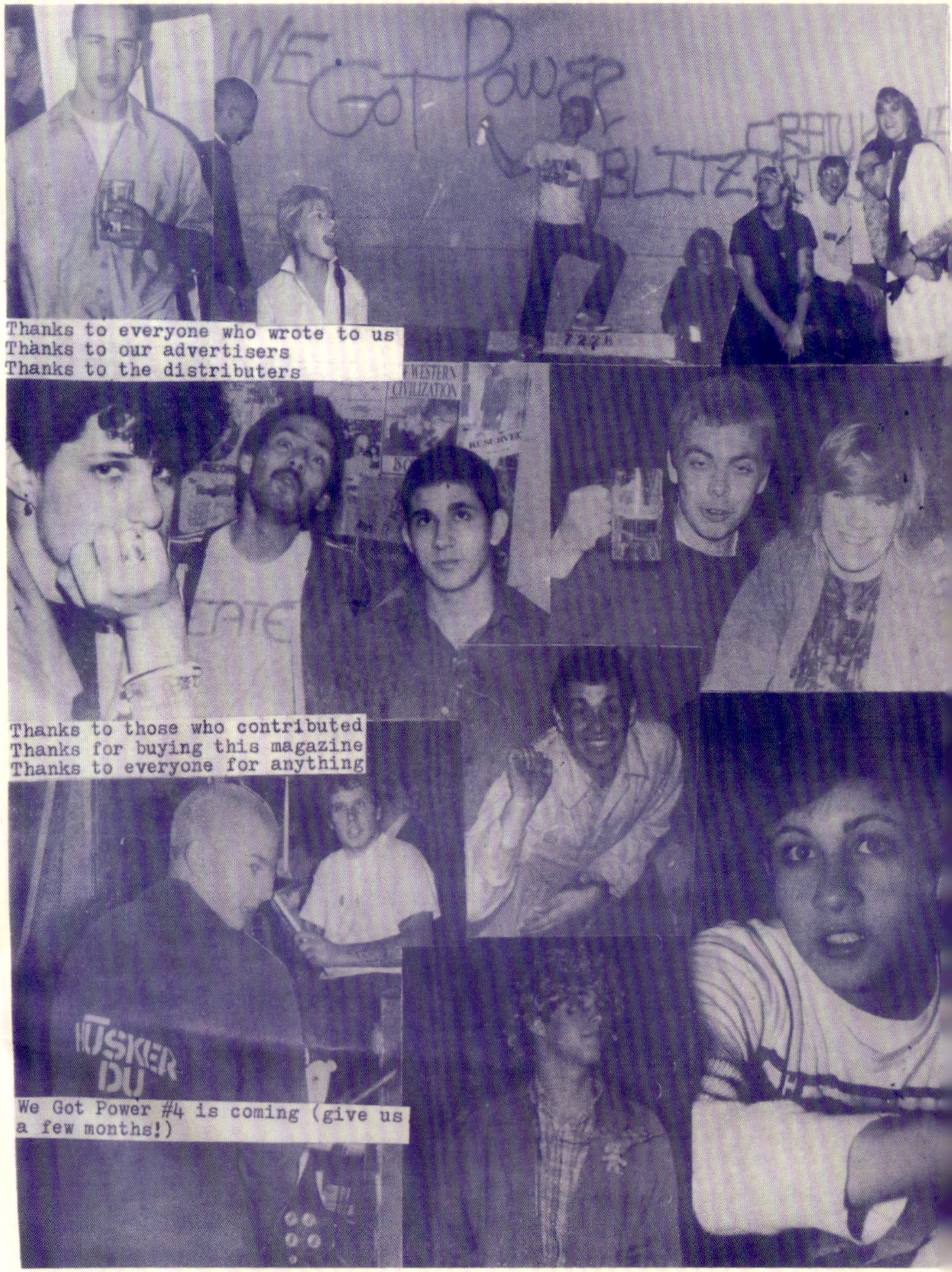
WE GOT POWER
BLITZ
Thanks to everyone who wrote to us
Thanks to our advertisers
Thanks to the distributers
Thanks to those who contributed
Thanks for buying this magazine
Thanks to everyone for anything
HUSKER DU
We Got Power #4 is coming (give us a few months!)

NOW OUT ON Smoke Seven

RED CROSS

- BORN INNOCENT -

This debut L.P. from RED CROSS includes Charlie, Linda Blair & Cease to Exist

RF7

- WEIGHT of the WORLD -

The band who first appeared on Public Service returns with their own L.P. picking up where Scientific Race left off

PUBLIC SERVICE

New music compilation featuring

RED CROSS · BAD RELIGION · RF7 · DISABILITY · CIRCLE ONE

Smoke 7 products distributed by: Greenworld, Rough Trade, Skydisc, Bomp Faulty Products, Win, Jem, Disc Trading, Systematic & Nu Music

WE GOT POWER #3
DoA
misfits
ch3
JFA
NO crisis

WE GOT POWER #4

SEPTEMBER 1982

Our inside joke about *We Got Power* #4 was that it was our hardcore sellout issue. The interviews with Black Flag, Dead Kennedys, Bad Religion, Minor Threat, Hüsker Dü, and Suicidal Tendencies—their first interview—were simply us leveraging the opportunities of having some killer bands coming through town. We were lucky to have some motivated people out there who got the scoop. Michel P. created the cover and masthead art.

Kim's scamming column returned in a Dear Abby format. We conducted an informal poll: "What does anarchy mean to you?" And I wrote some fiction about a punker's last stage dive. The highlight, though, is Kim's most insane gig review detailing her trip to see Chron Gen and Flipper in San Francisco—with her dad in tow.

—Jordan Schwartz

WE GOT POWER

magazine

number 4

1 dollar

L.A. at it's finest...

BLACK FLAG

dead kennedys

BAD RELIGION

Minor threat

byo

hüsker dü

suicidal TENDENCIES

MICHEL P. 82

WGP #4 magazine

Lots of different views expressed here. Many contributers, and various ideas all jumbled together. Loads of interviews, photos, articles, artwork, reviews, all revolving around the "current hardcore" scene in Southern California. One of the main purposes which keeps WE GOT POWER going is our effort to promote what we love and live for. If you don't like something, do something about it! IF YOU HATE IT, CHANGE IT. We did, and are going to continue till we can. All whats inside is what we want to promote. We cover what we see. If you would like to contibute, or comment on whats been said. YOU ARE INVITED!

THIS is YOUR MAG! (if you want it.)

PUBLISHED BY: jordan

LAYOUTS BY: dave

WRITTEN BY: kim, allison, jennifer, alan, mike, and various others

PHOTOGRAPHY BY: ed colver, allison jordan, and who ever we forgot to list

COVER & ARTOWRK: michel p.

PUT TOGETHER BY: everyone above

oh yeah, gremlin distribution strikes again!

NEXT ISSUE: WGP 7" Comp. EP with 14, count 'em, 14 bands! Comin' soon!

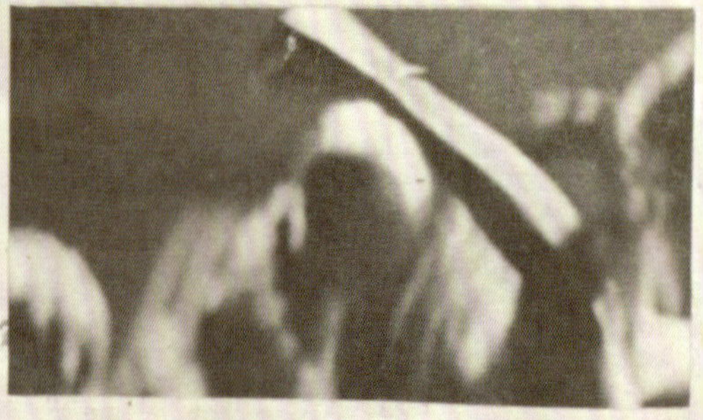

WE GOT POWER
3010 santa monica blvd.
no. 310 santa monica CA
90404

FUCKIN GREAT FANZINES:
* * * * * * * * * * * *
FLIPSIDE, OOPS, BORINGTON JOURNAL, FIRST OFFENSE, SICK TEEN, TOUCH & GO, RIPPER, MEDIA MASS, ATTACK, PHENIS, BURP, NOISE, PUNK LUST, PARANOIA, IDLE THOUGHTS, FORCED EXPOSURE, SCHRIK, MAXIMUM ROCK N ROLL, YOUTH PLAUGE, ASSASIN OF YOUTH, FRONTAL ASSAULT, XIPHOID PROCESS, SLAM, & BACKLASH.
(If you want to contact any or all of these US fanzines, write We Got Power).

FOR BACK ISSUES OF WE GOT POWER (#1, #2, #3.) SEND $2.00 FOR EACH ONE ORDERED. Postagepaid. Cash only, please. No personal checks. Money orders OK.

FOR ADVERTISING INFO, SEND US A S.A.S.E.

Support the coolest radio show of all time!! Ya!!

MAXIMUM ROCK'N'ROLL

THE Nationwide RADIO SHOW
Now HEARD IN California On:
KPFA—S.F. BAY AREA 94.1 FM TUES 9PM
KFCF—FRESNO CA 88.1 FM TUES 9PM
KPFK—LOS ANGELES CA 90.7 FM SAT MIDNIGHT

Any groups interested in submitting cassettes or records, or radio stations wishing to air MAXIMUM ROCK N ROLL sould write to: Tim Y., Maximum Rock, PObox 288, Berkeley CA 94701

BETTER YOUTH ORGANIZATION

I first came into contact with the Better Youth Organization while they were at Godzilla's. They were hired by Frank, and in turn hired bouncers on a trial and error basis. I saw a lot of the "error" bouncers (kids beating in the heads of those smaller).

They then managed to scam a show at the Hollywood Palladium, featuring LA hardcore acts. One of the largest hardcore gigs in history (nearly 3,000 peole) it was naturally a bouncer bloodbath but also a large accomplishment for the BYO. Besides, we sold a lot of mags.

Since then, the BYO have used their funds wisely and have established themselves as important figures in the LA hardcore scene. The three kingpins, Sean, Mark and Adam, (who also make up the band Youth Brigade) have, with their pals, put together an album ironically entitled,"Someone Got Their Head Kicked In". It features several local acts.

Though rather new, the Youth Brigade are on a national tour already, traveling in their own bus with Social Distortion. They also just completed an album of their own, "Sound and Fury". In the process, they accomplished another scam with Doug Moody of Mystic Studio/Record, a distribution company as an alternative to the poor treatment given to many independant labels by the big distributors. This organization will be a collection of several independant hardcore record companies, and they hope it will gain the power of a major label while maintaining full control of product and profits.

Anyone wishing to contact the BYO, write: Better Youth Organization, PO Box 67A64, Los Angeles, CA. 90067. --JORDAN

RECORDS

LIFE IS UGLY Nu Underground Records
Holy Moly, what a record, if you don't like something on this record youre fucked up in your head. Red Cross, Descendents, Anti Ill Will, Civil Dismay, China White, Mood of Defiance, Minutemen, 100 Flowers, Urinal, Zurich 1916, Plebs, Saccharine Trust, are on it, send money to New Underground 4305 W. 153rd st. Lawndale Cal. 90660. -Sam Slam

SOMEONE GOT THEIR HEAD KICKED IN (comp)
Adolescents don't belong here. The BYO added 2 cuts from their very early demo, it sounds funky. Aggression's cuts are good. Bad Religion's song was taken off their LP, but it's their coolest, I think. Battalion Of Saints effort is impressive, after hearing them a few times. I can pass on The Blades and The Jonses, tho the latter have a decent cut. Social D's turn gives us some sturdy, happening tunage, which reminds me slighly of The Weirdos. Finally, The Youth Brigade, a three piece now, caught me off guard, Sean can really sing! Looks like the BYO have their shit together. ($5.00 postpaid -great- BYO pob 67A64 Los Angeles, CA. 90067)

HUSKER DU "IN A FREE LAND" (New Allianc)
My favorite this issue! The title cut is sum fuckin' excellent shit! Wit them catchy melodys and all. Totalhardcore intense pop. "MIC" reminds me of Discharge kinda. If you don't get this EP, come clean my toilet.

BLACK FLAG "TV PARTY" (SST/UNI.)
Side 2 kicks. The cover is a gas! Get it. (Whatta long review!)-DAVE

LAST RITES FOR GENOCIDE & MIA
Smoke 7 does it again! Another MUST for your stack. One side is Genocide, from New York, with 11 songs! They're HOT. Even HOTTER is Las Vegas' MIA with 8 killer tunes.
(Smoke 7, 7230 DeSoto Ave. Suite 104 Canoga Park. CA 91303). -HECTOR

THIS IS BOSTON NOT L.A.
Modern Method records, 268 Newbury st. Boston, MA 02116
Side 2 rules, it starts with Gang Green a fast hardcore band, they do a real hot song called rabies. The Freeze have the best cuts on the album. Although the lyrics are nothing to get kicked out of the hous for, the music and the singing are really rad. Jerry's Kids and The F.U.'s shred side one. The Proletaiat cuts are okay. Get this record.

WHAT IS IT? What Records
This is a nice 77 comp with two neato cuts by the germs, "Forming" the regular version and another unreleased version that sounds different, Darby says "This This is no better than the last one, shit" All the songs on this comp are pretty good especially the Dils "I Hate the Rich" Check it out!
JORDAN

MINUTEMEN "WE NEED THE MONEY" ep (T8)
You can't get bored with these guys. They have so many recordings to their credit, and thats great. This 7" 5 song dude really happens. Best cuts: "If Reagan Played Disco" & "Afternoons". BUY IT!

NIGHEIST "WALKIN DOWN THE STREET" (T 10)
Record reviews are lame. You can't really say anything else but "it's great". SO WAT! IT'S GREAT. Come with me baby, I want to cum. Sounds like it was recorded on a tape recorder! Lets play this on KMET so those nummies can hear some real music.-WHOOYA! (T HERMIDOR, 912 Bancroft Way, Berkeley CA 94710).

The Meatmen "Blood Sausage ep"
Tesco's got a great voice! His band kicks some ass, too! FUCKYEAH. Definatly not for lame feminists or preps or sissy's. Someone says their like Fear and Sex Pistols- well. If you ignore the Meatmen, you don't know how to party. From Touch & Go (One of the rad labels) of Michigan.

The Fix "Jan's Room"
This rec. was done here in LA by that jazzman, Spot, but I'm not sure where the band is from. I know the rec. is put out on Tesco's Touch & Go label. Another standard hardcore beefy sounding 4 song ep that I'm glad I got for free. (Touch & Go records, box 26203 Lansing MI 48909). -DAVEO

Feeble Efforts (compilation)
New Alliance P.O.B. 21 San Pedro CA 90733
The more I listen to this The more i like it. The best cut is Jack Brewer's "a need", th Plebs and Fluid also have great cuts. Side" 2 is all instrumental, it's great to turn down the soun on the T.V. & to this. Radical Artcore - Jordo

ALSO ON NEW ALLIANCE: "THE PLEBS" e.p. get it Now

HEY BANDS: SEND WGP YOUR RECORDS DEMOS, LIVE TAPES, ETC. NOT ONLY WILL WE REVIEW THEM ON THIS PAGE WE"RE STARTING TO PUT TOGETHER.. "WGP RECORDS"! WE'RE LOOKING FOR TALENT...

WGP: We heard something went down in New York, something about hair length ...

Greg: No. Actually it had to do not with hair length, but cock sizes. Some of the girls in various parts of the counrty were dissapointed by the sizes of our cocks. We had this big image built up, Henry was on the cover of New York Rocker, all this shit, it was almost like Devo. They expected us to have big cocks like the Devo boys, you know, we couldn't deliver!

Chuck: I think maybe they get silicon inplants, to build up the placid size.

Greg: We figure if someone wants to listen to our music, our cock size shouldn't really matter. Whatever our cock size is doesn't have much to do with our music.

Chuck: Otherwise we'd be in the business like John Holms, and those guys.

Greg: We are a band because we like to play the music we like to play not for other reasons.

WGP: We heard you ran into a couple other troubles on this tour...

Chuck: I mean shit, our van caught on fire! What else?..!

WGP: So you guys stole Chuck Biskits, right??!

Greg: No. No. Chuck quit DOA, and now he's playin' with us. When we got up there (Vancouver) Emil decided he didn't want to be away from home all the time.

WGP: What's DOA gonna be doing for a drummer now..?

Chuck B.: They got Dimwit, that's my brother.

WGP: So, what do you think of the people who are getting pist at the $9.00 or $8.50 charge for Saturday nite. (Black Flag, 45 Grave, DOA, Descendents, & Husker DU)

Chuck: It's the minimum you can do, and pay the bills of the hall, the p.a. and stuff. Alot of good bands. We pay for advertising out of our funds.

Greg: That place (New Olympic) is the only place we can play, you have to rent a stage. Last time wa played there we ended up not making anything. Ya know.?

WGP: How are you working out with Unicorn?

Greg: They're distributing our records, I guess.

WGP: What about people sayin', "T.V. Party, oh, their 'sell out' record." ...

Greg: Most of the people sayin' that can trade me their apartment, and I can sleep at their place, they can sleep at my place. (Laughter). I don't know if we sold out, when do we collect?

Chuck: I think selling out is doing something you don't wanna do, because someone else is gonna give you something for it.

Greg: I think "T.V. Party" is hilarious. And if we would not do it because we think we might get some criticism that would be selling out, rather than saying, "well, we're gonna do what we like." For us, it's agreat break in our set to have some kind of humor in some of the songs because...

Chuck: It's us. We're not serious 100 percent of the time.

Greg: ... That's part of our thing, the zany-ness, I guess. What are we suppose to do, supress that because somebody might think it's not right?

Chuck: We broke somebody's rule, but wasn't that wat their made for? ... When Led Zeppelin was the big thing and when you went to play, they'd give you shit because the only thing they wanted to hear is Led Zeppelin, and if we had wanted to be popular at that point, then we'd be all playing Led Zeppelin songs. -interview by: Dave, Alan, & Jordan.

BAD RELIGION

Allison "Mouse" and Kim "Ru" interviewed Bad Religion at the New Florentine Gardens June 18. Special thanks to Sean Stern for the backstage passes.

Ru: So, we're all dying to know: are you going to go on tour?
Pete: (drummer) Never!
Roadie: We would go to New York but we're too new wave.
Mouse: So how is your album doing?
Jay: (bass player) Shitty!
Pete: Jay, shut up. The record's doing pretty good.
Mouse: Where's Brett? (guitarist)
Greg: (singer) Brett's not here.
Mouse: No kidding?
Roadie: Here's a relevant question. Greg, what was that in the LA Weekly about you and Greg Hetson doing a hardcore punk album together?
Greg: It's not punk, it's pop.
Jay: It's fuckin' Irish Spring.
Mouse: What did you think of doing New Wave Theater?
Jay: It sucked. They cut our interview.
Pete: Jay, shut up! It was pretty good.
Mouse: Did you get paid for doing it?
Pete: No way!
Greg: Yeah, we got about $1000.
Pete: Greg, shut up! Next question.
Ru: Do you have any plans for the futere that are worth talking about?
Greg: We're doing another album.
Mouse: Where did you get the money for this new album?
Jay: Do you know how rich we are now?? I'm buying a new bass!
RU: Are you aiming for commercial success?
Jay: NO!
Greg: Yes.
Jay: No. If it gets commercial I'll quit.
Greg: Good. We're in it for the Cause.
Pete: Yeah, the Cause!
Mouse: Jay, isn't it a conflict with you being in both Bad Religion and Wasted Youth?
Pete: No longer! He quit Wasted Youth.
Jay: It just wasn't working out. So we (Wasted Youth) decided that maybe Bad Religion needed a bass player, so I was back in.
Mouse: When you were playing with both bands did it ever conflict?
Jay: Yeah, once Wasted Youth had to go to Phoenix and Bad Religion went to Frisco.
Greg: So we got Greg Hetson to play bass.
Mouse: Did you get into any hassles when you played the Country Club?
Pete: None at all.
Jay: When Wasted Youth played we got through four songs before they kicked us off.

-ED COLVER

VALLEY DUDES!!!

Ru: What other bands do you like?
Jay: The Who!
Greg: Who?
Pete: You guys, shut up! Early Van Halen, Moterhead, and the Blades. They're great!
Mouse: Are you making any money tonight?
Pete: No, we're in it for the Cause!
Mouse: What is the Cause?
Greg: Pudding!
Jay: Jello Brand Pudding!
(Talk goes on about pudding-- the Cause being Bill Cosby).
Ru: Do you really think you're the best band in LA?
Pete: Do we think?? We know!!
Greg: We're the best band in the world!
Jay: Who said we're the best band in LA?
Ru: You did, onstage at the Music Machine.
Greg: Roger said it.
Mouse: Do you have a lot of followers?
Roadie: Yeah, they're into the Cause.
Greg: Come on, not again!
Ru: Do bouncers ever hassle you when you play?
Greg: Yeah!
Pete: Not me!
Greg: Fuck you.
Pete: Greg, shut up. Bouncers are cool guys.

EDITORIALS

— MORE —

POLICE ON MY BACK

I'm writing about that stupid punk from Santa Barbra that thinks the cops in his town are worse than those in L.A. because him and his friends got tickets for a six-pack That aint shit! I got arrested at Godzillas when the Damned played & was put in Juvy for 3½ months just for one stupid little beer. And that aint all. I got arrested at 9:30 at night for walking down Vista St. (By Oki-Dogs) because they said I was drunk. I was in jail for 5 days. So I say the pigs in S.B. aren't as bad as you think - Love, NICK (HAWKEYE) MORGAN

O.k. nick, enough of this bullshit of arguing over what city's cops are worse! Lets just say, "the badge means you suck". All coppers are bastards. Fuck city hall. We should all get together on this! I'm sure every one of us has had more than one bad experence with the men in blue. -WGP staff

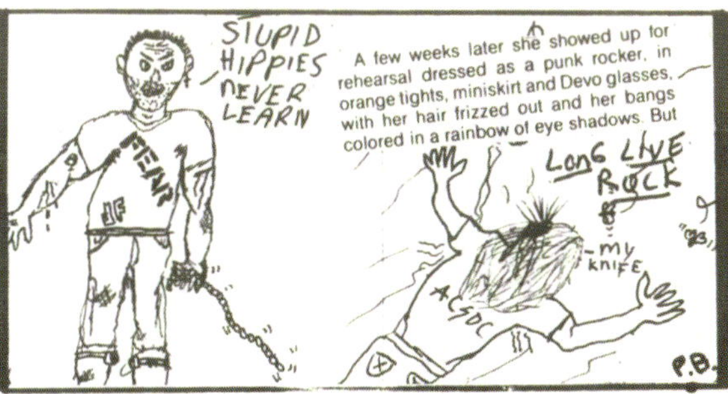

AN EDITORIAL REPLY TO AN EDITORIAL REPLY...

I'd like one last chance to support my editorial opinion printed in WGP #2. Apparently LA Reader recognized it, LINO LOUSY didn't read it, and Mr. Moreland in his speech printed in Flipside #31 was kind enough to see the "stupidity" of the editorial of which WGP supposedly "sermonizes," but I guess he fails to face reality and see all the hippies and hippie-punks which pose a threat to everyone's happiness. Don't get me wrong, I'd appreciate an intelligent editorial reply, but LINO, your a pathetic dumbfuck! You should carefully read something before ridiculing it, because I said none of those things you accused me of, except that hippies are loser outcasts and that its more constructive to pose a threat to an enemy rather than to yourself. Furthermore, I never said everyone shoud get a skinhead or dye their hair--two catagories which I myself don't fit into. I've never told anyone how to dress and so far I haven't beat up anyone either. It's unfortunate there are people as ignorant and worthless as yourself, LINO, who come across a zine with as much class as WE GOT POWER.

Sincerely -Mark
Seal Beach

And now about Serena Dank. I know alot of you are mad at her, and I dont blame you, but hear me out. Southern California (excluding punks, of course) is the most stupid, vacuous place on the face of the earth. I mean, it's a place where a woman can make her living blowing up baloons for parties. Now, while all the people are stupid idiots, the one thing they're good at is getting money out of each other, right? So this Serena Dank sees punks and thinks, "All those punks have parents, right?, and they're probably all outraged at their kids. So I'll set up an organization, right, and depunk them." I mean, I dont know what her reason is, could be for money, fame, power over the minds of people even stupider than her, but my point is: Serena Dank doesn't care about punks. She doesn't even hate them. But when you get mad at her, and tell her to fuck off, that's exactly what she wants... then all her points are made. So I say ignore her. Y'know if you wave the red flag in front of the bull, it just stands there. The whole thrill is gone. Personally I think she is a funny joke. Anyhow, enough about Serena Dank (I think she has the world's most appropriate last name) anyhow, I hate her. Stupid fucking bitch (snicker, snicker). -HARDCORE LIVES AND RULES, STRENGTH THRU OI, PAUL.

SUICIDAL TENDENCIES

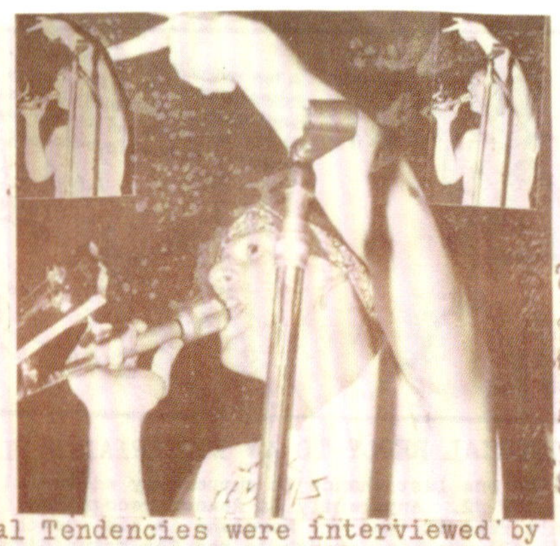

(PIC BY JORDI)

Suicidal Tendencies were interviewed by Kim and Jennifer. Also in the room were manager Dave Hutchinson and T-shirt artist, Bill Evans.

WGP: Who are those kids in the Suicidal Tendencies T-shirts?

Mike D.: They just like the band...

WGP: Are they friends of yours?

Louie: I know most of them.

Mike M.: There's a popular misconception that it's a gang, which it is'nt. Kids come up to me and ask, "How do I get in the Suicidal Tendencies gang?" And I tell them it's not a gang, it's just mostly people who live around here. We Hang out together , meet at the same places before shows to get rides, and if someone gets into a fight... but you don't see us fighting too much.

WGP: You still have quite a reputation.

Mike M.: That's because we have people like Bob Garvey's mom calling everyone's parents and saying, "Suicidal Tendencies played last night and another person got killed!" Everytime we play they say, "We read it in the papers, someone died at the party!" Last Wednesday night we played a party at Andre's house, there was no trouble.

WGP: Do you all live on your own?

Mike D.: I live on my own. Semi.

Louie: I live at home, but I'm on my own.

Mike M.: Sean, where do you live?

Sean: I don't have a brother.

Mike M: That's an inside joke..

WGP: Where do you live?

Mike M: I used to live in a resort home in the middle of Oakwood, but I moved back in with my parents. (Talk goes on about their house)...

MikeD.: And their kitchen never smelled.

Mike M: We used to practice in the kitchen. Mike D: There was a drum set right in front of the sink.

Mike M: That was a good excuse not to wash dishes! Our neighbors tried to get us evicted... Jezebel, RIP.

WGP: So what do you think of the big article on "Mike Suicide" in Penthouse?

Mike D: There were lies in there...

Mike M.: You gotta realize, the guy was working for a magazine. When you buy Penthouse, the only reason you buy it is to read the articles, so naturally you want them to be as interesting as possible. You don't want the people in the storys to be rational, thinking individuals, you want them to be psycotic and neurotic and crazy and not have a mind. You wanna have them look like they are not people, they are something else, freaks of society.

Mike D.: Ask us, "When's Suicidal Tendencies making their big break"?

WGP: Are you ever going to?

Sean: We'd like to be on an album.

Mike M: I'd like nothing more than to have our material on vinyl.

Mike D.: I get the feeling somebody's trying to screw us up somewhere. Like when someone takes a tape of us to the Whiskey and it's not us. Or they call and say they're our manager, and they're not our manager.

WGP: Isn't Dave your manager?

Mike M: He resigned to become president of The Mar Vista Skinheads Recreation Program. Every Tuesday night at the Mar Vista Bowl.

Mike D.: We're currently in eighth place out of eight teams, aren't we?

Dave: Yeah, we're doing good.

Mike M: We're getting a boxing team together, every Thursday night.

Louie: So, do you like our band?

WGP: If we didn't, we wouldn't interview you. WGP (Kim): Yeah, we might, I interviewed Bad Religion....

Mike M: I bet if you go to Uni Hi or Westchester High, I bet more people have heard of us than Black Flag, except maybe for "T.V. PARTY".

WGP: Alot of people say you bring your own audience to your shows...

Mike M: Who are we gonna bring? TSOL's audience?

Mike D.: Do you know what shock value is?

WGP (Kim): Of course, I have parents.

Mike D: Everything these days is shock value. Over the years, how many punks have you seen with swastickas on their shirts, how many of them are nazis? It's all for shock value..

Mike M: I've got a sawsticka shirt and I've got Jewish relatives. I'm not a nazi. I used to wear it to High School, people would freak out. You notice when you first cut your hair, who your friends are. And theye arent many.

L.Action '82 WGP

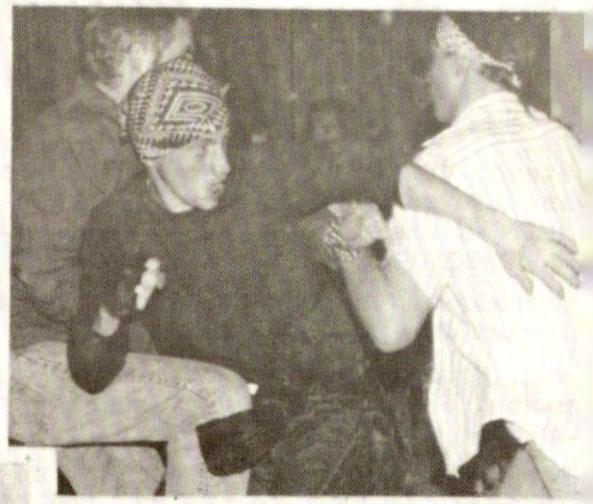

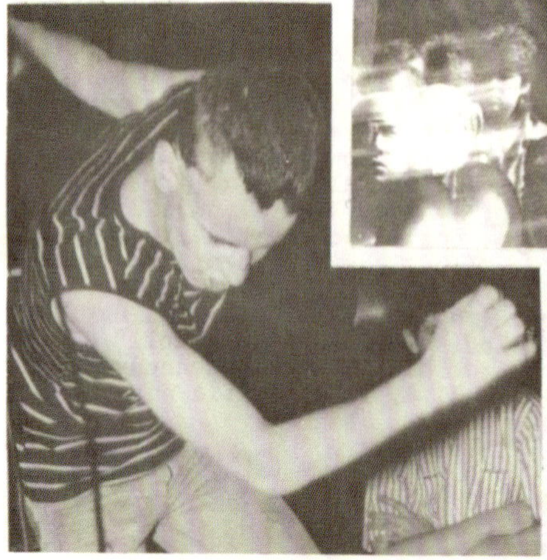

WHAT DOES ANARCHY MEAN TO YOU?

Stevo: "Anarchy, stands for freedom, and if you want to be free, order yourself an anarchy burger to go, HOLD THE GOVERNMENT!!"

Snickers: "Anarchy is for fools and losers!"

Meg: "Anarchy means, uh.. it means, it means. Uh huh. And don't you forget it buddy."

Kim: "Anarchy is going 100 mph on the freeway, on LSD, in the wrong direction."

Eddie Corbett: "The total punkrock attitude, man."

Dan: "Anarchy is a piece of shit."

Blaney: "No comment." "Okidogs suck".

Jody: "Anarchy means fuck the world, fuck the government, fuck society, thats why we're selling 'fuck the world' bumperstickers, and 'I hate Reagen buttons."

Some asshole: "Your mother."

Some other guy: "People are so beligerant."

iNUStRY NEWz

INDEPENDENT HARDCORE RECORD LABELS :

* *

SMOKE 7: Felix wants to do 3 12" 45's with three bands. Send him a demo and become a star if your band is good! Redd Kross second LP set for an October release."Public Service" going into it's third pressing, and "Last Rites" into it's second...

SST: Minutemen second LP out in Sept. One song is rumored to be 3 minutes long. Also dey is gwana be releasun St. Vidas, old Stains, and Overkill records sooon. Plus a Subhuman LP!, a SST comp "Blasting Concept", and maybe even an album by Texasgreats, The Dicks...

NEW ALLIANCE: Probably one of the best LP's this year, "Milo Goes To College" is out! There's still space on the truly hardcore "Mighty Feeble" comp. Must be recorded on cassete recorders! Send your entry's on in! Husker Du 12" in October. Minutemen 7" (outtakes of new album) out in December. The Plebs are looking for a bassist and a drummer call (213-548-1684) today!

EPITAPH: Vandals 12" ep, don't be afraid to pogo on frogs at the copacabana. Second Bad Religion Lp coming.

BYO: Youth Brigade LP out now! Get the comp, if you haven't. Aggression EP out whenever. Send tapes to get on next BYO comp.

SPINHEAD: Phil Botchman wants to do an LP wit a gohd band. Send demo tapes! Sin 34 7" "Die Laughing" EP going into second pressing... and then a Sin 34 LP packed with 20 songs! Eventually a comp will come from this label, too.

TOUCH & GO: Meatmen 7" second effort out?? Maybe a Process Of Elimination 2. Heck, we don't know, we live all the way out here in California!

DISCHORD: A Faith/Void LP out REAL soon. (Might be out already). heeer's sum newz... MINOR THREAT ALBUM in the works.

ALTERNATIVE TENTICALS: Bunches of EP's, Fartz, Seven Seconds, etc. etc. Get the fantabulous "Maximum Rock N Roll" double LP comp, or die. New Dead Kennedys LP comes out Sept. 1st, plastic surgery disaster. . . . . JORDAN

send us info about your record label!!

WGP: What do you think of LA?
Jello: I haven't seen all of LA. I keep telling myself to get hold of a car and take various freeway exits.
WGP: Does the crowd ever bother you?
Jello: Ah- it took a little getting used to at first, but over all it's healthy because it breaks down barriers (stage divers) between the audience and band. Everything gets blurred, and the band isn't up on a pedestal.
Klaus: Two years ago everybody was doing the worm-type thing and it evolved into the flying off stage-type thing.
Jello: But back to the original question what do we think of LA. It was alot more fun this time then during that Florentine disaster. It was fucked in the way it was run, and there was a certain eliment in the crowd that made people act like a bunch of derranged monkeys. Mainly it was the atmosphere of the place because they hired goons to provoke fights.
Klaus: There's alot less fighting and violence going on now.
WGP: What about people who wear DK shirts to DK shows, Fear shirts to Fear shows...
Jello: It's funny in a way because almost all the shirts are the proper color, corporate logos. But you wouldn't catch those people wearing a high school letter jacket, but the similarities are quite something. I think we mentioned that one night during Nazi Punks Fuck Off, that we weren't trying to tell people what to do. We just got some pretty damn strong opinions and if you have a better one, tell us.
WGP: What about the armbands that come in the Nazi Punks 45...
Jello: They were supposed to say destroy fascism, not just "Dead Kennedys say Nazi Punks Fuck Off." (Talk goes on about Al Haig and the likes....)
WGP: Are there any politicians you like?
Jello : I can't think of one right now.
Klaus: The couple I was fond of got killed in San Fransisco.
WGP: Do you find yourself losing control as far as people making shirts of you...
Jello: There's no way you can control that. The only ones that pissed us off was those fucking assholes at Poseur, who made the California Uber Alles buttons with the swastika and then refused to withdraw it, saying, "your just a bunch of vermin and we're here to make money off you." I'm surprised there still open or someone hasn't burned their building with them inside.
WGP: Are there any bands your against?
Jello: We are against right-wing bands, racist bands, bands like the Exploited who like to watch people beat each other up.
Klaus: We are against bands who say, "you have to think waht we say." We are not telling poeple to take everything what we say for gospel.
Jello: In places where punk is normal, like in LA, youve got bands who play it safe, commercial & safe, they really don't take a stand. (talk goes on about English bands...)
WGP: What do you think of the "real Cool" bands who "turn HEAVY METAL"!?
Jello: To us, they don't exist. I'd much rather see The Butthole Surfers every night of the week. They are one of a kind. They are not afraid to show their twisted, unique side to others, rather than trying to conform.
WGP: Some people wanted your autograph backstage, and some girl came up and kissed you on stage, what do you think of this?
Jello: Good question, um, well, if she wants to kiss me that bad, why the hell not? It's better than to tell people to fuck off. Occasionally I get tired of "the leach brigade".
WGP: And what's that?
Jello: 20 or 30 people surrounding you, asking dumb questions... We want to play in Japan, they are such an obedient society. I don't think they've seen a real thrash band before. I'd like to see some jaws drop, since we've been bigger, I miss that!
-INTERVIEW BY:MOUSE, DAVE, KIM, etc. and Jordan!

FICTION

"SATURDAY MORNING" By: Jordan

Jimmy kept his eyes closed when he woke up that morning. He let the light soak through his eyeballs which, from the inside, looked like orange movie screens. It was his favorite part of the day. He couldn't remember what he had to do today, or exactly what he had done last night.

Last night had been hectic. He had gone to the show sporting a new red, white and blue mohawk. As usual, he'd had a couple of beers, a few beauties, two more tall cans, and some Bacardi. He remembered being quite buzzed as he gave seven grimy dollar bills to the new wave chick at the door.

It seemed like someone was tilting the floor, trying to make him fall on his face, as he stumbled into the club. The P.A. was blaring a Sex Pistols album at an incredibly high volume, not to put the crowd in a good mood, but to stop communication between the punks so they wouldn't riot. Jimmy pushed through the sweaty bodies and rested himself against the stage.

Then the band began to play and Jimmy was overcome by an urgent need to work off energy, to do something, anything, but his wild, free spirit was trapped, like a butterfly in a cacoon, in a drugged-out student body. The band then started his favorite song, the one he listened to every morning to help him get through his dreary day. Electrified, Jimmy crawled out of the sea of perspiration and punks and onto the stage, to somehow show his appreciation to the band.

But as soon as he got onstage, a bouncer sent him flying head-first toward the ground. On the way down he looked right into the eyes of a fat insta-punk preppie wearing a manufactured Anarchy t-shirt like the ones for seven bucks at Posuers. "ANARCHY!!" he cried as his head slammed into the dance floor like a cigarette into an ashtray.

Then it was morning. Time to get up, Jimmy thought as he tried to open his eyes. They seemed to be glued shut with sleep. Something was wrong. He tried to move his body, but his joints seemed welded together. Finally he managed to open his eyes a bit, and he saw that he was in a hospital bed surrounded by all sorts of machines. His parents were crying at the foot of his bed, and a grave-looking doctor was coming toward him. Jimmy tried to say something, but there were too many tubes in his mouth. He watched helplessly as the doctor bent down and pulled a plug out of the wall.

Jimmy's spirit left his pale, dead body but clung on to a lifeless arm for a few seconds, reluctant to leave the world so soon. Then it dawned on him that he wasn't a punk no more, so he let go and was blown away by a gust of wind.

LIVE GIGS·

CHRON GEN, FLIPPER, WASTED YOUTH, SHATTERED FAITH, LEWD, JFA, CIRCLE ONE, CH3, HUSKER DU, ETC., EASTERN FRONT SHOW, AQUATIC PARK, BERKELEY, JULY 31.

This show was a real waste of plane fare. I brought my dad to see it, too. The gig was in a park, with all these pigs with guns surrounding it. It was ten dollars to get in, and I wasn't surprised that only about four hundred people showed up.

None of the bands were all that inspiring. Husker Du were the most interesting, and Circle One went over real well. Wasted Youth probably would've been good but someone threw a bottle and knocked out the drummer after 3 songs. My dad was upset about that. Incidentally, Shattered Faith were the cutest band there.

Negative comments: I hate Flipper so I'm not going to say anything nice about them, but the crowd loved them. Chron Gen were sort of boring (my dad liked them best, though). And the hot dogs were disgusting, and no one had any cigarettes, and I wanna know WHERE WAS ALL THAT GREAT SAN FRANSISCO ACID I'VE HEARD SO MUCH ABOUT? It wasn't at this gig. -RU

BAD RELIGION/ABANDONED/ISOLATION
MUSIC MACHINE, JUNE 7

The Music Machine in West L.A. was a pretty good club while it lasted, which was about two shows. Oh well. This was the second punk show at the club, and for a Monday night right before finals the turnout was pretty good. Isolation went on first. I've seen them several times and wasn't particularly impressed but this time I really listened and decided that they were pretty good---at least they have potential.

The Abandoned, next, were the best band of the evening. They were really good, doing an old Adolescents song as well as "House of the Rising Sun" and "White Rabbit". The singer has lost none of his energy and the others are equally dynamic---definitely a band to keep your eye on.

I didn't watch much of Bad Religion because I was outside scamming again. ...KIM

REVIEWS

Dead Kennedys, TSOL, Butthole Surfers
WHISKY JULY 4

Them Butthole Surfers were pretty rad! These guys are maybe too hardcore for hardcore, naw. Well. These Texans are lots of fun, esp. their guitarist, who got all the weird sounds and expressions. TSOL (JFK) did another standard set as the surprised audience didn't know that they were to play. Fireworks started to go off, as did the slammers. Dead Kennedys did a pretty cool set, the sound was better than the night(s) before at The Barn. Their new material looks like it just might top what was done on their classic "Fresh Fruit" lp! The crowd participation was kinda numb, untill the end of their set, which is a drag! I guess things are mellow and tame these days. -DAve

mike ness of social distortion and a unidentified fan singin' along at Meg's party. -pic by jordo.

CIRCLE ONE, SIN 34, BAD EXAMPLE, DR. NO
HATED PRINCIPALS, DJ Club July 24

Jorge of Youth Manifesto put this show on and it went great! This is the second show he has put on at places he just hunted for.

The DJ Club, just down the street from Bards, is happening. Four dollars and lots of fans keep the place real cool plus you can go in and out, and no backstage.

Hated Principals, from Culver City, were pretty bad except for the last two songs, Helter Skelter and HP theme song. Dr. No weren't to original but they were good. The singer Brandon Cruz used all of his acting talents in a stunning performance. Bad Example was scary; as for their music, I can't say. Sin 34 were real good, Mike Geek was a real geek. Julie was stylin' with humorous comments such as, "all the Suicidal Tendencies shirts go to one side and all the Circle One shirts on the other.

Circle One did the best set I've seen in a while, their new drummer Jody was jammin'. JJN

BLACK FLAG, REDD KROSS, DESCENDENTS, MDC at Dancing Waters JULY 30

The show was only 6.50, what a surpri Black Flag lowered their price so DW didn't charge nine bucks. MDC were a cool hardcore band, that's about it. The Descendents were great! They are or of LA's best bands and must be seen. They had a couple of good fast songs anc they played my favorite song "Kabuki". In between bands they showed videos of the Sex Pistols, Clash, Wierdos etc... they showed parts of CHiPs, news clips and Documentaries on punk rock. they were very entertaining. Redd Kross did a real fine set. Dez played guitar on some old songs like Stand in Front of Poseur. Jeff takes bong hits during the set. They're the best. Black Flag played good except for occasional power failure. They are better now then they ever have been. One of the better shows I've seen this summer. JENNIFER

BLACK FLAG, 45 GRAVE, DOA, DESCENDENTS, HUSKER DU, UXB July 17, Nude Olympic

I missed UXB and half of Jusker Du because I didn't think the show would start before dark. HD were great hardcore from Minnesota, buy their record! Descendents were way cool, that Milo sure can sing. DOA were happening, they are my favorite "big time" band. 45 Grave played too. I was in a bad mood until Flag played Nervous Breakdown. Henry was real good. Overall the sound was shitty, I must remember to get way drunk next time... JORDAN

Oi

People who always have a smile on their face are the ones to watch — they're holding it in.

OOOH NOO!

ANOTHER ONE BITES the dust

Looks like LA hardcore might have swallowed itself into the dreaded sto-mach of no shows, when three clubs clos-ed their doors to punk gigs in August.
The Dancing Waters seems to have prob-lems with a teen dance permit - and will not be accessable for a while, maybe a long while.
West LA's Music Machine has put a pad lock on the punk rock after a Fear show, when a record crowd turned out, kids couldn't get in, someone broke a window. In the neighborhood, that night, several punks were getting guns and knives pulled on them, by the locals.
Seems like the neighbors of The Whis-ky got a radical petition goin', and forced the club to cancel all punk shows at once. Lots of damage was done to store fronts and cars by punks and others, recently.. not to mention the "mini-roit" when a group of punks stormed Turners Liquor, after Bob Bone-head was beat up by the owner, or some-thing like that.
Everyone knows, The Country Club, The Palladium, and Devonshire wont host any more gigs, tho, the latter is rumored to be having a happening. The Florentine is to host 2 big hardcore gigs real soon, it's-alright-if-you-like-hall-gigs. And, for more good news, a second Godzillas is suppose to "open any day now"...DJCM

XTRA GIG REVIEW:
DESCENDENTS & VERONICA LAKE- at The Anti Club- August 23 '82
I knew Veronica Lake would be weird when she dedicated her set of "poetry" reading to the staff at BellVue, the last poem was most punk 'cos in it this chick rips off 20 cases of coke from a 7-11. The Descendents set tonite was RAD. Anyone who missed their show is eatin' life! Someone said that Kurt of Overkill (now heavy metal) played his drum set louder than the Descendent's Billy, NO WAY! When Bill hit that snare, it hurt my ears. Merrill got on stage to sing "Kabuki", which is important, since Milo is leaving (left)? When they finished their set, they received an encore by the enthusiastic crowd. Some how, the club owner didn't want them to play another tune. So I, Dave, and Cpt. Anarchy got mad and yelled for more and the fat lady owner came over and told us to stop clapping. Next thing we found ourselves kicked out! The wrong clubs are getting thrashed!! Twisted Roots played too. -JORDAN

SADISTIC EXPLOITS "Freedom/Apathy" ep
"Apathy" is a rad cut, real fast, short, to the point. The other cut is slower, and comes closer to "an English sound" type-of-thing. The singer has a real interesting sound and style, this band is from Pennsylvania. (SADISTIC EXPLOITS P.O.box 37 Upper Darby, Pen-nsylvania 19082.)

THE LEWD "American Wino" lp (ICI)
Side two is live at Target Video, and is like way groovy. This band is like pretty decent, kinda slower for "hardcore". On the whole, it makes for good kickback listening enjoyment. The studio side is faster, more standard, with a few fantastic songs. The cover has to be one of the better this month! (ICI RECORDS: 1765 N.Highland, Box 321 Hollywood, CA 90028).

MEAT PUPPETS lp (SST)
WOW! Next thing you know these guys will own limos and mansions and beach homes in Newport Beach! THIS IS MY CHOICE FOR THE NUMBER ONE LP OF THE DECADE... OF ALL TIME. It blows the Go-Gos away. "Our Friends" should be in heavy rotation at all the hip new wave discos across the country. Buy this record, don't be like a dip I know who plays this on 33. Sounds better on 45. WHOOPS, it was mastered at 45 speed.

WRUM ep (SST)
After five years, these old guys managed to paste together a little re-cord. "Time Has Come Today" is happen-ing, kinda twisted heavy pop, but of course, their claim to fame is that they have that Gary McDaniels guy from that band Panic playing bass. (SST re-cords P.o.box 1 Lawndale, CA, 90260)-Dave

oh no, we're running out of space, and we're going to print shop in 2 minutes EVERYONE BUY THE SIN 34 5 song ep NOW! (SPINHEAD REC.S 2265 Westwood Blvd. Suite # 541 LA CA 90064. $3.00 post paid)

WGP: So you guys broke up for a while?
Brian: 'Cos I went to college.
WGP: So college wasn't workin'...
Brian: No, it was working fine, straight A student. I just didn't like it. So I wanted to do the band...
WGP: How's things working out since you all re-joined?
Jeff: Great. Lyle: Just fine...
Ian: I think better than before.
WGP: So when are you gonna appear on vinyl next??
Jeff: As soon as we have enough new stuff... Brian: Probably by winter.. we'll do a album, yeah.
WGP: What have you came across on your tour, as far as different cities? Is this place alot different from DC?
Lyle : We don't have a beach in D.C.
Brian: What it is, basically, it's a-lot different what we heard it would be like. The way Flipside makes it sound, all the bands make it sound, like, A WAR, all the time. People have been cool, really positive.
Lyle: The most negative scene we've seen is probably San Fransisco.
Ian: Self destructive, bullshit.
WGP: Is there a differnce between punk and hardcore?
Brian: I nither know or care.
Ian: "Punk" became a really broad label. Like "rock n roll". When we first started out, we wanted to be different.
Jeff: Different from Richard Hell, The Exploited. Shit like that.
WGP: Tell LA about your "streight edge" concept...
Brian: We've answered this question a million times, straight edge is anti obsession with anything. Drugs, alcohol, religion, sex, anything. Personally some of us are straight, totally. Others drink, maybe take an occasional drug, but their is an outlook, a mental attitude that you have. That does not mean we are militant about it. It's not a club that you join.
Ian: It's not a set of rules...
WGP: Can't you be obsessed with straight edge?
Brian: Sure. There are people who are.
IAn: When you control a substance, a-nother substance control you..
I know when we play I speed more than twelve of your speed-sters combined! That's natural energy. If your able to do it on your own, it's that much better The line, "Don't fuck" doesn't refer to A-sexuality, or non-sexuality, the line refers to..
Brian: Following your dick around.
WGP: Are you gonna come to LA again?
Lyle: Eventually.
Ian: We're as big as Black Flag! (Just joking Black Flag.)

-int. by: JORDY & DAVEY

WHAT IS IT.

The Skulls.

The Dil s.

The Germs.

Controllers

The Eyes.

Kaos.

A compilation.

Soon. From What Records?

The streets of London have been overrun for months by grotesque, blood-lusting hoodlums — disciples of the most sadistic youth movement the world has ever known.

Now these sicko cults are spreading their poison to America, threatening to turn this country's children of the '80s into violence-loving freaks.

"It's coming — and it's not very pretty," said a worried New York police official.

Their king is Wattie Buchan, a fat buffoon the British press calls the most disgusting man in England.

The sneering Wattie is lead singer for a revolting rock band called Exploited. His favorite sport is splitting open the heads of his fans with bottles.

"It's the best laugh going," he said. "You can usually manage to get 40 stitches out of them."

These goofy-looking punks are typical of the blood-thirsty hoodlums who have wrecked England and menace America.

HA! HA! HA!!

Media Blitz

above is from "Weekly Enquirer". below is from "US" magazine. aren't these getting funnier?

While punk clothing and hairstyles may be disturbing, Dank says that the movement's "nihilistic, self-destructive" values are most dangerous. "A main part of punk thinking is to be as obscene and repulsive as possible," she says, attempting to explain the punk penchant for lacerating one's flesh with razors and burning the skin with lit cigarettes.

To those who would accuse her of overreacting to punk's dangers, Dank declares, "The whole movement is unbelievable to me. The scene lends itself to violence and suicide." She describes a radical strain of punk that has recently emerged in the U.S. called "Oi," 14- to 16-year-olds who have adopted the New Wave nihilism of punk rock music as a way of life.

movement that fosters racism and fascism.

"The whole thing is like *A Clockwork Orange*," she laments. "Frankly, it's horrifying." US

'Punk' Cats

I'm a dumb Hippy, I always mellow out and smoke Joints and write songs about how Good my girl gives the fucks to me ☮

I'm a Punk Rocker I'm not letting the society fuck me up, but these hippys are that why there so lame I'm trying to do something about it And the hippys are mellowing out like Geeks

drawing by Clarke 81

WE GOT POWER

7" comp. ep coming soon FEATURING 14 CUTS BY 14 BANDS ON A 7" DISC!

YES BANDS, there is still room. A little room. Songs must be under one minute (60 seconds or less). send demos WGP 3010 Santa Monica Blvd, #310, Santa monica Ca 90404......

GIG OF THE YEAR:

Meat Puppets do show in Phenoix and stun audience by doing the complete side one of "The Decline Of The Western Civilization" soundtrack, including the talking! Hey maybe, we can get 'em to do side two, here in LA!!

PEOPLE ON THE GO SSIP

WGP changes policy in attempt to better sales: we now kiss ass. Everything is wonderful. Everyone is having a real swell time.. Singer for Dr.Know Brandon C ruz, is Eddie Corbett of "The Courtship Of Eddies Father".. Michelle Bell gives up drugs and alcohol.. TSOL goes mellow . Jack Grisham catches the love bug.. Junior gets kicked out of house, now lives in abandoned trailor.. Mouse defects from WGP for No Mag Streight edge catches on.. Kim follows Donny Brooke down Bundy.. Okidogs sucks Too many palm trees, video games, flea-markets, assholes, & roaches, it's just like Disneyland.. Meg & brandon go all the way, to Frisco, for Easten Front, and pass out.. Kathy & Paula are New Waves Sluts.. Bloney.. Laura sees @narchy in France.. Jordan still loves chocolate, and Joannie still loves Cha-Chi.. Circle Jerks re-appear after long tour.. "Scranny wears Creepers on dates so he appears taller.".. WGP is lame.. Paul Nelson forms new band.. Nikki and Brian go broke.. managment opportunities available at McDonalds.. Phrank is cool.. Cool promoter: George Newberry.. Al Flipside is the king of cool.. Zizi carrots are specially made by Jah.. John Macias get arrested once again after leading punx on a wild pogo spree up and down Sunset.. Lizard Laduke The Ninth Grader gives Jug head.. Everyone joins BYO.."WGP Entertainment Corp." comin at ya.. Chuck The Duke goes bald after a while.. Minutemen coverboys went national on FS with skins.. Snickers shaves mohawk, now haas skin.. Anyone else?.. So what.. -WGP STAFF (Next issue we are starting "Song Dedications". If you wanna dedicate a song to anyone, send your letter on in. WGP SONG DEDICATIONS 3010 Santa Monica Blvd. #310, Santa Monica, CA 90404.)

(PICS BY JJN)

ISOlAtIon ↑

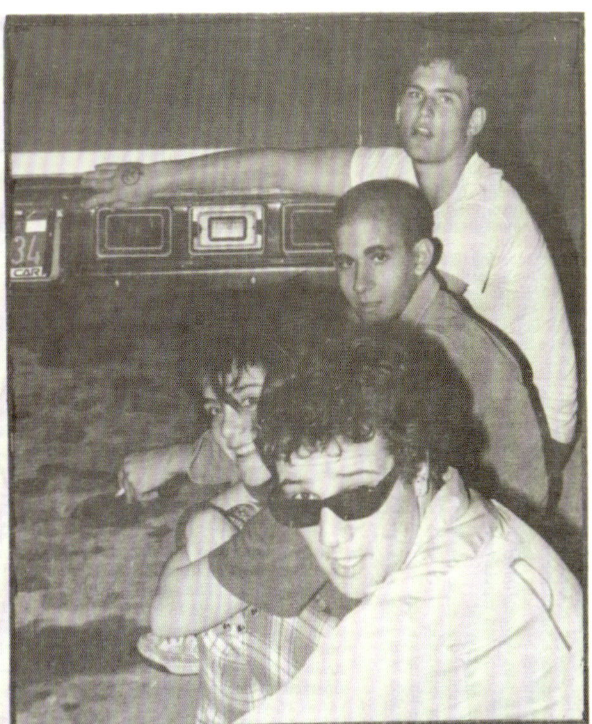

SIN 34 ↑

WGP WHOOYA PICS. PAGE

← mEat PUPPets

(ED COLVER)

HELP THE PUNK FIND A JOB

ANARCHY HOT DOG STAND NO

LAPD NO WAY

EF NO HUTTON

JOES DISCO SORRY

CITY GARBAGE DUMP NO

The only job he can find is working on a silly little punk rock fanzine!

SCAM

For lack of anything better to print this issue, we've decided to play "Dear Abby" and answer a letter that we actually received in the mail, supposedly written by some anonymous, frustrated scammer.

"RU: I am a 26-year -old woman and I love those young teen punkers. I'm very good-looking and I'd love to have sex with those highly energetic toughies. The problem is, I'm just not that aggressive, outside of bed! Is there a subtle way to let these teens in their prime know that I'm ready and willing to fuck?"

"Dear Frustrated: You shouldn't have to! If you're as attractive as you say you are, there's no reason why you shouldn't be propositioned 3-26 times a night! Perhaps, you being as old as you are, the young teen punkers don't think you'll be interested in a meaningless sexual encounter. You'll have to start hanging out and getting to be one of the crowd. Once you get a reputation as a slut, your problems will disappear.

Here is a truly brilliant plan. When you go to shows, dress provocatively and spend a little time sizing up the crowd. When you see a guy you'd like to get it happening with, first make sure he's free and available. Then, to get his undivided attention and eternal devotion, make him an offer he can't refuse. Offer him what he always wants, what he's always looking for, what's always on his mind, what he might even kill for. Offer him beer. Not only will you instantly have this guy in the palm of your hand, you'll have all his friends too. In fact, for the price of a six-pack,you could probably get gang-banged! Wouldn't that be fun?

If you're too shy to actually offer him the beer first, just stroll past a group of likely-looking anarchists with a couple brews and they may well attack you first. At least they'll offer some encouragement. At any rate, beer's the trick. As soon as your victim is a little buzzed, he'll be open and receptive to most suggestions, such as Merrill's favotite come-on line, "Hey, baby, wanna come home with me and meet my mother?"

If all this fails (for instance, if he's a non-drinker) I suggest you send WGP DATING SERVICE your name, phone number and photograph we'll set you up with more energetic young toughies than you can handle."----RU

FUN & GAMES

BEST BAND NAMES OF THE MONTH: Pop-o-pies, Easter Monkeys, Porch Monkeys, Wrecks, Young Iranians, Crewd, Lewd, Creedence Dirty Water Stinkpot, Liquid Shit Popsicles, The Dishrags, No Age Limit, Vomit Visions, Potty Trained, The Rotted, Special Rites, Hated Principals, Crucifux, Cricifix, Church Police, Moon Crestas, Youth Patrol, U.A.T., Green Chompy, Wall Flowers, 100 Flowers, Twisted Cross, Black Cross, Red Cross, Iron Cross, Ransid Youth, Varakers, Free Beer, Howdoyoudo, The New Christy Minstrels, BATMAN'S ENEMIES, & Sick Nurses.

WGP's FIRST ANNUAL, "HAVE YOUR MOM & POP COME UP WITH SOME GOOD PUNK BAND NAMES" CONTEST! yes, you heard it, kiddies! Just ask mom and/or dad if they could think of some repulsive names for your horrible punkrock bands. Write them on a card or letter, send them to WGP, "HAVE YOUR MOM AND POP COME UP WITH SOME GOOD PUNK BAND NAMES CONTEST". you might win!

HÜSKER DÜ

Greg & Bob from Husker Du were interviewed while in LA to record and play live.
WGP: We heard Tesco (Touch & Go) was giving some static to your band..?
Bob: He gave New Alliance static...
Greg: He said, "How did you get saddled with these guys." He says the record doesn't have any balls, or something. He seems to have a real hang-up about balls.

WGP: So, you set this tour up yourself?
Bob: Yeah, we usually do. It seems to work out better that way...
Greg: We always know, or at least have a pretty good idea of what's happening.
WGP: Where did you get your name?
Greg: Husker Du.. uh, there's that game. It's Danish, it means "do you remember". Thats kinda cool.
WGP: What kinda music do you consider yourself?
Bob: Everyone says the first thing was "progressive rock" and everyone that hears the album (Land Speed) says it's hardcore, and I bet alot of the people who hear the new single will say that it's pop, and when they hear the stuff we're working on now, they wont know what to call it. I guess it's just hardcore music...
WGP: What goes on in your hometown, Minneapolis? Any Labels? Fanzines?
Greg: Yeah. Twin Tone's the big label, a major independent like Bomp was before they made it big. Fanzines come and go, there's not that much to cover really.
WGP: So some kids will put out a zine...
Greg: Not so much kids. Old guard people Revillos & Jam fans. WGP:Oh no!
Bob: They try to write about us...
WGP: What bands do you like from LA?
Bob: Black Flag. The Minutemen.
Greg: The Minutemen are hot! More people should go out and see them instead of like 15-20 at a time.
Bob: That was sick last night, at the Grandia Room, there was like 20 people at the most...
ah lets see, who else is good around here? ah, Social Distortion. Greg: I sorta like Saccharine Trust.
(Talk goes on about "Ultracore", their total intense thrash sets, from one song into the next for 20 minutes... as recorded on their "Land Speed" New Alliance lp...)
WGP: What are the lyrics hitting up?
Greg: Kinda neat. The album had like personal stuff & political stuff. The new record doesn't have any political stuff on it. We're trying to get away from the bandwagon. Seems like everyone is ragging on death and famon.
Bob: What we've been working on out here with spot, is like personal polotics. Things for yourself. Not like "change the world"... it isn't working.
WGP: What good bands come from your city? Bob:Replacements, Man Sized Action.
Greg: From a little further east there's Nechmonsht and The Tar Babies from Madison and Die Kruzen hrom Milwauke, their hot! I guess they have something coming out on Noise Records, or Bob Moore's parent's Records!
WGP: What do you know about Bob Moore?
Greg: We got the dirt on him!...
Bob: If hardcore goes commercial, he'll go rasta (talk goes on about "rasta" trend & Bad Brains). Greg: It's just an excuse to get stoned all the time! You never see them pray to God, all they do is sit around and roll joints.
WGP: And, what are your hobbies?
Bob: I like to go bowling.
Greg: I like to take off for the day with friends and hide somewhere in the woods and drink beer, or go campin' on the northshore for the weekend.
-INTERVIEWED BY DAVE & MIKE

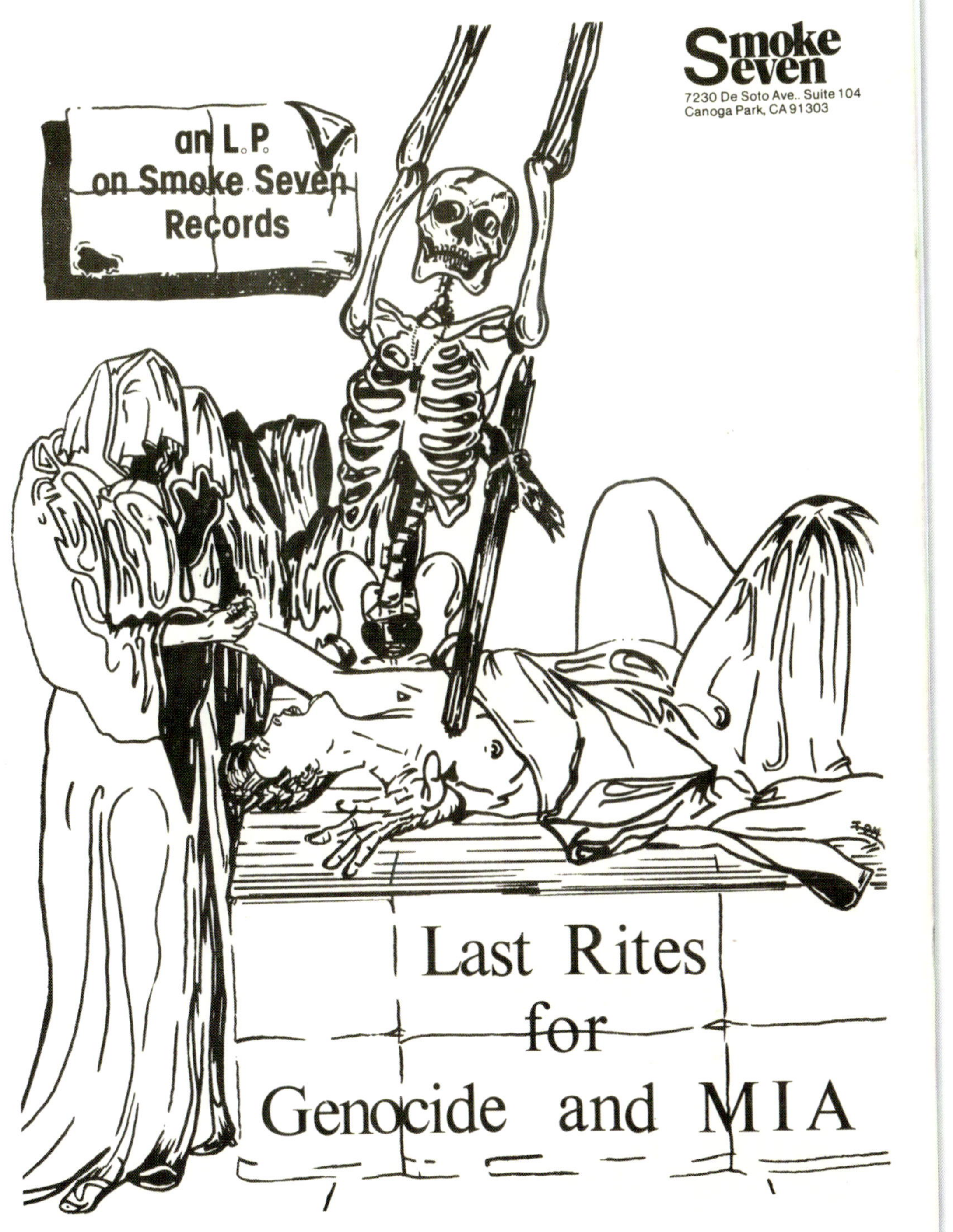
an L.P.
on Smoke Seven
Records
Smoke Seven
7230 De Soto Ave., Suite 104
Canoga Park, CA 91303
Last Rites
for
Genocide and MIA

From left: We Got Power Yearbook '82 *collected our first four issues and featured an Ed Colver photo of Tony Adolescent on the cover; Government Issue minus John Stabb (from left, Marc Alberstadt, Tom Lyle, Rob Moss, and stray kitty) turns the tables and reviews* We Got Power *#5, Shamus O'Brian's parking lot, 1983.* JORDAN SCHWARTZ

WE GOT POWER #5
MAY 1983

We broadened our mission with confidence for *We Got Power* #5, which includes my reviews of breakfast cereal, Kim's reviews of cheap beer, and Dave's reviews of LAPD police raids on punk shows—which used a one-to-five-star rating system.

Ed Colver's cover photo of a punker with a piece of a frog in his mouth was taken at a Vandals gig at Dancing Waters. During the tune "Frog Stomp," singer Stevo unloaded a bag of lab frogs on the stage for the crowd to tear apart. Our printer, Mr. Macias, tastefully loaded up the green ink for what would be our final run.

—*Jordan Schwartz*

MEDIA BLITZ — THEY ARE OUT TO GET YOU!

The stubbly hairdos are the latest rage amongst young boys, and barbers across the country link the trend to the faltering economy and the popularity of punk rock music.

THIS IS

4 36 QUINCY
After a boy is murdered at a nightclub, Quincy (Jack Klugman) claims punk rock was a contributing factor. Emily: Anita Gillette (60 min.)

GETTING REDICULOUS!

Culture Clubbers claim punk is passé. "I never liked it," says Boy George, 21, "because I like quality. That's why I like people like Tom Jones."

7 WE DESTROY THE FAMILY: PUNKS VS. PARENTS —Documentary

7 EYE ON L.A. A concluding report with punk-rock life-styles.

5 HOUR MAGAZINE Actress Betty White. Also: weight loss; the punk life style. (Repeat; 60 min.)

7 42 GENERAL HOSPITAL

Punk

Part 1 of three on "The Families of Punk Rockers"

stamp out punk music.

"Everything was mellow," he said. "It was fun until the cops came."

The philosophy of punk, Dank says, is to be as obscene and repulsive as possible.

2 42 IT TAKES TWO—Comedy
Lisa (Helen Hunt) flips over a punk rocker (Chip Van Eman) who aced Andy (Anthony Edwards) out of a job, but Sam (Richard Crenna) considers him "interplanetary fungus."

THERE WAS A CLOWN at Douglas Park named Frisbee. She had a wild get-up on topped with curly hair dyed three colors. At first, I thought the Jaycees had been infiltrated by a punk rocker.

Recently, a 14-year-old girl with cigarette burns on her arms came to see me," says Dank. "When I asked her about them, she told me she was a follower of the punk group Germs, and burning yourself is what you do to show you like them.

PUNK CONCERT

Punks roaming the streets of Hollywood yesterday dressed in black leather outfits, mohawks, orange-died hair and with staples in their ears

Amos, a punk rocker who sports an earring and a nappy crewcut, Newman issued a proclamation that stunned them both: He forbade Amos to get a haircut.

THE PUNK PUZZLE!

Enter the new wave world as puzzled parents try to cope with punk kids.

Punk Rock Fracas Leads to 5 Arrests

"Man, what's the matter with kids today?"

ATIONAL ENQUIRER

Inside the studio, the concert seemed to be a typically frantic punk affair

"A 13- or 14-year-old isn't sophisticated enough to understand the lyrics of many punk songs," says Dank, explaining that often they

Fashion designers predict punk styles will take over

AMERICA IS going punk — not only in music but in fashions.

What will the "with it" women be wearing? It's almost frightening to behold. At the top of the page are two actual "punk" looks. The others are drawings showing the bizarre eye makeup and other weird punk styles that could develop.

"Designers can thank the punk scene for fashion innovations that will be lining their coffers in the coming seasons," fashion consultant Mary Lou Double-U.

"When I play this one, my mother fights back with the vacuum cleaner."

What about punk rock?

UGLY BITCH

All of these people had real belligerent looks on their faces," one of the employees said. "We went up one of the catwalks and saw them spitting all over each other, cutting each other with razor blades.

Of course, the sure way to let it be known from a punk rocker is to walk up to the suspect with a balloon you've got up this way and if he or she is a punk rocker she will want a brick you to let go of a

Jennifer Kresch
Portola Valley
"Punk rockers are strange, but I like their music and the way they dress. It's too bad they are so violent toward each other. It's been around a long time in England, and now people are finally accepting it here."

Kennard Gray
Redwood City
"They are a degrading part of society. Punkers are just losers who want attention. Why can't they be happy about society? There are better ways to take out your aggressions than by this method.

Jay Mshuja
Palo Alto
"It's just another style of life and a lot of people try to imitate it. It's just the same as Valley Girls."

oh yeah!

Wendy Strickland
Redwood City
"I don't know why anyone would try hard to make themselves as unattractive as possible. I like some of the music but not the way most punkers look."

WHO WANTS TO LOOK LIKE YOU?

David Popovich
Redwood City
I know it's their life but I just don't understand why they'd want to act and dress that way."

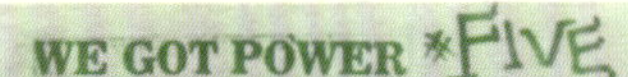

Laura: Tell us how to scam, Jughead...
Kim: Everyone wants to know how to scam.
Jughead: Well, the problem with all these guys is, they try their hardest to scam. Forget it. I gave up on scamming about a year and a half ago, two years ago. It's hopeless. All you do is get yourself all worked up and frustrated, hoping that you're gonna get laid, but it's all bullshit. I just hang out and if something drops in my lap, hey! that's happening!
Kim: If you saw a girl who was absolutly beautiful and you really wanted to fuck her and she wasn't going to approach you, what would you say to her?
Jughead: I'd smoke a joint with her. Make conversation, and wait for her to start feeling my balls.
Kim: Then what?
Jughead: Good old-fashioned American sex, done well.
Kim: You seem to get laid alot, what are your secrets?
Jughead: I'm good in bed.
Kim: Do you think sex is a very important part of any lifestyle?
Jughead: Heck yeah! You gotta have some fun along the line.
Kim: Do you beleive in the straightedge concept?
Jughead: The only reason a guy wont have sex is if he's got a little dick, and he can't use it right.
Kim: How big is your dick, Jughead?
Jughead: Alright. Better than average.
Kim: Average is 5½, 6 inches.
Jughead: What? You're crazy!
Kim: Hey, I should know.
Jughead: Oh man, most guys are hurtin'.
Kim: No kidding. Why do you think I'm celibate?
Jughead: No kidding. If I was a woman and I'd to put up with 6 inch pokers, I'd be celibate too.
Kim: Are you bisexual?
Jughead: No, I'm try-sexual. I'll try anything. Most of these guys today, you should see them. They're like a bunch of little kids. They'll have these really corny lines. "Hi, my name is Tom, what's your sign?"
Kim: Are you seriously bisexual?
Jughead: Heck no.
Kim: Now dude, I want some tips for scammers. If there is a guy who wants to pick up on a chick, what kind of tactical maneuvers should he use?
Jughead: "Hi. Do you smell good?"

edited by Dave

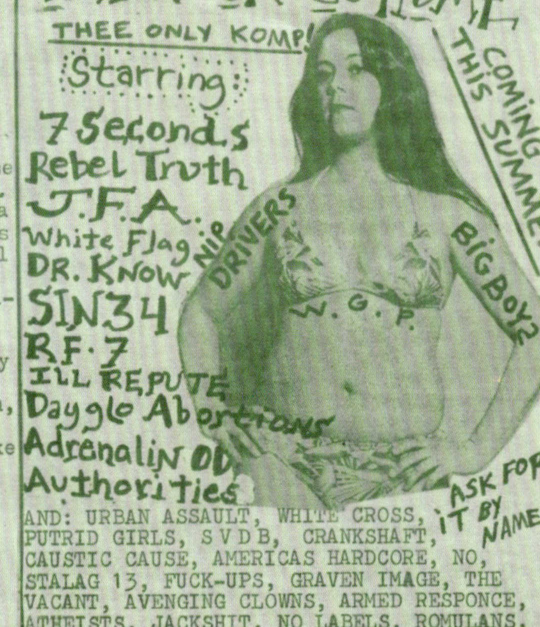

AND: URBAN ASSAULT, WHITE CROSS, PUTRID GIRLS, S V D B, CRANKSHAFT, CAUSTIC CAUSE, AMERICAS HARDCORE, NO, STALAG 13, FUCK-UPS, GRAVEN IMAGE, THE VACANT, AVENGING CLOWNS, ARMED RESPONCE, ATHEISTS, JACKSHIT, NO LABELS, ROMULANS, DERANGED DICTION, WILLFUL NEGLECT, TAR BABIES, MECHT MENSH, NEOS, HATED PRINCIPALS, MANIMAL, & maybe more!?

ASK FOR IT BY NAME!

A L L O N O N E 12" A L B U M ! ! !

WE GOT POWER — magazine

This mag is supposidly published by JORDAN SCHWARTZ. Layouts by DAVE MARKEY. Various writing and panicing by KIM who hasn't changed her name to "RU" yet. The cover shot was by ED COLVER, who took other pic's in here, too, along with ALLISON aka "MOUSE" and that five fingered GLENN E. FRIEDMAN ... Other writing and contribution were done by various peoples who have their name signed after their work.

BACK ISSUES ARE $2.00 EACH, POSTPAID.
WGP #1: Circle One, Wasted Youth etc.
WGP #2: Red Cross, Saccharine Trust, Henry, Overkill, club news & reviews etc
WGP #3: D.O.A., J.F.A, No Crisis, CH3, Misfits, Jack TSOL, & other shit
WGP #4: Black Flag, Dead Kennedys, Bad Religion, Minor Threat, Husker Du, + MORE

WE GOT POWER
3010 santa monica blvd.
no. 310 santa monica CA
90404

The Circle Jerks were interviewed by Kim and Jordan at one of their rehearsals, a few days after their show at the T-bird Rollerdrome. Present for the interview were Keith Morris (vocals), Greg Hetson (guitar), and new bass player Earl (formerly that big dude in Saccharine Trust).

Jordan: Question #1. What do you think of Peter Ivers being murdered?
Keith: It's really bad. Peter Ivers was a great host. (Note: Peter Ivers was host of "New Wave Theater").
Earl: What??
Kim: He was beaten to death. They found his body in his apartment last week.
Earl: For real?
Kim: Yeah. He's history.
Greg: He got blugeoned to death.
Jordan: Are you an Ⓐnarchy band?
Keith: We're a Yo band.
Greg: We're Yo.
Keith: Audience participation! We're a fun band.
Greg: We're a garage band.
Jordan: When did you get Earl, and why?
Greg: We got him about three weeks ago. We figured he was so ugly he'd fit right in.
Keith: As you can see, we're not one of the more glamourous bands.

Psychologist Serena Dank

NEW TV ALBUM!

Jordan: What's your new song, "Parade of the Horribles" about?
Keith: It's about religious fanatics--you know, the guy that stands on the corner and waves the Bible and says, "If you don't read the Bible you're all going to Hell".
Jordan: What do you believe happens when you die?
Greg: After about two weeks the maggots start eating your eyeballs.
Keith: When I die I wanna be a bird.
Earl: I wanna be a panther.
Jordan: Here's a question for Greg. Will you put us on the list if Kim fixes you up with her little sister?
Greg: You guys'll be on the permanent list.
Keith: I'll even set two extra plates at the table in case you appear.
Kim: Consider it done. What's the next question, Jordan?
Jordan: What are your influences?
Greg: Bad.
Kim: What're your favorite bands, and shit like that?
Greg: New Riders of the Purple Sage.
Keith: War, Iron Butterfly, Magazine, Motorhead, Bad Religion.
Kim: If you had a one-hour weekly t.v. show, what would you put on it?
Keith: I'd show pornography. It'd be like the PTL show. It'd be called, "Fucking for God".
Greg: I'd have my favorite bands on it, and comedians and stuff.
Earl: I'd do something like "In Search Of".
Kim: In search of what?
Earl: Women, drugs.

Mayhem

Kim: What if there was a Circle Jerks video game?
Greg: You'd have to dodge the slammers on-stage...
Earl: And you gotta make the kids in the audience catch the stage divers...
Keith: And you gotta be able to avoid the people at the door who want you to put them on the guest list...
Greg: And you also gotta make it to the liquor store by two.
Jordan: What have you done so far in 1983?
Greg: I bought a new guitar tuner.
Keith: We recorded a new album!
Kim: What about your personal lives? Any milestones?
Greg: I haven't got V.D. yet.
Jordan: What was your favorite gig, ever?
Keith: David Bowie at the Santa Monica Civic in 1972.
Greg: Motörhead at the Country Club!
Jordan: If you guys were ice-cream cones, what flavor would you be?
Greg: I'd be chocolate double fudge.
Earl: I'd be chocolate chip mint.
Keith: Neopolitan!
Jordan: Do you think we're being watched by beings from outer space?

SEX—BY COMPUTER

Greg: Yeah, they're watching us!
Keith: How do you think the pyramids were built? They're landmarks for people from outer space.
Jordan: Here's another great question. If Keith Richards walked onstage during one of your shows, would you let him solo or kick him off like Chuck Berry did?
Keith: Fuck yeah I'd let him play!
Jordan: What songs would you do?
Keith: We could play "Jumpin' Jack Flash" or "Brown Sugar"...
Kim: What were the last jobs you had before you became professional punks?
Earl: I worked at Safeway for four years.
Keith: I worked for my dad at a fishing tackle shop.
Greg: I delivered printing for STD in Santa Monica. I worked at USA gasoline for a day...
Jordan: Do you guys skate?
Keith: I used to skate.
Greg: I ice skate.
Earl: Ice hockey!
Jordan: Does t.v. cause cancer?

BALD?
Or otherwise?

Photo: Glen E. Friedman

USA NIGHT FLIGHT
Included: country singer Dottie West; rock group REO Speedwagon; "Stars over Harlem," with Joe Turner, Count Basie and Nat "King" Cole; clips from the movie "Six Weeks"; and episodes from "Space Cadet" and "Tales of Tomorrow." Also: Def Leppard on tour; David Johansen; Fleetwood Mac; Toto; the Spys; Circle Jerks. (4 hrs.)

YAAAAA!

"I was coming down Gower, over near Gower Gulch (shopping center), when I saw this mob of all these funny-looking people," Garvin said. "I parked my car and these people were running every place. There were as many people in front of my bar as there were during the Hollywood Christmas parade. But it looked like Halloween, the way everybody was dressed.

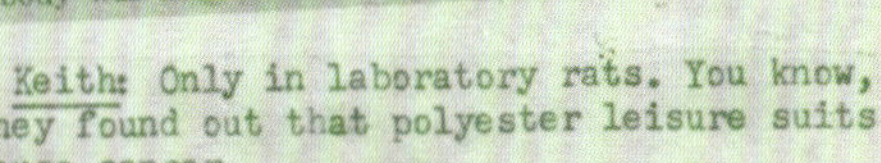

Keith: Only in laboratory rats. You know, they found out that polyester leisure suits cause cancer.
Greg: Posh Boy's gonna die pretty soon then, hopefully...sorry about that, Robbie.
Jordan: What was the first punk gig that you ever went to?
Greg: Dickies and Middle Class at the Whiskey in 1978.
Keith: The Ramones, with Blondie, at the Whiskey.
Earl: I can't remember who played, but it was at the Masque. My first big show was the Circle Jerks at the Fleetwood.
Keith: I saw the Sex Pistols in San Fransisco.
Jordan: When you take your farm animals out on a date, what hot spots do you usually go to?
Greg: Carlos and Charlie's.
Keith: Bennie-Hanna's of Tokyo.
Earl: Johnny's Steak House.
Kim: Where do you go afterward? Her place or yours?
Keith: We go back to the barn.
Jordan: Well, I guess that's about it.
Kim: No, we gotta have some more questions! Think of some!
Jordan: Uh...what's your favorite drug?
Keith: Chocolate long johns. Hostess twinkies.
Earl: Budweiser and acid!
Jordan: If you were God, what kind of religion would you have?
Keith: Budweiser! My church would be the Church of the Holy Party Keg. Keg party at Raleigh Hills!
Kim: Describe the perfect evening out.
Keith: The perfect evening out is: Dinner at Taco Bell, then going and seeing Missing Persons or Oingo Boingo, then to the Hot Tub Club, then down to the float tubs...
Earl: And then a walk on the Santa Monica pier.
Keith: In the nude.

—Kim

Stud tires out

J O R D A N's D A M A G E . . .

The "Party Or Go hOme" comp, complied by yours truly, on behalf of W G P mag is still in the works at press-time.. Still much mixing and some recordings are needed to finish the 40 band plus album... Mystic Records/W G P Records! are working (?) on getting the tapes (all one million of 'em) consistant 2 the same levels and all that technical bullshit. Only our Lord Jesus knows when this record will come out.

F L A S H ! Black Flag skateboard comin' at ya soon! Raymond Pettibone design! Write W G P for details... brought to you by Rip City Skates (213-828-0388) call 'em for more infoe dudez.

YE PUNKERZ. . . W G P ragazine needs U! Ol' We Got Power is lookin' for newww writers to help fill these pages here with more rad e. kal shit. Note: You need not know how to spell to qualify and you can write about what ever the fuck you want... just expect us to edit the heck out of it!

W G P industrys (no doubt) has creepy crawled into the video era with my new old $\frac{1}{4}$" Black & White Video Damage camera. Catch that hot punk flick... "The Slog Movie" with vintage footage of Circle One, Black Flag, Circle Jerks, more more more. All live, now on $\frac{1}{2}$" VCR for $18.00 postpaid. They might be available in da store one of these years.

Relax for the record, wait for the skate, the Slog video cassette will be with you shorty. Buy Buy.

-JORDAN

FUCKIN' FANZINE RUNDOWN SHIT!

Loads of hot shit... FLIPSIDE goin' on # 38! Al & the gang are doin' fuggin video 'zines now! U 've kum a long way babie! PoB 363 Whittier, CA 90608. TOUCH & GO has moved 2 D.C. Put out it's biggest ish yet #21! Box 25305 Wash. DC 20007. RIPPER more standard stuff: one of the more "technically advanced", nice lookin' layouts 1494 Teresita Drive, San Jose, CA 95129. MAXIMUM ROCK N ROLL being attacked for their political stance, but, whatever, this is one fine zine. They cover everything and everyone. An encyclopedia! The thikest zine yet. PoB 288 Berkeley, CA 94701. GRUDGE is a very well put together "up & comer" xerox-er 4343 Soquel Dr. #8 Soquel, CA 95073. SICK TEEN more teen insanityzany neglambamsham oh wow 708 St. Joeseph St. Green Bay, WI 54301. SLAM slam slam slam slam882 Bank St. Akron Ohio 44305. BIG CITY way rad gnarly koverage of da latest New Jork happenings. Good writin and all that jazz, you should order it today and be eligible for a free trip to Taheti 2329 Vance St. Bronx NY 10469. OUTCRY if only Steve would put out this finezine more often! (Boy, we shouldn't talk. WGP is published irregularly. Fuck. I kant spelll. Kim, korrect the erorz Break out the Liquid Paper!) Anyhow, get outcry or die (a rhyme!) 1001 Fremont, PoB 1194 So. Pasadena CA 91030. SUBURBAN RELAPSE excellent Floridain magazine with lotsa LA coverage PoB 610906 N. Miami, Fl. 33161. KILLER is pretty fuckin killer. (Isn't this fun? Loads of recordreviews & such. 84 Eldridge St. #5 NYC 10002. PHENIS upholding the rep to be Az's #1 (are there any more?!) 527 w 13st Tempe, Az 85281. PARANoiA more more more encore PoB 20391, Reno, NV 89515. XIPHOID PROCESS ok short little ditty outta texASS. Austin looks waaay hapenin' I wanna go! 401 W. 32nd Austin Tex 78705. FRONTAL ASSAULT 33 Adams St. Littleton, Mass, rad e. kal man, totally diffrent kind o' head. FORCED EXPOSURE "the biggest mag on the east coast", ok 76 Bromfield St. Watertown Ma 09172. AKA more fun than the TV Guide! As I said above, Tex is hip. PoB 191935 Arlington, Tx 76019. CONTEMPT in the vein of Slam mag & Sick Teen. I love strainin' my eyes to read the teeny type! Wat exorsize. I CANT FUCKING SPELL! 9135 Johnnycake Ridge Rd. MENTOR Ohio 44060. GAGGING DOG ANOTHER one of those neat-o xerox dudes, much like PHENIS (hey, this is from the same place! There is more!) Yeah, I really like this.. 1624 Gaylon Dr. Tempe, AZ 85282. YOUTH PLAUGE hey, wherez yer new ish? 4019 Hessington Place Victoria, B.C. Canada V8N 5C5. SCHRIK a long while ago, the editor of this fine zine sent some ishes to the irresponcible kids at WGP, we sold 'em at Rhino- We owe ya about $5.00, we'll get it ya soonest! Anyhow, get this zine..34 Longford Cres. Agincourt, Ontario M 1 W 1 P 4. BIG TAKEOVER continues Jack Rabid c/o Prudential Lines Inc, One World Trade Center #3701 NY NY 10048. Oops whhopaditty, OOPS! Get it. 4812 Eldo St. Willoughby OH 44094. My Degeneration if you've read this far, you're either a complete fanzine fanatic or you'be bored of readin' the side of toothpaste boxes. c/o Headbanger PoB 7038-A Denco 80207. OOH Myyyyy-DAVE

TWISTED IMAGE-R-

JORDAN IS A BIG FLAKE

YOU CAN'T MAKE IT BY YOURSELF
. . . THE WORLD IS GOING MAD.

"Oh my God, this could be my kid."

"It's really hard to be a good Catholic when you're young and wanting to enjoy life but when it all boils down, I'd rather have eternal life than a lot of wild parties."

EPIDEMIC:
Why your kid is on drugs.
A horrifying account of the ultimate social disease.

Beer Reviews
by Kim

Good Beer--G
Prep Beer--P
Cult Beer--C
Punk Beer--Ⓐ
Beer Your Parents Buy For You--A&W

Budweiser--Definitely the King of Beers, and my personal favorite. Cool horses, too. Buy bottled, 'cause cans won't break when you toss 'em out the car window. G.

Michelob--Something to drink when you can't find Bud. A little more expensive, but it tastes better and the packaging is classier. G.

Old English 800--This stuff tastes like soapsuds, but it gets you fucked up fast. How else can you get high for a dollar? Ⓐ

Heineken--I paid $3 for half a six-pack of this shit, and I barely got high. Also this beer tastes like bad coffee. Leave this brew to the West-wood crowd and other retards. P.

Mickey's--The Official Beer of Venice. Ask anyone in Suicidal Tendencies about this brew, they'll know. It tastes pretty rank, but it'll get you wasted pretty fast and you just can't top those cool 'big mouth' bottles. C.

Killian's Red--This beer looked interesting and I liked the commercials so I tried it out. A real disappointment. First of all it isn't even red. And it isn't very strong either. Definitely geared for the IRA crowd and other patriotic Irishmen. C.

Stevo - VANDALS

Kim: Stevo, what have you done to deserve the honor of being this month's Young Acheiver?
Stevo: I've fucked up a bunch of shit and I've told a bunch of people to fuck off and I've made a lot of friends.
Kim: Have you trashed any clubs recently?
Stevo: Every club we've been to.
Kim: Can you elaborate on the damage?
Stevo: Broken toilets, tore the towel dispensers off the walls--all the minor that happens at average clubs.
Kim: Who aids you in your vandalistic endeavours?
Stevo: Anybody who's into the scene knows that they should break stuff and fuck things up wherever they go, because if any club sticks around for too long, it stagnates and stands for the Establishment. Someone runs the club, someone makes money off of it--that can't happen.
Kim: So you are definitely into destroying your own scene?
Stevo: We have been known to fuck up our own scene, but when the time comes that we've fucked up our own scene so bad that we can't play anymore, we're not useful anymore, and our goal will be acheived.
Kim: What about girls? Have you had any interesting experiences with girls that would be worth printing, like that one last summer?
Stevo: Well, there was this chick, and she was too young, and I got in trouble and the cops were looking for me for kidnapping and rape, and that's all there is to it.
In my opinion, I am the best fuck-up-my-scene person that there is. I don't have a job, I don't have a car, I don't have any money and I'm getting evicted. I do lots of drugs--I had some blue shit the other night, it was pretty good. I heard it was morphine. The only way I can cope with reality is to get so fucked up everything looks cool.
Kim: Tell us about the Vandals. Are you serious musicians?
Stevo: No! We're fucked musicians. We don't want anyone to take us seriously.
Kim: What are your favorite bands?
Stevo: Favorite bands? I have no musical taste. Why do you think I'm in hte Vandals? I can't distinguish between a good band and a bad band.
Kim: How did you do in school?
Stevo: I was a failure. I did too many drugs. But I'm a fairly intelligent person.
Kim: So you have, acheived, as a failure.
Stevo: Yes.

Expects Little Sex

KIm: What sets you apart from every other failure in the world?
Stevo: I'm the best failure there could be! I'm alienated from my parents--they don't ever want to see me again. When I go over to friends' houses, they ask me to leave...my band even sometimes teels me to split when we have practice,,,and me , being the lead singer, I'm suppossed to be a real heavy guy and popular and stuff, but people always tell me to GET THE HELL OUT OF HERE and chicks just don't wanna have xxxenithing to do with me 'cause i'm such a damn slob.
Kim: You're bummin'!
Stevo: I'm not bummin'. I dig it! I love being depressed. I live in a studio apartment with a fold-out' "Three Stooges" bed. I sit by myself and drink vodka and watch TV all day, 'til it's time to go out. The only thing that keeps me going are these gigs. I see the people that come here, and I know that I'm not a freak. And I'm not alone. There are many failures here. I can relate to them. I talk to failures all night long, and I feel good as a failure. Failures unite!
Kim: Stevo, do you have any idols? Your favorite failures?
Stevo: Well, this may sound trendy, but Sid Vicious is one of my favorite failures.
kim: What about Richard Nixon?
Stevo: I wish he was still president. He was cool, but he fucked up, he got cought. Nixon's been over to my house a few times, I've rapped with the dude, he's really cool, he don't get high but he does drink. Every time I surf near his pla ce he lets me wash off with his hose.
Kim: That's graet.
Stevo: That's kill, 'cause I don't get sand in my friend's car that way.
Kim: Can you relate to Charlie Brown?
Stevo: Oh yeah, he's a fucked failure. He's a nerd, he's a fuck-up. Yeah, I can realteto him. I'm a cool failure, though, and he's a fucked-up failure. People appreciate me for being a failure. I'm a failure, but they still come around.
I've been turned down by so many girls that it's not funny. I co me up with the coolest pick-up lines. Like I walk up to chicks at a gig and I say, "Hey, how ya' doin"? I haven't bathed in a week". They dig it. Then I say, "I've got a mini-bike waiting outside. Would you like to come to my trash bin?" But I haven't had a chick in about two years.
Kim: What kind of girls do you like?
Stevo: I'm not that selective. I like anything with two holes and a heartbeat.
Kim: Does that include animals?
Stevo: As long as their heart is still beating and their body is warm. I will have sex with animals. I don't fuck anything thats dead 'cept frogs.
Kim: What is your fetish for frogs?
Stevo: I hate frogs. The reason we do the song "Frog Stomp", is because I saw the movie ("The Frogs") when I was young and it scared the shit out of me. They eat all the people, and thats not right, people should eat frogs, or stomp on them.
Kim: Do you think you could get the same responce from, say, hamsters?
Stevo: I never have seen a hamster movie.
Kim: You saw "Ben" didn't you?
Stevo: Yeah, they were cool, they ate the bad guys. They were cool rats.
Kim: What if you could train an army of frogs to attack? Would you like them?
Stevo: No, I'd stomp on them. In fact I'g get them to trust me and when their backs were turned I'D STOMP ON THEM TIL THEIR GUTS SHOT OUT THEIR MOUTHS!! I wanna meet the guy on the front cover of this magazine and I wanna congradulate him for his antica. He's ok by me.

LÖTSA RECORDS

State dinner featured cat, American food

VANDALS "PEACE THROUGH VANDALISM" (Epitaph)
This H.B.-based band's six-song e.p. is definitely this week's big thing, the trend of the future, etc., and if you don't have it or haven't taped it off a friend or something you are N.H. (not happening). Seriously, it's an incredible record, with brilliant production and hilarious songs. The tunes deal with topics such as the True Meaning of Anarchy, an old H.B. group house "Wannabe Manner", the Pirates of the Carribean ride at Disneyland, and the extremely anarchistic feats of one Mr. Pat Brown. I'm sure you've heard their famous KROQ crossover hit, "Urban Struggle", and they also do a real nice cover of "Heartbreak Hotel". This is definitely an album for the 80's--and besides, how can you not like a band that throws beers to the audience and makes such a joke out of "ruining their own scene"? Get this record.

NO CRISIS "SHE'S INTO THE SCENE" (Ultra-Mega)
Another extremely impressive six-song 12" 33 rpm e.p. from a very good local band. No Crisis have been around for a while, but they don't play very often so you may not have seen them. Anyhow, their record is great. Their songs are pretty thrash and mostly deal with the familiar anger/political frustration/rebellion/social disgust etc. themes, but they do it well. You probably have heard "Take It" on Rodney already. I think this is a different version. "She's Into the Scene" is a cool song with a relatively original topic, but my favorite is "On Your Head". Aggression also does this song. In fact, all the songs on this record are good. And it's printed on clear vinyl, and the singer did the vocal tracks in one take. How can you resist?

DOES ANYBODY REMEMBER THIS?!

BLACK FLAG KILLS ANTS ON CONTACT

CUT OUT & STICK ON YOUR CAR!

D.O.A. "WAR ON 45" (Alternative Tentacles)
Here's another 12" e.p. featuring eight "songs to march by" from God's gift to punk rock and the best band in the world, D.O.A. Actually, I don't think this is the best record they've ever done but it's still damn good music for your money. They do an inspiring version of "War" which is already a big daytime KROQ hit, and they also cover "Let's Fuck" in about four different languages (none of them pronounced with any accuracy whatsoever). They've redone the Dil's "Class War" and do a slow reggae tune, "War in the East" which is kinda monotonous. The good news are the four originals, which are as intense, aggressive and exciting as anything else they've ever done. "Liar for Hire", "I'm Right You're Wrong", "America the Beautiful", and "I Hate You" all display the sort of anger and political awareness that have always characterized D.O.A.'s attitude and earned them a reputation for musical integrity & honest indignation. (rarities these days, I might add). Also, Joey Shithead's voice has improved tremendously. He's really singing well now.
Remember, talk minus action equals zero.

TSOL NOW ↓ THEN ↓

TRUE SOUNDS OF LIBERTY "BENEATH THE SHADOWS" (Alternative Tentacles)
T.S.O.L. are annoying millions with this new album, and it's easy to see why. The last traces of thrash punk have disappeared from their music with the addition of a keyboardist, and hardcore fans are likely to be a bit bummed. However, that's nothing new as T.S.O.L. have always been known, and often disparaged, for changing their musical direction with each new record. They always manage to maintain their uniqueness and energy, however, but this is definitely their mellowest yet. You've probably heard a lot of their new stuff by now. It's sort of hardcore muzak. I like it a great deal, but then I'm real into Bach, too. You may not be. You know what I mean?

CRASS "HOW DOES IT FEEL?" (Crass Records)
This record was really my first serious encounter with Crass. I can't say they're ever going to be one of my favorite bands. The lyrics are cool if you're into British sociological problems. I'm not. The music is horrid. I'm sure Crass are brilliant etc., but I'll give this record away to the first person who writes in and asks for it.
-THIS PAGE BY KIM.

REVIEWZ

Maximum Rock "Not So Quiet" (Alt. Tent.)
Great package. Great deal. 47 bands on a double LP. Stand-outs include: **MDC, DKs, Deadly Reign, Juvenille Justice, 7 Seconds, Wrecks, Bad Posture, Social Unrest, UXB, Free Beer**, etc. SOOO MUCH! More! More! Yeah Tim! Lets get your radio show back on LA airwaves! (Alternative Tenticals POB 11458 San Francisco CA 94101).

BIG BOYS "Fun Fun Fun" EP (Moment)
Different. Good. They play sum kool jive here. Their cover of "Hollywood Swingers" drags, while their thrasher "Apolitical" (With J.Blafra singing back-ups) goes faster than a speeding bullet. "Prison" is a great song. A record with real personality. (Moment POB 12424 Austin Texas 78711).

CONFLICT "America's Right" (UNJUST TAPES)
From the land of Arizona, comes this h.c. outfit backed with female vocals (which ads to the growing list, which is ok by me). They put much thought into their lyrics, and the music sound great aswell. Someone should put this on vinyl & this band should try to make it up to LA sometime. (Write to them: Conflict c/o K.Allman 3033 E 6th St. B-2 Tuscon Az, 85716).

ANTI "I Don't Wanna Die In Your War"
Haven't we heard this stuff before? Uh, who cares, I ain't gonna nitpick. This 12" is very fast, and it often lacks diversity, but who gives a fuck! This ain't David Bowie. The singer's got one harsh & snotty voice, and in these grooves sits some neat guitar work. (New Underground Records 4305 W. 153rd St. Lawndale, CA 90260.)

ROCK AGNEW "All By Myself" (Frontier)
A solo LP full of mediocre material. Yes, he's fucking talented, BUT... Too bad the **Adolescents** couldn't of stayed together to do this one!

HUSKER DU "Everything Falls Apart" LP
Outstanding effort by one of my fave's. This disc isn't as "ultra-core" speed, but, remember tempo doesn't always determin if a song is hardcore! This record should make the "real critic" RAVE. Best cuts "Blah, Blah, Blah", "Wheels", "Gravity", and "Punch Drunk", which will appear on the WGP Comp LP!??? (Reflex 731 Pontiac Pl. Mendota Height's MN 55120)

WARF-RAT TALES sampler LP
Well-produced comp of "more LA bands". My fave's on here are **100 Flowers** (who have the best tracks), **The Leaving Trains** & **The Last**. (Warf-Rat POB 25A39, Los Angeles, CA 90025).

RF7 "Fall In" 12" EP (Smoke Seven)
Awsome! Hot production. Hot songs! These crankin' Valley dudes can sure rok. The guitar work stands out on this one. Felix really belts out them wordz. Good work boys. (Smoke Seven 7230 De Soto Ave Suite 104 Canoga Pk. CA 91303.)

BEASTIE BOYS "Poliwog Stew" 7" EP (Rat Cage) I love this record. Totally break neck speed, silly lyrics, thrashy guitar. A "fun" record. Damn, I hope this band (from N.Y.) comes to LA! Every tune on this 8 song ep is wickid. Especially, "Egg Raid On Mojo", "Transit Cop", and "Holy Snappers". Get this record, if you happen to come across it! (Rat Cage 307 E. 9th St. NY 10003)

MISGUIDED "Bringing It Down" EP
New York is hosting some hot new HC bands! This self-produced 3 song 7" is raw and powerful, but isn't as distintive as some.

A celebration of cowboys, cow ponies and cow country.

ZERO BOYS "Vicious Circle" LP (Nimrod..)
Blazing stuff here. Outstanding production, great tunes like "Civilizations Diein'", "Livin' In The 80's", & "Down The Drain". Oh yeah, "HighTime" is a killer tune too. If this band were from the West Coast, rather than the Mid West, we'd hear alot more from them. They broke up.

MASTER TAPE comp (Nimrod/Affirmation)
Put out by Zero Boys; their fellow Mid-West & East Coast H.C. bands is also radical! I especially like **Die Kreuzen**-man is this band intense, can't wait to hear more from them! **Articles Of Faith**, **Toxic Reasons**, & **The FU's** are great too. (Both Zero Boys & Master Tape are $5. postpaid -great- Affirmation POB 30253 Indianapolis Ind. 46220). Get 'em!

Die Kreuzen's Cows Beer rules

DAYGLO ABORTIONS "Out Of The Womb" LP
Fuckin' decent. Funny fun material. "1967" & "Scared Of People" are stand out cuts. Great guitar work and use of organs, back-up vocals, & hot drummin'. Crazy. (Write to 'em: Jesus Bonehead 567 Head St. V9A 555 Victoria B.C. Canada)

SCREAM ep (IMMORTAL NUTS)
Not to be confused with the **DC Scream**. This Nor. Cal. band put out this EP which is ok stuff, didn't leave a big impression on me. P.S. They changed their name: "Rebels & Inf." (Immortal Nuts 620 Santa Clara Ave. #31 Alameda CA 94501). THIS PAGE OF REVIEWS BY-DAVE J.C. MARKEY

DAVE REVIEWS MORE RECORDS....

NEGATIVE APPROACH ep (TOUCH&GO)
AaaaaUuuuUUhHhhhWaaaruuuUAAAgggggggGG Dis be one two one two breakneck stuff. Maybe this is even faster that HC! If you play the Pistols on 78, it's not even as fast as this. Get this record for your sister!! (T & G pob 716 Maumee Ohio, 43537). Rad. e. Kal

NO! PLEASE! NO MORE FUCKIN' RECORD REVIEWS! PLEEZE NO!!! ARRRG!!!

NECROS "Conquest For Death" 45
First listen I wasn't too stoked. Only 2 songs, went by too quick. Then I played it a few more times. I noticed I was humming the chorus of the title cut. Then I read the lyrics, and boy, they did apply. Kinda snuck up on me. The music is more complicated than before, great. We need to get more hectic. The cover looks way bitchen, and the other song is funny. (NECROS info P.O.B.421 Maumee, Ohio 43537).

FANG "Landshark"
Uh, I donno. Pretty fair stuff I recon. The opening cut sounds like X! The last cut, "Skinheads Smoke Dope" is funny 'cos the singer sings with an Oi/Cockney accent. Inbetween is some standard thrash and slower, easier, '77 punk stuffff. This SF band has a great song on the Max R komp too!!

DEAD KENNEDYS "Plastic Surgery Disasters"
Some have been criticizing the DKs for not progressing, or sounding the same. This LP is different from their other releases! I think this is great! The songs are well structured, the music alone is worth the price of admission. Be sure to look through the booklet inside while your listening to the LP, it's like a gnarly movie with a realistic soundtrack. This is the stuff they don't want you listening to. They'd rather have you buy and think Journey, Oliva Newton John, or any of the other million corporate "rock" groups. Too bad this doesn't get airplay, 'cos this IS rock. (ALTERNATIVE TENTICALS/FAULTY)

NOISE FROM NOWHERE comp EP
The sound "quality" isn't up to par. This doesn't help out these bands from "nowhere". **Moslem Birth** have a funny song about **Christian Death. Kent State** do "Breakout Breakfree". I've heard it before! (Toxic Shock Records, box 242 Pomona CA 91769). Surprise, no photos by Ed Colver! ha ha ha ho ho ho he he...

THE FUCKING US FESTIVAL MAN

manson youth rule!

Jordan's record reviews. . .

7 SECONDS "Skins Brains Guts" ep
Hot hardcore thrash from this tightly knit Rino trio. The music is really radical, the lyrics are kinda basic (like "Anti-Klan"), but what the fuck! (ALTERNATIVE TENTICALS)

ANGRY SAMOANS "Back From Samoa"
This is a kool album. The Samoans really jam their axe's, the lyrics are pretty funny... (BAD TRIP)

Artistic Decline 4 song ep
I don't want to fucking rank on this but this record just ain't hate kill and destroy enuff ya know? Theres this shit about Andy Warhol. OOPS the record plays man farout. ANYways, the guitar on here is pretty happening, and the bass was cool. Uh... (New Underground Records)

AUTHORITIES "Soundtrack For Trouble" ep
I first heard them do "I Hate Cops" on the Max R'n'R radio show (when it used to be on in L.A.) and I said "They must be on the WGP **Party Or Go Home** comp record (coming out sooon), and they are! This 7" 4 song ep is way cool and way short. BUY IT!!! (SELECTA RECORDS 261 Patricia Ave. Stockton, CA 95210

MEATMEN "Crippled Children Suck" ep
Kinda dull. "Blud Sausage" was much much better. They should try somthing new like keyboards. (Touch & Go) RULEZ)

EVEN WORSE "Mouse Or Rat" 45
Slower. Not "high energy", but the guitar sounds good.

OVERKILL 4 song ep
This is okay, but it's not totally Overkill, like their old punk shows. Merrill left the band, they now play the heavy metal circut but claim to still play their thrash, and get away with it 'cos their new singer looks like Robert Plant.

S.F. URBAN ASSAULT
"Burn down city hall, kill the pigs". Kinda basic, tho a good first record. They should be Real Hot if they stay together and keep playing.

S.F. FUCK UPS
First off, I hate 7" records. I have to keep getting up and turn them over.or I forget to turn knob from 12" to 7" and the needle does a gnarly grind on the turn table. Thrash. Not the best record in the world, but pretty stylin'. I like that "White Boy" song. Why do you even care what I say about these records? Buy it and find out for yourself!!

THE LEPERS 45
The B side lyrics are written by John Hinkley Jr. and they are prettygood. The vocals are happening too.

SHATTERED FAITH lp
Not my bag of dirt. Nice production work, this gay record is a fuckin' waste! ThEsE gUyS jUsT aIn'T WgP mAtErIaL! The fake applause and stoopid intro makes this lamer than Styx's "Mr. Roboto"!!!! CHEEZE!

WHITE CROSS 7" eepp
I was washing dishes their "Speed Of The Presses" came over my speakers YeAH yeAH YEAH hardoncore. I started jumping up & down and I broke all the dishes. A definate mood elivator.

MINUTEMEN "What Makes A Man Start Fires?" al bum
This record was recorded as good as the band is. There's lotsa songs (18), Happening. "Tin Roof" is one of my favorite songs.

MINUTEMEN

WHAT MAKES A MAN START BARBEQUES?

CONFUSED? KXLU F.M. 89.9

SUDDEN DEATH komp (Smoke 7)
If you don't have this record by now put this mag down and go to the record store and buy it, or tape it. A really worthwile comp with lots of different bands. **JFA** & **Sin34** are cool! THRASH! I dig that last line on the first **Moral Decay** track. **Crankshaft** are cool massacre killers. At this point I turn the record over making sure to miss The **Demented**'s "How Can I Kill You". (Sorry Nick.) **Red Kross** is totally happening, thrash trash thrash. **Youth Gone Mad**, now here's a band that's been around for a while and I've never heard, their songs are good & fuNNy. I had the **Naughty Women** song "Linda Is A Monster" running through my head today. Just because sumebody gots long hair and wears a dress don't mean they ain't hardcore. This is my favorite comp of the year, so far.

SCREAM RULE

URBAN WASTE 8 song EP
Oh wow, more New York stuff. The production on this is pretty tinny, but on first listen, it makes a decent impression, especially the vocals. Some of the lyrics are pretty tired ("Police Brutality", "No Hope",etc.) Basic and nothing new. Ah, so what, they play it well! (Mob Style Records 246-14 54th Ave, Douglaston, N.Y. 11362). -DJCM

VYNAL! (sic)

JFA "Beyond The Valley..." lp
Oh man, when's someone gonna invent some new adjectives to describe these radical disc's o' vinyl? FUCKIN AYEEEEE! I can pass on the surf music on there, though. butt this elpee is an excellent soundtrack for the summer! YEAHH!!

CIRCLE JERKS "Golden Shower Of Hits"
The two guitars on here work surprisingly well. The songs themselves, have never been better! ("Parade Of The Horribles", "High Price On Our Heads", "Junk Mail" ect.) This record is sooooo good. Forget their "Wild In The Streets" fiasco, this record is as good as "Group Sex" (Almost!) RAVE! RAVE! RAVE! Keith really sings swell on this hip 12-er. "Jerks On 45" is really funny. For surely a million seller....

LIVE

Punks battle police at rowdy concert

... Sunset Boulevard. Bottles and rocks flew through the air. One missile just missed a passing Los Angeles Police Department patrol car, and the riot was on.

MISFITS, CIRCLE ONE, DISCHORDS, DR. KNOW, REGIONAL CONFUSION. (Some gig in Watts 4-9)
R.C. opened and were okay, if they practice alot, the should shred by the end of summer. Dr. Know happened. It's about time for these boys to do a record. Their guitarist was really jamming on their "heavy metal song". Dischords, missed 'em, sorry guys. Circle One, this was the first I seeze dis band 4 a long tyme. Dagwood Bumstead (Danny) on bass really jams. Jody is an excellent drummer (for a hippy). They played mostly new songs, that remind me oF new TSOL. They are finally gonna do a record (after years of heresay). George Baby Newberry is doing it on his new label. Their old songs were great. (They did "Plastic Life", "Highway Patrolman", & "DeestrOI Exxon"!) I missed the end of their set because the street wise negros outside were throwin bottles and wuz gwanna start a riot if anybody went outside of the club. They don't like them punkrockers, they crazy, Whip It. The Misfits went on and the room got really hot. All the Misfits ~~fans~~ feinds were pogoing and slammin an singin along. I went to check out the raceriot scene.. the locals really bum when they see white kids dressing the way the want and having fun in their fucked neighborhood. They should start some bands down there. As far as the "riot" that was happenin outside, there was this black dude in the doorway of the club, charging people to escort them to their car!! -JORDAN ANDREW

250 of the punk rockers spilled onto the street, although rehearsal studio employees put the number at between 1,000 and 1,500.

Aside from a few minor hand abrasions among the 30 to 40 policemen, all wearing riot helmets, there were no reported injuries.

They took an assortment of chains and razor blades to the show at a Hollywood rehearsal studio, but they said they weren't looking for trouble.

They were just a bunch of punk rockers—about 2,000 of them, according to the studio's estimates—

By punk standards, Saturday night's show at Studio Instrument Rentals in Hollywood sizzled with good, clean fun. The kids spit in each other's faces, slashed each other with razor blades and slammed into each other on the dance floor.

Until midnight, the concert, featuring four punk bands, had been mild by punk rock standards, those who know said.

"They were just punching each other and cutting each other a little with razor blades," SIR's rental manager, who asked not to be identified, said. "But that's their forte. That's what they do.

Although there was no damage to SIR, the rehearsal hall probably won't be rented for punk rock again.

"They're semi-crazy people," SIR's rental manager said. "I wouldn't do it again."

It took 40 officers dressed in full riot gear to quell the disturbance by 1 a.m. yesterday. Eleven people — including six officers — were injured.

"If it wasn't a riot, it was the next best thing," said Sgt. Hugh Decker, a watch commander at the LAPD Hollywood division station. "I'd call it a riot. It was really a mess."

Jeff McDonald, 18, the lead guitarist and singer for Redd Kross, said the show itself was peaceful but that the ensuing disturbance outside could mean trouble for the future of punk concerts in the Los Angeles area.

BLACK FLAG, AGGRESSION, SECRET HATE, ILL REPUTE, CATHAY DE GRANDE 4·25
This was the last PUNX produced gig at the Cathay, and there was alotta groovy happenings here the past few months. Ill Repute were pretty decent, their sound mix wasn't so hot. Secret Hate are REALLY decent, but somehow dont ever get enough recognition. Aggression seem to be concentrating on a "metaL" sound of late. Their album should be hott. Black Flag did a nice set, pretty pretty. Their very old stuff comes off great these dayze, and their brand new stuff is XXcellent! Practically everyone snuck in, and had fun. Oh well, no more Cathay. -DJCM

T.S.O.L. REDD KROSS, DI, RHINO 39
Kuntry Club (or Culture Club) 4-18-83
We arrived early and casually strolled in the back door and hid out back stage with Redd Kross. Who wants to make the people that run this club any richer? Anyways, Rhino 39 opened to a thin crowd. Heres a band thats been around for years but NEVER plays. They we-re okay. DI (not the rockabilly DIs) did a warm set next. This relativly new band with Casey on vocals (ex-Adolescents drummer) are definatly the last of the 80-81 Beach bands. They play 77 style punk metal and do a fun cover of the Sweet's "Ballroom Blitz". Redd Kross (this show with Dez) came on and we're pelted with cups and spit from some of the kiddies. Why must people yell, "get a haircut."? Why must there be rules? It seems half the crowd loved 'em and half drained out their saliva. Jeff & Steve seemed to have fun antagonizing "the punkers". TSOL did another set. The managment announced, "anyone who gets on stage will be trown out". Jack then announced, "We'll never be able to play here again." I thought it was funny when that one dude got up to sing and he didn't know the words, and he COULDN'T sing. That was the best part of the show. -DAVE

LIVE

Members of CH3, friends, roadies, and Brawny Mouse

CH3, SIN34, KILROY, UNDERCITY KINGS
A benefit for Mitch's fanzine at the Rock N Roll Orphanage May 8
Missed the first band. Kilroy were happening but I wasn't there to see all of their set. (Oi covers-ed.) Their EP will be real nice when is comes out. Sin 34 were haaapening. Highlight of the set was a totally out of control version of "Uncontrollable Urge". CH3 were definatly Channel 3 with "My Generation" and way cool back-ups. Way cool. Way cool. -JORDAN

PARTY AT JOHN PRESS'S HOUSE MAY 7
Even though I'd just gotten back from the Mother's Day Banquet at Church, and was coming down from cocaine, I still decided to attend this party only two block from my house. Sin 34 played first and were fuckin' rad man. Mike Geek is my guitar hero, and Dave makes the best faces while he's drumming. The Patriots played next. They are good. I was too wasted to hear much more, so I broke coathangers into little pieces and carved things in my arm with pieces of aluminum beer can. Then we all tried to get Phil Newman to show us his dick. Fucking great party, man. -KIM

BLACK FLAG, SACCHARINE TRUST, THE FRONT gig in San Diego 4-29-83
Quite a drive! But what the fuck! We partied anyways. We arrived in time for the opener, The Front, who were real good. Kinda Clash-ish, UK Subs-ish, and Mugger said some of their stuff reminded him of Husker Du. If this is a sample of the local San D bands, give us more! ST did a ok set to a thickening crowd. The sound mix wasn't so hot. At least these guys haven't broken up as I thought dey did. Goody! Anyhoo, Flag did a loooong and goooood set. Their new songs, "Slip It In", "Beating My Head Into A Wall", & "You're One Of Them" are too great for words! Henry did a great job of crawlin all over da floor & cuttin him self up. Milo sung on Police Story. Everyone sung on Rise Above. Good show. Good show. DAVE

BLACK FLAG at Joe VEX's new place 2-29
Saccharine opened & did a very intense set. The crowd just stood and stared. They should get another record out with their new line-up. Minutemen played next, I haven't seen 'em for a while. They were happening, as usual. (What else?ed.) The buzz word for Flag's set was sweat. The small place (about the size of 2 living rooms) was packed. Everything sweated to the max! The walls, the floor, the valley girls, and Greg's guitar. I went by his amp and got a gnarly electro shock. I just heard Joe Vex was thrown is jail, so look for his new place is 5 to 10 years, maybe less if he gets out on good behavior. -JORDAN

More black and whites at Huntington Park fracas.

POLICE RAID REVIEWS

*****= Brilliant
****= Very well
***= Ok. Could of used more imagination
**= Trite, dull, expected
*= Inept

* Cove Theater: CH3, Redd Kross, Jonses. The Hermosa Beach Police Department blew it. They came too late. The place was trashed. They could of made some good arrests.

*** S I R: TSOL, Social Distortion, etc. The West Hollywood Police Division had a problem. They had to stop a punk rock riot (as seen on Quincy & Chips) but there was no riot, so they decided they would create one. They closed the show down and got cans and bottles thrown at them.

***** Mendeolas Ballroom: Exploited. The men in blue decided to throw a little party. What fun. Highlights of the evening were the two police officers who took into their hands to smash store front windows so it would look nice and violent on t.v. Hats off to the friendly neighborhood policemen who maced and batoned innocent bystanders, including a USC student who got his camera and his head smashed.

** T-Bird Rollerdrome: Circle Jerks, Battalion Of Saints, etc. They came. Punks went home as they were ordered.

** T-Bird Rollerdrome: CH3, MDC, SIN 34. This show was closed the day it was to be on. The reason: the sidewalk was two inches short, not enough room to escape incase of a fire. Good one.

*** Anti-Club: 45 Grave, etc. That same night of the show above saw hundreds of punks hanging around the small Hollywood location. Some fight errupted, it took the cops long enough to get there! Geeze. But when they did, two dozen units and a helicopted shut the neighborhood off, created havoc, and had one hell of a time! Whooya! Officer Reed to Officer Malloy: "Lets go beat the shit out of the punkers!"

Coming soon: 1984! - Dave

NEWS: DEZ OUT OF "", AND NOW IS IN REDD KROSS, WHO KICKED OUT TRACY, WHO IS FORMING A NEW BAND W/ TOP DAN!

BREAKFAST CEREAL REVIEWS

ratings: @ = Health cereals
$ = Good sugared cereals
¢ = Bad sugared cereals
! = Cereal your parents buy for you

@ "Puffed Rice" - You are not gonna make any friends with this cereal, not much taste and it doesn't fill you up. I eat it cuz its good for me.

! "Team Flakes" - Yeah. Hea are sum nice tasty cereal, not much sugar and four grains to boot.

¢ "Sugar Corn Pops" - Bad News Bears, these things are frosted barbwire. The little chrystals of sugar cut the inside of your mouth.

! "Cheerios" - An old favorite. Last Monday my mom bought a box of Cheerios and a box of Life cereal. Sorry Mikey, I will take that toasted oat taste of Cheerios any day of the week. I also break out the C & H to add a special treat!

$ "Frosted Flakes" - My favorite. Lots of sugar and good t.v. commercials.

@ "40% Bran Flakes" - No way am I gonna even touch this shit! The name is lame and it's geared for adults.

GEE SHERIFF, YOU LOOK SO CUTE WITH THAT GUN!

WE GOT POWER magazine

the inconsiderate, incomplete,....

WGP HOTT RECORD GUIDE of the month

(In alphabetical order) - -

AUTHORITIES "Soundtrack For Trouble" ep
BLACK FLAG "Everything Went Black" lps
CIRCLE JERKS "Golden Shower Of Hits" lp
DAYGLOS "Out Of The Womb" lp
DEAD KENNEDYS "Plastic Surgery Disasters"
DESCENDENTS "Milo Goes To College" lp
DIE KRUEZEN "Cows & Beer" ep
FANG "Landshark" ep
FLIPPER "Get Away" 45
HUSKER DU "Everything Falls Apart" lp
JFA "Beyond The Valley..." lp
MEATMEN "Crippled Children Suck" ep
MINOR THREAT "Out Of Step" ep
MINUTEMEN "What Makes A Man Start Fires"
MOOD OF DEFIANCE "Now" lp
NECROS "Conquest For Death" 45
NEGATIVE APPROACH ep
NOISE FROM NOWHERE comp ep
RF7 "Fall In" ep
SCREAM "Still Screaming" lp
SIN 34 "Do You Feel Safe" lp
SUDDEN DEATH comp lp
URBAN WASTE ep
VANDALS "Peace Through Vandalism" ep
WHITE CROSS ep

REDD KROSS put out that new record!
BUTTHOLE SURFERS please put out a lp!
WHITE FLAG where's your lp??!

what is happening to the sink?

LOOK OUT FOR THE NIP DRIVERS!

PAT - drums * TEd - bass * Vic - sings * VINCE - Guit

WGP: Question #1. Why did you change your name from Red Alert to Saint Vitus Dance Band?
Vince: Red Alert was pretty much a different band. We do play some of the stuff, though. Ted-Roy and I originally started the band. We found a freind of ours to play guitar, and we had a whole lot of names before Red Alert. Like The Nun Hunters. We were the original 4 Skins five fucking years ago. (Wow! -ed.) Well, this guitarist, Tommy, couldn't handle being in a band, I guess. The other members were too busy doing their own thing. But fuck, Red Alert could of been a real good band. We were just to stupid to see it.
WGP: What do you do in your spare time?
Pat & Vic: School.
Vince: I work on Mercedes-Benzes all day.
WGP: And you drive a Porsche...
What kind of music do you consider yourselves to be playing?
Vic: It's not rock n roll.
Ted-Roy: But it's not punker-dunker music either.
Vince: It's new-, and everybody's gonna love it once they catch a glimse of it.
WGP: How long have you been playing...?
Vince: Since I was 11. (He is 22).
Pat: About six years.
Ted: I've been playing bass for seven years. I'm the father of the band.
WGP: Does the fact that there is another band called "Saint Vitus" bother you? Pat: Oh, the big question...
VINCe: Well, we never print "St. Vitus Dance Band". We're just "SVDB". If I have to, I'll change the name to Severely Venerally Diseased Boys...
WGP: Is Saint Vitus a disease?
Pat: Yeah, I made up the band name.
WGP: What are your hobbies ?
Ted-Roy: Fishing.
Pat: Skateboarding.
WGP: What do you think of all those girls who love you?
Pat: The ones from the valley,? I hate their guts. - MOUSE

BEYOND THE VALLEY

The ol' "RU ON THE ROAD" column visits ARIZONA

We all frequently find ourselves pondering the question, "what exactly goes on in Arizona, and how does it compare to L.A.?"-- sometimes for hours, in fact. We've all heard that there is life in Arizona, some of it intelligent, but like any modern, well informed citizen, we naturally want first-hand reports to keep us up to-date on whats happening in other cities...

There are two cities worth mentioning in Arizona; Phoenix and Tucson. Phoenix is the clos-est, a mere seven-hour cruise down Interstate 10, with Tucson another couple hours away (from LA, that is). The drive is great if you are into romantic desert scenery-- you know, cactuses, dirt, dry stuff, etc. If this doesn't excite you, you'd better bring alot of pot,'cause 6½ hours don't exactly fly by.

Next thing you know, you find yourself in Phoenix, which has a rad scene, with about 400 or so active participants. The main club now is a boxing ring called Madison Square Gardens (original name, huh?) The bands play in this ring surrounded by rubber ropes and a ceiling high fence. Its like playing in a cage. Phoenix people even take drugs! There was alot of pot, acid, mushrooms, & pills going around when I was there, and of course the drinking age is a mere 19.

Some of the happening Phoenix bands are J.F.A, Meat Puppets, Soylent Green, Junior Acheivement, and an all girl combo, Putrid Girls. Also, the scene there boasts of this really cool party house called Spahn Ranch.

As exciting as Phoenix is, however, I must admit I found Tuscon more intriguing. Tuscon is a thrift shop heavan, there is a whole block of them on the street of the club; The Backstage. The bands work the door and get 100% of the receipts to split. The scene there is smaller (100-150) and it has alot of catching up to do. For instance, $4. is, to them, a lot of money to pay to see CH3, Circle One, & Aggression! The people there are cool & they have some decent bands; Conflict, Corporate Whores, & Civil Death, who totally thrash! Don't forget to bring some extra money, if you go, for the thriftshops. -KIM

FUN & GAMES

best BAND NAMES

AVENGING CLOWNS, PUTRID GIRLS, E.T.s, BREATHING TOOLSHEDS, WHITE CROSS, DOUBLE CROSS, IRON CROSS, CROSS TOPS, NIP DRIVERS, WHITE FLAG, WHITE SISTER, TWISTED SISTER, NEIGHBORHOOD WATCH, GBH (Go Back Home), JHB, NBJ, NEGLAM-BAM-SHAM, KILLER SMURFS, KILLER PREISTS, KILLER PUSSY, KILLER PUSSY, KILLER GUMBYS, E.T. THRASHMO, MDM (Millions of Dead Mods), FLOCK OF TRENDYS, Mv3 ANARCHY, UPSET JEWS, OBSESSION (Queens of leather rock), TAR BABYS, CHICKEN ON FIRE, CHAUCER, AUTHORITIES, NEW WAVE SECRETARIES, REFUGA, MIKEY JUREVICK BAND, TRACY MARSHACK PROJECT, SICK NURSES, ILL COMPUTER, VENICE PARTY BAND, RAGDOLL, BITCH, DANTE FOX, W.A.S.P., PLASMATICS KISS, SAM SLAM & THE ANARCHY FOUR, YESCACA, EGAR TEENAGERS, TFOT (True Fathers Of Thrash).

WHAT IS THE DIFFERENCE BETWEEN THE TWO SKINNERS ABOVE?

PUNKER PUZZLE

Enter the new wave world as puzzled parents try to cope with punk kids.

```
S C H I P S P I T C O P O G O O V E D
P L F I G H T E T I B P O T Y K A J B
I V A G U E S T L I S T C K N I X F R
T A V M E L R O S E P E A C E D U A I
X N A T H I P P Y S O Z Z Y R O E N S
D D L R F U C H S A L S M R E G T A T
A A L A B L A C K S A B B A T H I S L
E L Y S K I L L E R P U S S Y O N A E
H I G H N I K S O I O I O I S D U T S
R S I E P U N K N E S S N B U T D O A
O E R R K R O Q O A D I S C H A R G E
T L L O S H A M M N O I T R O T S I D
O R D I S C O B S E D G E R X T E M A
M M A N M V 3 O R P R U H L O N R L Y
N E W W A V E R O A L E T V E H U B H
Y O T N I A P Y A R P S A S K N U P C
S L O Q U I N C Y S I R E H T A E L R
A M N O I T C U R T S I D E T A H L A
S E V E N S E A S B E E R E D R U M N
M O H A W K H I G H S C H O O L O R A
```

find the punk terms, but beware of the hippy & new wave words!

SLAM SPIT MOHAWK ANARCHY OI OI OI
THRASH LEATHER BRISTLES STUDS
OKIDOG HIGHSCHOOL DEATH DESTRUCTION
DISTORTION QUINCY CHIPS PUNX PUNKS
UNITE FIGHT BITE POGO VANDALISE
SPRAYPAINT RAPE MURDER HATE
GUESTLIST BEER HEROIN DISCHARGE
GERMS DARBY SID

THANKS TO: ______ (YOUR NAME)

MOUSE INTERVIEWS the NECROS

NECROS Barry-vocals, Andy-guitar, Cory-bass, Todd-drums

WGP:So your like the Maumee's boys,right?

Band: Ha ha ha ha

WGP:What does "Necros" mean?

Cory:Like when your little, your neck grows. (Barry picks up an antique in our interviewer's home and starts to play with it).

Mouse: (Our interviewer)Put it down!

Barry: Is this you? Mouse: NO!

Barry: Does it fly?! Mouse: Please,put it down!

Barry: Necros is the latin word for dead.

There Will Be No Christmas for "Red"

WGP:How's the scene out in Maumee?

Barry:As good as it is out here.

Cory:Theres nothing in Maumee. It's a cool place to hang out 'cause there's no punk rockers...

Barry:...to make you sick and puke. Detroit is the center of the Midwest scene. So thats where we hang out.

Cory:Thats where we play. We hang out in Maumee.

WGP:Did the BYO Tour ever get to Detroit?

Andy:Yeah, half of them. Social Distortion

WGP:How did you like Youth Brigade?

Barry:Youth Brigade were better that SD.

Cory:They were. They were pretty decent.

Andy:As far as the crowd went, people were groovin' to Youth Brigade. Then during SD, they left.

Cory:But most of these people dont knew shit!

Andy:Do you want to know the true story?

Cory:Nigheist played first and blew everything away.

WGP:How do you feel about drugs?

Andy:I feel drugs often.

WGP:Why did it take you 3 years to come out here to LA?

Cory:Because we always had somebody in the band who for some reason or another couldn't get away to tour for a month. Somebody who was in school or then somebody had a job they couldn't lose--

Piggies

WGP:(to Cory)How did you hurt you leg?

Cory: Skating in Denver.

WGP:Oh, your skatepunks?!

Cory:No. Disco rollerskating. We were at a disco roller rink and some guy pushed me over.

WGP:What influounces your band?

Cory:B52's, Talking Heads, Flock Of Sea gulls.

Barry:No bands that exist now directly influounce us.

WGP:Get any groupies out here?

Barry:Fuck no.

Cory:Andy got laid in San Diego.

FICTION

The MODern Ripoff

Tim first noticed the change in himself when he realized that though his hair was nearly covering his ears, he had no desire to cut it.

"Strange", he thought, looking at a three-month-old photograph of himself with a skinhead. "Well, maybe it's just a phase I'm going through". His self-doubts quickly disappeared, as he still felt compelled to wear the same torn jeans, army boots and Circle Jerks t-shirt he'd been wearing to school for two weeks.

A few days later, though, it struck again. This time he was overcome by an uncontrollable urge to wear a neatly ironed dress shirt and a brand-new pair of tan corduroy pants his mother had bought him for "family occasions". He didn't think anything of it until he noticed the funny looks he was getting from his friends at the "punk table" during lunch.

"Some friends", Tim thought later, as he stood in front of his mirror trying to figure out how to wear a tie. He gave up and went to ask his mom. On the way out he stopped to stare at his autographed 8"x10" glossy of Henry Garfield-Rollins, and somehow it no longer seemed relevent.

He began shunning the company of the punks at school, looking away when he passed them in the halls. He couldn't understand what was happening, but whatever it was, it had a vise-like grip on his mind; like an obsession, only stronger, it controlled his every move. Sometimes he couldn't stand it anymore, and would black out for a few hours. When he came to, he'd invariably find he'd been shopping. Once he discovered several new records in his collection—the English Beat, the Untouchables, and a used Small Faces album he'd apparently bought for a dollar. Once, to his horror, he found a brand-new parka hanging in his closet. For a moment he was overcome by disgust, thinking of the connotations involved, but then he tried it on. It fit quite nicely, and he was happy.

And then came the morning when he went outside to his 1972 Plymouth Duster and found that it no longer existed, that during his last blackout it had miraculously changed into a shiny new Vespa scooter.

He stared at it in total shock, and then broke into hysterical screaming. Dashing into the house, he grabbed the phone and dialed his friend Jim's number.

"Jim! You gotta help me!" he screamed in desperation. "Something's...something's really wrong with me". Sobbing, he explained the occurances of the past month.

Jim's voice was grave. "What you're describing is very serious, Tim", he said. "You've somehow managed to pick up this really nasty virus that's going around, some new venereal disease that..well..it turns you into...a... well, Tim, you're a Mod. You must've fucked a Mod chick when you were drunk or something." He paused. "It's incurable".

"NO!" screamed Tim, completely breaking down. "NO! IT CAN'T BE TRUE! MODS BURN IN HELL!!!"

Jim remained calm. "There's only one way out, Tim."

"I know..I know..." Tim sobbed. "Please..you gotta help me..."

"Whatever I can do, Tim. You can borrow my razor blade...or I'll score you some junk cut with battery acid... or I could push you over a cliff... just do something, Tim, before it's too late!"

"I will", Jim promised.

But it was already too late. The disease had progressed too far, and soon Tim's mind was completely disintegrated. You can still see him sometimes, standing in front of the Roxy when the Untouchables play, or hanging out on Melrose on Saturdays. He's a happy vegetable now, concerned only with his clothes and the latest dance steps, and doesn't really mind enduring this fate worse than death. So you needn't pity him.

Just make sure it doesn't happen to you. ~KIMMEROO

A new lavender-colored booklet, entitled *How to Distinguish Decadent Songs*, explains the perils of "quivering rhythm," unruly notes and the "unclear, loose, drunken pronunciation" peculiar to imported popular music.

He picked up Betsy and put her on the train,
And promised he'd make our country strong again.
Rah, rah Reagan; Reagan save our land.
Hooray for Reagan; Reagan is our man.

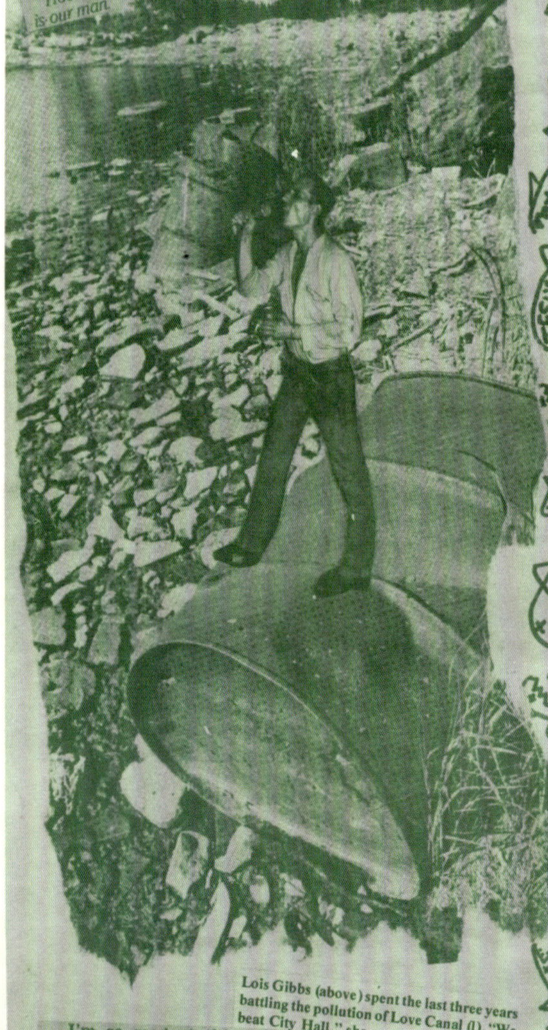

Lois Gibbs (above) spent the last three years battling the pollution of Love Canal (l). "We beat City Hall," she says.

I'm so mad at this current crop of wimpy draft dodgers I could twist their pony tails until their pimply faces explode.

FLIPPER

FAMOUS SAN FRAN NEW WAVE-HIGH TECH-BAND, WHO HAVE BEEN COMPARED WITH THE GREATS: DURAN DURAN, ADAM ANT, & OINGO BOINGO! FLIPPER HAVE THIS WEEKS NATIONAL SELLER, OUT TOPPING MICHAEL JACKSON! THEY'VE DONE AMERICAN BANDSTAND & ARE HEADLING THE US FESTIVAL!

INTERVIEWED BY KIM & ANITA HELPED...

Anita: So how do you like L.A. compared to San Fransisco?

Bruce: That question's been talked over lots of times with lots of fighting. It's getting better, as far as playing in LA. This is our third time down here.

Kim: So, I don't know too much about you guys. What's your basic philosophy or attitude?

Bruce: We write songs, we play 'em. We don't really define our attitude. It goes through changes. Whatever the situation is, we react to it at the time and we just play the songs we're playing and we don't particularly care whether we're making a million or we're fuckin' dying or what.

Kim: You seem to be one of those bands that people either love or hate. Why do so many people seem to hate you?

Bruce: Some bizarre form of jealousy.

Will: Some people may not enjoy the music.

Bruce: The music has been changing.

Kim: I saw you in San Fransisco at the Eastern Front show and you were--well, not really abusing the audience, but giving them a lot of shit. Why do you do that?

Bruce: We were playing off them. I was trying to give people shit tonight.

Kim: Why?

Bruce: Just to see what kind of mood they're in...to see how many intelligent people out there will make an intelligent comment back. I start off with a stupid comment, someone will make a smart one, I'll try to top his... just to get something going.

Anita: Why do you combine psychadelic and heavy metal and punk....

Bruce: We don't do it purposely...it just comes out that way.

Will: There is no theory or concept.

Bruce: It's just music.

Kim: How long have you been together?

Bruce: Three and a half years.

Kim: What label are you on?

Bruce: Subterranean.

Kim: What particular aspects of the whole punk thing--the music, the scene, the shows, etc., really bother you?

Bruce: What it's evolved into, as opposed to what it was.

John: (friend) High school.

Bruce: It's turned into high school. Before, it was people who were really trying to defy the system. I know that sounds cliche...

CORPORATE LOGO'S

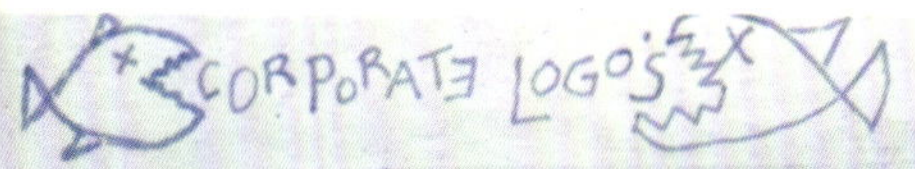

John: Let's put it this way. It's very easy for kids now to say, "O.K., I'm gonna be rebellious, I'm gonna break a lot of fucking laws".

Bruce: "I'm gonna be punk". They're really blatent about it. It used to be that if we went out to smash a lot of things--to be violent--we did it in a good, sneaky way. We just did terrorism, subliminal terrorism. During the time it was happening, like in 1977 I noticed it a lot around the Bay Area, it was very creative people standing up for themselves for once, defying the bullshit.

Will: A lot of misfits found out they weren't the only people breaking molds.

Bruce: A lot of misfits found out they weren't really misfits, and decided that the rest of society was pretty much made of misfits, which is because they all pretty much conform to the same structure. LA's a perfect example of the American structure--lots of cars and flat, wide open spaces, and all the industry and shit that goes on here.

Will: And now punk's turning into another structure.

John: It's just another mold, another format.

Bruce: Right. It's something that kids can go to now. I mean, it's almost expected of teenage kids now to go New Wave or--if so daring--punk. These are the kids who are a little out of hand.

John: They need to go see psychiatrists and such.

Kim: It's like the hippie thing, a symbol of the times, a Youth Movement...

Bruce: Yeah. There were hippies, and then there were hipsters...now, there're punks and then there're hardcores.

Kim: I've been to San Fransisco a couple of times in the past year and it seems a lot more laid back than LA. Do you think that's better?

Bruce: It's not necessarily better than anywhere else. It's just that in San Fransisco you have a lot of freedom. But it's like, you just don't go around abusing the place where you live. People in San Fransisco tend to respect the city for being what it is, and that's a very free place.

Will: San Fransisco tends to be more receptive to different things, off-the-wall things.

Bruce: There's still a lot of avant-garde jazz going on, there's still a lot of art bands, there're all kinds of weird electronic pop bands, there're all kinds of pretentious pop bands, there're all kinds of hardcore bands, there're psychadelic bands, there's a lot of art going on all over the place, a lot of political movements--everyone's really into the city government.

John: You don't have to spend half your time trying to break the mold, you can just do it--or do whatever you want.

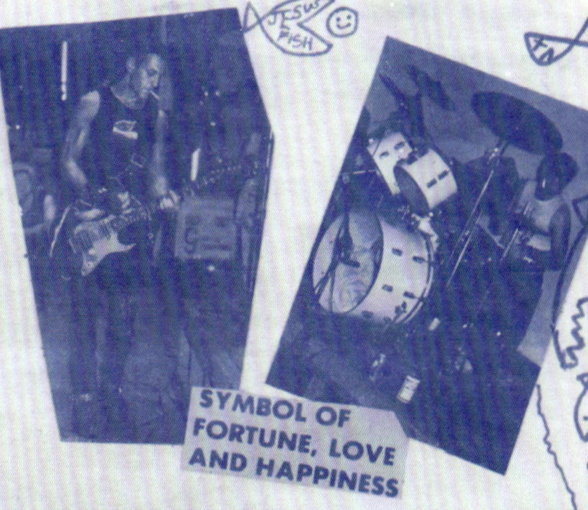

Kim: They seem to be more into their city up there.

Bruce: They're just more into being people and living where they live. They're not laid back...it's pleasant, but to me, laid back is some idiot getting wasted on ludes and beer and pot and watching a fuckin' color television all day.

Will: In San Fransisco you don't have to compete with everyone else to show how hardcore you are.

Bruce: You can just do whatever you want and people will appreciate it, if you're doing something worthwhile. A lot of people come to San Fransisco from New York to refine their art, and then go back to New York and make a million. —KIM

SYMBOL OF FORTUNE, LOVE AND HAPPINESS

JESUS FISH

SHAMOO TOO!

VENICE — Pac-Man has created a bit of controversy on Washington Street

MOUSE PHOTOS

DEVO

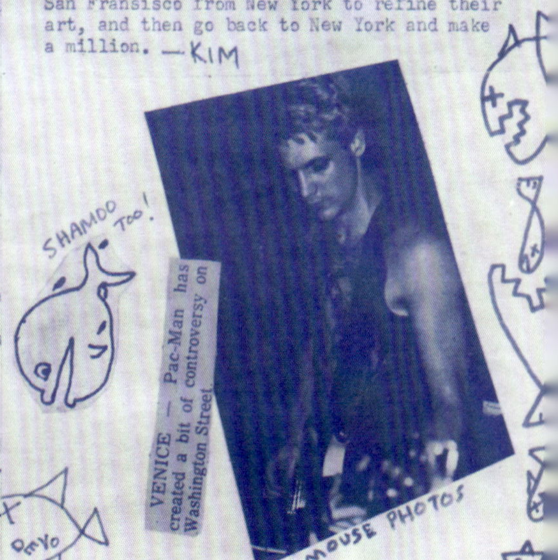

white flag: al, pat, & jello

AL: There's so much violence and hatred and stuff. Obscenities, people spitting on each other, people getting on people's backs because of hair length. See, in the begining, it was just... no rules. Now I feel like saying, "wake up guys". You want something that has no rules, then you set all these standards for people to live up to, and if they don't follow along, you bum on 'em. It happens when you get cliques. You should be able to hang out with anybody, but, for instance, preppy people don't want to hang out with hippies... I got gum thrown in my hair tonight. Stuff like that really bums me. I mean, if you don't like us, fine, but, I was really upset.

Laura: People are really closed minded.

Al: Well, we're trying to open people's minds back up again. Even if they don't like the music. We try to be entertaining.. The first time people see us, it's really hard for them to accept us. Like, Black Flag is God as far as punk rock goes, and if you do something like call yourselves White Flag, it bums 'em.

Pat: (Arriving) Jordan is a flake...

Kim: Jordan's criminally insane, but he's God.

Pat: I'm Pat Fear. I play guitar for White Flag.

Al: I'm Al Bum. And that's Jello B. Afro.

Kim: Are you trying to accomplish anything as a band? Are you trying to create art, or make money, or piss people off, or be cool, or do you just like controlling guest lists?

Jello: We just do this.

Pat: We don't really even do this.

Al: Its a habit. Like being a junkie.

Pat: I wanna say that Pat Smear is the best guitarist in the world.

Kim: Tell us about all the rotten things people do to you when they don't think you're cool and they hate you.

Pat: They throw raw meat and little animals on stage 'cause they think Al looks like Ozzy Osbourne and they expect him to bite their heads off.

Kim: Do you get beat up? Do you get hate mail? Do you get booed off stage? Do you get bombs in your car?

Pat: We've never been booed off stage. Every show we've played, we've gotten an encore, and I french kissed Tracy Lea of Redd Kross for a whole song tonight.

Al: So what?

Pat: We get love mail from Italy and Japan. We're huge in Japan. We have a record out in Germany, it's a live thing. This guy liked us, made a record out of us, so we're getting ripped off over there.

Pat: Lets talk about Chris Trent.

Al: I don't want to talk about him.

Pat: Lets talk about Rob Henley. Who thinks Mugger's gay? I do. I do.

Kim: He is not.

Pat: I know, but he pretends real well.

Kim: What pisses you off? What things do you hate? What Bums YOU out?

Pat: We don't hate anything. Nothing pisses us off. We love everything. I wanna say Social Distortion's the best band, Mike Ness is the ultimate guitar player. He's almost as good as me and Ace Frehley and Pat Smear.

Kim: And he's a brilliant guy too. Uh, how's your record doing, guys?

Pat: It's selling like hotcakes.

Kim: Oh yeah?

Pat: It would be if it was out!

Jello: My mom bought one.

Al: I sold one to my sister.

Pat: Ask Jello a question. He has the largest testicles in History.

Laura: How do you know pat?

Pat: He brags about them all the time..

Kim: He's got big balls, eh?

Pat: Yeah, ask Mugger.

Kim: Quit ranking on Mugger. Is there anything you would like to tell the world?? start talking.

Pat: Yes, I'd like to tell the world that life is beautiful, so you should experience it's surroundings

Al: Shut up!!

Kim: Do any of you go to college?

Pat: I go to Milo City College.

Al: Irvine.

Kim: Do any of you still live with your parents?

Pat: I live with Mugger.

Kim: One more joke about Mugger and I'll print your real name in this interview!

Pat: I live with Rick Agnew.

Al: I live with my mom.

Kim: If you werw playing a swank night-club in New York and Keith Richards got on stage to jam with you, would you kick him off like Chuck Barry did, or would you let him solo?

Al: I'd let him jam. I'd french kiss him like Mick did. To tell you the truth, I'd rather have Ron Wood on stage 'cause he used to be with the original cool guy, Rod Stewart.

Pat: We have a song about Pat Smears frogs.

INTERVIEWED BY KIM & LAURA LUDWIG

(Charly Watts was there, Joan Jett was there. Bianca Jagger was there. There was a beauty contest between Joan and Bianca. Joan won.)

ARE YOU BORED?
Do something about it!

SIN34

SIN34 were interviewed after they played The Galaxy by Kim. Jordan was there but he didn't help much.
SIN34 are Julie-vocals, Phil-bass Dave Hector-drums, Mike G.-guitar

Kim: Is it true your singer has a tatoo ?
Dave: Not anymore!
Julie: Yeah!
Mike: No!
Phil: Kinda...
Mike: Don't even talk about it! It's personal!
Kim: Mike, when did you die your hair blue?
Mike: A couple days ago.
Dave: Mike is stoned on pot! Look at his eyes.
Kim: Why has everyone died their hair? Julie's is blue, too, Drew's is green and Laura's is red.
Mike: Because we're punker than shit.
Kim: Mike, you have a reputation as a real geek. How did you get this reputation, which gave Sin 34 the label of "geek rock"?
Mike: Ask Dave. He made it up.
Dave: He was just being himself!
Kim: Do you mind being called "geek rock" ?
Dave: I don't give a damn 'bout my bad reputation, no no no no no. Joan Jett.
Kim: Why did the audience throw records at you at the Happy Times Roller Rink ?
Phil: They wanted us to autograph them.
Mike: They didn't like disco.
Dave: They were throwing records at us? Is that what they were doing?
Kim: Where are you guys from?
Dave: Half of us are from Santa Monica and the other half are from Beverly Hills.
Kim: Do you ever get "rich kid" shit?
Phil: I love Moon Unit Zappa.
Mike: I am broke all the time...
Dave: We're all college students, we're all rich millionaires. I go to Twilight Zone University. The hours are from 12 noon to 1, 5 days a week. On channel 5.
Mike: Drew Bernstien invented punkrock.
Kim: What big shows have you played?
Phil: Devonshire Downs. The Whisky. Cynthia's backyard...
Dave: Santa Monica Pier.
Kim: Do you think you've improved recently??
Dave: I think we're devolving.
Mike: I get worse everytime I play.
Phil: We're a dance band.
Dave: WE're a mod band, ska ska ska!

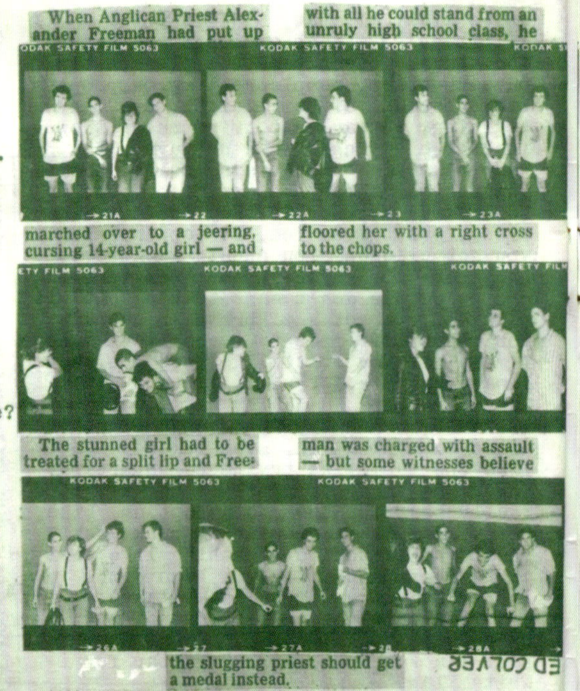

When Anglican Priest Alexander Freeman had put up with all he could stand from an unruly high school class, he

marched over to a jeering, cursing 14-year-old girl — and floored her with a right cross to the chops.

The stunned girl had to be treated for a split lip and Frees man was charged with assault — but some witnesses believe

the slugging priest should get a medal instead.

ED COLVER

Mike: Drew and I are straightedge. We drink beer for the taste.
Dave: I have a message for everyone in "the scene": DON'T UNITE!
Phil: Lets organize this interview...
Dave: Okay. Lets get serious!
Jordan: Let's ask Dating Game questions!
Dave: Mike is our sex symbol. Why does Mike's van smell like cat piss? (V.C. S)
Kim: Julie, who are your favorite bands and idols?
Juile: TSOL's my favorite band.
Phil: Kiss, Ozzy Ozborne, Yvonne O'neal trib.
Dave: Our goal is to be really cool.
Kim: Who are your favorite bands?
Mike: Dogma Probe. Pain. Mayhem. Devo.
Dave: Anarchistic Youth. White Flag.
Phil: Anarchistic Youth are the best. Backstage Pass, good 70's band.
Kim: Do you have any hobbies?
Phil: I like walking my dog.
Kim: What do you think of the scene?
Mike: It's punker than shit.
Dave: You said that already!
Phil: It's hunky-dory. We're for it.
Mike: I'm on the geeks' side.

But seriously folks, SIN34 have just finished work on an album which will be out by the time this maggg comes out. They are very active in playing live and they want to play at your house.

DENVER (UPI) — Mann Theaters Corp. has been sued for $400,000 by a couple who took their own popcorn to a Denver movie theater and were thrown out, arrested and charged with disturbing the peace.

DO YOU KNOW HIM?

STOP THOSE PUNKS!

John Denny of the long lost Weirdos

CREW CUT CRAZE

PIX BY ED C. MOUSE + JORDAN

GUITARIST

RUNAWAYS

Butthole Surfers

TALK DIRTY TO ME

Monique Dana Gregory said she barely escaped being murdered by fleeing in the nude.

MELTED VERSION

WHERE'S S.D.'s LP?

BOY GEORGE!

DESPERATE TEENAGE

WGP WHOOYA PIX PAGE

WE GOT POWER!

3010 santa monica blvd.
no. 310 santa monica CA
90404

GREG - BAD RELIGION

MARK STERN - YOUTH BRIGADE

PARTY OR GO HOME OUT BEFORE YOU CAN SAY REMEMBER THE GOOD OL' DAYS

New ALBUMS FROM SMOKE SEVEN . . .
R F 7
FALL IN
VIET VETS
666 HEAD
57 MILLION PEOPLE
REVOLUTIONARY WORKER
VAMPIRE LADY (COKE WHORE)
WHAT I'M TRYING TO SAY
& Fuck Money
"FALL IN" - A 12" E.P.
from R F 7
SUDDEN DEATH
RED KROSS
Moral Decay
Youth Gone Mad
Sin 34
Naughty Women
Demented
"SUDDEN DEATH"
compilation
Smoke Seven
STILL AVAILABLE!!
Last Rites for Genocide and M I A
RED CROSS
BORN INNOCENT
Last Rites
Genocide and M I A
PUBLIC SERVICE
RF7
Weight of the World
PUBLIC SERVICE
pre-war hardcore
ORDER NOW... BEFORE It's TOO LATE!!
For Mail Order
Send $5.00* for each to:
Smoke Seven
7230 De Soto Ave #104
Canoga Park, CA. 91303
Prices Include Postage !!
*"FALL IN" - 12" E.P. $4.50
*overseas residents add $2.00
*allow a couple of weeks for delivery
The 2nd L.P. from
Red Cross
could this happen only in America?

Jordan with the five-issue run of We Got Power, *sitting on the gas meters of David's mom's apartment building on Broadway and 26th.* DAVID MARKEY

WE GOT POWER #666

UNRELEASED CIRCA 1984

This unfinished issue, still pasted up with spray adhesive on its original yellowing layout board, has been unseen for almost thirty years. The Ray Pettibon cover, "We Survived the Pit," was apparently a rejected Black Flag *Damaged* LP cover. We used the art in 1988 for the Anarchy 6 *Hardcore Lives*! LP. Other salvageable relics include the usual inside cover photo collage I did for every issue; Jennifer Schwartz and Kim Pilkington's interviews with Würm and the Skoundrelz (featuring Tony Alva on bass). I wrote the reviews. Comic artwork is by Brian Walsby and San Fernando Valley's own Cameron Jamie. I lent a hilarious interview with Redd Kross's Steven McDonald in page layout form to Howie Pyro on behalf of Bryan Ray Turcotte for his *Fucked Up + Photocopied* book in 1999, and I never saw it again, so that's missing.

I lost interest in completing the zine once a certain Hollywood record label executive who bore a striking resemblance to Burgess Meredith's portrayal of the Penguin started barking orders at me. His fly-by-night record label and cheesy cashing-in on the punk scene put me off. He had put out our *We Got Power—Party or Go Home* compilation LP, and was planning his own sequel with *We Got Power* #6 included inside. I severed all ties to this character, but that didn't stop him from doing a total of three *We Got Power*—or, ahem, *We Got Party* compilations. Yes, it's true: Doug Moody killed *We Got Power* zine.

—David Markey

WE GOT POWER

NO. 666

Würm
Skoundrelz
Biscuit (Big Boys)
Steve McDonald
Redd Kross
Pettibon
Cameron Jamie
Record Reviews

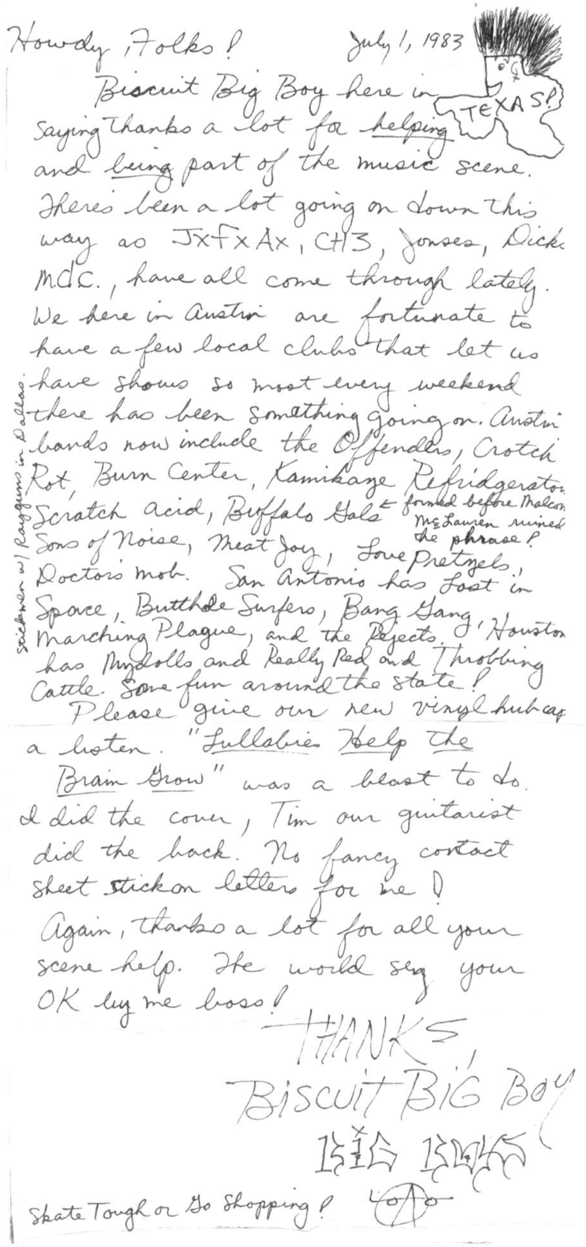

Howdy, Folks! July 1, 1983

TEXAS!

Biscuit Big Boy here in saying thanks a lot for helping and being part of the music scene. There's been a lot going on down this way as JxFxAx, CH3, Jonses, Dicks M.D.C., have all come through lately. We here in Austin are fortunate to have a few local clubs that let us have shows so most every weekend there has been something going on. Austin bands now include the Offenders, Crotch Rot, Burn Center, Kamikaze Refridgerator, Scratch acid, Buffalo Gals← formed before Malcom McLauren ruined the phrase! Sons of Noise, Meat Joy, Love Pretzels, Doctors mob. San Antonio has Lost in Space, Butthole Surfers, Bang Gang, Marching Plague, and the Rejects. Houston has Mydolls and Really Red and Throbbing Cattle. Some fun around the state!

stickmen w/ Rayguns in Dallas

Please give our new vinyl hubcap a listen. "Lullabies Help the Brain Grow" was a blast to do. I did the cover, Tim our guitarist did the back. No fancy contact sheet stick on letters for me! Again, thanks a lot for all your scene help. He would say your OK by me boss!

THANKS,
BISCUIT BIG BOY
BIG BOYS

Skate Tough or Go Shopping!

Randy "Biscuit" Turner, Big Boys, the Vex, 1983. JORDAN SCHWARTZ

WE GOT POWER
PARTY OR GO HOME!
NO. 666
Brian Walsby:
JOE HARDCORE BUYS THE W.G.P. ALBUM...
THIS BETTER BE GOOD... IT COSTS ME $5!!
SUDDENLY, ALONG COMES JULIE.
LET ME TELL YOU.. THIS RECORD IS GREAT!
HEY.. AREN'T YOU.
THEN ALONG COMES AL-BUM..
YOU'D BE A FOOL IF YA DIDNT BUY IT!
WOW MAN!
JORDAN COMES ALONG.
IT MAKES A GREAT XMAS GIFT!
ITS PAST XMAS, JERK!
EVERYBODY THATS ON THE ALBUM COMES BY!
..& WE'RE ALL ON IT!!
THIS BETTER BE FUCKIN GOOD
Edited by
Dave Markey
Published by
Dave Markey
Jordan Schwartz
Cover art by
Raymond Pettibon
Staff also includes:
Jennifer Schwartz
Kim "Ru" Pilkington

DAVE'S SCHOOL OF RECORD REVIEWS. . . .

HUSKER DU "Metal Circus" EP: Of course they don't fail to maintain their standard of releasing really rad shit. This band has something special, something undescribable, something different... Check out the track "Diane". Also my fave cuts on dis are "Deadly Skies" & "Lifeline". A-

BUTTHOLE SURFERS "Brown Reason To Live" EP: Too hardcore for hardcore? Actually, yes! This is a great record to scare your so-called "hardcore" friends away with! Just the way I like it. "Bar B Q Pope" & "Something" should be fuckin MTV videos dammit! B+

CIRCLE ONE "Patterns Of Force" LP: Mike Vallejo jams! His guitar work here is worth the price of admission alone. Also dig on Danny's funky bass manovers, if only they would give a little more room for "jams". Most of the material is good, tho I do have a hard time with a few of the 13 cuts here... particularly "The Gospel", "Our Sword", &"The Rapture". The lyrics sound more like tacky cliches from a t.v. evangelist. C'mon, dudes, we want "Nothing/One Chord", "In This City", & "Are You Afraid". What about "Highway Patrolman"?! Please release those tunes. C+

ANTI "Defy The System" LP: The last from the now defunct Anti. If only they would of steered away from those musical and lyrical typical-ness (Is that a real word?!). Anyhoo, amazingly so, there are some hot pop tunes on here("Five Downtown".) And the singer has improved 100% from their last disk. C+

STAINS LP: Another rave review! Goddamn, the guitar work here is just too insane for words. Rudy is a great singer, and there are some great songs on this. Note: This was recorded about 3 years ago and it's just comin' out now! A

PROLITARIAT "Soma Holiday" LP: After the first listen, I filed this record in my collection between my Wire "Pink Flag" & TSOL's first ep by accident, but this is very reminisant of those two. Also it seems like they've listened to Crass once or twice, maybe Gang Of Four aswell. Not to say Prolitariat is unoriginal, in fact this is one of the more innovative records this issue. You might remember them from "Boston Not LA" comp from a while back. I really didn't care much for them on that, but I do suggest the purchase of this. A-

AVENGERS LP: A great record made up of two of their earlier, rare, and out of print EP's, plus some unreleased tunes too boot. OK, for some of youse who may not know, The Avengers were this punk rock back from the 70's, who have been history even since the end of that decade. I'm sorry I never got the chance to see 'em! A

GOVERNMENT ISSUE "BOYCOTT STABB" & "MAKE AN EFFORT" EP's: I just plain out like this band & record. The songs have a light-hearted attitude, dare I say "fun". Definatly groovy man. DC strikes again and again.... B+

THE DICKS "KILL FROM THE HEART" LP: From the rockin' version of "Purple Haze" to "Right Wing/White Ring" to the title cut, here lies some cool (whoops, they're "anti-cool" remember!?!) material. Not exactly the best record in the world, butt.... I wish this band would play LA already!!! B+

RF7 "SUBMIT TO THEM FREELY" EP: "Fortunate Song"scores! The title cut is typical RF7; Felix's groans, Nick's rad guitarism, Walt's tight drumming... They;ve added a 2nd guitar, which fills in the rhythem a bit. B-

THE FREEZE "GUILTY FACE" EP: This is old, they now have an LP, which is supposed to be kill. Anywayz, first listen, no real impression. Then it starts to creep up on you. One of those things. C+

DETONATORS "EMERGENCY BROADCAST SYSTEMS" LP: Q" Who is this, CH3? A: No, it's the Detonators. Q:Who? A: The Detonators. Q:Where are they from? A:L.A. Q:I've never heard of them, have they played live? A:A few times, I gather. Q:Is this any good? A:Yeah, I guess. Nothing really special, not bad tho. C

SVDB/BATALLION OF SAINTS 45: From Mystic's "Destroy LA" comp. WOW, svdb finally get a record, a first great effort! Looks like we have another "BIG" band comin' up! And for the Batallion Of Saints side... well, I've never cared too much for the BATS, so... Uh, I guess it's pretty good!? C+

WE GOT POWER's PARTY OR GO HOME lp: Fuck everything else! Buy this record. What an amazing concept, what andamazing package! A++++++++++++++++++++++ god ok?

Wurm were interviewed by Kim and Jennifer quite some time ago. As of this writing, the future of the band is uncertain.

Wurm consist of Ed Danky on guitar, Loud Lou on drums, Simon on vocals, and Chuck Dukowski on bass. Simon is (or was) also in Dead Hippie, Ed is currently playing bass for the Mentors, and as we all know, Chuck recently left Black Flag.

Only Ed and Chuck managed to show up for this interview.

-Kim: Let's talk about the good old days. Where did you two meet?

Ed: At Chadwick, our high school.

Kim: What kind of teen-agers were you?

Ed: We were stoners.

Kim: How old are you?

Ed: I'm still 29. (30 by now).

Chuck: I'm 29, too. (Also 30 now).

Ed: We're infamous for being kicked out of our school, together.

Kim: For what?

Ed: Conspiracy of possession.

Kim: Does that mean you were selling weed?

Ed: It was a big schoolwide scandal. The junior classes' money was missing; it went for a couple pounds of weed. We got ripped off by a couple of guys on a boat.

Chuck: There was, like, Mafia action with the sophomore class student organization. They got burnt.

Kim: So you got kicked out of a private school?

Chuck: We were on probation. We had to sit in the library to eat lunch for a week. They wanted to keep us away from the other people.

Kim: Did Wurm exist in high school?

Chuck: Wurm didn't start 'til college.

Ed: About '73 or '74. This is our 10th anniversary.

Kim: After Chuck joined Black Flag, did you continue as a band?

Ed: He joined them when I split. We broke up and I went to Chicago for a few weeks. We got back together to do the first single.

Kim: Why did you name your band "Wurm"?

Ed: It's from physics. It's the center of a black hole. It's a mathematical curve where matter goes faster and faster, closer to the speed of light, and turns into pure energy.

Kim: What's the name of your first single?

Chuck: It's called "Wurm".

Ed: It has "We're Off", "I'm Dead", and "Time Has Come Today". We're on the Radio Tokyo Tapes with "Modern Man", and the Destroy L.A. comp with "Black Swan". And we're gonna do the Mystic cop-ilation.

Kim: What are your favorite bands? What bands were you raised with? What bands inspired you?

Ed: That's a big list! All the earliest, heaviest, trashiest bands. Like the MC5, Stooges, Dolls, Hendrix, Black Sabbath.

Kim: Chuck, what bands influenced and inspired your musical endeavors?

Chuck: Recent? Recent bands are, like, Saccharine Trust and the Minutemen.

Kim: What are you two going to do in the event of a nuclear holocaust? Ed Danky, are you going to fight or flee? Would you split with Chuck?

Ed: Yeah, I'll follow this guy! He knows where to bail.

Chuck: Check it out! It's Pompeii, you know? What do you think about all the people who didn't bail from Pompeii? Everybody there knew it was coming down in a matter of days (a volcanic eruption) but they just sat there and got cooked alive.

Kim: What kinds of jobs have you two had in the past?

Chuck: I've worked at McDonald's...we worked at Marineland...

Kim: What did you do at Marineland?

Ed: We were slide boys. We had to wax it. We trained dolphins for a while.

Chuck: Tell her about walruses.

Ed: OK. There was this main walrus at Marineland who had been there for ten years or something. He put on this show--every Sunday he'd go down to the big glass windows with all the families outside and he's start beating his meat with his flippers. It got about three or four feet long, and then all of a sudden a big white cloud would spurt out into the water. All the families would' take their little kids and run in terror. He got killed when somebody threw a golf ball in his tank and he snorted it.

Then we got promoted and were ushers at the Long Beach Arena. We ushered at rock concerts... we got to see Black Sabbath, Led Zepplin, the Stones, Elvis...

Kim: One last question: What does your band--Wurm--have to offer that we don't already have way too much of?

Chuck: I don't think you can get enough of my trip.

Kim: What is your trip?

Ed: Powerful playing! Pound-for-pound heavier weight. Loud and proud---we're just great.

Chuck: I wonder how many people...have you ever eaten Chef's Delight?

---------KIM

VERONICA LAKE - DESCENDENTS - TWISTED ROOTS @ ANTI CLUB

THE ANTI CLUB IS NEAR THE GRANDIA ROOM, BUT WHAT MAKES THE GRANDIA ROOM BETTER IS THAT THEY LET THE BANDS DO WHATEVER THEY WANT, ANARCHY. I VERONICA LAKE WOULD BE WEIRD WHEN SHE DEDICATED HER SET OF POETRY READING TO THE STAFF AT BELLVUE. SHE READ THREE POEMS WHICH HAD THE WORD BLUE IN IT, THE LAST ONE WAS THE MOST PUNK, THIS CHICK AND SOME RIPPED OFF 20 CASES OF COKE FROM A SEVEN ELEVEN. THE DESCENDENTS WERE RAD, ANY BODY WHO MISSED THIS SHOW IS HATIN' LIFE. SOMEBODY SAID THAT KURT FROM OVERKILL PLAYED DRUMS LOUDER THAN BILL, SORRY DUDE WHEN BILL HIT THAT SNARE DRUM IT MADE MY HEAD HURT. MERRIL GOT ON STAGE AND SUNG KABUKI, WHICH IS IMPORTANT BECAUSE MILO IS LEAVING THE BAND FOR COLLAGE IN SEPT. WHEN THE DESCENDENTS STOPPED PLAYING DAVE CAPT ANARCHY AND I YELLED FOR MORE AND THIS FAT LADY CAME OUT AND SAID THE DESCENTS COULDNT PLAY NO MORE, BASICALLY WE TALKED BACK AND GOT KICKED OUT, THE WRONG @ CLUBS ARE GETTIN TRASHED. TWISTED ROOT PLAYED TOO.

SKOUNDRELZ

Jordan: Alright, everybody say your name.
Dave: I'm Dave.
Kim: What do you do, Dave?
Dave: I sing.
Mike B: I'm Mike Ball, I play guitar.
Mike D. I'm Mike Dunnigan. I play the other guitar.
Tony: I'm Tony Alva. I play bass.
Jordan: So, Mike and Mike...you guys used to play guitar in a different band, right? You guys used to be in the Faction?
Dave: I, too, was in a band that plagerized.
Jordan: So you guys don't have plans to be on any records.
Tony: Not yet. We might be on the next Thrasher tape if Don Bolles will cough up the live tape that they made of us at the Cathay....
Dave: If he could just stop shooting dope for five minutes....
Jordan: What are your favorite bands to listen to?
Mike D: Throbbing Gristle.
Tony: I like heavy metal stuff. I like old heavy metal...I guess just rock'n'roll..I like Aerosmith.
Jordan: What would you say your sound's like?
Dave: Like the Dolls met Joy Division and they had Lemmy playing bass.

SOME TALL BLOND GUY COMES IN.

Mike B: This is Mondo. He does the faces. He's on brush.
Jordan: Yeah, what's the story behind the painted faces?
Tony: It's tribal. Just to look different on stage, instead of the typical jeans and high-tops.
Mike B: It's something we do so people will notice us.....
Jordan: Yeah, it looks really cool.
Tony: It's really just to put on a good show.
Mike B: we're not trying to be like Kiss...
Mike D: Yeah we are! Don't lie.
Tony: I worship Gene Simmons.
Mike B: Ace can bend over backwards and touch the ground with his back. He has lead boots. The guys in Redd Kross should learn how to do that.
Mike D: They might step on their hair though.
Kim: What drugs do you guys like?
Tony: Everything!
Dave: Opiates!
Tony: We like pot.
Mike B: Speed!
Tony: Mike likes meth.
Kim: I like meth.
Tony: I like mushrooms and pot. I don't like coke that much...I think I like meth a little better than coke.
Dave: I like dope!
Mike D: I like root beer. I'm on sugar.
Jordan: Yeah, me too.

THE DRUMMER, DELLA, COMES IN.

Tony: Della, sit down and shut up.
Jordan: So what's the Jack's Team influence on the band?
Tony: Raging fucking skateboarders and absolute music! We did the Fascist Regime thing to Bill Waler.. we mugged him and took his president's bracelet back before he went to San Fransisco so the other Jacks couldn't steal it. We want to keep the presidency in LA. My little brother is president now.
Jordan: You guys play a bit up in Frisco?
Tony: As much as possible. Our favorite place to play is Down the Drains, a play-and-no-pay thing. We like to go there and play at the Tool and Die with the Black Athletes or Swivel.
Mike D. We want to make friends.
Jordan: What bands would you like to make friends with?
Tony: The Faction! No, seriously, we want Kiss to come over to our house.
Jordan: But you'd settle for Redd Kross. If you guys did a video for MTV, what do you think it would be like?
Dave: It would have lots of girls in bathing suits.
Tony: And fast cars.
Mike D: The underlying themes would be lust and flashy G-spots.'
Dave: I'd smoke a doobie.
Jordan: So what are your songs about?
Dave: Depression.. lust... waking up with a boner...
Jordan: I heard that when Mike Dunnagin joined the band, he laid a whole bunch of songs on you, but you didn't want to use them because they all sounded like "Suicidal Failure". Mike, how did you conquer the Flock?
Mike D: Mike Ball wrote "Suicidal Failure"! We'll see you in court, Glenn.
Jordan: So where do you guys skate?
Dave. I skate ay Paul Revere.
Tony: Jack's Dam, Shaw's Ramp...Mondo and I hunt out pools here and there. We're riding the one in Palos Verdes that was on the cover of Thrasher magazine...we rode a pool in the Valley...we went to Arizona and skated this pipe out there...regularly, we just get all the boys together and go to Revere. There's a good combination of banks there and stuff. That's where I learned to skate when I was like ten.
We wanna tell all the kids who saw us at Perkin's Palace that we all used to be bald.
Jorden: Get that straight!
Mike D: Lond hair's back! Your girlfriends loved it.
Jordan. Let's end it with that. Now we're gonna go home and cut up the interview and change all the words aroung.

—KIM

The Skoundrelz.
PHOTOS BY JENNIFER FINCH

oi!
punkers
Don't let your building
look like a bathroom wa
the upper and middle class suburbs
Southern California "the last bastion of punk in
America."
Punkers Ponder
Altar-ations

1136

RED MESSAGE

REBELLING AGAINST THE REBELLION
JEFF AND STEVEN McDONALD

Steven McDonald: Yesterday I was on Facebook, and I ended up on the Godzilla's club page. What a weird-ass feeling. That's *time* you're talking about. I felt a lifetime of pain in my stomach looking at it. Well, there was only one flyer on the page that had Red Cross. It was Red Cross, Mau Maus, and UXA.

Jeff McDonald: I remember one show with a bunch of hardcore bands from the period when we would play with bands like Circle One. Those shows were just a nightmare. There would be guns; everyone was so drugged out.

Steven: We were little kids in the later stages of early punk rock in Los Angeles, in an environment with people who were left over from the glitter world, and graduates from the first wave of Cal-Arts students, and people like the Weirdos and X. They were real outsiders, older than us, but very kind. They thought it was really cool that kids from the suburbs were opening their minds. When they learned I was a twelve-year-old kid playing bass, everyone was receptive and cool to us. Later, suddenly it was people our age—it was our peer group at shows. The things Janet Housden is talking about in her piece in this book about the Tony Alva disaster—all that was really hard for me. This world was my escape from high school, with this music that I loved, and I was accepted. We were freaks; it was peaceful, and it was really creatively inspiring. At least that's the way I remember it.

Facing page: *Avid reader Jeff McDonald and the* Red Message.
DAVID MARKEY

Jeff: That's what it was like when we first met Black Flag and all of our South Bay friends. We were fans of the Alley Cats, and they were playing in the South Bay at a Moose Lodge Hall with Black Flag and some other bands. That was unheard of, a show in the South Bay, and it was fantastic. Black Flag got kicked off the stage. I got Black Flag's EP, and it had a Lawndale P.O. Box address. So I thought they were from Lawndale, which is next to Hawthorne, where we lived. Somehow I got their phone number and I called Greg Ginn and asked if we could play a show with them. He told me they had a practice space in Hermosa Beach, and he invited us and about ten other people, Dez Cadena being one of them, and Ron Reyes, Joe Nolte from the Last, and Janet Housden. She lived about a half mile from the Church, where Black Flag lived and played.

Steven: They were real weirdos, and they had their own little oasis in Hermosa Beach, which was luckily really close to us. We all sat and watched Black Flag rehearse. After they were done, they handed us their guitars. Chuck Dukowski gave me his Flying V Ibanez bass, and I'm like this five-foot-one-inch eleven-year-old.

We went for it. We did our original six-song EP, and a cover of the Beatles' "I Want to Hold Your Hand," where the first verse was done in Beatles tempo and the second verse was done in a punk rock tempo. We also did "Who Are the Mystery Girls?" by the New York Dolls. They basically made us audition to hang out with them. Their minds were probably blown.

Jeff: They were older than us; we were little kids, but we had listened to a lot of music they had listened to. That was the glorious year before the period that's documented in *The Decline of Western Civilization*.

Steven: In the early '80s, a couple of years later, came Godzilla's, one of the places in an industrial part of the Valley. That was the first time there were other sixteen-year-olds there, suburban sixteen-year-olds. They were same kids who were beating me up in school; now it was like punk became the new extreme sport. I felt even more alienated by that than I did in gym class at school. It was sad to have this world invaded, a world that encompassed so many things I needed: music, people to relate to, and something to call my own. Before the Internet, it was hard to find a niche; then we had it flipped upside down. But we had no choice—it was the only place that we kinda still fit in.

Jeff: We didn't fit in at all. We did one show at the Country Club with Poison, because people kept telling us: "You're gonna love this new band Poison... They're just like the New York Dolls." I hadn't even met them or seen their sound check, but I was suspicious when I saw the sign on their dressing room door: THE GLAM SLAM KINGS OF NOISE. They didn't even have the nerve to call themselves the "queens" of noise! Sure enough, they got onstage and they were this bad Van Halen imitation band. But during that Godzilla's era, at the height of all that nonsense when suburban kids and hardcore was created, we still found an oasis within that. The *We Got Power* crew had its own sort of thing in Santa Monica. We all started hanging out together. It was inspiring to be rebellious within this rebellious movement. It was fun to fuck with those people. Without that, what would we have rebelled against? Nothing. There was always someone to fuck with you, so we had to be creative and just keep moving forward.

Jennifer Schwartz: You used to fuck with those people, all right. I remember when you played the Santa Monica Pier. The Suicidal Tendencies gang was all there, already wanting to kill you for having long hair, wearing velvet jackets, cutoff shorts, and giant Kiss platform boots. They were really violent. They were from Venice and Santa Monica. I went to high school with a lot of them, and had seen them beat the shit out of people. But on the pier that day, between songs, Jeff said into the mic: "This next song is from a record I bought at a garage sale at Mike Muir's mom's house. It's the Partridge Family." I have never seen a crowd get so mad and so close to killing a band. The Suicidal guys tipped over a fruit stand and started pelting you with strawberries, kiwis, everything. They could've killed you with an orange!

Jeff: That's the power of the electric guitar. You always have this false sense of empowerment. The thing is, we've been booed throughout our whole career. From the very first time we ever played in front of a live audience we were booed. We've always had people throwing shit at us.

Steven: To put it into context, that gang eventually became the band Suicidal Tendencies and Mike Muir was the leader of it. We knew of these infamous people and for whatever reason, we just decided to, like, pick a fight as if we were tough. We weren't tough; we just had a bad attitude.

Facing page: *Jeff and Steven McDonald of Red Cross, playing in an upstairs bedroom at a Hollywood house party, 1982.* JORDAN SCHWARTZ

Jeff: Our first show was at an eighth-grade graduation party. We talked this girl into letting us play. We had just met Black Flag, so we invited them, too. So it was all these eighth graders at a house party in Hawthorne. Then all these fucking gearhead idiots showed up while we were playing. They were staring at us. So I said: "This next song is an unreleased Black Sabbath number."

Steven: And they were like, "Oh cool!" But we'd go into some Teenage Jesus jam. Just because we had guitars, they thought we had some inside scoop on Black Sabbath prereleases.

Jeff: And I'd say it over and over, before every song. They were like: "You suck!" after every song. That was an empowering incident and our very first experience playing live. So we were definitely able to deal with gangs later. But imagine having Black Flag play at this little kid's house, with their full stacks and full energy.

Steven: When we played, all the kids our age thought they could take us on. They gave us hell the whole time. But when Black Flag played, those kids just evacuated from the living room. And we got a private Black Flag concert. Keith Morris's memory of that party was that some girl was passed out, she OD'd on a pot of coffee.

Jeff: That was another weird thing during that period; you'd just do these weird gigs in people's houses or backyards. I just remember, as a musician, those were always such a drag to play. They were just not fun. I have this video Dave Travis shot. During the *My War* period, Black Flag were playing at this horrible house in Lawndale with no furniture. It's the funniest footage: Black Flag in their really slow, aggro period, playing with a backdrop of a big '70s decorative wicker basket on the wall behind them. That was around the time that the LAPD clamped down on all Hollywood venues. The Starwood closed down. The Whisky was closed in the early '80s. Remember, it was vacant for five years. We played the last show. The police would riot every time they had shows. We played the S.I.R. Studios riot with TSOL. We were inside during the riot. We came outside, and there were cop cars that had been destroyed. We were like, What the hell happened? Then there would be a big punk show, like then the Ramones would play. We were at the riot at the Palladium with Black Flag when Melanie Vammen of the Pandoras got hit across the back with a billy club. I think the LAPD was extremely corrupt.

Jennifer: That drove everybody into these weird pockets of L.A., to weird clubs and to parties.

Steven: Like the Vex in East L.A., and Godzilla's, and all these places. I didn't feel safe outside the venue, and I didn't feel safe inside the venue.

Jeff: And if you were in a place like San Pedro, you were never safe. Once there were no shows in L.A., they started doing them in places like San Pedro, where gangs ruled the area. There were times they had to lock the doors because of the local gangs outside. Why were so people stupid about these things? Los Angeles was really segregated at the time, and you were not safe if you were white teens in certain areas. Why did we go? I never watched the bands in that period. We just hung out. It wasn't until a little bit later in the '80s that there were any good bands. All the arty bands like the Minutemen were good, and there were these little bands here and there, but not enough to sustain going out every weekend. I mean, there were like six bands with people you could have a conversation with, who were weirdos and fun. All the other bands were like stupid idiots and they were terrible and that's the truth.

Facing page: *Steven McDonald photo session, Serra Vista Townhomes, Santa Monica, 1983. Jennifer's interview with Redd Kross bass player Steve McDonald was planned to run in the final issue of* We Got Power. *The issue didn't happen, but the photo shoot sure did. Jennifer and her friend Hilary Rubens, along with a wardrobe, an electric fan, a bottle of Jack Daniel's, and some chemical enhancers, photographed Steve in the living room of the Schwartz's mom's Santa Monica condo, where we shot most of* Desperate Teenage Lovedolls. PHOTOS BY JENNIFER SCHWARTZ

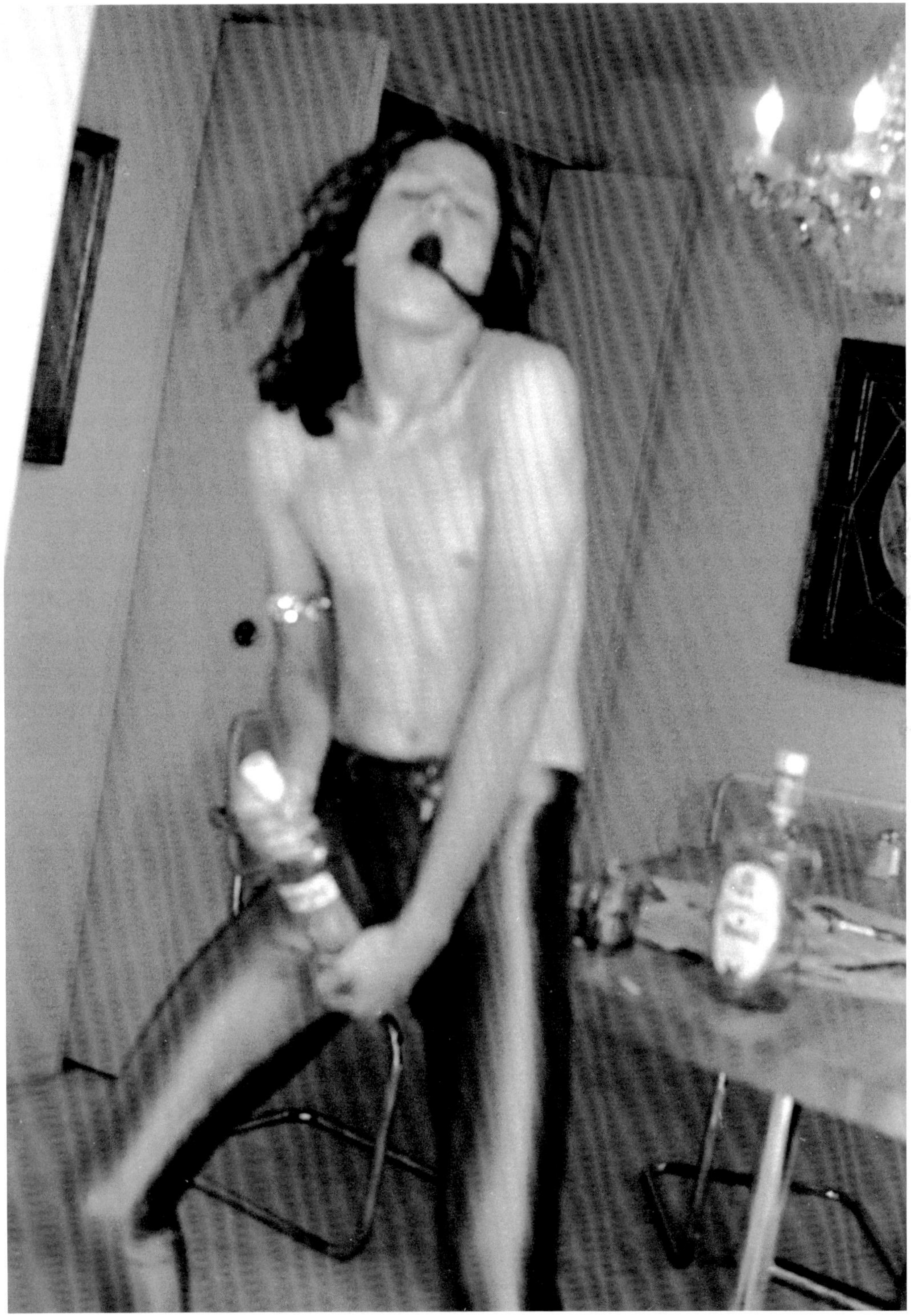

Steven: Well, we didn't identify with them, that's for sure. The first *Decline* depicts an era that we were first a part of, with X and the Germs. It was a transition. You have to understand, our perspective at that time was bitter and weird. Ron Reyes was fronting Black Flag. We had had a very nasty experience with him as the drummer of Red Cross. He left the band one night because Jeff was drunk in the parking lot, and a girl had put Magic Marker around his eyes—it was Iggy Pop Egyptian style. Ron said: "I'm quitting because I'm not playing in a band with a fag." Then Greg Hetson left the band. And when Circle Jerks came out, much of their set was comprised of Black Flag and Red Cross riffs. At the time there was bad blood. It was a heated, sensitive moment. Black Flag and Circle Jerks gave birth to this scene that we then had to live in. The only places we could play were places like the Vex, and it was nightmare. It was like, beware of what you care about, beware of putting your heart into anything, because not only are these people going to fuck you, they're going to give birth to someone who's going to destroy the music of the scene you love.

Jeff: That's what inspired phase two, the rebellion against the rebellion, like I was saying. It totally inspired me. I loved rebelling against the Circle Jerks and Black Flag at that time. They had started marketing themselves to this new, huge crop of people, very successfully. All of a sudden they were playing shows to thousands of people, playing the Santa Monica Civic. We weren't. I took pride in not doing it that way. I thought, "Fuck this. We're going to do our own thing. I listen to the Beatles and the Rolling Stones, I don't give a shit about this band, Circle One or whatever." I don't mean to keep name-checking them but they're the only ones I can remember. It was a fun adventure. And we had friends. And all of us did our creative things. We got into other things, like movies and stuff.

Steven: But the way I'm articulating it now, that's in retrospect that I can look at that Godzilla's page and relive the pain and suffering. How did I survive that? Now I'm in Off! So you can imagine how psychedelic my experience is all the time. It's like, "We're saving a genre, hardcore." I'm always the problem child in that band. I was interested in doing Off! because it reminded me of very early Black Flag, which I have a fondness for. That was the beginning of my involvement in a musical community, and I loved it. I still love it. In my mind, I could play a Dee Dee Ramone–style role, you know, which is awesome; I'd love to bring that to the kids of today. But when people talk about saving hardcore and that genre being elevated as an important art form...I've had to hold my tongue.

Facing page: We Got Power, *Steven McDonald photo session, Serra Vista Townhomes, 1983. "This photo shoot was like living out the Johnny Tramaine freak-out scene in* Desperate Teenage Lovedolls*, except that I hadn't been slipped 'Manersha Blue'—I was knowingly under the influence."—Steven McDonald.*
JENNIFER SCHWARTZ

This page and facing page: *Anarchy 6. Venice Beach, 1988.* Facing page, hanging left to right: *Mark Davey, Spike Geek, and H.C. Skinner.* Front and center: *Chemical Warfare. Many were hoodwinked into thinking Anarchy 6 was a real band, and we have the fan letters to prove it! Of course, maybe some of those were fake, too. But the act was done straight-faced, and the music and execution were perfect. The lyrics are ridiculous, just every hardcore cliché turned up to 11. What the Rutles did to the Beatles, Anarchy 6 did to hardcore. It was beyond anti-PC. You have to love something very much if you are going to go that far, and Anarchy 6 went there. Even Tesco Vee was fooled!* PHOTOS BY JOE COLE

We got power! From left: *David Markey at sea, Sutro Baths, San Francisco, 1987.* JORDAN SCHWARTZ; *Jordan Schwartz at SST/Global, Redondo Beach, 1987.* NAOMI PETERSEN

WE GOT POWER!
CONTRIBUTORS

HENRY ROLLINS was born February 13, 1961, in Washington, DC. Henry formed State of Alert in 1980, then joined Black Flag as front man in July 1981 until the band's end in 1986. His Rollins Band was active from 1987 until 2006. His 2.13.61 is an independent book publishing imprint and record label. Rollins has also acted in films, starting with David Markey's *The Slog Movie* in 1982. "The Henry Rollins Show" appeared on IFC. His radio program airs on KCRW. He has not stopped touring the world in over three decades.

CAMERON JAMIE, born in Los Angeles in 1969, is an American visual artist and filmmaker. His work has been shown widely and internationally. He lives and works in Paris and Berlin.

PAT FEAR formed White Flag in 1982, in Sunnymead, CA, and the band has since released 23 albums. His Gasatanka Records has released music by Redd Kross, the FU's, Melvins, the Cowsills, Anarchy 6, Tater Totz, and the *Flipside Vinyl Fanzine* series. Pat backed Rodney Bingenheimer in Rodney and the Tube Tops, with David Markey on drums. He helped popularize Japan's Shonen Knife, and Brazil's Os Mutantes dedicated their 2009 reunion album to him. Pat has also worked as a songwriter and producer for Dot Wiggin of the Shaggs, the Go-Go's, Susanna Hoffs, Redd Kross, and Sean Lennon.

JENNIFER SCHWARTZ is a cowriter and star of *Desperate Teenage Lovedolls* and *Lovedolls Superstar*, and she fronted the Lovedolls. She graduated from UC Santa Barbara with a BA in psychology, and currently lives in Del Rey, CA, filling in boxes on entertainment web sites with words. While longing for the days of punk rock, the Z Channel, and staying up past 10 p.m., she enjoys modern technology and benefits from the current bounty of hair-straightening techniques.

CHUCK DUKOWSKI was bassist and a songwriter in Black Flag from 1977 through the end of 1983; for Würm from 1973 through 1977 and 1981 through 1985; for SWA from 1984 through 1990; for October-faction from 1984 through 1988; for United Gang Members in 1992; for Fishcamp in 1998; and for the Chuck Dukowski Sextet since 2002. He was a partner in SST Records from its launch in 1978 until 1990.

KEITH MORRIS was born in 1955. He was a good little kid until 1976, when, as lead vocalist in Black Flag, he helped turn a few people's planets upside down. Once on the musical (or nonmusical) map, and in the sights of the LAPD, he jammed on up to Circle Jerkdom. Reveling in wacky sarcasm and humor, the Circle Jerks became the soundtrack to punker-dunker fiestas across Malibu, Cahuenga Pass, Hollywood, Flintridge, Huntington Beach, Inglewood, and the rest of Southern California. Running out of venues to play, they traveled across the USA for over thirty years. Morris's new band, OFF!, is already heading out to new rock-and-roll adventures in faraway places.

JOE CARDUCCI is a former coowner of SST Records and founder of Systematic Record Distribution. He is the author of *Rock and the Pop Narcotic, Enter Naomi: SST, L.A. and All That...*, and *Life Against*

Dementia: Essays, Reviews, Interviews 1975–2011. His blog The New Vulgate appears regularly at newvulgate.blogspot.com.

MIKE WATT was born in 1957 in Portsmouth, VA. His family moved to San Pedro, CA, and in 1971 he met Dennes Boon, whose mother suggested Watt pick up the bass so the boys could form a band and keep out of trouble. They became inspired by the L.A. punk scene, and in 1978 formed the Reactionaries with drummer George Hurley and singer Martin Tamburovich. Watt, Boon, and Hurley became the Minutemen in 1980, releasing records like *Paranoid Time*, *Double Nickels on the Dime*, and *Three Way Tie for Last*—until D. Boon died in a tragic van accident in 1985. Watt and George Hurley continued in fIREHOSE from 1986 to 1994. Watt also formed the bass duo Dos with Kira Roessler. He joined the Stooges in 2003, appearing on their 2006 release *The Weirdness*. He has played and recorded with countless bands, has released several solo albums, and hosts the *The Watt from Pedro Show* at www.twfps.com.

DEZ CADENA joined Black Flag as vocalist in 1980. His hoarse voice became a recognizable and often imitated signature in hardcore punk. In 1981, Dez switched to playing guitar in Black Flag alongside founder Greg Ginn, and he appears on the album *Damaged*. Afterwards, Dez formed DC3, and was a member of Redd Kross, Twisted Roots, Carnage Asada, and Vida. He appeared on Hüsker Dü's *Zen Arcade*, and circa 1999 he toured in Duff McKagan's solo band. He is now guitarist for the Misfits, while working on a solo album, which will include many guests.

JACK BREWER was born in Havana, Cuba, before the revolution. He started Saccharine Trust with Joe Baiza, released six albums on SST Records, toured the U.S. four times with Black Flag, and had songs covered by Sonic Youth and Superchunk. Kurt Cobain listed Saccharine Trust's *Pagan Icons* as his ninth favorite album. He has recorded with the Jack Brewer Band and Bazooka, and created a spoken-word CD. Now at work on an album with Thurston Moore and Mike Watt, he performs and records with the Lofty Canaanites, Lord Ransom and His Ranch Knaves, and the Exxtras.

DANIEL WEIZMANN has written fiction and humor for the *L.A. Reader*, *Jewish Journal*, *Buzz*, the *L.A. Weekly*, and anthologies including *Too Cool* and *Drinking with Bukowski*. At age 13, he started the punk rock fanzine *Rag in Chains* under the nom de plume "Shredder." He released two spoken-word CDs on New Alliance/SST. He collaborated on Dee Dee Ramone's *Lobotomy* and edited Timothy Leary's final memoirs. He also edited several volumes of *Mad Libs*.

STEVE HUMANN, aka Stephen Oliver Pfauter, was born in 1963. He dropped out of high school in 1979 and played in Jim Jones and the Koolaids, the Vandals, Detox, and Ken, All-Night Rocker. Nicknamed "Human T-Shirt," he designed and printed shirts for TSOL, Black Flag, the Germs, and the Dead Kennedys. Steve spent many years working in the film industry on swing gangs. Now fatter and balder, he is probably angrier at the bullshit and injustice he sees on a daily basis than he ever was as a callow youth stabbing tires out of cars.

EUGENE TATU, aka Euge from the Coast, was born in the Los Feliz section of L.A. He played bass for the Atoms, Nig-Heist, No Crisis, Agression, Friends of Mine, the Wayward Caines, and—at their last show—the Cheifs. Today he travels the world as a recording artist and folksinger.

LOUICHE MAYORGA joined Suicidal Tendencies in June 1981. He cowrote the hit "Institutionalized," propelling the band into the mainstream. He wrote the title track and "Possessed to Skate" for *Join* *the Army* in 1987, drawing new audiences with crossover metal. In 1988 Louiche was kicked out of Suicidal Tendencies. He joined Santa Monica band Horny Toad, and remains with them today. He has also played with Los Cycos, Uncle Slam, Agony, and Beowülf.

SEAN WHEELER was born in 1966 and started playing music in Mutual Hatred as a 15-year-old desert rat in Palm Springs, CA. In 1993 he formed the raucous Throw Rag. He has recorded with Queens of the Stone Age/Eagles of Death Metal members as Sun Trash, and currently performs as a duo with American treasure Zander Schloss. Sean enjoys burritos, the L.A. Clippers, and spending time with sons Devo and Desmond.

TONY ADOLESCENT is a schoolteacher, parent, autism activist, punk rock singer, and sometime writer. A product of the vinyl age, he still makes what he calls "records." He likes projects like this one because he would rather hold and smell a book than a flashing pad with words. He spends more time than necessary watching television, eating fried pork products, and going to the movies. And after all this time, he believes that Dave and Jordan are nice young men, even if they insist on hanging around those punk rock types.

JANET HOUSDEN has spent the last 32 years playing in a metric fuckton of L.A. bands, including the Disposals, the Lovedolls, and the Shakes. She is probably best known as the Pete Best of Redd Kross—and as the evil hippie who kills Kitty Carryall's mom in *Desperate Teenage Lovedolls*. She hardly ever hits people with bottles anymore.

JULA BELL was born in Los Angeles. She has played in Bulimia Banquet, Bobsled, Marc Spitz Freestyle, Miss Derringer, and Nip Drivers. She has contributed to numerous film and TV soundtracks, including a song with Devo for *Tank Girl*. Her work in film production includes *Twin Peaks*. Jula has a black belt in kenpo jitsu ryu karate, and can chop people's heads off, if need be. She currently runs a camp for dogs and a dog-walking service in Silver Lake, CA.

JEFF and **STEVEN McDONALD** formed the Tourists in 1978 at the ages of 14 and 11, respectively, and have since worn every fabric ever created as core members of Red Cross and Redd Kross. They appear in the films *Desperate Teenage Lovedolls*, *Lovedolls Superstar*, and *The Spirit of '76*. Steven McDonald plays bass in the group OFF! They are lifers.

EDWARD COLVER documented the birth of punk music, fashion, art, and lifestyle in L.A. His iconic images appear on album covers by Circle Jerks, Black Flag, D.O.A., the Germs, CH3, TSOL, the Gun Club, Bad Religion, Christian Death, Aerosmith, Red Hot Chili Peppers, Social Distortion, Wall Of Voodoo, Alice Cooper, and Ice Cube. His work graces the cover of *We Got Power #5*, and his book *Blight at the End of the Funnel* can be found at www.edwardcolver.com.

SPOT is a musician, writer, photographer, audio engineer, pit mechanic, and late-night counter bum. He has always believed in doing the right thing, then disappearing quietly. The traces are located at www.spotinator.com.

ABOUT THE AUTHORS

DAVID MARKEY was born December 3, 1963, in Burbank, CA. He made his first film at the age of 11 and published a neighborhood newspaper at 12. In 1980, he became involved in the local underground music scene. He helped form Sin 34 in 1981, and captured the punk scene in the Super 8 film *The Slog Movie*. Markey was a part of *We Got Power* fanzine from 1981 to 1983, then kept the name alive through his We Got Power Films. He cowrote and directed *Desperate Teenage Lovedolls* in 1984. He photographed, edited, cowrote, and directed *Lovedolls Superstar* in 1986. Also that year, his band Painted Willie toured with Black Flag for six months, a period depicted in his film *Reality 86'd*. Later, he traveled with Sonic Youth and Nirvana across Europe to make *1991: The Year Punk Broke*. Markey has directed music videos for Meat Puppets, fIREHOSE, Shonen Knife, Mudhoney, and Pat Smear, and collaborated with visual artists Cameron Jamie, Raymond Pettibon, and Kim Gordon. In 2005, he accidentally discovered he was adopted, leading to work on the autobiography *Dark Circles*. Markey directed the documentaries *The Reinactors*; *Dinosaur Jr. Bug (Live) at 9:30*; and the Circle Jerks film *My Career as a Jerk*. More at www.wegotpowerfilms.com.

JORDAN SCHWARTZ met David Markey while skateboarding in a flooded Santa Monica parking garage in 1979. As they discovered the growing Los Angeles hardcore punk rock scene, Jordan teamed up with David, his sister, Jennifer, and Alan Gilbert to found *We Got Power* magazine. Jordan contributed in many roles, including that of staff photographer. Jordan had producing and acting roles in *Desperate Teenage Lovedolls* and the sequel, *Lovedolls Superstar*, notably appearing as the rock star Brews Springstein. Jordan facilitated the release of three Black Flag skateboards featuring original artwork by Raymond Pettibon. In 1984, Jordan began working and living at SST Records' Global Network Agency booking gigs and tours for various high-profile bands on and off of the label during the pioneering years of the U.S. independent scene. In 1988, Jordan began a career working with computers connected to the Internet. He lives in Santa Monica with his wife and dog, still hangs out at Rip City on the weekends, and makes it to local gigs.

EXTRA CREDITS

Front cover: Jordan Schwartz in front of the Punk Shack, Yale Street and Santa Monica Blvd. Ray Pettibon artwork displayed to his left. Sin 34 and Red Cross logo and skateboard to his right, along with original artwork by David Markey titled *Flipper*. The Punk Shack was an abandoned real estate office in our neighborhood that we took over. We still lived with our mothers at the time; this became the hangout where we listened to tapes of Rodney Bingenheimer's *Rodney on the ROQ* show and added to the graffiti. DAVID MARKEY

Back cover: David Markey behind the Punk Shack; Miller High Life bottles pictured were personally consumed by underaged punks Markey and Schwartz, after being procured illegally from Kings Liquor a few blocks to the east. JORDAN SCHWARTZ

Front endpapers: Facing east toward Lincoln Blvd., Santa Monica, 1980. This photo was taken from the rooftop of a Ramada Inn across the street from "Samohi"—Santa Monica High School. Behind a moving van is the original Jack in the Box sign, before they blew him up. That big clown head used to scare the crap out of me. DAVID MARKEY

Flip side of front endpapers: Flyer wallpaper was the way to go. We started out with a few, then added more each week. I had my bedroom walls and ceiling completely plastered with flyers. How my mother allowed it, I will never understand. I do recall occasionally losing one or two with questionable graphics, like a Raymond Pettibon flyer that depicted an erect penis. DAVID MARKEY

Left overleaf following title page: Jordan Schwartz and Mike Roth in front of the Punk Shack. We would leave graffiti there, and next time we came back, there would be fresh punk graffiti alongside ours. Eventually we met the culprits, Mike and his friend Junior. They lived nearby and were into the same bands, but were way younger than us, probably 12 and 13. We ended up taking them into Hollywood and beyond. DAVID MARKEY

Right overleaf following title page: Dave Markey with Zizi Carrot, publisher of *Lowest Common Denominator* fanzine. PUNKERS SUCK SHIT is evidence of our ongoing turf war with the local anti-punk faction that broadsided our hangout regularly, like the mods vs. rockers struggles in *Quadrophenia*. "Punk sucks" is no longer a concept, but we used to hear it all the time, usually yelled from a moving Camaro. JORDAN SCHWARTZ

Flip side of back endpapers: Graffiti for a good cause: artwork for our *We Got Power: Party or Go Home* compilation LP featuring more than forty blasts of hardcore punk fun by White Flag, Nip Drivers, Minutemen, JFA, Ill Repute, Adrenalin OD, Big Boys, Sin 34, Red Cross, 7 Seconds, Dr. Know, and more. Available for free download while supplies last at www.wegotpowerfilms.com. JORDAN SCHWARTZ

Back endpapers, from left: "Goodbye!" Backyard punker party. JORDAN SCHWARTZ; All roads lead to Hermosa. DAVID MARKEY

Snickers from the Simpletones and the Stains gets the last dance, Dancing Waters, 1982. JORDAN SCHWARTZ